FINANCING THE 2016 ELECTION

FINANCING THE 2016 ELECTION

David B. Magleby

editor

Brookings Institution Press
Washington, D.C.

Library of Congress Cataloging-in-Publication data are available.

ISBN 978-0-8157-3659-2 (pbk. : alk. paper)
ISBN 978-0-8157-3660-8 (ebook)

9 8 7 6 5 4 3 2 1

Typeset in Sabon

Composition by Westchester Publishing Services

To Waisale, Emma, Ephraim, Zachary,
Jeeta, Colin, Theodore, and Louis

Contents

Preface and Acknowledgments

For a twenty-year period between 1976 and 1996, the United States had a quite stable and transparent system of financing federal elections. This changed as the result of a surge in party soft money, largely spent for candidate-specific electioneering and interest group issue advocacy, which was mostly spent attacking individual candidates. The Bipartisan Campaign Reform Act (BCRA) banned party soft money and defined what constituted an election ad to include elements beyond a few magic words.

Since BCRA, the pace of change in campaign finance has greatly accelerated. These changes have largely been deregulatory in nature. Groups can now form and make independent expenditures without contribution limits as to source of funds (corporations and unions can contribute from their general treasuries, which they otherwise cannot do), and these independent-expenditure-only political action committee (Super PAC) donors can give in unlimited amounts. Other court decisions have stricken the aggregate contribution limits in place for four decades for money contributed to candidates, party committees, and PACs. The Supreme Court has also revised again what constitutes an election ad, returning to a definition that allows individuals and groups to claim an ad is an issue ad when it is likely seen by voters as about electing or defeating a particular candidate. Such a change has made campaign finance less transparent again. Another development that has made campaign finance less transparent is the surge in spending by nonprofit social welfare organizations organized under section 501(c) of the Internal Revenue Code. The law governing these groups has not changed, but the advent of Super PACs has seemed to encourage those who anonymously fund these groups to spend more this way. Much of this activity could be subject to regulatory oversight, but both the Federal Election Commission and Internal Revenue Service have been largely absent as regulators.

At the same time as the campaign finance system was becoming deregulated, presidential candidates were rejecting in increasing numbers the partial public financing of the nomination phase and the public grant for funding the general election phase of presidential elections. This shift has amplified the importance of candidate fundraising, a topic explored in some detail in this volume.

These post-BCRA changes themselves would have made 2016 an interesting election to study, but the success of a very unconventional candidate, Donald Trump, in securing the Republican nomination and then, with an Electoral College majority but not a popular majority, the presidency makes understanding how 2016 was financed all the more noteworthy. As discussed in this book, Trump's campaign was substantially outspent, but much of that fundraising gap was made up for with earned media, the free media coverage Trump generated through tweets, newsgenerating personal attacks on his opponents, and his celebrity status, which helped him lead in a crowded field of Republican candidates. While self-financing was part of his strategy, he never hit his announced $100 million target in self-financing.

The 2016 presidential race was unusual in the extent to which candidates in both parties labeled the system as "corrupt." Trump first attacked his GOP rivals for their reliance on Super PACs and wealthy donors such as the Koch brothers, only to then do the same against Hillary Clinton. Trump's opposition to Super PACs was not enduring. Near the end of the general election, Trump benefited from Super PAC support, endorsed by his son Donald Trump Jr. and his campaign manager, Paul Manafort. For the 2020 presidential race, he already has a Super PAC staffed by close associates, very much in the mold of other presidential candidate Super PACs in 2012 and 2016.

As this book goes to press, there are important details we do not know about the financing of the 2016 election. The most important of these details is the extent to which the Russian government and foreign nationals spent money to help elect Donald Trump and defeat Hillary Clinton.

This series of quadrennial books on the financing of U.S. federal elections dates to 1960. *Financing the 2016 Election* is the fifteenth book to continue Herbert Alexander's commitment to documenting and analyzing how American elections are financed. Alexander, for more than three decades, provided detailed books and articles on American campaign finance. As in prior editions, the chapter authors bring a wealth of expertise to their chapters. Anthony Corrado provides an insightful summary of campaign finance law and administrative rulings that set the stage for the 2016 election. The presidential nomination phase in 2016 had no incumbent president or vice president seeking either party's nomination. Hillary Clinton faced a surprisingly strong challenge from Vermont senator Bernie Sanders for the Democratic nomination. In the Republican Party, a crowded field divided resources and public attention, a factor that assisted the best-known contender, Donald Trump. John Green examines this phase, showcasing the relative success of the candidates in fundraising but also the role played by Super PACs. David Hopkins contributes a chapter on the presidential general election.

Congressional elections feature wide variation in the ability of challengers to mount visible campaigns. In their chapter, Molly Reynolds and Richard Hall provide data and analysis on how incumbents, challengers, and open seat candidates financed their campaigns. Outside groups were also part of the story in congressional races in 2016. These included Super PACs, both candidate-specific and those aligned with congressional leadership. There was again substantial activity by party committees through independent expenditures in battleground races. Some had speculated that by banning soft money, the Bipartisan Campaign Reform Act of 2002 would greatly reduce the role parties play in elections. However, party committees have substituted independent expenditures funded by hard money for much of what they once did with soft money. Diana Dwyre and Robin Kolodny then assess the role of party committees in 2016 and also the further expansion of parties thanks to the *McCutcheon* v. *Federal Election Commission* decision in 2014. Long before the advent of Super PACs, interest groups were important in funding elections. Jay Goodliffe and I discuss the role of traditional PACs as well as Super PACs and section 501(c) organizations in chapter 3, on interest groups in 2012. Finally, chapter 8 concludes the book by looking at the political and policy implications of how the 2016 election was financed and lessons for reformers that can be drawn from the 2012 election.

I am grateful for the financial support provided to this project by the William and Flora Hewlett Foundation. Financial support for the project also came from Brigham Young University. Once again, this volume greatly benefited from the assistance of Stephanie Perry Curtis, who is skilled at navigating the complex datasets at the Federal Election Commission. The project also benefited from a capable team of BYU undergraduate research assistants, specifically Hyrum Clarke, Ben Foresgren, John Geilman, Elise Hall, Jake Jensen, Jacob Nielson, Blake Ringer, Alena Smith, Wen Je (Fred) Tan, and Sam Williams. Caroline Dove of Colby College assisted in the research for chapter 2. At BYU, grant management support was provided by Gary Reynolds at the Office of Research and Creative Activity and Kathleen Rugg in Research Accounting.

Our friends at Brookings were helpful and patient with us as we produced this volume. We express appreciation especially to Janet Walker, and Hal Henglein provided a thorough copyedit. We also express appreciation to the two anonymous reviewers whose comments and suggestions improved the book.

Finally, I would like to dedicate this volume to my grandchildren, who will inherit our shared national experiment in self-government.

DAVID B. MAGLEBY

Financing the
2016 Election

ONE

Change and Continuity in the Financing of the 2016 U.S. Federal Election

DAVID B. MAGLEBY

The 2016 election had both continuity and change in how it was financed and in the underlying dynamics of the election. When measured in dollars raised and spent, the gap between nominees Hillary Clinton and Donald Trump was the greatest in any election since the era of more reliable reporting began in 1976. The gap between Clinton and her joint party fundraising committees and Trump and his joint party fundraising committees was more than $285 million.

Given this disparity, how Donald Trump financed and ran his campaign was different from other candidates in his ability to exploit free media coverage, his limited fundraising in the nomination phase, and his claims that his opponents in both the nomination and general election phases of the contest were corrupted by their donors. The financing of Trump's campaign became more conventional in the general election, where he relied heavily on a joint fundraising agreement with his party, used their voter mobilization infrastructure, successfully tapped into contributions from small donors, and benefited from spending by Super PACs and nonprofit groups late in the campaign. Whether another presidential candidate can mount a Trump-like campaign in the future is uncertain, and Trump himself has signaled that when he seeks reelection in 2020 he intends to mount a more conventional campaign by aggressively fundraising earlier than his predecessors and endorsing a Super PAC, America First.[1]

The financing of campaigns by other participants in the 2016 federal elections was more conventional. Consistent with previous cycles, more money was raised and spent overall in 2016 than in 2012 or earlier presidential election cycles. In the presidential contest, the party that had held the White House for two consecutive terms was not able to retain it. Since 1960, only George H. W. Bush—in 1988—was able to secure a third consecutive term for his party.

With both Clinton and Trump viewed so negatively, the broader mood of the country received less attention in the media. Other fundamentals that were in the Republicans' favor were that the economy was only gradually recovering from the great recession of 2008 and that recovery was much less evident in some parts of the country, especially rural areas and places with concentrations of non-college-educated whites. Income inequality had grown, and for some seemingly stuck in low-paying jobs, there appeared little hope for a better future. A substantial number of white non-college-educated voters were angry with the government, and those who had lost jobs feared for their future. Among this set of potential voters, there was also a distrust of politicians, many of whom had promised Americans a better future but, in the view of these voters, had not delivered on those promises. It was this set of individuals who most resonated with Donald Trump's message of change ("make America great again," "drain the swamp," "bring back jobs," and "America first").

Beyond Trump, the 2016 election was unusual in some other ways. For only the second time since 1896, the Electoral College winner did not win the popular vote.[2] For the first time, a major party nominated a candidate with no previous government or military experience, and, as noted, the gap in spending between the two party standard-bearers was unprecedented.

This gap prompted some observers on both sides of the ideological spectrum to express the view that money no longer matters in presidential elections. The day after the 2016 election, Scott Blackburn of the Center for Competitive Politics (now the Institute for Free Speech) published a blog post titled "Money Doesn't Buy Elections" and suggested that the election outcome demonstrated that "elections are not 'bought' by millionaires and billionaires."[3] Other conservatives echoed the theme that the 2016 outcome proved concerns about unlimited spending were overblown. Kyle Sammin, a contributor to the online conservative magazine *The Federalist*, titled his piece "Trump Proved *Citizens United* Doesn't Let Big Money Control Democracy."[4]

Those with the view that money is no longer as important as it once was not only perceive the 2016 election outcome as evidence that Super PACs lack potency but also believe that the importance of fundraising by candidates is exaggerated. For example, many point to Donald Trump, who won the election despite being heavily outspent by Hillary Clinton. Others point to Jeb Bush's unsuccessful candidacy for the Republican presidential nomination even though he far surpassed all his competitors in money raised by his closely aligned Super PAC, Right to Rise. However, in his candidate campaign committee fundraising, Bush lagged well behind Texas senator Ted Cruz, whose campaign committee raised $89 million compared to the $34 million raised by Bush's candidate campaign committee. Cruz had multiple aligned Super PACs that together raised $53,681,251.[5]

Assumptions about fundraising and the importance of early money were also questioned by liberals, who pointed to the ability of Bernie Sanders, a little-known senator from Vermont, to challenge Hillary Clinton in the Democratic primaries and caucuses. Clinton had tremendous fundraising assets, including a large network of donors to her previous campaigns for president and for senator for New York (some of whom had also donated to her husband's two presidential campaigns). She also had an experienced staff, some of whom had been integral to Barack Obama's fundraising in 2008 and 2012. Despite these advantages, Sanders, a Democratic Socialist from a small state, raised more money in the first three months of 2016 than Hillary Clinton did. Sanders's success is seen by some as evidence that candidates no longer need to host fundraisers and court megadonors. Mike Lux, who joined the Democratic National Committee (DNC) staff with Donna Brazile in September 2016, observed, "One of the things that I think both the Sanders campaign and Elizabeth Warren's senate campaign four years prior proved conclusively was that candidates for major office can raise most or all, in Sanders' case all, of what they need to raise from small donors. If their brand is right."[6] Small donors were also important to the fundraising of Donald Trump, especially in the general election.

That campaign money is now less important is not a new claim. For example, political scientist Thad Kousser, writing more than a year before the 2016 general election, stated that "the impact of money in November's election will likely be the same non-story that it was in the era of public financing."[7] Kousser's view was that several candidates were more than adequately financed, several having a Super PAC "patron," and that in the general election both nominees would "have enough to run a strong campaign."[8] This was the case in 2012, when both presidential candidates, their parties, and their outside group supporters were at parity in spending,[9] but as this book will explore, the two major-party nominees were not near parity in spending in 2016. This raises the question of how much of a fundraising gap a candidate can overcome. Are there substitutes for money? Did Trump's dominance of the media mitigate Clinton's superior fundraising?

Campaign Finance as an Issue in the 2016 Presidential Election

In 2012 and again in 2016, nearly all presidential candidates had one or more supportive independent-expenditure-only committees (Super PACs) that were clearly identified as supporting a particular candidate but met the minimum legal requirements for being independent of the candidate. During the nomination battle in both parties, Super PACs were part of the debate and also substantial spenders in the Republican contest. Both Donald Trump and Bernie Sanders made a point of not wanting a Super PAC. In an October 2015 Republican presidential candidate debate, Trump said, "Super PACs are a disaster. They're a scam. They cause dishonesty. And you better get rid of them, because they are causing a lot of bad decisions to be made by some very good people."[10] In a March 2016 debate, he returned to this theme: "Super PACs are a disaster, by the way, folks. Very corrupt. It's going to lead to lots of disasters."[11] Speaking to a group of steelworkers in Iowa, Sanders said that "the campaign finance system that exists today is corrupt and undermining American democracy."[12] Sanders, who had strong support at the time from a nurses union Super PAC, also said, "I don't have a Super PAC, and in the best of all possible worlds, which I hope to bring about, we will get rid of Super PACs, we will overturn Citizens United."[13]

Trump's and Sanders's criticism of the current campaign finance system was not limited to Super PACs; rather, it extended to the broader claim that the current system is rigged in favor of wealthy individuals and special interests. Sanders's critique encompassed the speaking fees Hillary Clinton received from Wall Street firms, implying that taking such fees was corrupt. Clinton, in her postelection book, said of these speeches and fees: "That was a mistake. Just because many former government officials have been paid large fees to give speeches, I shouldn't have assumed it would be okay for me to do it. Especially after the financial crisis of 2008–2009, I should have realized it would be bad 'optics' and stayed away from anything having to do with Wall Street. I didn't. That's on me."[14]

A similar theme was expressed in an early Republican primary debate, where Trump said, "I will say this—people control special interests, lobbyists, donors, they make large contributions to politicians and they have total control over those politicians. I don't want anybody to control me but the people right out there. And I'm going to do the right thing."[15] At this same Republican nomination debate, Trump also said,

> I know the system far better than anybody else and I know the system is broken. . . . I was on both sides of it, I was on the other side all my life and I've always made large contributions. And frankly, I know the system better than anybody else and I'm the only one up here that's going to be able to fix that system because that system is wrong.[16]

Donald Trump further criticized his opponents for catering to wealthy donors, and he attacked the donors as well. In recent years, some of the most prominent donors to the campaigns of conservative candidates have been brothers David and Charles Koch. The Koch brothers own the second-largest privately held company in the United States and helped create a network of nonprofit groups that spend heavily on politics. Much of their spending has not been disclosed, but it is estimated that they spent as much as $400 million in 2012[17] and about $400 million in 2014,[18] and they had stated they planned to spend $889 million in the 2016 election.[19] Later reports revealed that the Koch brothers scaled back their spending to about $40 million.[20]

The influence of the Koch brothers extends to other wealthy conservatives, many of whom gather at an annual event to meet each other and candidates. Speaking of such an event in 2015, Trump tweeted, "I wish good luck to all of the Republican candidates that traveled to California to beg for money, etc., from the Koch Brothers. Puppets?"[21] Later, he criticized Las Vegas casino magnate Sheldon Adelson, one of the largest donors to Republican Super PACs, tweeting, "Sheldon Adelson is looking to give big dollars to Rubio because he feels he can mold him into his perfect little puppet. I agree."[22] Trump even went so far as to seemingly threaten Joe Ricketts—another major Republican donor, who had given $5.5 million to Our Principles PAC, a Super PAC that attacked Trump during the nomination phase of 2016—in the following tweet: "I hear the Rickets [*sic*] family, who own the Chicago Cubs, are secretly spending $'s against me. They had better be careful, they have a lot to hide."[23] Later in the 2016 cycle, Joe Ricketts joined Sheldon and Miriam Adelson and others in donating to Future 45, a Super PAC supporting Trump. Joe Ricketts's son, Todd Ricketts, ran Future 45[24] and was also active with 45Committee, a nonprofit group that also spent money to help elect Trump.[25]

Like Trump, Bernie Sanders frequently made claims of a corrupt campaign finance system, but he went further, calling for comprehensive campaign finance reform. Hillary Clinton and Martin O'Malley joined Sanders in the chorus, deploring the role of money in presidential elections. O'Malley described the current campaign finance system as "corrupt," though "technically legal," and he stated that "big money special interests have taken over our elections."[26] Clinton's views were similar: "We have to end the flood of secret, unaccountable money that is distorting our elections, corrupting our political system, and drowning out the voices of too many everyday Americans." She also said, "Our democracy should be about expanding the franchise, not charging an entrance fee."[27]

Sanders referred to his campaign's success among small donors as evidence of public support for a different way to fund campaigns. He repeatedly pointed out that his average contribution was twenty-seven dollars. Sanders, Clinton, and O'Malley all agreed that a major reform of the campaign finance system was needed. Trump's comments were consistent with his promise to "drain the swamp" of Washington, D.C., but he did not propose specific reforms, and since his election, campaign finance reform has not been on the agenda. Rather, Trump filed paperwork for candidacy for the 2020 presidential election on his inauguration day, and his campaign commenced fundraising soon thereafter. This was the earliest a sitting president had announced a reelection bid since the election of Ronald Reagan in 1980.[28] In addition, at least two Super PACs supporting Trump's agenda and looking to the 2020 election were formed, and they raised a combined total of over $5 million through the first half of 2017.[29]

Foreign Money and the Financing of the 2016 Election

The idea that foreign nationals or a foreign government might actively work to elect or defeat a particular presidential candidate occurred to the authors of the Federal Election Campaign Act (FECA) in the 1970s, who made it illegal, and it remains illegal today. In 1996, there were news reports about a Department of Justice investigation into whether foreign nationals from Taiwan had given funds to the Democratic National Committee, the Bill Clinton Defense Fund, or the Clinton/Gore 1996 campaign.[30] Some individuals involved were convicted of campaign finance violations, and some of the funds were returned to their source.[31] The issue resurfaced in Gore's own presidential campaign in 2000 and was part of opposition ads in that race.[32]

In 2016, U.S. intelligence services concluded that the Russian government had mounted a large and sophisticated effort to influence the 2016 presidential election. The evidence that Russians did this with the intent to help elect Donald Trump and defeat Hillary Clinton is compelling. While some aspects of the Russian activity have not been disclosed by Department of Justice special counsel Robert Mueller, we know that the Russians, operating through various front organizations, successfully hacked into the computers at the Democratic National Committee (DNC) and those of scores of Clinton and DNC staff, obtaining large numbers of e-mails, which they later selectively leaked through WikiLeaks and a Russia-based site, DCLeaks, with the intent of doing maximum damage to Clinton and the Democrats. In May 2018, the *New York Times* reported that there was also possible involvement by the United Arab Emirates and Saudi Arabia in the 2016 election. As with Russia, this latter case includes a reported meeting with Donald Trump Jr., son of the president, and others at Trump Tower in New York City before the election.[33]

Much more has come to light about the level and nature of Russian activity.[34] For example, the leaks that led to the resignation of DNC chair Debbie Wasserman Schultz came just three days before the start of the Democratic National Convention.[35] Republicans, especially Donald Trump, referenced the leaked e-mails on the campaign trail to point out divisions within the Democratic Party and to perpetuate concern about the private e-mail server used by Hillary Clinton during her service as secretary of state. Trump expressed his hope that Russia would find and publish the Clinton e-mails that, because of their personal nature, had not been shared with investigators. At a news conference about the Clinton e-mails, Trump directly urged Russia to hack into and release them. Trump's critics responded, saying it was "a serious threat against the security of the West" for a presidential candidate to invite a foreign adversary to intervene in an election by conducting illegal espionage against a political opponent.[36]

   Russian operatives actively used social media to campaign for Trump and against Clinton. They did this primarily on Facebook but also on Twitter, Instagram, and Google. Some of the ads placed on Facebook were paid for with Russian rubles. Other campaign activities were paid for using bitcoin, a digital currency, to register internet domains, purchase servers, and fund hacking operations.[37] In October 2017, Facebook disclosed that 126 million people saw content from the Internet Research Agency, a Russian firm with connections to the Russian government.[38] The Russian campaign was sophisticated, using trolls within Facebook, for example, to target particular segments of the population with messages intended to influence whether they would vote at all and, if they decided to vote, who they would vote for. There were an estimated 288 million automated election-related tweets after Labor Day paid for by Russian accounts. Some of these tweets falsely told people they could "vote by text."[39]

   According to the Department of Homeland Security, the Russians also attempted to gain access to voter files in twenty-one states before the 2016 election.[40] Voting systems in the United States are decentralized in most states to the county level, but the potential to create chaos by altering the voter files is real and remains an ongoing concern.

   For much of President Trump's first two years in office, the issue of Russian activities in the 2016 election has generated extensive news coverage. Multiple committees in the House of Representatives and Senate have been investigating the matter. The Mueller investigation has secured criminal charges against fifteen Russians, five Americans, and one Dutch citizen, as well as three corporations.[41] One of the indicted Russians, Maria Butina, is charged with spying for Russia while seeking to cultivate relationships with interest groups such as the National Rifle Association (NRA) and Republican operatives.[42] Some of the legal issues have to do with possible violations of campaign finance laws, which will involve the Federal Election Commission (FEC) and the Department of Justice. The extraordinary involvement by Russia in 2016 may also prompt legislative responses, a topic revisited in chapter 8.

   So is money now less important than it used to be? Can small donors be substituted for "max-out" or Super PAC donors? Does the public agree with the Sanders/Trump view of Super PACs as corrupting? What are the longer-term implications of the involvement by foreign nationals and a foreign adversary actively working to elect a presidential candidate? This book looks at how the 2016 election was financed, with a particular focus on the changing emphasis of parties, candidates, and outside groups on both small and very large donors.

2016 Election Financing in Context

The answer to the question of whether money matters is much more nuanced than the view that Trump's victory shows that money no longer matters; it is not yet clear whether any candidate can assume that using the internet and social media will result in the same kind of attention it did for Donald Trump in 2016. Sanders's success with small donors confirms that candidates who are perceived as authentic messengers with an appealing message can hope to mount a successful presidential or congressional campaign largely funded by small donors. Having a mix of donors at all levels, including those donating to aligned Super PACs and other outside groups, remains a likely strategic advantage. If one side is being outspent, Super PACs offer a quick way to address a shortfall. In 2016, this was the case for Republicans in some competitive U.S. Senate races. Steven Law, who heads the Senate Leadership Fund, described how his Super PAC responded:

> About two weeks into October, [we] put out an APB [all-points bulletin] to all of our donors and indicated that as generous as they've been, we really needed them to help further to try to even out the financial spending gap. We ended up raising about $38 million in about 10–11 days. We were able to deploy that to equalize what was on the air. We didn't actually achieve parity in most of the states. We just started getting close. I think that another axiom of spending in politics is you don't have to spend the same amount. You can be outspent, but just not massively.[43]

As this quotation illustrates, Super PACs and their donors recognize the potential impact of large contributions at critical times in a contest. With the expanded array of ways in which donors can inject large sums of money into an election, it is not surprising that these donors weigh the full range of their giving options and the strategic advantages of each. It is thus important not to limit analysis of campaign finance to the candidates' campaign committees but also include independent expenditures by party committees, by conventional PACs and Super PACs, and by non-profit organizations in assessing how money was raised and spent in 2016.

Donald Trump

Whereas the financing of the 2016 Republican presidential nomination was unusual, Donald Trump's general election fundraising was more conventional. In the general election, he relied heavily on a joint fundraising effort with the Republican National Committee (RNC). Despite his earlier claim that Super PACs are "very corrupt," Trump benefited from their late spending. Just as Trump used social media in fundraising, he also stretched his resources by spending more heavily on social media advertising, especially Facebook, and much less on television—a reminder that expenditures are just as important as receipts when assessing campaigns. Brad Parscale, who oversaw the Trump social media campaign, noted after the election that "Facebook and Twitter helped us win this."[44] He continued, "We knew the 14 million people we needed to win 270. We targeted those in over 1,000 different universes with exactly the things that mattered to them. . . . And we spent the money on digital to do that because we couldn't compete with them [the Democrats] on TV."[45]

Donald Trump's candidacy is a striking departure from the norm of past presidential candidacies. Although he had no experience in government or in military service, he had substantial name identification as a result of his role on two prime-time television shows, *The Apprentice* (2004–15) and *The Celebrity Apprentice* (2008–15), both on NBC.[46] He also had built brand identification through high-end real estate (including hotels, high-rise condos, and resorts), self-promotion, and his penchant for generating media coverage. He used these strengths to make himself the dominant force in the Republican nomination contest. His unconventional style included personal attacks, seemingly unscripted speeches, and his promise to self-fund his campaign.

Trump could be called the first Twitter president; he used social media more extensively than any other presidential candidate did. Mike Podhorzer, political director of the American Federation of Labor and the Congress of Industrial Organizations (AFL-CIO), stated, "I think digital was hugely important."[47] Although the public knew about Trump's frequent tweets, little was known about how his campaign used Facebook. At the postelection conference for Harvard University's Institute of Politics, there was a revealing exchange between Mandy Grunwald, senior media adviser of the Clinton campaign, and Brad Parscale of the Trump campaign.

> MANDY GRUNWALD: I give them credit. We gave you the material to work with. Comey gave you the material to work with. But do not underestimate the power of that negative campaign. Brad, you haven't had time to talk about some of the Facebook stuff you were doing on the negative side. I'm fascinated to hear all about that because it's so hard for us to track.
> BRAD PARSCALE: It is very hard. I agree.
> MANDY GRUNWALD: That was a very powerful piece.
> BRAD PARSCALE: The media had no idea unless I told them.
> MANDY GRUNWALD: I know, and more power to you for being candid about it.
> BRAD PARSCALE: That's the beauty of Facebook.[48]

Trump surprised many with his success in the GOP nomination contest. The field of candidates was large, including nine sitting or former governors, five sitting or former senators, a pediatric neurosurgeon, and two successful business leaders.[49] The crowded field meant Trump could "win" contests with less than a majority of the vote. He won two-thirds of the primaries and caucuses before the New York primary on April 19, 2016, with most of his losses in caucus states. After New York, he won all contests with a majority of the vote. Before New York, his mean share of the vote was 40.9 percent—he had not won a majority of all votes cast in any state. His name recognition made him the best-known candidate, which helped his standing in the polls, and his position as the leader in the race meant that he had the center position in all but one of the televised nomination debates. The exception was the one he bypassed in Iowa. Coming out of the 2014 midterm elections, the presumed front-runner was former Florida governor Jeb Bush. Building on his father's and brother's fundraising network, he established supremacy in his "lane" of mainstream Republican contenders.[50] Mike DuHaime, chief strategist for New Jersey governor Chris Christie, said of Bush, "Jeb being in [the race] was a huge obstacle for everyone. Any time any one of us got any oxygen and started to shoot up—for Christie, it was after the *Union Leader* endorsement—Jeb's Super PAC hammered whoever got oxygen."[51] But Bush, like the other contenders, was not able to distinguish himself from the other candidates and directly challenge Trump.

Campaigns spend money to get the attention of voters, communicate their messages, and mobilize people to vote. They do this through paid advertising, nomination conventions, presidential debates, an organized ground game of voter contact designed to mobilize people to vote, and campaign events designed to generate favorable news coverage and build support among potential voters. Experienced Democratic pollster Geoff Garin observed that Trump's "ability to dominate cable news coverage and news coverage in general more than compensated for any shortfall in fundraising."[52] Donald Trump was able to set the agenda and reach large audiences through well-timed and provocative statements and tweets. Trump's messages often dominated media coverage for any given news cycle of one or two days, after which a statement or tweet on a different subject would recapture attention. In speeches, at debates, and on Twitter, he defined his opponents in negative terms ("Lyin'" Ted, "Little" Marco, "Low Energy" Jeb, etc.). He personally attacked an opponent's spouse (Heidi Cruz) and questioned whether anyone would vote for a woman with Carly Fiorina's face.[53] At the same time, he presented himself as "strong" and a "winner" and promised that he would "Make America Great Again."[54]

Trump also broke with convention by attacking former Republican standard-bearers and the most recent Republican president. Referring to John McCain's roughly five years spent in a North Vietnamese prison, Trump said, "He's not a war hero. . . . He was a war hero because he was captured. I like people who weren't captured."[55] Of Mitt Romney, the 2012 nominee, Trump said that he was a "stiff" and a "catastrophe" and that he had "choked like a dog" in his race against Obama.[56] Trump made a point of criticizing former president George W. Bush for "[getting] us into the war with lies" (referring to the Iraq War) and said that "the World Trade Center came down during [Bush's] reign."[57]

For fundraising purposes, Trump's attacks posed challenges because he ran the risk of alienating major donors who had helped fund the candidacies of the three most recent nominees, Bush, McCain, and Romney, and had been longtime supporters of the RNC. Trump's ability to dominate news coverage of his campaign—and his characterizations of his opponents, former GOP standard-bearers, and even the pope—meant he could achieve widespread coverage at little or no cost to his campaign. Free media attention, referred to by media scholars as *earned media*, is an objective of every campaign.[58] According to one estimate, the value of Trump's earned media in the primaries was $2 billion by March 2016.[59]

Trump also sustained an earned media advantage over Clinton in the general election, with his earned media valued at $5.9 billion compared to $2.8 billion for Clinton.[60]

Trump was not the first wealthy businessman to largely finance his own nomination campaign. Steve Forbes did so in the Republican nomination contests of 1996 and 2000. However, Forbes spent $37.4 million of his own funds in 1996 and $32 million in 2000,[61] compared to the $65 million of his own wealth spent by Trump in 2016.[62] Furthermore, Forbes never generated media attention the way Trump did. In 2016, former New York mayor Michael Bloomberg considered a self-funded run for the presidency as an independent, and he "indicated to friends and allies that he would be willing to spend $1 billion of his fortune on it."[63] Other wealthy candidates, such as Mitt Romney in 2008, have loaned their campaigns substantial sums, in Romney's case $44.6 million.[64] In 2012, Romney and his wife, Ann, contributed $150,000 to his campaign and his joint RNC Romney committee, the maximum amount allowed, but he did not loan funds to his campaign in 2012, even when it was strapped for funds that summer. As Mark Halperin and John Heilemann learned from senior Romney staff in 2012, the reason was "that to self-fund in 2012 would make Romney look like a 'rich guy trying to buy the [presidential] race.'"[65]

Trump's decision to self-fund was part of a broader strategy "to run the most unconventional race in the history of the presidency, without assembling the greatest political consultants ever, and by embracing Mr. Trump's wealth and not running from it."[66] Trump's claim that he was self-funded allowed him from very early in the campaign to characterize his opponents as having been "bought" by wealthy interests and lobbyists. He tweeted, "By self-funding my campaign, I am not controlled by my donors, special interests, or lobbyists. I am working for the people of the U.S."[67] In a later tweet, he criticized his opponents for their funding sources in comparison to his self-financed campaign. He tweeted, "I am self-funding my campaign and am therefore not controlled by the lobbyists and special interests like lightweight Rubio or Ted Cruz."[68] However, most of Trump's general election campaign was not self-funded, and Trump himself tweeted, "I'll be putting up money, but won't be completely self-funding."[69]

In the second presidential debate, Trump contrasted his self-financing with Clinton's "taking money from special interests that will tell you exactly what to do."[70] A Clinton campaign aide later described this as the "bought and paid for" argument and viewed Bernie Sanders's campaign as having initially raised the argument during the primaries.[71] During the nomination phase of the 2016 election, Trump was critical of the RNC and Chairman Reince Priebus. Frustrated by Senator Cruz's success in states such as Colorado and North Dakota, Trump said, "Our Republican system is absolutely rigged. It's a phony deal."[72] In an interview, he described the party's system as a "scam" and a "disgrace."[73] Once Trump had secured the nomination, however, his campaign became fully integrated with the RNC. Brad Parscale described the joint RNC/Trump operation as follows:

> Our ground game was operated through the RNC instead of operating more independently. The RNC was the best blessing that we had as we came out of the convention. The RNC was ready for a plug-and-play ground operation with a data-centric view. That was a huge win for us. We didn't have to build our own ground game. The RNC had built an operation. We didn't need offices because we had an app. We didn't have to rely on old paper, door-to-door knocking.[74]

Trump's general election effort benefited greatly from the groundwork laid by RNC chair Priebus in building an improved data file on voters and donors and establishing field offices and trained voter mobilization staff well before Trump was the nominee. In a detailed report titled "The Growth and Opportunity Project Report," the RNC mapped out the need for the 2016 nominee to have a state-of-the-art database and ready-to-use field staff by July 2016.[75] Trump also formed a fundraising partnership with the RNC. Trump, like Sanders in the primaries, had success among small donors during the general election, especially when considering his joint fundraising with the RNC.[76] However, much of Trump's fundraising came late, and therefore so did much of his spending.

In sum, Trump and the RNC raised $372 million through joint fundraising, in addition to the funds his campaign committee raised.[77] Together, his earned media, his campaign account, the spending by outside groups, and the joint activity with the RNC gave Trump enough of a financial footing to mount a campaign that won the majority of electoral votes. Though he did not match Clinton in spending, he and his allies spent enough to secure a majority of the electoral votes. Looking to the future, are Trump's skills in setting a campaign agenda through social media, debate performances, and campaign rallies transferable to other candidates? Has Trump opened up a new way to mount campaigns, or was his campaign sui generis?

Hillary Clinton

The Democrats had a clear presumptive nominee in Hillary Clinton. Her prior candidacy for the presidency and her network of donors and supporters, which included many who had supported her husband in his 1992 and 1996 presidential campaigns, provided a jump-start in fundraising and a national network of advocates. While Clinton fell short of matching Obama in small-donor fundraising, she was able to apply some lessons learned from his 2008 and 2012 campaigns. Clinton followed a strategy of starting early and using all the fundraising mechanisms available to her under the law; by 2016, these mechanisms included an exploratory committee, a Super PAC, a substantial joint fundraising effort with her national party, and a large and specialized campaign staff.

Clinton's fundraising was consistent with the approach taken by other mainstream candidates in both parties. She focused on individual donors who could make the maximum legal contribution to her campaign and to a joint fundraising committee formed with the DNC. She included small donors in her overall fundraising approach but did not enjoy nearly the level of success with them that Obama had. Mike Lux, who joined the DNC with Donna Brazile in September 2016, observed, "The big advantage with Obama completely went away this cycle and I think it was like a vicious cycle because Hillary would turn off small donors by raising money from big donors and then she couldn't go back. . . . People didn't think that she cared that much about small donors."[78] In this sense, her strategy was more like Romney's in 2012. Like Romney, Clinton fully endorsed a candidate-specific Super PAC, Priorities USA Action, and, like Romney, she emphasized large donors over small ones.[79]

In 2016, it was Vermont senator Bernie Sanders who mounted an Obama-like campaign with small-dollar fundraising and volunteers. His success in challenging Clinton, especially in caucus states and in fundraising, was a surprise. Democrats have had "outsider" campaigns in the past, such as those of Governor Howard Dean (another Vermonter) in 2004, Senator Bill Bradley in 2000, and—in some respects—Senator Barack Obama in 2008. Sanders drew policy distinctions from Clinton, an element of the contest that frustrated Clinton.[80] Sanders built an organization reliant on volunteers and used the internet to raise funds and mobilize a base of supporters who were more ideological and energized. Sanders expanded on Obama's small-donor fundraising approach and did not hesitate to talk about the need for a revolution in America. Unlike Clinton, Sanders shunned fundraising events, instead using the internet as his primary fundraising tool. He and his team understood that, to remain competitive, he would need to maintain the flow of small donations by winning an early contest and then continuing to regularly win at least some states along the protracted primary schedule. His supporters were mostly young people, a group that Clinton later had difficulty winning over.[81] Robby Mook, Clinton's campaign manager, commented that the Clinton campaign fell short of the necessary 60 percent of young voters because so many of them voted for "third party candidates."[82]

Sanders exposed some of Hillary Clinton's weaknesses and raised an issue that was later used by Trump as well. For example, President Bill Clinton had signed a crime bill that resulted in much higher incarceration rates for young African American males. Though Hillary Clinton had not voted on this bill, she had said in 1996, in the context of high crime rates, that members of this demographic "are often the kinds of kids that are called 'superpredators,' no conscience, no empathy, we can talk about why they ended up that way, but first we have to bring them to heel."[83] This issue was later raised in the Trump campaign, especially through Facebook ads and messages late in the campaign, with video clips of Clinton mentioning the word *superpredators*.[84]

Early in the cycle, the Clinton campaign negotiated a joint fundraising agreement (JFA) with the DNC. Because party contribution limits are annual limits, there is an advantage to starting early with such a committee, both for the party and the candidate. Sanders and the other Democratic candidates were also invited to negotiate such an agreement. Sanders objected to some of the DNC expectations, especially since his campaign was not generally hosting events for large donors, a mode often used when raising funds for joint fundraising committees. Thus, while an agreement was reached, it never took effect. Hillary Clinton was not the first candidate to form a joint fundraising committee more than a year before the election. Obama had also signed a JFA early in 2011 for the 2012 general election,[85] but he was an incumbent president who had no intraparty challengers. Obama and Clinton had signed an unusual JFA with the DNC in 2008. Donors could give to a Democratic White House Victory Fund, with whoever won the nomination then able to use those funds in the general election.[86]

Tensions between the Sanders and Clinton campaigns rose further when it was reported that Sanders staffers had accessed data in the DNC voter file that should have been restricted to the Clinton campaign. The Sanders campaign apologized for the staffers' mistake but believed that being barred from using the data that the DNC had previously been sharing with it was excessive; consequently, the Sanders campaign sued the DNC to regain access.[87] Only hours after filing suit, the Sanders campaign regained access to Sanders/DNC data. However, it was the leaked e-mails from the DNC and John Podesta, Clinton's campaign chairman, that Sanders and his supporters saw as evidence that the DNC had been showing favoritism toward Clinton. These events culminated in the resignation of DNC chair Debbie Wasserman Schultz shortly before the Democratic National Convention in July 2016.

The new DNC chair, Donna Brazile, and the associates she brought with her, thus had to take charge of a party just over three months before voting started. Brazile later learned that the DNC had signed a JFA with the Clinton campaign that severely limited the DNC. Brazile wrote in her postelection book that

> the agreement—signed by Amy Dacey and Robby Mook with a copy to Mark Elias—specified that in exchange for raising money and investing in the DNC, Hillary would control the party's finances, strategy, and all the money raised. Her campaign had the right of refusal of who would be the party communications director, and it would make final decisions on all the other staff. The DNC also was required to consult with the campaign about all other staffing, budgeting, data, analytics, and mailings.[88]

Two Negatively Viewed Nominees

Voters see candidates in both positive and negative ways, but Clinton and Trump were the most negatively viewed candidates since the early 1950s, when polling on positive and negative candidate appeal became more common.[89] Most voters said neither Clinton nor Trump were trustworthy (61 percent said Clinton was untrustworthy, and 64 percent said Trump was untrustworthy). A bare majority (52 percent) believed that Clinton was qualified to serve, while 38 percent believed Trump was qualified to serve. Furthermore, 55 percent of voters believed that Clinton had the temperament to be president, and 35 percent believed that Trump did.

Two negative issues stood out in the 2016 campaign. One was the release of a tape of Donald Trump from the studio of the television show
Access Hollywood, where he spoke graphically and in vulgar terms about
how he violated women. Republican leaders such as House Speaker Paul
Ryan, Senate Majority Leader Mitch McConnell, and Trump's running
mate Mike Pence called on Trump to apologize, others called on him to
withdraw from the race,[90] and some major RNC donors reportedly withheld financial support after hearing the recording.[91] Responses to exit poll
questions about Trump's treatment of women indicated that half of all voters were strongly bothered by Trump's treatment of women, and 83 percent
of this group voted for Clinton. Though Trump suffered a slight drop in
the polls after the release of the *Access Hollywood* tape, many conservatives and Republicans ultimately voted for him anyway. Even among conservative and Evangelical voters who were offended by Trump's *Access
Hollywood* tape and his tweets, the prospect of replacing deceased Supreme Court justice Antonin Scalia with another conservative on the
Supreme Court, as well as Trump's promise to be antiabortion and overturn *Roe* v. *Wade*, overrode concerns about his character.[92] Other character-
related negatives for Trump included his unwillingness to release his tax
returns (something other candidates for the last four decades had done),
his business bankruptcies, his xenophobic comments about undocumented
immigrants and Muslims coupled with his refusal to condemn the Ku Klux
Klan and David Duke, his mocking of John McCain for being captured as
a prisoner of war, and his mocking of a disabled reporter.

The other major negative candidate-appeal issue was Hillary Clinton's
use of a private e-mail server for her e-mails during her time as secretary
of state. Clinton, while serving as secretary of state, used a computer
server in her home to receive and send both personal and work-related
e-mails. This had been done before by others holding her office, but it
posed a security risk. Clinton later acknowledged that having the private server was a mistake. This issue became major campaign news, in
part because of an unprecedented announcement that a candidate for
president was under investigation by the FBI. After the initial investigation, FBI director James Comey stated that criminal charges would not
be brought against Clinton, but he also said that Clinton had been "extremely careless in [her] handling of very sensitive, highly classified
information."[93]

Months later and only eleven days before Election Day, Comey announced that the FBI was reopening the investigation because a laptop

owned by the husband of a Clinton staffer being investigated for an un-related matter may have contained classified information. One week later, Comey announced that no new evidence had been found, and reiterated his earlier conclusion that no criminal charges would be brought forward.[94] This issue bothered 45 percent of voters significantly, and of this group, 87 percent voted for Trump.[95] Clinton herself has said that setting up a private e-mail server was a "dumb mistake."[96] In June 2018, the Department of Justice auditor general released a report stating that the decisions by the FBI in pursuing the investigation and not prosecuting the matter were reasonable. The report also found that Comey had deviated from long-established policies in speaking publicly about the investigation at the July news conference and by sending the letter to Congress late in the campaign announcing the reopening of the investigation.[97]

How critical the Comey announcements were to the outcome of the election will be debated for years to come. Comey's second announcement, which came after the release of the *Access Hollywood* tape, reinforced the sense that both candidates were flawed. Democratic pollster Geoff Garin saw the second Comey announcement as creating "a permission structure for people to ignore *Access Hollywood* and ignore lots of other things that concerned them about Trump."[98]

E-mails were important to the campaign in a second and unrelated way. As noted, Russians hacked into e-mails at the DNC and in the account of John Podesta. The hacked e-mails were later made public by WikiLeaks over several weeks and received widespread media coverage. Clinton has likened the WikiLeaks e-mail dumps to "Chinese water torture. No single day was that bad, but it added up, and we could never get past it."[99] While none of the DNC or Podesta e-mails conveyed criminality, they revealed that the Clinton campaign had a close relationship with the DNC, something that greatly upset Clinton's primary opponent, Bernie Sanders, and his staff. For most voters, the lasting impression was not of the "inside baseball" nature of the leaked DNC and Podesta e-mails; rather, it was that there was lingering controversy surrounding Clinton and e-mails.

That voters viewed the candidates so negatively is, in part, a reflection of the 2016 campaign strategies, as each standard-bearer made much of the opponent's failings, either through paid advertising by Clinton or tweets and campaign rallies by Trump. The personalization of the negative attacks was extraordinary and included chants of "lock her up" (referring to Clinton's alleged illegal use of the nonsecure e-mail server) at the Republican National Convention.

Much of the campaign message shared by Clinton and allied groups concerned how unfit Trump was for office. Peter Hart, a leading Democratic pollster who, along with prominent Republican pollster Bill McInturff, did the NBC/*Wall Street Journal* polls in 2016, told *NBC News* that "Donald Trump's message was the fear of what was happening to America, and Hillary Clinton's was about the fear of Donald Trump."[100] In contrast to those of the Trump campaign and previous presidential nominees, the Clinton TV ads focused far more on the personal characteristics of her opponent and far less on policy differences.[101] The problem with this strategy, for Clinton, was that many people also had serious reservations about her. Others may have been hesitant to defend her for reasons expressed by Teddy Goff, the Clinton campaign's chief digital strategist. He said, "It was uncomfortable for people to be full-throated in their support of Hillary Clinton . . . [because of the] private server."[102]

The media provided extensive and protracted coverage not only of the FBI investigation of Clinton's e-mails but also of the hacked e-mails released to the media in batches. Analysis of what people remembered about the Clinton campaign indicates that voters tended to associate the Clinton candidacy with e-mails.[103] This view was confirmed by focus groups the Clinton staff conducted late in the campaign. Clinton quoted some participants in the focus groups as follows: "'I have concerns about this whole Weiner thing. I find it unsettling. I had been leaning toward Hillary, but now I just don't know,' said one Florida voter. 'I was never a fan of either one, but this e-mail thing with Clinton has me concerned the past few days. Will they elect her and then impeach her? Was she giving away secret information?' said another."[104]

Whereas Clinton failed to present a positive message, Trump promoted his positive message of change, and many of those who voted for Trump overlooked his flaws. Sharon Wolff Sussin of the National Federation of Independent Business (NFIB) reported that some NFIB members said, "[Trump] really just needs to be quiet, but he is the business guy. I know I can trust him to be a smarter businessman, and we need to get our business back on track."[105] Despite Trump's shortcomings, various individuals voted for him because of a combination of factors, including his message that he was successful, his commitment to appoint a conservative judge to the U.S. Supreme Court to replace Antonin Scalia, his appeal to some infrequent voters, and his relentless focus on change.

Finally, as Harold Ickes, a close confidant of the Clintons, observed, "Republicans really came home."[106]

Financing the 2016 Election: The Big Picture

While much of the focus during the 2016 election was on Donald Trump's unconventional presidential campaign, much of how the 2016 election was financed was similar to the financing of other recent presidential elections. Individuals remained the most important source of funding to candidates, party committees, PACs, and Super PACs. The 2002 Bipartisan Campaign Reform Act (BCRA) legislation sought to expand the role of individuals in financing federal elections by increasing the limits for individual contributions to candidates and party committees, while leaving static the limits on how much individuals could give to PACs. Table 1-1 presents the individual contribution limits in place before and after BCRA was enacted.

By the 2016 election cycle, a politician could raise more from a couple contributing at the maximum allowed for the primary and the general election, $10,800, than he or she could from a PAC, whose limit was $10,000 combined for the primary and general election. Because of the Supreme Court's decision in *McCutcheon* v. *Federal Election Commission*, for the first time since the Federal Election Campaign Act, individuals giving in the 2016 cycle no longer had aggregate limits on how much they could give to candidates, party committees, or PACs; the limits on contributions to any single candidate, party committee, or PAC were not stricken. The *McCutcheon* decision is discussed in greater detail in chapter 2; here, it suffices to note that *McCutcheon* and BCRA elevated the potential role of individual donors in financing candidates' campaign committees and party committees.

Have the aggregate amounts given by individuals increased in the period since BCRA? Table 1-2 presents the amounts of money contributed by individuals to candidates, party committees, and PACs since 2000.

In 2016, individuals contributed more than $5 billion to federal candidates, party committees, and PACs. This amount is a new high and is consistent with the rise in aggregate individual donations since the implementation of BCRA. The total dollars contributed by individuals to candidates, party committees, and PACs rose most dramatically between 2000 and 2004. The total amount given by individuals in 2004 was $1.5 million more than in 2000.[107] The surge in individual contributions was

Table 1-1. *Individual Campaign Contribution Limits over Two-Year Election Cycle, Pre- and Post-BCRA*
Dollars

Year	To any candidate committee (per election)[a]	To any national party committee (per year)	To any state or local party (per year)	To any PAC or other political committee (per year)	Aggregate total per election cycle		
					To candidates	To parties and political committees	Overall
Pre-BCRA	1,000	20,000	5,000	5,000[b]	25,000	25,000	25,000
2004	2,000[b]	25,000[c]	10,000[d]	5,000[b]	37,500	57,500 (37,500)[e]	95,000
2006	2,100[b]	26,700[c]	10,000[d]	5,000[b]	40,000	61,400 (40,000)[e]	101,400
2008	2,300[b]	28,500[c]	10,000[d]	5,000[b]	42,700	65,500 (40,000)[e]	108,200
2010	2,400[b]	30,400[c]	10,000[d]	5,000[b]	45,600	69,900 (45,600)[e]	115,500
2012	2,500[b]	30,800[b,c]	10,000[d]	5,000[b]	46,200	70,800 (46,200)[e]	117,000
2014	2,600[b]	32,400[b,c]	10,000[d]	5,000[b]	48,600	74,600 (46,200)[e]	123,200
2016	2,700	33,400	10,000	5,000	n.a.[f]	n.a.[f]	n.a.[f]

Source: Adapted from Center for Responsive Politics, "Campaign Contribution Limits" (www.opensecrets.org/overview/limits.php), as of May 2017.
a. Per election refers to primary election, general election, or runoff election.
b. Subject to aggregate limit.
c. Per party committee.
d. Levin funds, subject to state law but not subject to the aggregate limit.
e. Figure in parentheses is maximum amount of larger total to political committees.
f. Following *McCutcheon v. Federal Election Commission*, there is no longer an aggregate limit on how much an individual can give to all candidates, PACs, and party committees combined. Absent the *McCutcheon* ruling, the aggregate limit on giving to candidates would likely have been $50,100; to parties and political committees, $76,900; and $127,000 overall. Unofficial estimate based on data provided by Christian Hilland, deputy press officer, Federal Election Commission, e-mail to the author, June 16, 2017.

Table 1-2. *Levels of Individual Contributions to Candidates, Party Committees, and PACs in Presidential Election Years, 2000–16*
Millions of 2016 dollars

	2000	2004	2008	2012	2016
Presidential					
Democrats	109.9	468.2	1,029.2	577.2	644.0
Republicans	230.3	345.3	436.4	462.5	439.3
Others	27.7	5.5	5.4	3.8	23.1
Total	367.9	819.0	1,471.0	1,043.5	1,106.4
Senate					
Democrats	133.9	219.4	163.7	256.7	243.1
Republicans	213.9	202.0	130.0	223.8	179.6
Others	2.7	0.5	0.3	9.0	1.5
Total	350.5	421.9	294.0	489.5	424.2
House					
Democrats	198.0	226.7	315.5	298.0	270.7
Republicans	223.5	267.2	257.6	367.0	270.9
Others	3.5	6.1	6.0	4.1	4.8
Total	425.0	499.9	579.1	669.1	546.4
Parties					
Democrats	271.3	642.2	441.2	438.9	418.2
Republicans	549.8	832.0	567.3	452.6	355.3
Others	16.7	8.8	9.9	5.4	5.7
Total	837.8	1,483.0	1,018.4	896.9	779.2
PACs					
Conventional	782.0	1,040.3	1,235.2	1,151.9	1,242.5
Super PACs	n.a.	n.a.	n.a.	534.4	1,044.9
Total	782.0	1,040.3	1,235.2	1,686.3	2,287.4
Combined total	2,763.2	4,264.1	4,597.7	4,785.3	5,163.6

Source: Compiled from Federal Election Commission data.
Note: Data adjusted for 2016 dollars using the CPI inflation calculator from the U.S. Bureau of Labor Statistics (www.bls.gov/data/inflation_calculator.htm).

greatest for presidential candidates in 2008, when in the aggregate they received 32 percent of all individual contributions in the 2007–08 cycle. The surge resulted in large part from the contested nomination among Democrats that year. Democrats also saw larger percentage gains for Senate candidates and party committees than Republicans did. When all individual contributions to candidates, political parties, and PACs are combined, we find that in 2000, political parties received 30 percent of the contributions, and in 2004 the share increased to 35 percent. In 2012 and 2016, the share of all individual contributions that went to political parties fell relative to candidates and PACs. In 2012, it was 19 percent, and in 2016, it was 15 percent.

The amount given by individuals to Republicans was down in 2016—and not just for Republican presidential candidates. The drop in aggregate contributions to the GOP from individuals is most notable for Senate candidates; Senate Republican candidates raised $24 million less from individuals in 2016 than in 2012. This trend is not unique to 2016, as Senate Republicans raised $3 million less in 2014 than in 2012, and $50 million less in 2014 than in 2010. Since 2000, when Senate Republicans outraised Senate Democrats by $80 million, Republicans have raised less from individuals than Democrats have. House Democrats and Republicans were at parity in the amounts each party raised from individuals in 2016. This is a departure from the greater success House Republicans have had over House Democrats in raising money from individuals since 2008.

Until 2016, Republican Party committees raised more from individual donors than did Democratic Party committees; in 2004, Republican Party committees raised $190 million more than Democratic Party committees did. But, in 2016, Democratic Party committees surpassed Republican Party committees by over $62 million. The RNC's decline in raising money from individuals cannot all be attributed to Donald Trump. Rather, the decline since 2004 has been continual, with each presidential cycle seeing fewer dollars raised from individuals than was the case in the preceding cycle. While the aggregate receipts for the RNC in 2016 were down compared to any cycle since 2000, these more limited funds were very important to Trump's general election campaign. As discussed in chapter 7, the joint Trump/RNC spending on the ground and in the use of the voter and donor database the RNC had built were important to Trump's victory because, before he won the nomination, he had invested very little in field offices and in a large database suitable for targeting and mobilizing voters in a general election.

While the maximum contribution limits to conventional PACs were not changed by BCRA, individuals gave $258 million more to conventional PACs in 2004 than they did in 2000, which was followed by an increase of $195 million from 2004 to 2008. Since 2008, aggregate individual contributions to PACs have leveled off, with a decline in 2012. In some ways, the absence of a decline in individual contributions to conventional PACs is surprising, given the surge in individual contributions to Super PACs. The large amounts that a small number of individuals give to Super PACs might have discouraged some conventional PAC donors, but, in the aggregate, individual contributions to conventional PACs have not declined.

Most of the increase in individual dollars contributed in 2016 came from the money individuals gave to Super PACs. Individuals gave $510 million more to Super PACs in 2016 than they did in 2012. In 2012, individual contributions to Super PACs exceeded $500 million, and in 2016 the amount exceeded $1 billion. These amounts are greater than the total increase in money given by individuals in every other way in 2012 and 2016. As chapter 3 will explore, much of this money came from a relatively small number of individuals who made large contributions. Some of these donors were not inclined to work with each other in their support of specific candidates. Hence, multiple large Super PACs supported Texas senator Ted Cruz. Other billionaires had mixed feelings over whether to spend large sums in support of Donald Trump. Two donors who sat out 2016 were Charles and David Koch.[108] Sheldon Adelson stayed on the sidelines in the presidential race until close to the end, when he invested in a Trump-aligned Super PAC.[109]

Super PACs again played an important role in battleground Senate races, with most of the money being raised and spent by Super PACs organized by party leaders but with some candidates having their own candidate-specific Super PACs. A prominent example is the Super PAC of Republican senator Rob Portman of Ohio.

As discussed in chapter 3, independent expenditures, which have grown in importance since 2010, were an even larger part of the financing in 2016 than they were in 2012. While Donald Trump and Bernie Sanders both shunned Super PACs in their respective party's nomination contests, other Republicans and Democrats did not; in the Republican nomination contest, spending not controlled by candidates again prolonged the contest, just as in the GOP presidential nomination phase of 2012. Super PACs spent more in congressional contests in 2016 than in 2012 or 2014. In the presidential general election, both the Clinton and Trump campaigns had supportive Super PACs and section 501(c)(4) groups. What was new in the use of money not controlled by candidates in 2016 was the expanded use of 501(c)(4) groups in the presidential contest. Much of the spending by 501(c) groups is not reported to the FEC, and therefore the magnitude of the spending is uncertain. One marker is that the 501(c)(4) group One Nation reported spending $3.4 million but actually spent over $40 million.[110]

While independent spending is, to some degree, independent of the candidate, a key element of U.S. campaign financing is that the spending is very much candidate centered. Much of the spending by outside groups focuses on attacking opponents, leaving the candidate's campaign to focus on positive messaging.

In addition to the importance in 2016 that spending not be under the direct control of the candidates, another big story was the success some candidates had with small-donor fundraising. Bernie Sanders stands out as the candidate propelled most by funds from small donors. Sanders answered a question lingering from Obama's successes as a small-donor fundraiser. Could another candidate repeat his success among small donors? The answer is yes! Sanders had a clear and consistent message that resonated with his donor base. Though an unconventional candidate, he had an authenticity that was also appealing. Finally, he used social media to broaden his base of donors and built on Obama's use of internet tools in online solicitations and contributions.

As major-party nominees have done in previous campaigns, both Donald Trump and Hillary Clinton had successful joint fundraising committees involving their respective national party committees and saw surges in donations before and after their conventions and during key moments in the general election campaign. Trump's campaign signaled that he welcomed Super PAC support (after opposing it during the primaries),[111] and he, like Clinton, benefited from independent expenditures.

Given all these changes in how individuals, party committees, and groups spend money, what is the long-term trend in overall spending in federal elections? Table 1-3 presents overall spending figures for different types of participants since 2000, the last pre-BCRA presidential election.

Presidential candidate campaign expenditures in inflation-adjusted dollars peaked in 2008, largely as the result of Obama's success in raising contributions from individuals but also because of the crowded field seeking the nomination for president with no incumbent running (see figure 1-1). Expenditures dropped in 2012 because Obama ran uncontested for the nomination, and in the general election, Romney relied heavily on Super PAC spending. Interestingly, individual contributions to Senate and House candidates dropped in 2016 compared to 2012, while individual contributions to presidential candidates rose. This was driven in part by the Sanders and Clinton campaigns' successes with individual

Table 1-3. *Overall Spending in Federal Elections, 2000–16*
Millions of dollars

	2000	2004	2008	2012	2016
Presidential candidates[a]	674	988	1,829	1,396	1,523
Congressional candidates[b]	978	1,099	1,297	1,766	1,512
National parties (federal)[c]	544	1,214	1,219	1,274	1,356
National parties (nonfederal)[d]	498	n.a.	n.a.	n.a.	n.a.
State and local parties (federal)[e]	171	201	318	893	354
State parties (nonfederal)[f]	330	67	94	0	10
PACs[g]	320	532	767	1,120	2,473
Super PACs[h]	n.a.	n.a.	n.a.	809	1,756
Section 527 organizations	101[i]	442[j]	258[j]	155[j]	143[j]
Section 501(c) groups	10[k]	60[l]	196[m]	640[n]	205[o]
Issue advocacy	248[p]	n.a.	n.a.	n.a.	n.a.
Individuals[q]	4	2	2	1	2
Total	3,876	4,605	5,981	8,056	9,333

Source: Data from Federal Election Commission except as otherwise noted.

a. Includes all spending related to presidential election in prenomination, convention (including spending by host committees and the convention grant), and general election periods. Candidate transfers to party committees are deducted from the total to avoid double counting.

b. Includes all spending by congressional candidates. Candidate transfers to party committees are deducted from the total to avoid double counting.

c. Includes all spending by national party committees, including independent expenditures and coordinated expenditures on behalf of candidates. Contributions to candidates are deducted from the total to avoid double counting.

d. Transfers among party committees are deducted from the total.

e. Includes all spending by state and local party committees, including money contributed to candidates, independent expenditures, and coordinated expenditures on behalf of candidates. The national party transfers were deducted from the Democratic and Republican state and local party disbursements.

f. Includes nonfederal (soft) share of state party expenses that must be paid with a mix of federal (hard) and some soft money during election cycle (Levin funds).

g. Total includes independent expenditures and internal communication costs incurred by PACs. PAC contributions to federal candidates and Super PAC independent expenditures (in 2012 and 2016) are deducted from the total to avoid double counting.

h. Includes all spending of independent-expenditure-only committees but does not include independent expenditures made by individuals or single candidates. In 2016, $50 million reported by Get Our Jobs Back was removed from totals because of no visible campaign activity.

i. Major transfers removed. Estimate is much lower than the actual amount because 527 spending was not disclosed until July 2000, because of the adoption of the new disclosure law.

j. See Center for Responsive Politics, "527s: Advocacy Group Spending" (www.opensecrets.org/527s/index .php). Total includes spending by groups that either were thoroughly committed to federal elections or were heavily involved in federal elections but also doing substantial state and local work. Total includes electioneering communications made by 527 organizations.

k. Total includes independent expenditures made by 501(c) groups.

l. See Campaign Finance Institute (www.cfinst.org/pr/prRelease.aspx?ReleaseID=71). Total includes groups spending at least $200,000 and consists of independent expenditures, electioneering communications, and other expenditures (including internal communication costs) made by 501(c) groups.

m. See Campaign Finance Institute (www.cfinst.org/pr/prRelease.aspx?ReleaseID=221). Total includes groups spending at least $200,000 and consists of independent expenditures, electioneering communications, and other expenditures (including internal communication costs) made by 501(c) groups.

n. See Center for Responsive Politics (www.opensecrets.org/outsidespending/). Total includes independent expenditures, electioneering communications, and other expenditures (including internal communication costs) made by 501(c) groups. Estimates of spending by 501(c) groups given to the authors for the 2012 edition of this book are included as well.

o. See Center for Responsive Politics (www.opensecrets.org/outsidespending/). Total includes independent expenditures, electioneering communications, and other expenditures (including internal communication costs) made by 501(c) groups.

p. Compiled from Campaign Media Analysis Group data. This money was spent on broadcast ads in the top seventy-five media markets between March 8 and November 7, 2000. This figure may include some money reported by parties, PACs, 527s, or 501(c) groups elsewhere in the table.

q. Total includes independent expenditures made for or against candidates by individual donors.

Figure 1-1. *Inflation-Adjusted Congressional and Presidential Candidate Campaign Expenditures, 1976–2016*

Millions of 2016 dollars

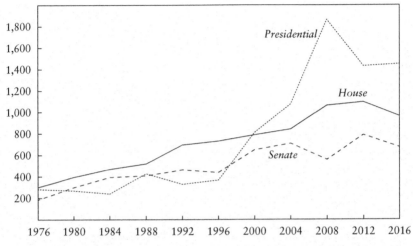

Sources: Data for 1972–98 from *Financing the 2008 Election*, edited by David B. Magleby and Anthony Corrado (Brookings, 2011); data for 2000–16 from Center for Responsive Politics (www.opensecrets.org).

fundraising and by the crowded field of Republicans seeking the presidential nomination.

In the 2012 volume of this series on the financing of federal elections, I argued that federal elections are best understood as a team sport, with candidates at the center. Both major-party nominees aggressively raise money for their candidate campaign committees and their joint fundraising committees (partnering with the national party committees). They also rely on aligned Super PACs and other outside groups. As discussed, the area that saw the most growth in 2016 was Super PACs. Table 1-4 summarizes spending by the two major presidential teams in 2012 and 2016.

Whereas in 2012 the two major parties' presidential teams were near parity in overall spending, that was not the case in 2016. Team Clinton outspent Team Trump by over $360 million. This difference comes largely from the Trump candidate committee's lower level of spending, Trump's joint fundraising with the RNC, and RNC expenditures more generally. Super PAC independent expenditures in 2016 were nearly the same for both teams. An important missing element in table 1-4 is earned media. As discussed earlier in this chapter, Trump had a $3.1 billion advantage

Table 1-4. *Total Expenditures by the Two Presidential Election Teams in 2012 and 2016*

Dollars

	2012		2016	
	Team Obama	*Team Romney*	*Team Clinton*	*Team Trump*
Candidate expenditures[a]	755,753,668	501,321,779	585,346,281	342,883,682
Contributions from other federal candidates[b]	6,250	101,722	202,481	38,610
Joint fundraising committee expenditures[c]	116,589,192	148,248,025	153,644,963	110,533,515
National party-committee expenditures[d]	143,631,224	134,422,297	190,724,764	105,360,563
Super PAC independent expenditures	136,303,062	251,178,045	301,653,805	278,785,550[e]
PAC independent expenditures	10,462,338	24,926,812	11,680,183	50,193,539
PAC internal communications	9,614,987	1,356,433	11,729,142	813,632
Section 527 organization expenditures[f]	1,461,145	2,327,544	14,956,823	12,281,011
Section 501(c) group expenditures[g]	12,947,843	127,316,180	21,219,278	22,399,264
Other independent expenditures[h]	953,582	2,106,839	247,844	1,790,946
Total	1,187,723,291	1,193,305,675	1,291,405,564	925,080,312

Sources: Data compiled from Federal Election Commission and Center for Responsive Politics.

a. Candidate expenditures include candidate committee and convention grant expenditures. Candidate transfers to party committees are deducted from the total to avoid double counting.

b. Contributions from other federal candidates include in-kind contributions.

c. Transfers to affiliated committees and offsets to operating expenditures are deducted from the joint fundraising committee disbursement totals to avoid double counting.

d. National party-committee expenditures include all expenditures of the DNC and RNC, including coordinated expenditures, independent expenditures, and other expenditures directly linked to the presidential campaigns. Operating expenditures were deducted from each organization's totals. Contributions to candidates are deducted from the total to avoid double counting.

e. $50 million reported by Get Our Jobs Back was removed from Trump's total because there was no visible campaign activity.

f. Section 527 organization expenditures include electioneering communications and independent expenditures made by 527 organizations.

g. Section 501(c) group expenditures include independent expenditures, electioneering communications, and other expenditures (including internal communication costs) made by 501(c) groups.

h. Other independent expenditures include those from individuals and groups not otherwise registered as political committees who undertake independent expenditures, as well as single-candidate independent-expenditure committees.

over Clinton in earned media. This estimate is not included in the table because we do not have similar estimates for the 2012 election to use for comparison.

The 2016 presidential campaign was marked by a proliferation of groups actively spending to influence the election outcome. These groups took multiple forms, many of which existed before 2016 but had not been used as extensively before then. Evidence of this is that presidential candidates used more modes of fundraising during the early stages of the 2016 contest. In the fundraising process, candidates are required to form and register their campaign fundraising committees, and these committees are then required to report receipts and expenditures. During the period when candidates are contemplating running and before they officially file for a campaign committee, they may raise funds subject to contribution limits in exploratory or "testing the waters" committees. Candidates can also form a leadership PAC, an entity that raises money to assist other candidates and PACs. A leadership PAC can contribute to another candidate's campaign committee. Leadership PACs can also be used to fund expenses for travel, staff, and other costs associated with the exploratory stage of a campaign. Candidates may form joint fundraising committees with other candidates with their party's joint fundraising committees. This practice has been most common at the presidential election level.

Aside from forming candidate campaign committees, leadership PACs, and joint fundraising committees, candidates also form organizations that operate independently of their campaigns. Specifically, candidates can form Super PACs, to which individuals may contribute unlimited and undisclosed amounts, or nonprofit social welfare organizations, which are 501(c)(4) organizations under the Internal Revenue Code. Additionally, existing PACs can create a segregated account for contributions to an independent-expenditure-only fund, forming a hybrid PAC. Last, candidates and their affiliated Super PACs may also form limited liability companies (LLCs), which Jeb Bush did in 2016 to own his campaign logo.[112]

In the 2016 election, presidential candidates of both parties used outside groups far more than in the 2012 presidential election and the 2014 midterm election. Table 1-5 shows the types of groups formed to support each presidential candidate; all of the types of groups were at least minimally endorsed by the intended beneficiary. Virtually all presidential candidates had a range of supporting groups, including their own

Table 1-5. *Candidates' Types of Supporting Groups, 2015–16*

Candidate	Super PAC	501(c)(4)	Leader PAC	Joint fundraising committee	Hybrid PAC	Exploratory/ testing waters	LLC	527
Jeb Bush (R)	x	x	x				x	
Ben Carson (R)	x		x			x		
Ted Cruz (R)	x	x	x	x				
Chris Christie (R)	x		x					
Marco Rubio (R)	x	x	x	x				
Mike Huckabee (R)	x	x	x			x		x
Rick Santorum (R)	x	x			x	x		
Donald Trump (R)	x	x		x	x	x		
John Kasich (R)	x	x						x
Carly Fiorina (R)	x							
Lindsey Graham (R)	x		x			x		
George Pataki (R)	x	x				x		
Rand Paul (R)	x		x	x				
Rick Perry (R)	x	x	x					
Bobby Jindal (R)	x	x	x			x		x
Scott Walker (R)	x					x		x
Hillary Clinton (D)	x	x		x	x			
Martin O'Malley (D)	x		x					x

Sources: Democracy in Action, "Building Campaign Organizations" (www.p2016.org/chrnprep/organization2015.html); Center for Responsive Politics, "Behind the Candidates: Campaign Committees and Outside Groups" (www.opensecrets.org/pres16/outside -groups?type=A); Federal Election Commission, "Campaign Finance Disclosure Portal," April 1, 2017 (http://fec.gov/pindex.shtml); Ian Vandewalker, "Shadow Campaigns: The Shift in Presidential Campaign Funding to Outside Groups," Brennan Center for Justice, 2015. See this chapter's appendix for additional source details.

Note: Bernie Sanders did not have a candidate-specific Super PAC or an allied 501(c)(4) group.

candidate committee, a leadership or other PAC, and a Super PAC. Some also had a 501(c)(4) group, and some had a limited liability company.

One change in the way money flowed into the nomination phase of the 2016 election was the expansion of candidate-specific tax-exempt nonprofit groups, such as 501(c)(4) organizations. Unlike Super PACs, these organizations do not disclose their donors and cannot direct all their spending to electioneering. Several 501(c)(4) groups were active in a wide range of campaign functions in 2016. Table 1-5 lists the types of outside groups used by candidates in the 2016 presidential contest.

Before 2016, outside money for presidential campaigns was largely spent on television ads. In 2016, we saw a diversification of activities that Super PACs engaged in. Using media reports and interviews as sources, table 1-6 lists the different kinds of campaign assistance provided by out-side groups to presidential candidates in 2015 and 2016.

Table 1-6. *Campaign Assistance Provided by Outside Groups to 2016 Presidential Candidates*

	Fiorina	Clinton	Kasich	Jindal	Paul	Huckabee	Carson	Bush	Cruz	Rubio	Trump
Video production	x	x	x		x	x		x	x	x	x
Press	x	x	x					x		x	
Rapid response	x	x								x	
Advance events	x			x	x	x					
Google calendar	x				x	x					
List / data	x	x	x	x			x	x	x	x	
Field	x	x			x		x		x		x
Policy research	x	x						x			

Sources: Compiled from press reports. See this chapter's appendix for source details.
Note: Bernie Sanders did not have a candidate-specific Super PAC or an allied 501(c)(4) group.

Carly Fiorina relied more heavily than any other candidate on a wider array of services from groups independent of her campaign. Her Super PAC helped stage events, manage merchandise sales, and coordinate volunteer lists. The Super PAC CARLY for America would post on its website upcoming travel plans for the candidate and manage the event. Super PACs working to support Mike Huckabee and Rand Paul completed similar tasks.[113] The Super PAC Keep the Promise I, supporting Texas senator Ted Cruz, had six to ten field staff working in Iowa and another fourteen working in South Carolina.[114] A Super PAC supporting Ben Carson, 2016 Committee, was also active on the ground.[115]

These groups and the functions they completed for candidates were once thought to be the sole province of candidates and their campaign committees. The numerous ways candidates benefited from spending by groups operating without the constraints of contribution limits led to an even larger role for wealthy individuals in 2016. These same developments affected competitive congressional races, in which a small number of individuals directed very large sums of money to battleground contests through Super PACs and 501(c) organizations. These changes and their implications are a recurrent theme in this book.

The 2016 Congressional Elections

The 2016 election was about more than the election of the forty-fifth president. A majority in the U.S. Senate was up for grabs, and while partisan control of the U.S. House was more predictably Republican, there was a time when Democrats entertained the idea that they might control both houses of Congress and the White House—and with that unified control, appoint and confirm Supreme Court justices. The intense media focus on Donald Trump also meant that less attention was given to congressional races and that the attention given was often about his impact on House and Senate contests. Rob Simms, executive director of the National Republican Congressional Committee (NRCC), reported, "National reporters . . . really started writing the 'Trump is a disaster' story in March. . . . Then as we got into the fall and particularly after the Billy Bush audio release, it was just overwhelming."[116]

The financing of congressional elections in 2016 was quite consistent with previous cycles in that incumbents benefited from their relationships with PACs and raised much more money than the candidates running against them. Most congressional races were not seriously contested, and in those that were, there was a concentration of fundraising

Table 1-7. *Expenditures by the Democratic and Republican Congressional Election Teams in 2012 and 2016*
Dollars

	2012		2016	
	Democratic	*Republican*	*Democratic*	*Republican*
Candidate expenditures[a]	679,876,980	776,582,914	810,907,133	913,872,782
Contributions from other federal candidates[b]	5,883,690	7,032,434	4,232,645	7,115,543
National party-committee expenditures[c]	192,512,403	159,797,634	231,501,424	180,291,573
Super PAC independent expenditures	121,294,632	97,414,294	211,277,211	270,249,025
PAC independent expenditures	33,197,175	23,080,443	49,220,111	18,915,914
PAC internal communications	7,722,657	1,784,502	3,100,705	2,225,331
Section 527 organization expenditures[d]	40,306,920	19,626,077	27,942,696	18,280,783
Section 501(c) group expenditures[e]	33,191,291	108,732,184	13,820,415	74,637,683
Other independent expenditures[f]	102,311	1,486,136	18,749	127,903
Total	1,114,088,059	1,195,536,618	1,352,021,089	1,485,716,537

Sources: Data compiled from Federal Election Commission and Center for Responsive Politics.

a. Candidate transfers to party committees are deducted from the total to avoid double counting.

b. Contributions from other federal candidates include in-kind contributions.

c. National party-committee expenditures include all expenditures of the Democratic Senatorial Campaign Committee, Democratic Congressional Campaign Committee, National Republican Senate Committee, and National Republican Congressional Committee, including coordinated expenditures and independent expenditures. Operating expenditures were deducted from each organization's totals. Contributions to candidates are deducted from the total to avoid double counting.

d. Section 527 organization expenditures include electioneering communications and independent expenditures made by 527 organizations.

e. Section 501(c) group expenditures include independent expenditures, electioneering communications, and other expenditures (including internal communication costs) made by 501(c) groups.

f. Other independent expenditures include those from individuals and groups, not otherwise registered as political committees, who undertake independent expenditures as well as single-candidate independent-expenditure committees.

by candidates and independent spending by party committees and outside groups (congressional elections are the subject of chapter 6, while chapter 7 discusses political parties).

Congressional campaign financing is also a team sport, especially in competitive contests that may determine which party controls one or both legislative chambers. Table 1-7 presents the different ways the Democratic and Republican teams financed their campaigns in 2012 and 2016.

The presidential race clearly overshadowed most contests for other offices. As with House races, Republican senators faced the dilemma of whether to run with Trump or run away from him. Jennifer Duffy, who monitors Senate races for the *Cook Political Report*, summarized the challenge as follows: "Running away from [Trump] was putting yourself in the crosshairs of two different guns. The Democrats, who called you opportunistic, who asked why you didn't do it sooner, who beat the crap out of you for doing what they asked you to do; and Republicans who thought you were being disloyal."[117]

The close margin enjoyed by the Republicans in the U.S. Senate going into the election meant that control of the chamber was up for grabs. The most intense battlegrounds for campaign fundraising and spending are the competitive environments (states for the presidential and U.S. Senate contests, congressional districts for U.S. House contests), in which far more money is spent. In 2016, congressional campaigns continued to focus on individual contests for seats in the House or Senate. Thus, there was a second, more national focus on which party would secure majorities in the House and Senate following congressional elections.

At some point in the 2016 campaign, many of the battlegrounds for Senate control overlapped with presidential battlegrounds (Colorado, Florida, Nevada, New Hampshire, North Carolina, Ohio, Pennsylvania, and Wisconsin). The exceptions were Illinois, Missouri, and Indiana. In most states, this meant that the voter mobilization effort was the joint task of the presidential or senatorial committees and the state or national party committees. The exception was in Pennsylvania, where the Trump and Pat Toomey campaigns were largely separate, with Toomey consciously distancing himself from Trump[118] and only in the last hour of voting revealing he had voted for Trump.[119] In competitive Senate contests in states that were not presidential battlegrounds, the voter mobilization effort was mounted by the senatorial campaigns and the national party senatorial campaign committees.

Overview of the Book

Political parties and Super PACs associated with the partisan congressional leadership played important roles in the 2016 election. For presidential candidates, they were especially important in raising additional funds through candidate/party joint fundraising committees. Trump's funding was unconventional, especially in the nomination phase. The

Trump/RNC agreement came late but, as noted, was critical to his success.

The party leaders in both parties and in both chambers had very active party-centered Super PACs raising unlimited amounts of money to gain or retain a majority in their respective chamber. Until 2016, Senate Republicans depended on American Crossroads, a Super PAC that also was a major player as a Super PAC for Mitt Romney in 2012,[120] but in 2016, Senate Majority Leader Mitch McConnell joined the other congressional party leaders and established the Senate Leadership Fund. As discussed in chapters 6 and 7, these party-centered Super PACs, when combined with party-committee independent expenditures, make the parties counterbalances to interest-group and single-issue Super PACs.

Super PACs are examined at length in chapter 3. Since they became part of the campaign finance landscape, they have grown in importance. In 2016, as in 2012, the spending by candidate-specific Super PACs in the Republican nomination contest prolonged the candidacies of several candidates. Both major parties have now embraced Super PACs at the congressional level. Presidential candidates, with the exception of Bernie Sanders, did as well. There are no signs that spending by outside groups will diminish in the 2020 election. Although as a candidate Trump spoke of the rigged and corrupt campaign finance system, as president he has not recommended any policy changes. As discussed in chapter 8, the policy agenda in this area has several important unresolved issues, including the need to appoint one vacated position on the Federal Election Commission as well as name individuals to replace the five other commissioners, whose terms have now expired. The policy agenda also includes providing clearer regulatory guidance on what types of coordination candidates may engage in with Super PACs and 501(c) groups. There is also uncertainty about the implications of President Trump's executive order about churches being given greater latitude as 501(c)(3) groups.

Data and Methodology

The data used in this book come largely from the Federal Election Commission, and much of this information is available on the FEC website. The FEC campaign finance data are frequently updated in response to amended reports and coding or other errors. For the most current data, it is best to consult the FEC website. The FEC data used in this book were downloaded from the FEC's disclosure database (FTP server). This source provides the most up-to-date campaign finance records. The data also feed into a variety of maps, charts, and summary tables that are available for viewing on the FEC website. When using summary tables cited in FEC press releases, users should be aware that these tables are not updated if there are changes to the original data from which the tables, figures, or maps were created. Because the FEC data are frequently adjusted to reflect amended reports, it is best to use the FEC disclosure database.

For analytic purposes, it is important to note the difference between receipts and expenditures. When the research question pertains to how much money a particular committee raised compared to other committees or over time, the metric used will be receipts. When the interest is in how much money was spent by a particular committee, the reported expenditures will be examined. Committees do not always spend all the money they raise; thus, using receipts as a measure of electoral activity by a committee would be problematic.

Because money is often transferred between committees, such as from PAC to PAC or from 501(c)(4) group to Super PAC, it is important to account for double counting. Therefore, when calculating overall election expenditures, candidate transfers to party committees are deducted from the candidate committee totals, contributions to candidates are deducted from party disbursements, national party transfers are deducted from state and local party totals, and PAC contributions to candidates are deducted from PAC expenditures. The footnotes below the tables and figures in this book indicate whether these deductions were necessary for the data being summarized.

Receipts for and expenditures by political committees are reported on a set schedule. In this report, such data are generally presented for the full two-year election cycle. When a shortened reporting period is used, such as the presidential general election, this will be indicated.

When comparing receipts or expenditures over time and inflation is considered, it will be indicated at the top of the table that the data are in "2016 dollars." There are many acronyms and abbreviations used both in this book and in writing about campaign finance generally. Table 1-8 lists commonly used acronyms and abbreviations.

Table 1-8. *List of Commonly Used Terms and Abbreviations*

Term	Abbreviation
Bipartisan Campaign Reform Act	BCRA
Democratic Congressional Campaign Committee	DCCC
Democratic National Committee	DNC
Democratic Senatorial Campaign Committee	DSCC
Federal Election Campaign Act	FECA
Federal Election Commission	FEC
Internal Revenue Service	IRS
Joint fundraising agreement	JFA
Joint fundraising committee	JFC
Leadership political action committee	LPAC
National Republican Congressional Committee	NRCC
National Republican Senate Committee	NRSC
Political action committee	PAC
Principal campaign committee	PCC
Republican National Committee	RNC

APPENDIX

Sources for Table 1-5

Jeb Bush

SUPER PAC RIGHT TO RISE USA
Beth Reinhard and Patrick O'Connor, "Jeb Bush Moves Quickly to Build Policy and Fundraising Arms," *Wall Street Journal*, January 6, 2015.

501(C)(4) RIGHT TO RISE POLICY SOLUTIONS
Ed O'Keefe and Matea Gold, "How a Bush-Allied Nonprofit Could Inject More Secret Money into '16 Race," *Washington Post*, March 31, 2015.

LEADERSHIP PAC RIGHT TO RISE PAC
Reinhard and O'Connor, "Jeb Bush Moves Quickly to Build Policy and Fundraising Arms."

LLC BHAG LLC
Russ Choma, "Why Does Jeb Bush Have a Mysterious Shell Company?" *Mother Jones*, June 29, 2015.

Ben Carson

SUPER PAC THE 2016 COMMITTEE
Katie Glueck, "Pro-Carson Super PACs Join Forces," *Politico*, October 22, 2015.

LEADERSHIP PAC USA FIRST PAC
Center for Responsive Politics, "USA First PAC" (www.opensecrets.org/pacs /lookup2.php?cycle=2016&strID=C00567685).

EXPLORATORY COMMITTEE
Reid J. Epstein, "Ben Carson Creates Committee to Explore Presidential Bid," *Wall Street Journal*, March 2, 2015.

Ted Cruz

SUPER PAC KEEP THE PROMISE I, II, III
Nicholas Confessore, "Network of 'Super PACs' Says That It Has Raised $31 Million for Ted Cruz Bid," *New York Times*, April 8, 2015.

501(C)(4) SECURE AMERICA NOW
Theodore Schleifer, "Cruz Super PAC Claim: More than $37 Million Raised," CNN, June 3, 2015.

LEADERSHIP PAC JOBS, GROWTH, AND FREEDOM FUND
Kevin Diaz, "Cruz, Cornyn Focus on Senate Republicans, Not Trump," *Houston Chronicle*, October 31, 2016.

JOINT FUNDRAISING COMMITTEE
Center for Responsive Politics, "Ted Cruz Victory Cmte" (www.opensecrets .org/jfc/summary.php?id=C00542423).

Chris Christie

SUPER PAC AMERICA LEADS
Jose A. DelReal, "Christie Allies Launch Super PAC," *Washington Post*, March 12, 2015.

LEADERSHIP PAC LEADERSHIP MATTERS FOR AMERICA
Center for Responsive Politics, "Leadership Matters for America" (www.open secrets.org/pacs/lookup2.php?cycle=2016&strID=C00571778).

Marco Rubio

SUPER PAC CONSERVATIVE SOLUTIONS PAC
Ed O'Keefe, "Marco Rubio Gets a Super PAC," *Washington Post*, April 9, 2015.

501(C)(4) CONSERVATIVE SOLUTIONS PROJECT
Robert Maguire, "Two (at Most) Secret Donors Funded 93% of Pro-Rubio Nonprofit," Center for Responsive Politics, May 3, 2017.

LEADERSHIP PAC RECLAIM AMERICA PAC
Center for Responsive Politics, "Reclaim America PAC" (www.opensecrets.org /pacs/lookup2.php?strID=C00500025).

JOINT FUNDRAISING COMMITTEE RUBIO VICTORY COMMITTEE
Center for Responsive Politics, "Rubio Victory Cmte" (www.opensecrets.org/jfc
/summary.php?id=C00494617).

Mike Huckabee

SUPER PAC PURSUING AMERICA'S GREATNESS
Philip Bump, "Mike Huckabee Kicks Off His 2016 Bid with a Violation of
Campaign Finance Law," *Washington Post*, May 5, 2015.

501(C)(4) AMERICA TAKES ACTION
Tom Hamburger and Robert Costa, "Mike Huckabee Rebuilds Political Team with
Eye on Another Presidential Run," *Washington Post*, November 12, 2014.

LEADERSHIP PAC HUCK PAC
Center for Responsive Politics, "Huck PAC" (www.opensecrets.org/pacs/lookup2
.php?cycle=2016&strID=C00448373).

EXPLORATORY COMMITTEE
Adam Wollner, "Mike Huckabee Says He's Formed an Exploratory Committee
for a Presidential Run," *The Atlantic*, April 17, 2015.

527 ORGANIZATION PROSPERITY FOR ALL FUND
P2016 Race for the White House, "Building Campaign Organizations (2015)"
(www.p2016.org/chrnprep/organization2015.html).

Rick Santorum

SUPER PAC TAKE AMERICA BACK PAC
Ben Gittleson and Shushannah Walshe, "Rick Santorum Staffers Switch Tactics,
Form Super PAC," *ABC News*, August 6, 2015.

501(C)(4) PATRIOT VOICES
Rachel Weiner, "Rick Santorum's Next Move: 'Patriot Voices,'" *Washington
Post*, June 8, 2012.

HYBRID PAC PATRIOT VOICES PAC
Center for Responsive Politics, "Patriot Voices PAC" (www.opensecrets.org
/pacs/lookup2.php?cycle=2016&strID=C00528307).

EXPLORATORY COMMITTEE
Andrew Rafferty, "Rick Santorum Sets Up 'Testing the Waters' Account for 2016
Run," MSNBC, April 9, 2015.

Donald Trump

SUPER PAC REBUILDING AMERICA NOW
Alex Isenstadt, "Trump Super PACs Revving Up for Final Stretch," *Politico*,
September 15, 2016.

501(C)(4) 45COMMITTEE
Kenneth P. Vogel, "Secret Money to Boost Trump," *Politico*, September 28, 2016.

JOINT FUNDRAISING COMMITTEE
Alex Isenstadt, "Trump, RNC Enter Joint Fundraising Pact," *Politico*, May 17, 2016.

HYBRID PAC GREAT AMERICA PAC
Rebecca Ballhaus, "Pro-Trump Group Great America PAC Bags Two Billionaire Backers," *Wall Street Journal*, June 2, 2016.
Note: Get Our Jobs Back did not make any contributions to a single campaign or other political entity during the 2016 cycle. It received a single $50 million donation, which it immediately returned to the donor. The two other donations were much smaller. One was immediately returned to the donor, and the other, a $15,477 donation, was given in part to an organization owned by the treasurer of Get Our Jobs Back. This figure removes the $50,010,116 reported by Get Our Jobs Back.

EXPLORATORY COMMITTEE
Jeremy Diamond, "Donald Trump Launches Presidential Exploratory Committee," CNN, March 18, 2015.

John Kasich

SUPER PAC NEW DAY FOR AMERICA
Darrel Rowland, "Kasich Jumps into the Murky Waters of Modern Fundraising," *Columbus Dispatch*, July 12, 2015.

501(C)(4) BALANCED BUDGET FOREVER
James Hohmann, "John Kasich's Crusade," *Politico*, December 14, 2014.

527 NEW DAY INDEPENDENT MEDIA COMMITTEE
Rowland, "Kasich Jumps into the Murky Waters of Modern Fundraising."

Carly Fiorina

SUPER PAC CARLY FOR AMERICA
Reid J. Epstein, "Carly for America? Bad. CARLY for America? Fine," *Wall Street Journal*, June 17, 2015.

Lindsey Graham

SUPER PAC SECURITY IS STRENGTH
Katie Glueck, "Graham Super PAC Raises $3 Million," *Politico*, July 30, 2015.

LEADERSHIP PAC FUND FOR AMERICA'S FUTURE
Center for Responsive Politics, "Fund for America's Future" (www.opensecrets.org/pacs/lookup2.php?cycle=2016&strID=C00388934).

EXPLORATORY COMMITTEE SECURITY THROUGH STRENGTH
Jose A. DelReal and Sean Sullivan, "Lindsey Graham Officially Launches Presidential Exploratory Committee," *Washington Post*, January 29, 2015.

George Pataki

SUPER PAC WE THE PEOPLE, NOT WASHINGTON
David A. Fahrenthold, "Heard of George Pataki? Every Four Years He Thinks about Running for President," *Washington Post*, May 28, 2015.

501(C)(4) AMERICANS FOR REAL CHANGE
Center for Responsive Politics, "George Pataki (R)" (www.opensecrets.org/pres16 /candidate?id=N00028981).

EXPLORATORY COMMITTEE
Dan Friedman, "Presidential Hopeful George Pataki Fails to List Party on Committee Form—But Is Still Running as a Republican, Spokesman Says," *New York Daily News*, June 5, 2015.

Rand Paul

SUPER PAC AMERICA'S LIBERTY PAC
Center for Responsive Politics, "America's Liberty PAC" (www.opensecrets .org/pacs/lookup2.php?cycle=2016&strID=C00532572).

LEADERSHIP PAC REINVENTING A NEW DIRECTION PAC (RANDPAC)
Center for Responsive Politics, "Reinventing a New Direction" (www.open secrets.org/pacs/lookup2.php?strID=C00493924).

JOINT FUNDRAISING COMMITTEE
Rebecca Ballhaus, "Rand Paul Sets Up Combined Fundraising Committee," *Wall Street Journal*, April 6, 2015.

Rick Perry

SUPER PAC OPPORTUNITY AND FREEDOM PAC
Carrie Levine, "Perry's Finance Chairman Does Super PAC Two-Step," *Texas Tribune*, July 22, 2015.

501(C)(4) AMERICANS FOR ECONOMIC FREEDOM
"Perry Group Launching National Anti-Washington Ads," CBS DFW, October 14, 2013 (http://dfw.cbslocal.com/2013/10/14/perry-group-launching-national -anti-washington-ads/).

LEADERSHIP PAC RICK PAC
Kurtis Lee, "Campaign Cash: 'Leadership PACs' Becoming Vehicle of Choice for Presidential Candidates," *Los Angeles Times*, March 11, 2015.

Bobby Jindal

SUPER PAC BELIEVE AGAIN
Rebecca Ballhaus, "Jindal Supporters File Paperwork for Super PAC, 'Believe Again,'" *Wall Street Journal*, January 22, 2015.

501(C)(4) AMERICA NEXT
James Hohmann, "Jindal Group Bids to Win 'War of Ideas,'" *Politico*, October 16, 2013.

LEADERSHIP PAC AMERICA NEXT
Center for Responsive Politics, "Bobby Jindal (R)" (www.opensecrets.org/pres16 /candidate?id=N00026786).

EXPLORATORY COMMITTEE JONATHAN TOPAZ
"Bobby Jindal Forming Exploratory Committee for White House Run," *Politico*, May 18, 2015.

527 AMERICAN FUTURE PROJECT
Internet Archive, "2016 Political Ad by American Future Project," February 1, 2016 (https://archive.org/details/PolAd_BobbyJindal_1rw68).

Scott Walker

SUPER PAC UNINTIMIDATED PAC
Patrick Marley, Mary Spicuzza, and Kevin Crowe, "Scott Walker Super PAC Nets Nearly $20 million," *Journal Sentinel*, July 31, 2015.

EXPLORATORY COMMITTEE
Jason Stein, "Scott Walker Forms Committee to Explore Presidential Run," *Journal Sentinel*, January 27, 2015.

527 OUR AMERICAN REVIVAL
Jenna Johnson, "Groups Supporting Scott Walker Have Raised $26 Million," *Washington Post*, July 21, 2015.

Hillary Clinton

SUPER PAC PRIORITIES USA ACTION
Glenn Thrush, "Messina in the Cross Hairs at Pro-Clinton Super PAC," *Politico*, May 20, 2015.

501(C)(4) AMERICAN BRIDGE 21ST CENTURY FOUNDATION
Dave Levinthal, "Inside Hillary Clinton's Big-Money Cavalry," Center for Public Integrity, April 7, 2016.

JOINT FUNDRAISING COMMITTEE HILLARY VICTORY FUND
Matea Gold and Tom Hamburger, "Democratic Party Fundraising Effort Helps Clinton Find New Donors, Too," *Washington Post*, February 20, 2016.

HYBRID PAC CORRECT THE RECORD

Center for Responsive Politics, "Correct the Record" (www.opensecrets.org
/pacs/lookup2.php?strID=C00578997&cycle=2016).

Martin O'Malley

SUPER PAC GENERATION FORWARD

John Wagner, "O'Malley Backers Launch Super PAC Ahead of Democrat's
Presidential Bid," *Washington Post*, May 27, 2015.

LEADERSHIP PAC O' SAY CAN YOU SEE PAC

John Wagner, "O'Malley Launches Federal PAC as Profile Rises," *Washington
Post*, July 26, 2012.

527 O' SAY CAN YOU SEE PAC (NONFEDERAL 527)

O'Malley website (https://martinomalley.com/); Jill Lawrence, "Is It Time to
Take Martin O'Malley Seriously? The Maryland Governor Is Determined to
Be Part of the 2016 Conversation. If Hillary Clinton Lets Him, That Is," *The
Atlantic*, June 24, 2013.

Sources for Table 1-6

Carly Fiorina

Hannah Levintova, "Fiorina Super-PAC Makes Its Own Abortion Video,"
Mother Jones, September 24, 2015.

Carly for America, "Carly for America Committee," April 22, 2016 (www
.p2016.org/fiorina/fiorinasuperpacorg.html).

Matea Gold, "It's Bold, but Legal: How Campaigns and their Super PAC Backers
Work Together," *Washington Post*, July 6, 2015.

Nick Corasaniti, "Carly Fiorina's 'Super PAC' Aids Her Campaign, in Plain
Sight," *New York Times*, September 30, 2015.

"Super PACS Find Ways to Skirt Campaign Finance Laws," *PacTrack*, March 11,
2016.

Hillary Clinton

Madeline Conway, "Clinton Super PAC Ad Capitalizes on Trump Video," *Politico*, October 10, 2016.

Chris White, "FEC Complaint Accuses Clinton Campaign of Illegally Coordinating with David Brock Super PAC," *Law and Crime*, October 6, 2016.

Lee Fang and Andrew Perez, "Hacked Emails Prove Coordination between
Clinton Campaign and Super PACs," *The Intercept*, October 18, 2016.

Chloe Nurik, "Correct the Record," *Fact Check*, January 22, 2016.

Patrick Caldwell, "How Two Hillary Clinton Superfans Became Super-PAC
Power Players," *Mother Jones*, February 18, 2014.

Kate Kaye, "The Super PAC Big Data Election: Ready for Hillary Was Just the Beginning," *AdAge*, April 13, 2015.
"Pro-Clinton Super PACS," *Priorities USA Action*, January 23, 2014 (www .p2016.org/clinton/clintonsuperpacorg.html).
Paul Blumenthal, "How Super PACs and Campaigns Are Coordinating in 2016," *Huffington Post*, November 14, 2015.

John Kasich

Paul Blumenthal, "How Super PACs and Campaigns Are Coordinating in 2016," *Huffington Post*, November 14, 2015.
"New Day for America," *P2016*, April 26, 2016 (www.p2016.org/kasich/kasich superpacorg.html).
Dan Tuohy, "Presidential Hopeful Kasich Combines Data Mining with Traditional Campaigning," *Government Technology*, December 28, 2015.

Bobby Jindal

Katie Glueck, "Pro-Jindal Super PAC Fueled by Louisiana Cash," *Politico*, July 31, 2015.
Paul Blumenthal, "How Super PACs and Campaigns Are Coordinating in 2016," *Huffington Post*, November 14, 2015.
Darrel Rowland, "Super PAC Rules Are Super Vague," *Columbus Dispatch*, October 5, 2015.
David M. Drucker, "Can Bobby Jindal Ride His Super PAC to an Iowa Upset?" *Washington Examiner*, November 5, 2016.
Nick Corasaniti, "Carly Fiorina's 'Super Pac' Aids Her Campaign, in Plain Sight," *New York Times*, September 30, 2015.

Rand Paul

Ashley Killough, "Rand Paul Supporters Envision NSA Fight as WWE Match," *CNN*, May 29, 2015.
David Weigel, "A New 'Pro-Rand Paul' Super-PAC Is Making Paul's Official Super-PAC Nervous," *Bloomberg*, June 19, 2015.
Nick Corasaniti, "Carly Fiorina's 'Super Pac' Aids Her Campaign, in Plain Sight," *New York Times*, September 30, 2015.
Alex Isenstadt, "Rand Paul Super PAC Launches Ad Buy Ahead of Iowa, N.H.," *Politico*, November 25, 2015.
"Legal Blog Network," *Find Law* (http://news.findlaw.com/prnewswire /20150724/24jul20151800.html).

Ted Cruz

"Pro-Cruz Keep the Promise Super PACS to Announce Grass Roots Creative Contest," *Business Wire*, June 12, 2015.

Tom Hamburger, "Cruz Campaign Credits Psychological Data and Analytics for Its Rising Success," *Washington Post,* December 13, 2015.

Matea Gold and Sean Sullivan, "Ted Cruz Leans on Allied Super PAC as GOP Nomination Fight Rolls On," *Washington Post,* April 4, 2016.

Jeb Bush

Reid J. Epstein and Rebecca Ballhaus, "Roles of Presidential Super PACs Expanding," *Wall Street Journal,* April 30, 2015.

Ian Vandewalker and Eric Petry, "The Shift in Presidential Campaign Funding to Outside Groups," *Brennan Center for Justice,* August 4, 2015.

Andrew Kaczynski and Ilan Ben-Weir, "We Crashed Jeb Bush's Super PAC's Donor Call, and Here's What They Said," *Buzzfeed,* June 17, 2015.

Marco Rubio

Scott Bland, "Secret-Money Group Tied to Marco Rubio Super PAC Has Been Researching Presidential Primary Voters," *The Atlantic,* April 10, 2015.

Robert Maguire and Anna Massoglia, "New Tax Forms Show Strong Ties between Pro-Rubio Group and Campaign," *OpenSecrets,* May 24, 2016.

Paul Blumenthal, "How Super PACs and Campaigns Are Coordinating in 2016," *Huffington Post,* November 14, 2015.

Richard Skinner, "Marco Rubio Breaks New Ground in Dark Money," *Sunlight Foundation,* November 24, 2015.

Matea Gold, "The Rubio Campaign Tweets—and the Rubio Super PAC Airs an Ad," *Washington Post,* February 4, 2016.

Ben Carson

Brent Ferguson, "Candidates & Super PACs: The New Model in 2016," Brennan Center for Justice, 2016.

Joseph Tanfani and Seema Mehta, "Super PACs Stretch the Rules That Prohibit Coordination with Presidential Campaigns," *Los Angeles Times,* October 5, 2015.

Eliana Johnson, "Trump Campaign Turns to 'Psychographic' Data Firm Used by Cruz," *National Review,* August 5, 2016.

Mike Huckabee

Nick Corasaniti, "Carly Fiorina's 'Super PAC' Aids Her Campaign, in Plain Sight," *New York Times,* September 30, 2015.

Max Brantley, "Here Comes Huckabee," *Arkansas Times,* May 1, 2015.

Donald Trump

Dave Levinthal, "Donald Trump Embraces Donors, Super PACs He Once Decried," *Time Magazine,* June 17, 2016.

"Future 45: Expenditures, 2016 Cycle," *OpenSecrets*, 2016 (www.opensecrets
.org/pacs/expenditures.php?cycle=2016&cmte=C00574533).

OpenSecrets: No vendor payments found for Cambridge Analytica in 2016
(www.opensecrets.org/expends/vendor.php?year=2016&vendor
=Cambridge%2BAnalytica).

Notes

1. Julie Bykowicz, "Trump Makes Quick Work of Re-election Fundraising: President and His Super PAC Appeal to Supporters Big and Small to Build Massive War Chest—Faster than Any Prior White House Occupant," *Wall Street Journal*, February 1, 2018.

2. The other president who won office this way was George W. Bush in 2000.

3. Scott Blackburn, "Money Doesn't Buy Elections: 2016 Presidential Election Edition," Center for Competitive Politics, November 9, 2016.

4. Kyle Sammin, "Trump Proved *Citizens United* Doesn't Let Big Money Control Democracy," *The Federalist*, February 20, 2017.

5. Center for Responsive Politics, "Ted Cruz (R)" (www.opensecrets.org /pres16/candidate?id=N00033085).

6. Mike Lux, cofounder and president of Progressive Strategies, LLC, and senior adviser for progressive outreach for the Democratic National Committee, interview by David Magleby, January 6, 2017.

7. Thad Kousser, "Election 2016: Why Money Won't Matter," Institute of Governmental Studies, September 18, 2015.

8. Ibid.

9. David B. Magleby, "The 2012 Election as Team Sport," in *Financing the 2012 Election*, edited by David B. Magleby (Brookings, 2014), pp. 21–23.

10. Donald Trump, "Transcript: Read the Full Text of the CNBC Republican Debate in Boulder," *Time*, October 28, 2015.

11. Donald Trump, "The CNN Miami Republican Debate Transcript, Annotated," *Washington Post*, March 10, 2016.

12. American Presidency Project, "Remarks in a Meeting with Steelworkers in Des Moines, Iowa," January 26, 2010 (www.presidency.ucsb.edu/ws/index .php?pid=117514).

13. Nicholas Confessore, "Bernie Sanders Tops His Rivals in Use of Outside Money," *New York Times*, January 28, 2016.

14. Hillary Rodham Clinton, *What Happened* (New York: Simon and Schuster, 2017), pp. 45–46.

15. Trump, "The CNN Miami Republican Debate Transcript, Annotated."

16. Ibid.

17. Kenneth Vogel, "The Kochs Put a Price on 2016: $889 Million," *Politico*, January 26, 2015.

18. Nicholas Confessore, "Koch Brothers' Budget of $889 Million for 2016 Is on Par with Both Parties' Spending," *New York Times*, January 26, 2015.

19. Nancy Benac, "Who Are the Koch Brothers?" *PBS NewsHour*, January 28, 2015.

20. Gabrielle Levy, "Cashed Out: Koch Bros. Sit on Wallets in '16: They Spent $900 M. in 2012 but Won't Bankroll a Third Party Bid—or Anyone Else in the GOP," *U.S. News*, May 19, 2016.

21. Donald Trump, Twitter post, August 2, 2015, 7:00 A.M. (https://twitter.com/realdonaldtrump/status/627841345789558788?lang=en). See also Theodore Schleifer, "The Year When Money Won Nobody Nothing," CNN, November 12, 2016.

22. Donald Trump, Twitter post, October 13, 2015, 3:46 A.M. (https://twitter.com/realdonaldtrump/status/653884577300267008?lang=en). See also Schleifer, "The Year When Money Won Nobody Nothing."

23. Donald Trump, Twitter post, February 22, 2016, 6:42 A.M. (https://twitter.com/realdonaldtrump/status/701779181986680832?lang=en). See also Schleifer, "The Year When Money Won Nobody Nothing."

24. For more on the Joe Ricketts reversal on opposing Donald Trump, see Matea Gold, "After Opposing Trump in the Primaries, Joe Ricketts Will Give at Least $1 Million to Support Him," *Washington Post*, September 20, 2016.

25. Katherine Skiba and Kathy Bergen, "Todd Ricketts, Cubs Co-owner, Picked to Serve as Deputy Commerce Secretary," *Chicago Tribune*, November 30, 2016.

26. Martin O'Malley, "Campaign Finance Reform," October 1, 2015 (http://martinomalley.com/the-latest/campaign-finance-reform/).

27. Sam Frizell, "Hillary Clinton Announces Plan to Limit Money in Politics," *Time*, September 8, 2015.

28. Lee Morehouse, "Trump Breaks Precedent, Files as Candidate for Reelection on First Day," AZfamily.com, January 30, 2017.

29. Ashley Balcerzak, "Super PACs Already Racing toward 2018—and 2020," Center for Public Integrity, August 1, 2017.

30. Anne Farris, "Unfolding Story Swelling Like a Sponge," *Washington Post*, April 6, 1997.

31. Terry Frieden, "Former Democratic Fund-Raiser John Huang Pleads Guilty," CNN, August 12, 1999.

32. Neil A. Lewis, "Longtime Fund-Raiser for Gore Convicted in Donation Scheme," *New York Times*, March 2, 2000.

33. Mark Mazzetti, Ronen Bergman, and David Kirkpatrick, "Trump Jr. and Other Aides Met with Gulf Emissary Offering Help to Win Election," *New York Times*, May 19, 2018.

34. Ibid.

35. Anne Gearan, Philip Rucker, and Abby Phillip, "DNC Chairwoman Will Resign in Aftermath of Committee Email Controversy," *Washington Post*, July 24, 2016.

36. Max Fisher, "Donald Trump's Appeal to Russia Shocks Foreign Policy Experts," *New York Times*, January 20, 2018.

37. Nathaniel Popper and Matthew Rosenberg, "How Russian Spies Hid behind Bitcoin in Hacking Campaign," *New York Times*, July 13, 2018.

38. "Inside the Internet Research Agency's Lie Machine," *The Economist*, February 22, 2018.

39. Anne Claire Stapleton, "No, You Can't Vote by Text Message," CNN, November 7, 2016.

40. Callum Borchers, "Analysis | What We Know about the 21 States Targeted by Russian Hackers," *Washington Post*, September 23, 2017.

41. Katelyn Polantz and Stephen Collinson, "12 Russians Indicted in Mueller Investigation," CNN, July 14, 2018.

42. Josh Meyer and Darren Samuelsohn, "U.S. Officials Charge NRA-Linked Russian with Acting as Kremlin Agent," *Politico*, July 16, 2018.

43. Steven Law, president and CEO of Senate Leadership Fund, interview by David Magleby, March 15, 2017.

44. Institute of Politics, *Campaign for President: The Managers Look at 2016* (Lanham, Md.: Rowman and Littlefield, 2017), p. 228.

45. Ibid., p. 229.

46. In 2015, Donald Trump and NBC agreed that Trump would not host *The Celebrity Apprentice* during his presidential campaign. The show continued with Arnold Schwarzenegger as host. See Cynthia Littleton, "Donald Trump to Remain Executive Producer on 'Celebrity Apprentice,'" *Variety*, December 8, 2016.

47. Mike Podhorzer, political director for the AFL-CIO, interview by David Magleby, March 17, 2017.

48. Institute of Politics, *Campaign for President*, p. 244.

49. The governors were John Kasich (Ohio), Jeb Bush (Florida), Chris Christie (New Jersey), Scott Walker (Wisconsin), Bobby Jindal (Louisiana), Jim Gilmore (Virginia), George Pataki (New York), Rick Perry (Texas), and Mike Huckabee (Arkansas). The senators were Ted Cruz (Texas), Marco Rubio (Florida), Rand Paul (Kentucky), Lindsey Graham (South Carolina), and Rick Santorum (Pennsylvania).

50. Sasha Issenberg, "Mike Murphy of Right to Rise Explains His Theory That Jeb Bush Is Still the Candidate to Beat," Bloomberg, October 20, 2015.

51. Institute of Politics, *Campaign for President*, p. 138.

52. Geoff Garin, president of Hart Research Associates, interview by David Magleby, June 1, 2017.

53. Jessica Estepa, "Donald Trump on Carly Fiorina: 'Look at That Face!'" *USA Today*, September 10, 2015.

54. In the early stages of the campaign, Trump focused many of his personal attacks on Jeb Bush. Included among the labels he gave to Bush in tweets and speeches were the following: "low energy, no clue, failed campaign, lightweight, desperate and sad, weak, weak, by far the weakest of the lot, Sad!, total disaster, low energy guy, sad sack, too soft, pathetic, weak on illegal immigration, will NEVER Make America Great Again." See "Donald Trump Twitter Insults," *New York Times*, January 28, 2016.

55. Ben Schreckinger, "Trump Attacks McCain: 'I Like People Who Weren't Captured,'" *Politico*, July 18, 2015.

56. Madeline Conway, "Trump and Romney's 10 Harshest Insults," *Politico*, November 25, 2016.

57. Michael Addady, "Donald Trump Backtracks on His Criticism of George W. Bush," *Fortune*, February 14, 2016.

58. For a discussion on how the term *earned media* came into use, see Dotty Lynch, "How the Media Covered the 2008 Election," in *Campaigns and Elections American Style*, 3rd ed., edited by James A. Thurber and Candice J. Nelson (Boulder, Colo.: Westview Press, 2010), pp. 157–92. On earned media in the 2004 campaign, see Matthew Dowd, "Campaign Organization and Strategy," in *Electing the President, 2004*, edited by Kathleen Hall Jamieson (University of Pennsylvania Press, 2006), pp. 21–24.

59. Nicholas Confessore and Karen Yourish, "$2 Billion Worth of Free Media for Donald Trump," *New York Times*, March 15, 2016.

60. Niv Sultan, "Election 2016: Trump's Free Media Helped Keep Cost Down, but Fewer Donors Provided More of the Cash," Center for Responsive Politics, April 13, 2017.

61. Leslie Wayne, "The 2000 Campaign: The End; Forbes Spent Millions, but for Little Gain," *New York Times*, February 10, 2000.

62. Jeremy W. Peters and Rachel Shorey, "Trump Spent Far Less than Clinton, but Paid His Companies Well," *New York Times*, December 9, 2016.

63. Alexander Burns and Maggie Haberman, "Bloomberg, Sensing an Opening, Revisits a Potential White House Run," *New York Times*, January 23, 2016.

64. John C. Green, Michael E. Kohler, and Ian P. Schwarber, "Financing the 2012 Presidential Nomination Campaign," in *Financing the 2012 Election*, edited by Magleby, p. 91.

65. Mark Halperin and John Heilemann, *Double Down: Game Change 2012* (New York: Penguin Press, 2013), p. 334; Jonathan Alter, *The Center Holds: Obama and His Enemies* (New York: Simon and Schuster, 2013), p. 214.

66. Institute of Politics, *Campaign for President*, p. 28.

67. Donald Trump, Twitter post, September 5, 2015, 2:50 P.M. (https://twitter.com/realdonaldtrump/status/640280850182090752?lang=en).

68. Donald Trump, Twitter post, February 27, 2016, 7:25 A.M. (https://twitter.com/realdonaldtrump/status/703601762876305409?lang=en).

69. Monica Langley and Rebecca Ballhaus, "Donald Trump Won't Self-Fund General-Election Campaign," *Wall Street Journal*, May 4, 2016.

70. Donald Trump, "Transcript of the Second Debate," *New York Times*, October 10, 2016.

71. Jonathan Allen and Amie Parnes, *Shattered: Inside Hillary Clinton's Doomed Campaign* (New York: Crown, 2017), pp. 217–18.

72. Jeremy W. Peters and Jonathan Martin, "Donald Trump, Losing Ground, Tries to Blame the System," *New York Times*, April 12, 2016.

73. Bob Cusack, "Trump Slams RNC Chairman, Calls 2016 Process 'a Disgrace,'" *The Hill*, April 12, 2016.

74. Institute of Politics, *Campaign for President*, p. 228.

75. Republican National Committee, *Growth and Opportunity Project Report* (2013), pp. 24–32, 34–35.

76. Campaign Finance Institute, "President Trump, with RNC Help, Raised More Small Donor Money than President Obama; as Much as Clinton and Sanders Combined," February 21, 2017 (www.cfinst.org/Press/PReleases/17-02-21/President_Trump_with_RNC_Help_Raised_More_Small_Donor_Money_than_President_Obama_As_Much_As_Clinton_and_Sanders_Combined.aspx).

77. Trump had two joint fundraising committees with the RNC. The Trump Make America Great Again Committee raised $264 million, while Trump Victory raised $108 million. See Center for Responsive Politics, "Joint Fundraising Committees" (https://www.opensecrets.org/jfc/).

78. Lux, interview.

79. David B. Magleby, Jay Goodliffe, and Joseph A. Olsen, *Who Donates in Campaigns? The Importance of Message, Messenger, Medium and Structure* (Cambridge University Press, 2018).

80. Clinton, *What Happened*, p. 227.

81. In 2016, Clinton received the votes of 55 percent of those under the age of thirty. In contrast, in 2012 Obama received 60 percent of the votes of this group. See CNN (www.cnn.com/election/2012/results/race/president/ and (www.cnn.com/election/results/exit-polls).

82. Institute of Politics, *Campaign for President*, p. 53.

83. Heidi Gillstrom, "Clinton's 'Superpredators' Comment Most Damaging by Either Candidate," *The Hill*, September 30, 2016.

84. Joshua Green and Sasha Issenberg, "Inside the Trump Bunker, with Days to Go," *Bloomberg Businessweek*, October 27, 2016.

85. Dan Berman and Kenneth P. Vogel, "Team Obama Raises $1 Billion," *Politico*, October 25, 2012.

86. "Obama, Clinton Sign Joint Fundraising Agreement with the DNC," *Economic Times*, May 15, 2008.

87. Catherine Treyz, Dan Merica, Jeremy Diamond, and Jeff Zeleny, "Sanders Campaign Sues DNC after Database Breach," CNN, December 21, 2015.

88. Donna Brazile, *Hacks: The Inside Story of the Break-ins and Breakdowns That Put Donald Trump in the White House* (New York: Hachette Books, 2017), p. 97.

89. Angus Campbell, Philip E. Converse, Warren E. Miller, and Donald E. Stokes, *The American Voter* (New York: Wiley, 1960), pp. 54–65.

90. Alexander Burns, Maggie Haberman, and Jonathan Martin, "Donald Trump Apology Caps Day of Outrage over Lewd Tape," *New York Times*, October 7, 2016.

91. Jonathan Swan, "Republican Donors in 'State of Panic' over Trump," *The Hill*, October 8, 2016.

92. Meghan McCarthy, "Republican Voters Remain Loyal to Trump in First National Poll after Video," *Morning Consult*, October 9, 2016.

93. Corky Siemaszko, "FBI Recommends No Criminal Charges against Hillary Clinton," *NBC News*, July 5, 2016.

94. Eric Brander, Pamela Brown, and Evan Perez, "FBI Clears Clinton—Again," CNN, November 7, 2016.

95. "2016 Exit Polls," CNN, November 23, 2016.

96. Clinton, *What Happened*, p. 220.

97. U.S. Office of the Inspector General, U.S. Department of Justice, "A Review of Various Actions by the Federal Bureau of Investigation and Department of Justice in Advance of the 2016 Election," June 2018 (www.justice.gov/file/1071991/download).

98. Garin, interview.

99. Clinton, *What Happened*, p. 349.

100. Mark Murray, "NBC News/*Wall Street Journal* Poll: 2016 'An Election about Fear,'" *NBC News*, November 6, 2016.

101. Erika Franklin Fowler, Travis N. Ridout, and Michael M. Franz, "Political Advertising in 2016: The Presidential Election as Outlier?" *The Forum* 14, no. 4 (2016), pp. 457–59.

102. Institute of Politics, *Campaign for President*, p. 232.

103. Chris Cillizza, "Hillary Clinton's 'Email' Problem Was Bigger than Anyone Realized," CNN, May 26, 2017.

104. Clinton, *What Happened*, pp. 403–04.

105. Sharon Wolff Sussin, national political director of the National Federation of Independent Business, interview by David Magleby, January 5, 2017.

106. Harold Ickes, previous president of Priorities USA and cofounder of Ickes and Enright Group, interview by David Magleby, December 12, 2016.

107. This surge came after BCRA, as total individual contributions in 2006 were also much higher than in 2002, rising from $2.2 billion in 2002 to $3.2 billion in 2006.

108. Kenneth P. Vogel, "Behind the Retreat of the Koch Brothers' Operation," *Politico*, October 27, 2016.

109. Ed Henry, "Adelson Pours $25 Million into White House Race, More May Be Coming," *Fox News*, October 31, 2016.

110. Robert Maguire, "One Nation Rising: Rove-Linked Group Goes from No Revenue to More than $10 Million in 2015," Center for Responsive Politics, November 17, 2016.

111. They did this by having Eric Trump, Donald Trump's son, speak at a fundraiser for the Great America PAC and by having Paul Manafort speak via telephone at a donor event for Rebuild America Now, another Trump-supporting Super PAC. On the Eric Trump connection, see Shane Goldmacher, "Eric Trump Attends Pro Trump Super PAC Fundraiser," *Politico*, September 9, 2016. On Paul Manafort and Rebuild America Now, see Alex Isenstadt and Kenneth Vogel, "Trump Blesses Major Super PAC Effort: Candidates' Top Aides Participate in Briefing with Major Donors for Super PAC That Raised $5 Million in Recent Days," *Politico*, July 20, 2016. Later, vice presidential nominee Mike Pence was quoted as saying the Rebuild America PAC was "one of the best ways to stop Hillary Clinton." See John McCormick and Bill Allison, "Paul Manafort's Friend Is Still Making a Ton of Money on a Mostly Dormant Trump Super PAC," *Time*, December 11, 2017.

112. Russ Choma, "Why Does Jeb Bush Have a Mysterious Shell Company?" *Mother Jones*, June 29, 2015.

113. Nick Corasaniti, "Carly Fiorina's 'Super PAC' Aids Her Campaign, in Plain Sight," *New York Times*, September 30, 2015.

114. Patrick Svitek, "Pro-Cruz Super PACs Focus on Ground Game, Wait on TV," *Texas Tribune*, November 25, 2015.

115. Jonathan Easley, "Iowa Ground Game Under Way for GOP Prize," *The Hill*, November 14, 2015.

116. Rob Simms, executive director of the National Republican Congressional Committee, interview by David Magleby, December 12, 2016.

117. Jennifer Duffy, senior editor of the *Cook Political Report*, interview by David Magleby, November 21, 2016.

118. Cathleen Decker, "A Republican Senator's Strategy to Save His Seat in One of the Country's Tightest Races: Avoid Trump," *Los Angeles Times*, October 24, 2016.

119. Anna Orso, "Pat Toomey, on Election Day, Finally Reveals He's a Trump Voter," *BillyPenn*, November 8, 2016.

120. David B. Magleby and Jay Goodliffe, "Interest Groups," in *Financing the 2012 Election*, edited by Magleby, p. 229.

TWO   *The Regulatory Environment*
           of the 2016 Election

ANTHONY CORRADO

Recent elections have been characterized by a steady dismantling of the federal campaign finance regulations erected by the 1974 Federal Election Campaign Act (FECA) and the 2002 Bipartisan Campaign Reform Act (BCRA). Courts have struck down key provisions of campaign finance law, and the Federal Election Commission (FEC), which is responsible for administering it, has proven to be an ineffective watchdog, interpreting rules in ways that have diminished their efficacy and often failing to reach decisions on enforcement matters.[1] As a result, the regulatory environment has become increasingly permissive, and political actors have been encouraged to test the limits of the law. In this regard, the 2016 election cycle was no exception, with the courts, FEC, and Congress all involved in efforts to further dismantle what little remains of a system designed to ensure that the financial activity in federal campaigns was based on limited contributions and transparency to the public. This chapter will explore the impact of these changes on the 2016 election.

The Supreme Court's 2010 decision in *Citizens United* v. *Federal Election Commission* created new paths for unlimited spending and contributions in federal elections.[2] The court struck down the long-standing ban on the use of corporate money to advocate for federal candidates by affirming the right of corporations—and by extension labor unions—to spend funds from their general treasuries to finance independent expenditures in support of candidates. The court also struck down BCRA's prohibition on the use of corporate and labor union money to finance electioneering communications, which are broadcast advertisements aired close to an election that feature a candidate. The ruling paved the way for a subsequent appellate court decision, *SpeechNow.org* v. *Federal Election Commission*. This decision gave rise to Super PACs, which are political committees that spend money independently in support of candidates and do not make contributions to candidates.[3] In *SpeechNow.org*, the court held that such PACs do not have to abide by federal PAC contribution limits because they only make independent expenditures and thus pose no risk of quid pro quo corruption of candidates. Super PACs may therefore spend unlimited sums from unlimited contributions, including contributions from corporations, labor unions, and interest groups.

While each of these court decisions upheld the disclosure rules requiring independent spenders to report their contributions and expenditures, the FEC had significantly diminished these requirements by adopting regulations in 2007 that required contributions to be disclosed only if given for the purpose of financing an electioneering communication or independent expenditure. Consequently, tax-exempt organizations established under section 501(c) of the Internal Revenue Code, including social welfare advocacy groups, trade associations, and labor unions, which as a result of *Citizens United* are allowed to make independent expenditures, may raise money without disclosing their contributors, since donors typically do not specify the purpose for which their money should be used. This ability to raise undisclosed money spurred the growth of 501(c) groups, especially 501(c)(4) social welfare groups, as a source of campaign funding. Often called "dark money" groups by advocates of strict regulation, these organizations are subject to only two major restrictions: (1) they may not coordinate their efforts with candidates; and (2) they may only use a minor share of their overall funding for political activity, since their tax-exempt status under the Internal Revenue Code is based on the fact that election activity is not their principal purpose.[4]

Furthermore, the presidential public funding program, which gave $239 million to candidates at its peak in 2000, has deteriorated into no more than a last resort for candidates with no viable alternative. In 2016, all the major-party presidential candidates rejected the public funding option, with one exception.[5] Democrat Martin O'Malley, who gained little support in his bid for the nomination, qualified for $1.09 million of primary matching funds, which was largely used to pay off campaign debts.[6] Jill Stein, the Green Party presidential nominee, also accepted primary matching funds, receiving $456,000 before her formal nomination.[7]

In the lead-up to the 2016 election, the dismantling of the regulatory structure continued. Congress eliminated public grants for party nominating conventions, which was the last actively used component of the public funding system. The Supreme Court also struck down BCRA's aggregate limit on individual contributions, thus allowing an individual to give an unlimited sum in total contributions, so long as the limits on contributions to a specific candidate, party committee, or PAC were followed.[8] The FEC and then Congress amplified the significance of this decision by raising party contribution limits so dramatically that the limits became meaningless for all but a small number of extremely wealthy donors. In addition, the FEC and Congress took no meaningful action to address the issues raised by the growing role of Super PACs and section 501(c) groups. As a result, the 2016 election was conducted in the most permissive regulatory environment since the adoption of FECA after the Watergate scandal.

Eliminating Aggregate Contribution Limits

Limits on contributions to individual candidates, parties, and PACs are the cornerstone of federal campaign finance regulations. These limits, first established by FECA in 1974 and later revised by BCRA in 2002, seek to limit donor influence and safeguard the political process against corruption in two ways. First, the law establishes base limits that restrict the amount a donor may give to a specific candidate, party, or PAC. Second, the law imposes an aggregate limit on the total amount an individual may give to all candidates, parties, or PACs. This latter limit is designed to reduce the influence of wealthy donors by preventing a donor from giving the maximum contribution to a large number of candidates or political committees. The limits in place for 2016 and earlier election cycles are in chapter 1, table 1-1.

Ever since the 1976 *Buckley* v. *Valeo* decision, courts have consistently upheld these contribution limits as a constitutionally valid safeguard against corruption or the appearance of corruption, which the courts recognize as the sole government interest involved in the right of free speech associated with a political donation.[9] Even though many other aspects of campaign finance law had changed, the limits on donations to candidates, parties, and PACs, as well as the aggregate limit, remained intact,

but in 2014, the Supreme Court took the first step toward dismantling
these contribution limits by striking down the aggregate limit imposed on
a donor's total contributions.

To put the Court's decision in context, a review of the contribution
limits in place before the decision is necessary. In 2012, an individual was
allowed to give $2,500 per election ($5,000 total for a primary and the
general election) to a candidate, $30,800 per year to a national party
committee, $10,000 per year to a state party committee, and $5,000 per
year to a PAC. In addition, a donor's total giving was subject to a biennial
aggregate limit established by BCRA, which revised FECA's aggregate
limit of $25,000 per year. BCRA's aggregate limit was based on separate
sublimits established for contributions to candidates, parties, and PACs.
In 2012, these limits allowed an individual to donate a total of $46,200
to all federal candidates and $70,800 to all party committees and PACs.
Of the $70,800, no more than $46,200 could be contributed to state or
local party committees and PACs. Thus, in all, an individual was limited
to contributing $117,000 in a two-year election cycle. This aggregate
limit affected relatively few donors, since most contributors lack the
means to give such a large sum. In the 2012 election, for example, only
646 donors reached this overall contribution limit.[10] This elite group of
donors gave a total of $93 million to candidates and committees active
in federal campaigns.[11]

In June 2012, Shaun McCutcheon, an Alabama businessman and
Republican donor, filed a joint lawsuit with the Republican National
Committee (RNC) that challenged the constitutionality of the aggregate
limit. McCutcheon had contributed a total of $33,088 to congressional
candidates as of June 18, 2012, giving $1,776 to each of fifteen challeng-
ers attempting to unseat incumbents.[12] He also contributed $1,776 to
the RNC, National Republican Senate Committee (NRSC), and National
Republican Congressional Committee (NRCC), as well as $27,328 to
several other noncandidate committees. He wanted to contribute $1,776
to twelve other congressional candidates and an additional $25,000 to
each of the three national Republican party committees. He did not make
these additional contributions, however, because doing so would have
violated the aggregate contribution limits.[13]

McCutcheon claimed that the aggregate limit violated his First Amendment rights by preventing him from making contributions that were
permitted by the base limits. The law's principal effect, he contended,
was to limit how many candidates or political committees an individual

could support, which is different in kind from a limit on how much a donor may give to a candidate or committee.[14] He further contended that the government's interest in preventing corruption was served by the base limits and that aggregate limits "serve no purpose other than to 'equalize' the relative ability of individuals to participate in the political process."[15] He also challenged the anticircumvention rationale advanced in *Buckley*, which upheld the aggregate restriction as a means of preventing an individual from circumventing the limit on contributions to a candidate by giving large sums to party committees that would then spend the money in support of the candidate. McCutcheon posited that party contribution limits established in BCRA that limited how much a donor could give to a national, state, or local party committee addressed the concern that a donor could give unlimited amounts to a candidate by using party committees as conduits to a candidate. In addition, rules adopted against earmarking contributions, which require that any contribution to a party or PAC earmarked to support a candidate or otherwise directed by a donor to be used to support a candidate be considered a contribution to the candidate subject to the candidate contribution limit, addressed the concern that a donor would give to other entities as a way to circumvent the limit imposed on donations to a candidate or committee.[16] The aggregate limit was therefore, McCutcheon contended, an overly broad safeguard that unnecessarily restricted his First Amendment freedoms.

The U.S. District Court for the District of Columbia rejected McCutcheon's arguments by a vote of 3-0. Following *Buckley*, the court upheld the constitutionality of the limit, specifically noting its role in preventing evasion of the base limits.[17] In support of this reasoning, the court acknowledged the argument, made by defenders of the law, that without the aggregate limit, a single donor could contribute to multiple committees, including all national party committees and state party committees, either through separate contributions or, in the scenario presented to the court, through a joint fundraising committee (JFC) created by these committees, which is allowed by the law. In this way, a single donor could contribute a large sum to a JFC that might consist of all national and state party committees. Because the law permits unlimited transfers among party committees, the funds could in turn be transferred to a single party committee, which might then use this large gift to support a particular candidate.[18] In the view of the court, such a scenario was not "hard to imagine."[19] The district court thus upheld the limit as part of a system to prevent corruption or the appearance of corruption.

The Supreme Court did not share this view. In a 5-4 decision issued on April 2, 2014, the Court struck down the aggregate limit, ruling that it was an unconstitutional restriction on First Amendment rights.[20] Although *Buckley* had supported the aggregate limit as no more than a corollary of base contribution limits, the Court did not consider *Buckley* dispositive. The Court noted that *Buckley* had devoted only a paragraph to the aggregate limit, which was not "separately addressed at length by the parties" in the case.[21] In addition, the Court recognized that the regulations had changed since *Buckley*. Statutory safeguards against circumvention had been strengthened since 1974, particularly rules on earmarking, and BCRA had established a "different statutory regime" than FECA, particularly given the limits on contributions to political parties.[22] The Court therefore concluded *Buckley* was not a controlling precedent on the matter.[23]

In judging the limit's constitutionality, the Supreme Court adhered to the narrow interpretation of corruption employed in *Citizens United*, which limited corruption to quid pro quo exchanges between a donor and a recipient. This understanding excluded the spending of large sums of money or efforts to "garner influence over or access to" elected officials or party officials through large donations from the concept of corruption.[24] Accordingly, the Court viewed base limits as the primary safeguard against corruption. While the aggregate limit may serve as an additional means of achieving this objective, the Court noted that it does limit the number of candidates or committees a donor may support, assuming that a donor wanted to give the maximum permissible contribution to many candidates and party committees. It therefore ruled that the aggregate ceiling is not a modest restraint on an individual's speech and associational rights; it imposes a substantial burden. The Court noted, "The Government may no more restrict how many candidates or causes a donor may support than it may tell a newspaper how many candidates it may endorse."[25] It therefore found "a substantial mismatch between the Government's stated objective and the means selected to achieve it" and struck down the aggregate limit.

The Court's majority did not acknowledge that a donor could support a large number of candidates or committees simply by giving small contributions or amounts well below the maximum permitted. Nor did it give much credence to the possibility of parties raising large sums from donors through JFCs or other scenarios highlighting the ways donors might circumvent base limits in the absence of aggregate limits. The Court determined that these scenarios were "either illegal under current campaign finance law or divorced from reality,"[26] and it concluded that each scenario "is sufficiently implausible that the Government has not carried its burden of demonstrating that the aggregate limits further its anti-circumvention interest."[27]

This aspect of the Court's decision was surprising because JFCs had become a common feature of federal campaign fundraising. A JFC allows candidates, parties, or other political committees to join together to raise money and solicit large sums from donors. These sums are then allocated based on applicable contribution limits. For example, in 2012, both President Obama and his Republican challenger, Mitt Romney, formed JFCs with their respective national party committees and state parties to seek contributions of more than $75,000, which included the maximum contribution to a presidential candidate and the $70,800 aggregate limit on party contributions. The Obama Victory Fund raised more than $454 million, including more than $176 million for the Obama campaign and $155 million for the Democratic National Committee (DNC) and state party committees. The Romney Victory Fund raised $492 million, including more than $146 million for the Romney campaign and $197 million for the RNC and state party committees.[28] After *McCutcheon*, nothing in the law prohibited a party from soliciting very large individual contributions through a JFC consisting of a presidential candidate, the national committee, and every state party committee, with all of the proceeds except the money received by the candidate spent by the party in support of its presidential nominee. This approach would allow a donor to give as much as $3.6 million in 2016 in support of a nominee within the scope of contribution limits. The ruling thus weakened the efficacy of contribution limits and enhanced the potential influence of donors capable of making six- or seven-figure contributions. But the *McCutcheon* decision proved to be only the first step in expanding the role of wealthy donors in federal elections, since its consequences were soon amplified by the actions of the FEC and Congress.

Reforming Convention Funding

The day after the Supreme Court issued the *McCutcheon* opinion, President Obama signed the Gabriella Miller Kids First Research Act, which was sponsored by House Majority Leader Eric Cantor, a Republican, and named for a young girl from Virginia who had died from a brain tumor after publicly advocating for increased funding for cancer research. The law eliminated the public subsidy for presidential nominating conventions, shifting the funding to the National Institutes of Health by authorizing $126 million over the next decade for pediatric medical research.[29] Bipartisan cooperation in passing legislation has been rare in recent years,[30] but the bill to abolish public funding for party conventions received broad support, with the Republican-controlled House passing the bill by a wide margin and the Democrat-controlled Senate adopting the measure by unanimous consent.[31] In 2014, Congress thus ended the last actively used remnant of the presidential election public funding system.

Even after presidential candidates had forsaken public funding, both parties had continued to accept the public convention subsidy. In 2012, each of the major parties received $18.2 million of public money to help defray the costs of a presidential nominating convention. In practice, this subsidy represented only a share of convention funding, since both parties supplemented these funds with private donations raised by their convention committees.[32] Parties also benefited from the fundraising efforts of host or municipal committees established by local organizations in convention cities. These committees are not subject to federal contribution limits and can accept unlimited donations, including corporate contributions, to pay for events and other activities associated with a convention, such as promoting local commerce and the city's image.[33] The share of convention funding from these private sources had grown significantly over time. In 1980, private sources of funding, including party convention committees, host committees, and municipal committees, were responsible for 7 percent of the $16 million total raised for the Republican and Democratic national conventions.[34] By 2008, private sources were responsible for more than 70 percent of the $118 million raised for the two conventions.[35] In 2012, private sources provided almost 75 percent of the $74 million spent on the Republican National Convention and $66 million spent on the Democratic National Convention.[36] Thus, while public money offered a substantial subsidy, it constituted a dwindling share of overall convention financing.

With the public subsidy ended, national party committees faced the prospect of additional fundraising to cover the costs of their conventions or a need to lower expenses, perhaps by reducing the length of the convention, or doing both. The parties responded by asking the FEC for additional fundraising authority to compensate for the loss of the public subsidy. The DNC and RNC jointly requested FEC approval to establish a separate account, or convention committee, which would operate under separate contribution limits for the sole purpose of financing convention expenses.[37] Any moneys raised would be governed by the same rules previously applied to public funds, which meant that they would be used for the costs of administering the conventions and not for general party-building expenses or the costs related to the campaigns of individual primary candidates.[38]

What the parties sought was a decision that would treat a convention committee as a fourth national party committee comparable to the existing national party committees (the DNC and RNC), U.S. Senate campaign committees (NRSC and DSCC), and U.S. House campaign committees (the Democratic Congressional Campaign Committee, DCCC; and National Republican Congressional Committee, NRCC). They based their argument in part on the need to replace the "entitlement" lost because of the end of public funding and in part on prior FEC opinions that permitted a candidate or party committee to establish a separate account with separate contribution limits to pay election recount expenses.[39] Advocates of campaign finance regulation countered these arguments by noting that public funding was a voluntary program, not an entitlement, and that the law already provided rules for private contributions to party convention committees, which did not include an additional limit for convention expenses. Furthermore, Congress did not consider an additional limit when it repealed public funding. Opponents viewed the proposal as no more than an attempt "to eviscerate the hard money contribution limits bit by bit by creating separate limits to fund activities of the National Party Committees" and claimed FEC approval would be "contrary to law and is outside of the FEC's authority."[40]

However, the FEC approved the DNC and RNC's request in October 2014, allowing them to establish convention committees to raise funds under a separate contribution limit of $32,400 for an individual donor and $15,000 for a PAC. The commission based its decision on the determination that a convention committee met the definition of a "national committee" under the law and was thus subject to its own contribution limit.[41] In effect, the decision increased the potential maximum aggregate contribution an individual could give to a party from $97,200 per year ($32,400 to each of the three national committees) to $129,600 per year ($32,400 to each of four committees). Similarly, the maximum aggregate PAC contribution to a party rose from $45,000 per year

($15,000 to each of the three national party committees) to $60,000 per year ($15,000 to each of four committees).

The FEC's decision represented a major change from earlier understanding of the law, but it constituted a limited step, because its principal practical consequence was to allow a donor who had already given the maximum permissible contribution to the DNC or RNC to give additional money to the party's convention committee. Whether this action would have allowed the parties to generate the sums needed to replace the public subsidy was an open question. However, before it could be answered, the commission's action on convention accounts was overshadowed by a bolder and more significant change in party contribution limits enacted by Congress.

Increasing Party Contribution Limits

The FEC decision did not allay the concerns of some party leaders about the parties' ability to generate adequate funds for the cost of a convention. Nor did it provide much help in allowing parties to compete against Super PACs and independent 501(c) groups that could receive unlimited contributions, including donations from corporations and labor unions. Republicans generally favored lifting the limits on party contributions to address these concerns. Democrats generally opposed higher limits, fearing that such a move would expand the influence of millionaires and billionaires, thereby providing an advantage to the Republicans. Any effort to ease the restrictions placed on parties would also contrast with the political messaging of many Democratic congressional campaigns, which condemned the influence of big money donors, especially the conservative Koch brothers, and urged an overturning of the *Citizens United* decision.[42] This partisan divide made any prospect for campaign finance reform legislation highly unlikely. Nonetheless, congressional leaders found a way to assist their parties by using a must-pass budget bill as a vehicle to roll back the restrictions that BCRA had placed on parties and raise contribution limits.

In December 2014, Congress needed to pass an omnibus budget bill or face the possibility of a government shutdown, since a stopgap budget measure adopted to continue government funding was set to expire on December 11. Congress avoided a shutdown by passing a $1.1 trillion omnibus spending package, which was voted on by the House on December 11, two days after the final text was released, and approved by the Senate two days later.[43] The final version of the bill included provisions that had been inserted at the last minute in the section titled "Other Matters," which began on page 1599 of the 1603-page bill.[44] These provisions revised the law on party fundraising and were the result of negotiations involving House Speaker John Boehner and Senate Minority Leader Mitch McConnell, both Republicans, and Senate Majority Leader Harry Reid, a Democrat. The provisions had not previously been discussed by the House or Senate, or publicly mentioned before the release of the bill. Through this secretive approach, Congress enacted the most significant legislative reform of campaign finance law since the adoption of BCRA in 2002.

The party-funding provisions inserted into the Consolidated and Further Continuing Appropriations Act, 2015,[45] which is often called the "CRomnibus" legislation, with the CR standing for continuing resolution, restructured the rules on party fundraising, dramatically increased party contribution limits, and significantly undercut the ban on party soft-money fundraising established by BCRA. The legislation, which was signed into law by President Obama on December 16, 2014, allowed national party committees to establish new, segregated accounts or committees that were distinct from the general account each party committee traditionally used to raise and spend money. Three new accounts were sanctioned: one to finance party conventions, one to finance buildings or facilities, and one to finance recounts or other legal matters. These new accounts would raise money under their own contribution limits, separate from the limit imposed on contributions to a party committee's general account. The rules applied to any national party committee, including those of minor parties. Thus, the DNC and RNC, in addition to their general or traditional account, were permitted to establish a convention account, a building or facilities account, and a recount and legal expenses account. Only the DNC or RNC may create a convention account, which was limited to spending no more than $20 million per convention for increased contribution limits to apply. Other national party committees (the NRSC, DSCC, NRCC, and DCCC) were permitted to establish two new accounts: a building account and a recount or legal expenses account.

More important, Congress *tripled* the party contribution limit for each of these new accounts. At the time the legislation was enacted, an individual could donate a maximum of $32,400 per year to a national party committee. The new rules maintained this limit for a committee's general account but allowed individuals to give three times as much, $97,200 per year, to each of the new accounts. Adjusting for inflation, in 2016 an individual could give a maximum of $33,400 per year to a committee's general account and $100,200 to each of the new accounts. In the wake of *McCutcheon*, these limits exponentially increased the amount an individual could contribute to a party. An individual who gave the maximum contribution to each account could give a total of $334,000 per year to the DNC or RNC ($33,400 to the general account and $100,200 to each of the three new accounts), and since these are annual limits, for those wanting to give in each year of a two-year election cycle these limits would be doubled. They could also give a maximum of $233,800 to a party's House or Senate campaign committee ($33,400 to the general account and $100,200 to each of the two new accounts). Thus, an individual could give a total of $801,600 per year by giving the maximum contribution to each account of a party's three national committees (the DNC, DSCC, and DCCC or the RNC, NRSC, and NRCC). In a two-year election cycle, an individual who gave the maximum to every account of each of the three national committees in one party could give a total of $1,603,200. If an individual chose to give the maximum amounts to both major parties, the total permissible sum would be more than $3.2 million. This latter possibility, however, was unlikely in practice, since most large individual donors typically support one party or the other.

That an individual could give $1.6 million in aggregate to a national party over the course of a two-year election cycle in itself indicates the scope of the change embedded in the CRomnibus. When combined with the $10,000 per year federal contribution limit on contributions to a state party's federal election account, which Congress did not change, an individual who gave the maximum to all state parties in both years of the election cycle could give another $1 million, increasing total permitted giving under the new hard-money limits to $2.6 million. To put this sum in perspective, in 2012, the total amount an individual could give to all party committees under BCRA's biennial aggregate limit was $70,800. The new rules therefore allowed an individual donor to give twenty-two times more to a national party in 2016 than the amount permitted in 2012. Overall, with state or local party contributions included, an individual could give thirty-six times more to a party in 2016 than in 2012.

The new rules similarly increased the maximum permissible PAC contribution to the new party committees. The $15,000 per year limit was maintained for contributions to a party committee's general account, but the limit on contributions to the new accounts was tripled to $45,000 per year. As under previous law, these limits were not adjusted for inflation. A PAC that gave the maximum to each party account could give an annual total of $150,000 to the DNC or RNC and $105,000 per year to the House or Senate campaign committees. A PAC that gave the maximum donation to every account of each of the three national committees in one party could give an annual total of $360,000 or $720,000 in a two-year election cycle. If a PAC chose to give the maximum amounts to committees in both major parties, the maximum permissible total contribution equaled $1,440,000. No PAC reached this threshold in 2016, but five PACs gave to all six committees at levels of $30,000 or more per party committee,[46] and two PACs gave to the House and Senate party committees in both houses at levels of $30,000 or more.[47]

Why this more complicated approach was adopted instead of simply raising the party contribution limit can be gleaned from subsequent news accounts of the negotiations.[48] Initially, Senator McConnell supported a rider that would eliminate party-coordinated spending limits to make it easier for the parties to work with their candidates, but this proposal was not included in the bill.[49] Speaker Boehner's staff first proposed unlimited contributions to convention accounts to address concerns about convention funding, which Senate Majority Leader Reid's representatives countered with the proposal for higher convention committee contribution limits, with spending capped at $20 million. Democrats were also interested in provisions that would permit higher contribution limits for building funds (at the time, the DSCC was in debt and held a $5.2 million mortgage for additional office space it had purchased) and for legal costs, which led to these accounts being added to the text of the bill.[50] Consequently, whether intended or not, the provisions followed the framework suggested by previous FEC advisory opinions on recounts and convention funding: separate committees with separate contributions and separate contribution limits. The law served to codify the FEC's opinions but went beyond them by adding a building account and significantly higher contribution limits.

Response to the new rules was immediate and highlighted the ongoing lines of debate between supporters of stronger campaign finance regulations and proponents of political parties. Advocates of stronger regulations and limited contributions criticized the process used to change the law and expressed outrage over the new rules. They decried the easing of BCRA's contribution limits and the advantage given to wealthy donors. House Minority Leader Nancy Pelosi, a Democrat, who was not included in the negotiations on the campaign finance provisions, declared that the law would "drown out the voices of the American people and massively expand the role of big money in our elections."[51] Fred Wertheimer of Democracy 21, a campaign finance reform advocacy organization, depicted the change as "the most destructive and corrupting campaign finance provisions ever enacted by Congress" and warned that they would "return our nation to the auction block in the same way that existed at the time of the Watergate scandals in the 1970s and the 'soft money' scandals in the 1980s."[52]

Proponents of political parties welcomed the change, arguing that the higher limits would help the parties raise needed funds and encourage wealthy donors to give to the parties rather than to Super PACs and independent groups.[53] Higher limits would thus help to restore the role of parties in campaign financing, in part by freeing up money received in general accounts to be used on campaign activities instead of other costs. Before the change, party committees had to hold aside funds raised by their committees for legal, recount, and building expenses. With these new designated committees with their own accounts and separate contribution limits, they could direct more of their general party-committee funds to election-related spending.

Moreover, increased party fundraising would increase the transparency and accountability of the process, since moneys raised by parties are disclosed to the public, unlike moneys raised by 501(c) groups. As Tony Herman, a former FEC general counsel, noted, the change "will thus help calibrate the balance away from secret contributions and from unaccountable Super PACs and toward open contributions to the parties by opening the door to higher contributions to the parties from wealthy individuals. . . . And for that reason, in a post–*Citizens United* world, champions of disclosure should applaud the legislation."[54]

The CRomnibus did not completely roll back BCRA's party soft-money prohibitions. Individual contributions were still subject to limits, albeit much higher ones than those established by BCRA, compared to the unlimited contributions that were allowed under the soft-money regime. The prohibition on corporate or labor union contributions also remained untouched. Super PACs and 501(c) groups therefore continued to hold a relative advantage with respect to the contributions they could receive, while 501(c) groups could still raise money outside the realm of public disclosure. Even so, parties gained a substantial potential benefit from the new structure. In all, the major parties raised a total of more than $135.5 million through their new accounts, with the Republicans taking in $87.7 million and the Democrats $47.8 million.[55] The RNC replaced the convention financing that would have been received from public funding, raising $23.8 million for this purpose, while the DNC fell just short, raising $16.8 million. The parties received $67.2 million in building funds, with the Republicans taking in $45.9 million to the Democrats' $21.3 million. For recounts and other legal expenses, they raised $27.8 million, with the Republicans receiving $18.1 million and the Democrats $9.7 million. Had a major recount been needed in 2016, the parties could have asked donors to give additional funds to their recount committees within these committees' contribution limits.

These higher party contribution limits, combined with the *McCutcheon* ruling, greatly enhanced the value of joint fundraising strategies. The parties and their candidates were thus encouraged to establish JFC structures that were more elaborate. In 2015, the Democrats established the Hillary Victory Fund, which was a joint effort of the Clinton campaign, DNC, and thirty-two state party committees.[56] By the time of the general election, it included thirty-eight state party committees.[57] The Republicans formed Trump Victory, a joint effort of the Trump campaign, RNC, and eleven state parties, which eventually grew to twenty-one states.[58] The Trump campaign and RNC also formed the Trump Make America Great Again Committee, which focused on small contributions.[59] These JFCs allowed both parties to solicit large contributions: a single donor could give more than $400,000 to the Hillary Victory Fund or Trump Victory.[60] In all, Hillary Victory Fund raised $530 million, while Trump Victory raised $108 million and Trump Make America Great Again $264 million.[61] The hypothetical JFC scenarios presented in *McCutcheon* thus quickly began to reflect reality.

The use of JFCs obscures the distinction between a candidate and the party committees.[62] While JFCs are entities legally separate from a candidate's campaign committee, they in effect allow a donor to give sums far in excess of the candidate contribution limit to help elect the candidate. The moneys raised by JFCs are in part transferred to the candidate's committee and otherwise directed to the party to be spent in ways coordinated with the campaign or on activities, such as voter identification and turnout programs, that indirectly benefit the candidate. In effect, they are indistinct from funds given to the candidate; the major difference is that the candidates do not wholly control how the parties spend the money placed in party coffers. Furthermore, since the moneys raised by both candidate committees and JFCs are disclosed to the FEC, there is little doubt that the candidate is aware of the large donors who give to JFCs. For these reasons, JFC fundraising highlights the limited efficacy of the former aggregate contribution limits in safeguarding against evasion of the candidate contribution limits, while at the same time demonstrating the enhanced role of wealthy donors in the absence of aggregate limits, which was the central concern of defenders of these ceilings.

Although the money raised in the new party accounts was restricted to particular purposes, the law contained no statutory definitions, had no legislative history, and had not been a subject of legislative debate. Therefore, the exact purposes for which these funds could be used were not clearly specified. For example, the new legal account is to be used to "defray expenses incurred with respect to the preparation for and the conduct of election recounts and contests and other legal proceedings."[63] What do "other legal proceedings" include? Could this fund be used to finance research and litigation related to voter identification laws, absentee ballot rules, voter registration laws, campaign finance regulations, redistricting plans, and analyses of the potential consequences of districting proposals, as well as the day-to-day legal work related to the administration of national and state parties? Similarly, the building fund is to be used solely "to defray expenses incurred with respect to the construction, purchase, renovation, operation, and furnishing of one or more headquarters buildings of the party."[64] This broad language suggests that funds may be used for both national and state party headquarters, including not only construction and renovation but also their operations and furnishings. What might be included in party operations?

While such questions were not presented to the FEC for resolution before the election, they are certain to arise in the future as parties seek ways to gain the greatest advantage from these new pools of money. In this regard, it is important to recall that party soft money began with an exemption to contribution limits for building funds used to finance construction costs and a subsequent exemption for moneys raised for generic party-building purposes.[65] These narrow exemptions were later interpreted by the parties and the FEC to include candidate-specific electioneering. The broader consequences of the new rules will depend on the FEC's interpretation of the statute. Given the FEC's approach in other areas of the law, the parties are unlikely to face tight restrictions should they seek legal avenues for expansive use of these moneys.

The Evolving Role of Super PACs

Super PACs are federally registered political action committees that only make independent expenditures in support of candidates and do not make contributions to candidates. These committees, which were first sanctioned by the 2010 *Speechnow.org* decision and were first established in advance of the 2010 midterm election, are allowed to accept unlimited contributions and spend unlimited amounts in support of candidates, so long as they do not contribute funds to candidates. Therefore, they differ from traditional PACs because they are not subject to contribution limits and are not established to make contributions to candidates, but like traditional PACs, they are required to disclose to the FEC any contribution or expenditure of more than $200. Because Super PACs may accept unlimited contributions, they have a major advantage over other PACs and party committees. Super PACs have therefore become a primary alternative for wealthy donors who want to give extremely large amounts, because these committees may accept such large gifts and spend all the money advocating the election of specific candidates. It is therefore not surprising that the number of Super PACs and the amounts they raise have grown dramatically over the course of the past three elections. Indeed, Super PACs have increasingly aligned their efforts with those of the parties and the candidates they support to become a common component of the team approach to campaign finance.

Before the 2016 election, the FEC took no action to stem the growth of Super PACs and their role as de facto campaign organizations that mirrored candidate and party committees. Although Super PACs were supposed to operate wholly independently of the candidates they supported, the FEC did not promulgate regulations governing these committees and offered little guidance on the activities that are permitted or prohibited under the rules barring coordination with candidates or party committees. In 2012, the FEC had deadlocked on a number of issues concerning the permissible activities of Super PACs, and these deadlocks were not resolved before the 2016 election.[66] Consequently, Super PACs were largely left to their own devices, with any restraint on their activities being primarily a function of the willingness of committee managers or lawyers to test the limits of the law. Not surprisingly, many of these committees were willing to push the limits of the law, increasingly blurring the distinction between candidate committees and Super PACs with respect to the activities traditionally carried out in a political campaign.

Super PACs have become a major source of federal campaign funding because they are allowed to accept unlimited contributions from individuals and sources that are prohibited from giving to candidates, parties, or traditional PACs, including corporations, labor unions, trade associations, and 501(c)(4) organizations. Their financial activity is subject to public disclosure, with any contribution or expenditure of $200 or more reported to the FEC. The major restriction on their activities is the prohibition on coordination with the candidates, a key factor in whether they are truly independent. To determine coordination, FEC rules set forth a three-pronged test, which includes coordination, conduct, and content standards. For example, an expenditure may be deemed to be coordinated with a candidate if it is either (a) made in cooperation, consultation, or at the suggestion of a candidate, a member of a campaign staff, or a candidate's authorized agent, or (b) made after substantial discussions with a candidate, and (c) involves one of the content standards, such as a republication of campaign materials or a public communication that expressly advocates the election of a candidate.[67] An activity that does not meet these criteria is not considered a coordinated expenditure.

The coordination rules are focused on activities in relation to a candidate, since they are used to determine whether any campaign support offered by a group should be considered a contribution to the candidate. They do not prohibit coordination among Super PACs or coordination among Super PACs and 501(c) groups. These minimal rules leave ample room for Super PACs to support their preferred candidates without violating the coordination restrictions. In fact, the only case of illegal coordination between a candidate committee and a Super PAC prosecuted to date was brought by the Department of Justice and involved a blatant violation of law in which a congressional candidate's campaign manager also knowingly controlled and was paid by a Super PAC supporting his candidate.[68]

Super PACs have therefore become a common component of federal campaigns. Almost every presidential candidate during the presidential primaries, with the notable exceptions of Bernie Sanders and Donald Trump, was supported by a candidate-specific Super PAC established by former staff or political advisers. Trump, however, was supported by candidate-specific Super PACs endorsed by campaign aides in the general election (see chapter 7). Super PACs closely allied with congressional leaders, including the Congressional Leadership Fund and Senate Leadership Fund on the Republican side and House Majority PAC and Senate

Majority PAC on the Democratic side, supplemented the activities of the party campaign committees. Dozens of others acted as partisan allies or sought to assist specific candidates in battleground congressional contests. In short, Super PACs have quickly become incorporated as part of the overall financial strategies employed in campaigns. Competitive campaigns are now typically financed through a team effort involving a candidate committee, Super PAC, and, in some cases, a 501(c) group, joined by the party in the general election, in a common endeavor to win office, even though members of the team are legally presumed to operate independent of each other.

One restriction the FEC has been willing to enforce is the prohibition on the use of a candidate's name in the name of a Super PAC. To avoid voter confusion, the rules require a committee authorized by a candidate to use a candidate's name in its name or title and prohibit an unauthorized committee from doing so. In accord with this rule, the FEC took action against Stop Hillary PAC, informing this Super PAC that it was in violation of the law.[69] The commission also determined that Carly for America, a Super PAC supporting Carly Fiorina for president, was in violation of the law. The Super PAC responded by simply changing its name to CARLY for America, an acronym for "Conservative, Authentic, Responsive Leadership for You and for America."[70] These signals caused other Super PACs using a candidate's name to change their names. Stand with Rand, a Super PAC organized to support the presidential bid of Senator Rand Paul, changed its name to SWR PAC.[71] Ready for Hillary, which was organized to rally support for Hillary Clinton before she became a candidate, changed its name to Ready PAC once Clinton entered the race and soon thereafter closed down its operations, but not before it shared its list of Clinton supporters with the political organization EMILY's List, which eventually shared this list with the Clinton campaign.[72]

Super PACs, however, did not need to use a candidate's name to make clear their role as surrogate campaign organizations for the candidates they were organized to support. These committees can engage in a wide range of traditional campaign activities and, in effect, coordinate their activities with the candidates without violating the rules on coordination. The FEC allows candidates or campaign officials to be a guest or featured speaker at Super PAC fundraisers, and meet with donors or prospective donors, so long as the candidate or campaign representative does not directly ask donors for contributions of more than $5,400. Super PACs may also follow the public schedules and statements of candidates and organize their own efforts based on their understanding of the candidate's strategy. They may use the same vendors as a candidate's campaign, and in 2016 they increasingly moved into grassroots organizing and other tasks typically carried out by a candidate's campaign. For example:

- Grassroots organization: Super PACs organized town hall meetings and other grassroots events, and sponsored other organizational activities. Believe Again, which supported Republican presidential candidate Bobby Jindal, organized town hall events in Iowa that featured Jindal as the invited guest. CARLY for America hosted events in Iowa and New Hampshire, recruited endorsements for Fiorina, and hosted conference calls with Fiorina on which she fielded questions from members of the press.[73]
- Advertising footage: Super PACs can use video footage of candidates, so long as they do not republish campaign materials. New Day for America, which supported Republican presidential candidate John Kasich, broadcast ads that featured Kasich speaking directly to the camera. The video used in the ad was shot before Kasich announced his candidacy. Other committees used video of the candidate campaigning or other typical scenes from a candidate's life, commonly called "b-roll" footage, which were not campaign ads and were often posted online. Such material placed online, for example by being posted on Vimeo, can be used by Super PACs in crafting their own ads, since it is publicly available as a result of being posted online. Super PACs can also simply shoot their own video of the candidate campaigning and then use this footage in their ads.[74]
- Opposition research and response: Correct the Record, which supported Hillary Clinton, focused its efforts on defending Clinton's record and responding to attacks against her, as well as carrying out opposition research on her opponents. The committee confined its activity to online distribution of information about Clinton through social media sites, posting its defenses of Clinton and its opposition research on her prospective opponents, which the Clinton campaign could then download and reuse. The Clinton campaign also paid a market rate to the Super

PAC for its nonpublic research.[75] The Super PAC contended that it could coordinate its activities with the Clinton campaign because FEC regulations exempt content posted online for free from the coordinated communications regulations, which only apply to paid political ads.[76]

Republican presidential contender Jeb Bush took the boldest and most controversial approach to Super PAC funding by essentially launching his presidential campaign by forming his own Super PAC. Bush participated in the formation and fundraising of a Super PAC, Right to Rise, and an affiliated traditional PAC, before he declared his candidacy in June 2015.[77] The committee, which Bush described as "tasked with 'exploring a presidential bid,'" was launched in early January 2015 and mounted an aggressive fundraising effort, with Bush serving as principal fundraiser.[78] By the time he entered the race, Right to Rise had raised $103 million, which primarily came from donors who gave $100,000 or more.[79] This tactic provided Bush with a dominant financial advantage early in the race, leading to the expectation that spending by the Super PAC would propel him to the presidential nomination. But Bush's lackluster performance on the campaign trail and his consequent poor showing in the early primaries led to his early exit from the race, despite aggressive spending by the Super PAC.

Bush's action raised the issue of whether his activity with the Super PAC before becoming a candidate was permissible under the law. Specifically, his use of a Super PAC raised two questions: When does a candidate become a candidate? And what activities are allowed a prospective candidate before triggering one's status as a candidate subject to federal campaign finance rules? The Campaign Legal Center and Democracy 21, two nonpartisan campaign finance watchdog groups, filed a complaint with the FEC on March 31, 2015, alleging that Bush had violated the law by failing to register as a candidate and exceeding the "testing-the-waters" regulations that restrict an individual exploring a candidacy to receiving contributions limited to $2,700.[80] Under the definitions set forth in the law, an individual qualifies as a candidate if he or she raises or spends more than $5,000. This financial threshold automatically triggers the registration and reporting procedures required of a candidate. The regulations contain a limited exception for "testing-the-waters" activities that an individual may undertake to explore the possibility of running for office. Such activities include private meetings with political officials, conducting a poll, appearing at political meetings or conventions, and incurring expenses for travel and administrative costs.[81] Individuals who are exploring a candidacy are not required to register as a candidate with the FEC, but they must pay for these expenses with contributions allowed by the candidate contribution limit. If a candidate decides to run for office, any moneys received in exploring a candidacy count as contributions to the candidate's campaign. The complaint charged that Bush exceeded the testing-the-waters exemption and violated the reporting requirements as a result of his activity with Right to Rise. Furthermore, he had accepted contributions in violation of the contribution limits and BCRA's ban on the solicitation of soft money. The complaint thus raised the issues of whether a Super PAC could be used to explore a candidacy and, more broadly, whether a prospective candidate's participation in a Super PAC's political activities could trigger FECA reporting and disclosure requirements.

The issues raised by Bush's use of a Super PAC were yet to be answered by the end of the election. Whether they will be resolved before the next election is difficult to discern, given the FEC's recent pattern of deadlocking on enforcement issues associated with Super PACs. Indeed, in November 2015, the FEC responded to an advisory opinion request by the Senate Majority PAC and the House Majority PAC that included a number of questions regarding the activities that might be undertaken with the involvement of *prospective* candidates, including the formation of single-candidate Super PACs that would collaborate with these potential candidates on strategy and advertising. The request included questions asking whether a single-candidate Super PAC could raise and spend funds after a prospective candidate involved in the formation of the committee becomes a candidate; whether a candidate's agent could raise money for a Super PAC; whether information shared with single-candidate committees and Super PACs by prospective candidates about their plans, projects, and needs could be used in public communications; whether video footage filmed before an individual becomes a candidate could be used after the individual becomes a candidate; and whether the filming of a prospective candidate or some amount of Super PAC money raised by a prospective candidate would indicate an actual candidacy. The six-member FEC divided on each of these questions and could not muster the fourth vote needed to issue a decision. The commission did vote 4-2 to allow a candidate's agent to raise money in excess of federal contribution limits for a Super PAC that supported the candidate, so long as the fundraising was done "on their own" and "not at the request or suggestion of a candidate" and was done at a "different time" from campaign fundraising. But the commission deadlocked on the question of whether a candidate's agent could raise money for a Super PAC that solely supported that candidate. The issues associated with a precandidacy Super PAC or coordination between a prospective candidate and a Super PAC thus remained in limbo.[82]

The FEC's failure to make regulatory decisions or pursue enforcement issues was not confined to Super PACs. A number of complaints were filed with the agency contesting the failure of tax-exempt organizations (501(c)(4) groups) to report their contributions and, in some cases, their expenditures as well. Complaints also pointed to the failure of these groups to file as political committees, given their levels of campaign spending. Specific complaints were filed against American Crossroads GPS, Americans for Job Security, American Action Network, American Future Fund, and Commission on Hope, Growth, and Opportunity. In each of these cases, the FEC's Office of General Counsel found evidence that offered a reason to believe that a violation of the law had occurred, and it recommended an FEC investigation and further enforcement proceedings. However, in every case, the FEC deadlocked 3-3 and no further action was pursued.[83]

In complaints against Americans for Job Security (AJS) and American Action Network (AAN), for example, FEC staff found evidence indicating the major purpose of these organizations was actually to influence federal elections and that they should have been registered as political committees and required to comply with federal disclosure rules. According to their calculations, AJS had spent roughly 76 percent of its $12.4 million of total spending in 2010 on independent expenditures in support of candidates, while AAN had spent almost 63 percent of its overall spending between 2009 and 2011 on federal campaign activity. Yet, the FEC deadlocked on both matters, with the three Republican appointees refusing to open an investigation. Citizens for Responsibility and Ethics in Washington (CREW), a government watchdog group, filed a lawsuit seeking to force the FEC to act. In September 2016, a federal district court held that the commissioners had acted arbitrarily and capriciously, as well as contrary to law, and remanded the case to the FEC to conform to its ruling within thirty days.[84] Regardless, the FEC failed to do so.

With the FEC failing to take action, enforcement of the law was left to the IRS, which is responsible for approving an organization's 501(c)(4) status and reviewing such committees to ensure that they are abiding by the law, including the rules governing the level of political activity allowed such organizations. In the years after *Citizens United*, this responsibility became more demanding, as the number of organizations applying for 501(c)(4) status rose from 1,741 in 2010 to 2,253 in 2013.[85] In an effort to manage this workload and attempt to identify organizations that might qualify as political organizations rather than social welfare groups, the IRS began using BOLO (Be on the Lookout) advisory lists in August 2010 that identified certain words in an organization's title that might indicate political activity. These terms included "tea party," "patriot," "freedom," and "occupy," and were eventually extended to include specific policy issues or groups.[86] When this approach became public, congressional Republicans criticized the agency for targeting conservative groups, which led to a political firestorm that focused on Lois Lerner, director of the Exempt Organizations Unit of the IRS, and then expanded to include other IRS officials. The "scandal" led to a prolonged process of investigations into the agency by the House Ways and Means Committee, the Treasury Inspector General for Tax Administration, and the FBI.[87] These investigations, which began in June 2012 and extended into 2016, revealed no criminal wrongdoing, but the political pressure placed on the agency, which included budget cuts and even consideration of an impeachment charge against the IRS commissioner, led the agency to abandon efforts to pursue more effective regulation and oversight of the political activities of 501(c)(4) groups.[88]

The lack of effective enforcement with respect to the political activities of tax-exempt groups has encouraged more electioneering on the part of these groups. As long as a 501(c)(4)'s principal purpose or primary activity is to promote social welfare or advocate policies, a group may spend funds on political activity, provided these political expenditures constitute a minor portion of their spending. These organizations are therefore spending substantial sums on activities advocating the election of candidates, including advertising, direct mail, and voter mobilization programs. In addition, they may spend unlimited amounts on issue advertising and policy advocacy, which can have the effect of promoting a candidate's policy agenda. Moreover, some of these organizations are becoming more candidate centered, in some instances supporting a single candidate (see chapters 1 and 7). Tax-exempt organizations thus are expanding their role in election campaigns while providing donors who seek to avoid public disclosure with an effective means of doing so, since 501(c) organizations are not required to disclose their donors under FEC rules.[89]

Conclusion

Changes in campaign finance regulations continue to sap the law of its ability to limit the sources of funding in federal elections and ensure the transparency of campaign financing. The piecemeal deconstruction of the regulatory structure has produced a system consisting of two separate regulatory spheres: one encompassing candidates, parties, and PACs, in which contributions are limited and fully disclosed, and another encompassing Super PACs and tax-exempt organizations, in which contributions are unlimited and in some instances undisclosed. This bifurcation gave Super PACs and 501(c) organizations a financial advantage over candidates and parties by allowing them to rely on wealthy donors and previously prohibited entities as sources of campaign funding. The changes adopted in advance of the 2016 election extended the role of wealthy donors by allowing individuals to give limited but very large sums to party committees. This rendered the party contribution limits meaningless to all but the relatively small group of individuals who might be willing to make multimillion-dollar donations. The strict contribution limits established by BCRA thus continue to unravel, and those that remain, particularly candidate and PAC contribution limits and BCRA's ban on soft money, are easily circumvented through contributions to Super PACs or other groups aligned with specific candidates or parties.

The failure of the FEC and IRS to effectively administer the law has led to a regulatory environment in which behavior is increasingly shaped by decisions made by political actors rather than by regulators. On a growing number of substantive issues, the failure of regulatory agencies to provide clear guidance or pursue enforcement actions has placed political actors in a position to decide whether inaction means that an activity is permitted, because it has not been prohibited, or not allowed, because it has not been approved. The lack of regulatory oversight has thus left Super PACs and 501(c)(4) organizations with the leeway to decide whether they want to test the limits of the law and assume actions are permitted until an agency or a court says otherwise or pursue a more conservative approach and avoid actions that have not received specific sanction.

Given the FEC's recent deadlocks on enforcement matters, and an absence of visible enforcement by the IRS, political actors are encouraged to pursue innovative strategies and challenge the law, because they face little risk of FEC action. Super PACs and 501(c)(4) groups are therefore delving into campaign activities traditionally carried out by candidates and are interacting with candidates or their staffs in ways that question their independence. These committees are likely to continue to press the boundaries of the law as they seek better ways to capitalize on their ability to raise and spend unlimited money. Such actions will serve to heighten calls for looser restrictions on candidates and parties as a way to level the playing field with Super PACs and independent groups. They will also provoke continued calls for stricter regulation, including options ranging from coordination rules that are more stringent to a constitutional amendment designed to reverse *Citizens United*.

Throughout the election, Donald Trump promised to "drain the swamp" in Washington and reform the current culture of money in politics.[90] One place to begin is to ensure that the laws on the books are vigorously enforced. A necessary change in this regard is reform of the FEC or at least the appointment of commissioners willing to exercise effective oversight. While such a change is unlikely, without it the regulatory regime will continue to promote the move toward unlimited and unaccountable funding in federal elections.

Notes

1. Fred Wertheimer and Don Simon, *The FEC: The Failure to Enforce Commission*, American Constitution Society for Law and Policy, January 2013; Ann M. Ravel, "Dysfunction and Deadlock at the Federal Election Commission," *New York Times*, February 20, 2017.

2. *Citizens United* v. *Federal Election Commission*, 558 U.S. 310 (2010). For a discussion of the case and its implementation by the FEC, see Anthony Corrado, "The Regulatory Environment of the 2012 Election," in *Financing the 2012 Election*, edited by David B. Magleby (Brookings, 2014), pp. 55–65.

3. *SpeechNow.org* v. *Federal Election Commission*, 599 F.3d 686 (D.C. Cir. 2010).

4. For a summary of the rules governing political activity by tax-exempt organizations, see John Francis Reilly and Barbara A. Bragg Allen, *Political Campaign and Lobbying Activities of IRC 501(c)(4), (c)(5), and (c)(6) Organizations* (Washington: Internal Revenue Service, n.d.); Campaign Legal Center,

"CLC Chart: CLC Disclosure Chart Defining Types of 501(c) Groups," November 1, 2010 (www.campaignlegalcenter.org/document/clc-chart-501c-disclosure-chart-defining-types-outside-groups).

5. The public funding option offered a candidate matching funds on the first $250 received from an individual donor in the primaries and a $96 million general election grant in exchange for agreeing to abide by spending limits.

6. John Fritze, "O'Malley Campaign Secures Public Cash before Dropping Out," *Baltimore Sun*, February 6, 2016; Federal Election Commission, "Federal Election Commission Certifies Federal Matching Funds for O'Malley," press release, April 6, 2016.

7. Federal Election Commission, "Federal Election Commission Certifies Federal Matching Funds for Jill Stein," press release, August 2, 2016.

8. *McCutcheon v. Federal Election Commission*, 572 U.S. ___ (2014).

9. *Buckley v. Valeo*, 424 U.S. 1 (1976).

10. Bob Biersack, "McCutcheon's Multiplying Effect: Why an Overall Limit Matters," Center for Responsive Politics, September 17, 2013.

11. Ibid.

12. Ronald Collins and David Skover, "Symposium: *McCutcheon v. Federal Election Commission*," *SCOTUSblog*, August 12, 2013; "Brief for Appellant Shaun McCutcheon, McCutcheon v. Federal Election Commission," *SCOTUSblog*, May 6, 2013.

13. "Brief for Appellant Shaun McCutcheon," pp. 11–12.

14. Ibid., p. 17.

15. Ibid., p. 19.

16. Ibid., pp. 40–48.

17. *McCutcheon v. Federal Election Commission*, 893 F. Supp. 2d 133 (2012), p. 140.

18. Ibid.

19. Ibid.

20. *McCutcheon v. Federal Election Commission*, 572 U.S. ___ (2014).

21. Ibid., p. 9, quoting the *Buckley* decision.

22. Ibid., p. 11.

23. Ibid., quoting the *Buckley* decision.

24. Ibid., p. 19.

25. Ibid., p. 15.

26. Ibid., p. 28.

27. Ibid., p. 23.

28. Anthony Corrado, "Fundraising Strategies in the 2012 Presidential Campaign," in *Campaigns and Elections American Style*, 4th ed., edited by James A. Thurber and Candice J. Nelson (Boulder, Colo.: Westview Press, 2014), p. 114.

29. Dan Roberts, "Obama Signs Ban on Public Funding of Political Conventions into Law," *The Guardian*, April 4, 2014; Robert Costa, "In Rare Bipartisan

Effort, Congress Votes to Shift Convention Money to Health Research," *Washington Post*, March 11, 2014.

30. See Thomas E. Mann and Norman J. Ornstein, *It's Even Worse than It Looks: How the American Constitutional System Collided with the New Politics of Extremism* (New York: Basic Books, 2012), pp. 44–50.

31. Costa, "In a Rare Bipartisan Effort, Congress Votes to Shift Convention Money to Health Research"; Ramsey Cox, "Senate Votes to End Taxpayer Funding of Political Conventions," *The Hill*, April 11, 2014.

32. For details on the sources of funding for presidential nominating conventions from 1980 to 2008, see the data on national party conventions compiled by the Campaign Finance Institute (www.cfinst.org/federal/conventions.aspx).

33. For background on the development of convention committees and host committees and the rules governing convention financing, see Lawrence M. Noble and Brendan M. Fischer, *Funding the Presidential Nominating Conventions: How a Trickle of Money Turned into a Flood* (Washington: Campaign Legal Center, July 2016). For a review of the public sources of convention funding, see R. Sam Garrett and Shawn Reese, *Funding of Presidential Nominating Conventions: An Overview*, Congressional Research Service Report R43976, May 4, 2016.

34. Campaign Finance Institute, "Sources of Funding for Major Party Presidential Nominating Conventions, 1980–2004" (www.cfinst.org/pdf/federal /conventions/FundingSources_1980-2004.pdf).

35. Campaign Finance Institute, "Heavy Hitters ($250,000 to $3 Million Donors) Supplied 80% of Private Financing for 2008 Party Conventions, Recent Filings Show," press release, December 10, 2008.

36. Sarah Mimms, "2016 Conventions Face Massive Shortfall Thanks to Congress," *The Atlantic*, March 19, 2014.

37. Federal Election Commission, Advisory Opinion Request 2014-12. This advisory opinion request and all other advisory opinions can be found at http://saos.fec.gov/saos/searchao.

38. Ibid., pp. 2 and 4.

39. Ibid. See Federal Election Commission, Advisory Opinions 2006-24, 2009-04, and 2011-03.

40. Comment on Advisory Opinion Request 2014-12 by Campaign Legal Center and Democracy 21, pp. 1 and 3 (http://saos.fec.gov/saos/searchao;jsessionid =C574C5F8E37A7A92BDFF975ABD0CD370?SUBMIT=continue&PAGE _NO=0).

41. Federal Election Commission, Advisory Opinion 2014-12.

42. Kenneth P. Vogel, "Behind Reid's War against the Kochs," *Politico*, July 7, 2014; Dana Bash, "Democrats Take On the Koch Brothers," CNN, May 16, 2014.

43. R. Sam Garrett, *Increased Campaign Contribution Limits in the FY2015 Omnibus Appropriations Law: Frequently Asked Questions*, Congressional Re-

search Service Report R43825, March 17, 2015, p. 1; Kenneth P. Vogel, "Budget Rider Would Expand Party Cash," *Politico*, December 10, 2014.

44. Matea Gold, "Spending Deal Would Allow Wealthy Donors to Dramatically Increase Giving to National Parties," *Washington Post*, December 9, 2014.

45. P. L. 113-235, 128 Stat. 2130. The provisions on party contribution limits are found in Division N, sec. 101 of the law at 128 Stat. 2772.

46. The five PACs were the National Automobile Dealers Association, Honeywell International, ATT Incorporated Federal PAC, Comcast Corporation, and Lockheed Martin Corporation Employees PAC.

47. Those two PACs were the American Society of Anesthesiologists PAC and the Mortgage Bankers Association PAC.

48. See Nicholas Confessore, "G.O.P. Angst over 2016 Led to Provision on Funding," *New York Times*, December 13, 2014; Gold, "Spending Deal Would Allow Wealthy Donors to Dramatically Increase Giving to National Parties"; Kenneth P. Vogel, "The Man Behind the Political Cash Grab," *Politico*, December 12, 2014.

49. Vogel, "Budget Rider Would Expand Party Cash."

50. Confessore, "G.O.P. Angst over 2016 Led to Provision on Funding."

51. Pelosi quoted in Vogel, "Budget Rider Would Expand Party Cash."

52. Democracy 21, "Fred Wertheimer Statement on Reid-McConnell 'Bipartisan' Deal to Eviscerate Anti-corruption Campaign Finance Laws," press release, December 10, 2014.

53. For a representative summary of these arguments, see Raymond La Raja, "CRomnibus Pays Off for Parties," *MassPoliticalProfs* (blog), *WGBH News*, December 17, 2014.

54. Herman quoted in Gold, "Spending Deal Would Allow Wealthy Donors to Dramatically Increase Giving to National Parties."

55. Federal Election Commission, "Party Table 10: Contributions to Accounts of National Party Committees, January 1, 2015 through December 31, 2016" (http://classic.fec.gov/press/summaries/2016/tables/party/Prty10_2016_24m .pdf). All figures in this paragraph are drawn from this table.

56. Hillary Victory Fund, "FEC Form 1: Statement of Organization, November 2, 2015" (http://docquery.fec.gov/pdf/234/201511029003261234 /201511029003261234.pdf).

57. Hillary Victory Fund, "FEC Form 1: Statement of Organization, Amendment 1, July 1, 2016" (http://docquery.fec.gov/pdf/028/201607019020110028 /201607019020110028.pdf).

58. Trump Victory, "FEC Form 1: Statement of Organization, Amendment 2, September 21, 2016" (http://docquery.fec.gov/pdf/548/201609219032063548 /201609219032063548.pdf).

59. Trump Make America Great Again Committee, "FEC Form 1: Statement of Organization, May 25, 2016" (http://docquery.fec.gov/pdf/030/2016 05259017296030/201605259017296030.pdf).

60. Libby Watson, "How Political Megadonors Can Give Almost $500,000 with a Single Check," Sunlight Foundation, June 1, 2016. Hillary Victory Fund was structured to accept up to $5,400 for the Clinton campaign ($2,700 each for the primary and the general election), $33,400 for the DNC general account, and $10,000 for each state party. Trump Victory was structured to accept up to $5,400 for the Trump campaign, $33,400 for the RNC general account, $100,200 for each of the RNC special accounts (convention, headquarters, and legal), and $10,000 for each state party.

61. Center for Responsive Politics, "Joint Fundraising Committees, 2016" (www.opensecrets.org/jfc/top.php?type=C&cycle=2016).

62. The Hillary for America and DNC joint fundraising agreement was seen by interim DNC chair Donna Brazile as giving the candidate unusual control over the DNC. See Donna Brazile, *Hacks: The Inside Story of the Break-ins and Breakdowns That Put Donald Trump in the White House* (New York: Hachette Books, 2017).

63. P. L. 113-235, Division N, Section 101, 128 Stat. 2772.

64. Ibid.

65. Anthony Corrado, "Party Finances," in *The New Campaign Finance Sourcebook*, edited by Anthony Corrado, Thomas E. Mann, Daniel R. Ortiz, and Trevor Potter (Brookings, 2005), pp. 162–163.

66. For a discussion of the FEC's decisions on Super PACs, see Corrado, "The Regulatory Environment of the 2012 Election," pp. 55–65.

67. 11 C.F.R. 109.21 (January 1, 2017).

68. Peter Overby, "Crossing the Line: Political Operative Gets 2 Years in Prison," N P R, June 12, 2015.

69. Federal Election Commission, MUR 7086 (www.fec.gov/data/legal/matter -under-review/7086/).

70. Ben Kamisar, "Carly Fiorina-Aligned PAC Changes Name," *The Hill*, June 17, 2015.

71. Ibid.

72. Annie Karni, "Clinton Campaign Scores Ready for Hillary Email List," *Politico*, May 30, 2015.

73. Adam Wollner, "10 Ways Super PACs and Campaigns Coordinate, Even Though They're Not Allowed To," *The Atlantic*, September 27, 2015.

74. Paul Blumenthal, "How Super PACs and Candidates Are Coordinating in 2016," *Huffington Post*, November 14, 2015.

75. Ibid.

76. Matea Gold, "How a Super PAC Plans to Coordinate Directly with Hillary Clinton's Campaign," *Washington Post*, May 12, 2015.

77. Andrew Desiderio, "Jeb Bush's Fundraising Haul: $114 Million," *Real Clear Politics*, July 9, 2015.

78. Jose DelReal, "Jeb Bush Forms PAC to Explore Presidential Run," *Washington Post*, December 16, 2014.

79. Desiderio, "Jeb Bush's Fundraising Haul"; Campaign Finance Institute, "Million-Dollar Donors Dominate Presidential Super PAC Giving," Table 2, press release, June 17, 2016.

80. The complaint can be found at www.democracy21.org/wp-content /uploads/2015/03/CLC-D21-v-Jeb-Bush_Complaint_3-31-15_file-stamped.pdf.

81. For a detailed discussion of the "testing-the-waters" regulations in the context of the 2016 election, see Paul S. Ryan, "'Testing the Waters' and the Big Lie: How Prospective Presidential Candidates Evade Candidate Contribution Limits While the FEC Looks the Other Way," Campaign Legal Center, February 2015.

82. Federal Election Commission, Advisory Opinion 2015-09; Paul Blumenthal, "FEC Deadlocks on Whether Candidates Can Coordinate with Their Own Super PACs," *Huffington Post*, November 10, 2015.

83. These complaints and the FEC responses are summarized in Ann Ravel, *Dysfunction and Deadlock: The Enforcement Crisis at the Federal Election Commission Reveals the Unlikelihood of Draining the Swamp* (Washington: Federal Election Commission, February 2017), pp. 14–19.

84. *Citizens for Responsibility and Ethics in Washington* v. *Federal Election Commission*, No. 1:14-cv-01419 (D.D.C. September 19, 2016).

85. Julie Patel, "Hobbled IRS Can't Stem 'Dark Money' Flow," Center for Public Integrity, July 15, 2014.

86. Ibid.; Lee Aitken, "There's No Way to Follow the Money," *The Atlantic*, December 16, 2013.

87. For a timetable noting key developments in the IRS controversy, see Kelly Phillips Erb, "IRS Targeting Scandal: Citizens United, Lois Lerner and the $20M Tax Saga That Won't Go Away," *Forbes*, June 24, 2016.

88. Patel, "Hobbled IRS Can't Stem 'Dark Money' Flow"; Stephen Ohlemacher, "Trump DOJ Declines to Charge Lois Lerner, a Key Figure in IRS Scandal," *Chicago Tribune*, September 8, 2017.

89. Corrado, "The Regulatory Environment of the 2012 Election," pp. 67–69.

90. Isaac Arnsdorf, Josh Dawsey, and Daniel Lippman, "Will 'Drain the Swamp' Be Trump's First Broken Promise?" *Politico*, December 23, 2016.

THREE · *Interest Groups in the 2016 Election*

DAVID B. MAGLEBY AND JAY GOODLIFFE

Interest groups play an important role in American campaign finance, and their role grew in 2016 through increased spending by Super PACs and 501(c) groups independent of candidates and parties, especially at the congressional level. At the same time, organized interests and interested individuals continued to be the major source of funds for candidates and political parties, contributing directly to candidate campaign committees and party committees. Interest groups also participate in the electoral process by helping to fund groups that spend money in ways not controlled by the candidates or parties. Besides providing money, interest groups provide volunteers who help with campaign events, voter identification, and voter mobilization. They communicate with their members about preferred candidates, and on occasion they actively recruit a group member to run for office.

Groups are organized in many ways and can be large or small. Some, such as businesses or unions, are based on common economic interests. Others are organized by a shared perspective on an issue such as abortion or the environment. Some are based on a specific ideology. Very few individuals spend money on elections by themselves. Rather, individuals typically participate in funding campaigns to elect or defeat candidates by giving to the candidate's campaign committees, by contributing to groups that share their interests, or by donating to political parties. For the purposes of this analysis, we treat individuals acting alone as an interest group.

Interest groups spend money to influence federal elections through several methods. As discussed in chapter 2, campaign finance laws passed by Congress and interpreted by the courts have influenced and extended the number of methods available. We divide these into six methods. The first three methods have been used since the passage of the Federal Election Campaign Act (FECA) and its amendments in 1974. First, interest groups can organize political action committees (known as PACs) to contribute directly to candidates' campaign committees and party committees; there are limits on how much individuals can contribute to the PAC and how much the PAC can contribute to candidate and party committees, and these transactions are reported to the Federal Election Commission (FEC) (see table 1-1). Second, interest groups can spend unlimited funds communicating with their members; these internal communication costs must also be reported to the FEC. Third, standard PACs can raise funds in limited amounts from individuals but spend those funds without limits to influence federal elections if the expenditures are "not coordinated with a candidate." These are known as independent expenditures.

The three other methods came after court decisions and reflect interest group entrepreneurship. The fourth method, available since 2010, is independent-expenditure-only PACs, known as Super PACs, through which interest groups can create separate political action committees that do not contribute directly to candidates or parties but only make independent expenditures. Like other PAC activities, the contributions and expenditures of Super PACs are reported to the FEC. Unlike other PAC activities, Super PACs can raise funds in unlimited amounts from individuals and organizations. Interest groups can also organize a "hybrid" PAC that includes both a standard PAC and a Super PAC. Fifth, interest groups can create 501(c) organizations, organized under section 501(c) of the Internal Revenue Code. The primary purpose of 501(c) organizations cannot be to elect or defeat a candidate, but these organizations can still raise and spend money on federal elections. Unlike the previous methods of influence, 501(c) organizations are not required to disclose their donors. Finally, interest groups can create 527 organizations, which receive their designation from their regulation by section 527 of the Internal Revenue Code. Section 527 organizations must report their transactions, though not always to the FEC, and their donors are not always publicly disclosed. Super PACs are 527 groups, but not all 527 groups are Super PACs. Examples of 527s fitting this description would be the Republican Governors Association and the Democratic Governors Association.

Interest groups may use as many of these methods as they like. The National Rifle Association (NRA), for example, uses standard PACs to make contributions directly to candidates as well as spend money on independent expenditures, uses internal communications, and has a 501(c)(4) group. EMILY's List has a standard PAC for contributions and a 527 organization. The Club for Growth has a standard PAC, a Super PAC, and two 501(c) organizations that spend in elections. The Service Employees International Union has a standard PAC, a Super PAC, a 527, and a 501(c), and it spent $1.5 million on internal communications. In the following section, we discuss the three methods involving standard PACs, after which we discuss the remaining three methods in separate sections.

Standard PACs

Political action committees (known as PACs) are the most common form of financial participation in elections by interest groups. In 1936, John L. Lewis, president of the United Mine Workers of America (and later the first president of the Congress of Industrial Organizations) created Labor's Non-Partisan League, which was the first forerunner of PACs and contributed more than $1 million to support Franklin D. Roosevelt's reelection and a pro-labor Congress.[1] Though the law prevented labor unions and corporations from using their treasuries to fund campaigns, both used PACs to spend money in elections. Organized labor requested that their committees be given further legal protection by friendly members of Congress, expecting "that corporations would not take full advantage of a clear and direct ruling on the constitutionality of PACs. As it turned out, they were greatly mistaken."[2]

Since the passage of FECA in 1971 (and its amendments in 1974, 1976, and 1979), interest groups have organized political action committees to contribute directly to candidate campaign committees and party committees. Contributions to a PAC are limited, as are contributions made by PACs directly to candidates and political parties (see table 1-1). PACs must report these transactions to the FEC. PACs associated with corporations, trade associations, or labor unions must set up organizations with "separate segregated funds," and they may solicit funds only from individuals associated with the sponsoring organization. Before 1971, most PACs were associated with labor rather than with business. In the 2016 election, 289 PACs were associated with labor unions, while there were 1,907 corporate PACs and 736 PACs associated with trade associations. Thus, business PACs now far outnumber labor PACs.[3]

Besides PACs associated with sponsoring organizations that have separate segregated funds, there are PACs that the FEC calls "nonconnected
committees." Nonconnected committees are usually issue or ideological
groups that have no parent or sponsoring organization. Unlike labor or
business PACs, whose administrative costs can be paid for by the associated organization, nonconnected committees must pay their own administrative costs but can raise funds from the general public. In 2016, there
were 1,981 issue-oriented PACs. Another type of nonconnected committee is a leadership PAC, which is formed by political leaders such as members of Congress. In 2016, there were 572 leadership PACs. The last type
of nonconnected PAC is the Super PAC, which is discussed separately.[4]

In the 2016 election, business-associated PACs spent $548 million,
while labor-associated PACs spent $332 million, and both figures are
higher than in 2012 (controlling for inflation). Thus, while business-
associated PACs outnumber labor-associated PACs 10 to 1, they outspend
them by only about 1.6 to 1. Issue/ideological PACs spent $234 million
in 2016 (about a 20 percent increase over 2012), and leadership PACs
spent $125 million, which was less than in 2012.[5]

Expenditures by congressional candidates have generally been increasing over time. Figure 3-1 shows the (inflation-adjusted) total expenditures by congressional candidates from 1976 to 2016. The same figure
shows that PAC contributions have increased over time, but not nearly
as much as candidate spending. About 28 percent of candidate expenditures in 2016 were funded by PAC contributions, a proportion similar to
that of previous election cycles. In the 2016 election cycle, PACs contributed $441 million to congressional candidates, a slight decrease from the
(inflation-adjusted) $466 million contributed in 2012. Although business-
related PACs maintained or increased their contributions to congressional
candidates from 2012 to 2016, labor PACs decreased their contributions from (inflation-adjusted) $60 million in 2012 to $47 million in 2016.
However, as will be discussed, Super PACs increased their spending from
2012 to 2016.

PAC Contributions

Over time, overall spending by congressional candidates has grown
more than the share of funds contributed to candidates by PACs. PACs
gave $97 million to congressional candidates in 1976 and $441 million
in 2016. Over this forty-year span, total congressional candidate expenditures rose from $489 million to $1.6 billion. The percentage of

Figure 3-1. *PAC Contributions to Congressional Candidates and Congressional Candidate Expenditures by Election Cycle, 1976–2016*

Millions of 2016 dollars

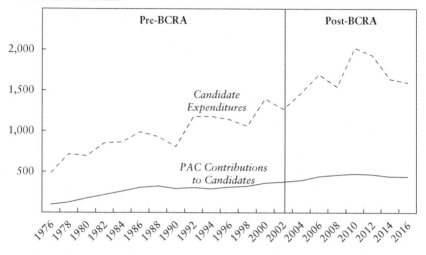

Sources: Harold W. Stanley and Richard G. Niemi, *Vital Statistics on American Politics 2015–2016* (Thousand Oaks, CA: CQ Press, 2015); Federal Election Commission, "Congressional Candidate Data Summary Tables: House and Senate Financial Activity" and "Political Action Committee (PAC) Data Summary Tables: PAC Contributions" (www.fec.gov/press/campaign_finance_statistics.shtml).
Note: Vertical line indicates when BCRA took effect.

congressional candidates' total spending that came from PAC contributions ranged from a low of 18 percent in 1978 to a high of 36 percent in 1990, and in 2016 it was 28 percent. Table 3-1 lists the top PACs by total contributions in 2016 and provides the percentages each contributed to Republican and Democratic candidates.

In 2016, the National Association of Realtors (NAR) PAC contributed the most to congressional candidates, giving $3.9 million. Seven of the top dozen PACs in contributions to candidates were trade associations (NAR, National Beer Wholesalers Association, National Automobile Dealers Association, Credit Union National Association, American Bankers Association, National Association of Insurance and Financial Advisors, and the National Association of Home Builders). One expressly partisan PAC, the Majority Committee, is also on the top PAC donors list, as are two PACs representing unions.

Most corporations and trade associations contribute more to Republicans than to Democrats, and all labor unions contribute much more to

Table 3-1. *Top PAC Contributors to Federal Candidates,*
by Recipient Party, 2015–16
Dollars

PAC	Total[a]	% to Democrats	% to Republicans
National Association of Realtors	3,942,700	42	58
National Beer Wholesalers Association	3,279,700	43	57
Honeywell International	2,835,866	41	59
AT&T Inc.	2,763,750	37	62
National Automobile Dealers Association	2,681,750	28	72
Lockheed Martin	2,610,750	38	62
International Brotherhood of Electrical Workers	2,470,400	96	4
Credit Union National Association	2,375,850	47	53
American Bankers Association	2,342,361	21	78
Comcast Corp. and NBC Universal	2,230,700	36	63
National Association of Insurance and Financial Advisors	2,182,150	33	66
National Association of Home Builders	2,169,625	17	83
Boeing Co.	2,156,000	43	56
Northrop Grumman Corp.	2,135,500	39	61
United Parcel Service	2,108,353	34	65
Majority Committee	2,071,513	0	99
American Crystal Sugar Co.	2,043,000	51	48
Machinists/Aerospace Workers Union	2,003,500	94	6

Source: Compiled from Federal Election Commission data.
a. Totals include subsidiaries and affiliated PACs, if any.

Democrats than to Republicans. The National Association of Homebuilders, a trade association, contributed 83 percent of its $2.2 million to Republicans, while American Crystal Sugar Co., a corporation, contributed 48 percent of its $2.0 million to Republicans. The other corporations and trade unions contributed between 53 and 78 percent to Republicans. The two labor unions on the list, International Brotherhood of Electrical Workers and Machinists/Aerospace Workers Union, contributed 96 percent and 94 percent, respectively, to Democrats. The only other PAC on the list, Majority Committee, which is a leadership PAC associated with House Majority Leader Kevin McCarthy, contributed 99 percent of its $2.0 million to Republicans.

This breakdown of top PAC contributors has not changed much over the past few election cycles. Table 3-2 displays the PACs that have contributed the most to federal candidates since 2000 and the proportion they have contributed to each major party. The NAR has contributed the most

Table 3-2. *Ten PACs That Gave the Most to Federal Candidates,*
2000–16
Millions of dollars

PAC	Total	% to Democrats	% to Republicans
1. National Association of Realtors	37	48	52
2. International Brotherhood of Electrical Workers	28	98	2
3. National Beer Wholesalers Association	27	37	63
4. National Auto Dealers Association	26	32	68
5. American Federation of Teachers	25	99	1
6. Laborers Union	25	89	11
7. AT&T	24	39	61
8. International Brotherhood of Teamsters	24	93	7
9. Honeywell International	23	41	59
10. Service Employees International Union	23	97	3

Source: Federal Election Commission, "Top 50 PACs by Contributions to Candidates" (www.fec.gov/press /campaign_finance_statistics.shtml). Includes activity through December 31, 2016.

to federal candidates since 2000, with over $36 million, roughly equally to Democrats and Republicans. The other contributors in the top ten since 2000 are other trade associations (beer wholesalers, automobile dealers) and corporations (AT&T and Honeywell), both of which give substantially more to Republicans than to Democrats, and labor unions (International Brotherhood of Electrical Workers, American Federation of Teachers, Laborers Union, International Brotherhood of Teamsters, Service Employees International Union), which give mostly to Democrats.[6]

As in previous election cycles, PACs contributed most of their funds to incumbents. Figure 3-2 shows how much PACs donated to incumbents, challengers, and open seat candidates in U.S. House general elections from 1996 to 2016. Of the $352 million that PACs contributed to House candidates in the 2015–16 election cycle, 89 percent ($314 million) went to incumbents. Only 5 percent ($18 million) went to challengers, while 6 percent ($20 million) went to open seat candidates. This is the lowest spending for challengers in recent election cycles. Most PACs, especially business PACs, want to have good relationships with incumbents, who often request donations from them. In the House, PACs contributed 58 percent ($204 million) to Republican candidates and 41 percent ($145 million) to Democratic candidates. This pattern results partly because there are more Republican incumbents and partly because business PACs donate more frequently to Republicans.

Figure 3-2. *PAC Contributions to U.S. House General Election Candidates, 1996–2016*

Millions of dollars

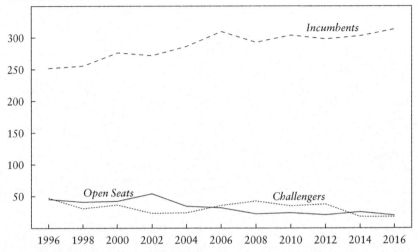

Source: Federal Election Commission, "PAC Contributions" (www.classic.fec.gov/press/campaign_finance_statistics.shtml).

In the 2016 election cycle, PACs contributed $90 million to U.S. Senate candidates, which was 20 percent of their total contributions to federal candidates (House candidates received 79 percent, and presidential candidates received 1 percent). This is mostly because the House has many more candidates than the Senate and because PAC contributions are capped at $5,000 for the primary election and $5,000 for the general election. Of the $90 million PACs contributed to the Senate, 76 percent ($68 million) went to Senate incumbents, 10 percent ($9 million) to Senate challengers, and 13 percent ($12 million) to open seat Senate candidates. PACs give relatively more to Senate nonincumbents than to House nonincumbents, perhaps because Senate incumbents lose elections more often than House incumbents. In 2016, PACs gave two-thirds ($60 million) of their Senate contributions to Republicans, whereas in 2012 PACs gave only 47 percent to Republican Senate candidates. This difference is explained by the number of seats each party had up for election in each cycle: in 2016, Republicans had twenty-four seats up for election, whereas in 2012 they had only ten seats up for election.

Table 3-3. *Internal Communication Costs, Presidential Election Years, 1980–2016*
Millions of 2016 dollars

	Presidential candidates		House candidates		Senate candidates	
Year	For	Against	For	Against	For	Against
1980	5.8	1.7	2.3	0.3	0.9	0.1
1984	10.9	0.1	2.3	0.1	1.4	0.0
1988	4.1	0.2	2.2	0.0	2.4	0.04
1992	7.2	0.1	3.9	0.02	3.3	0.1
1996	3.7	0.5	4.1	0.8	2.6	0.1
2000	15.2	0.8	5.0	0.3	3.2	0.1
2004	30.9	0.0	2.3	0.01	3.6	0.01
2008	17.8	2.3	2.6	0.004	1.0	0.002
2012	8.0	2.8	4.4	0.4	4.2	1.0
2016	11.9	0.7	1.9	0.2	2.9	0.4

Source: Federal Election Commission (ftp://ftp.fec.gov/FEC), as of August 14, 2017. Data adjusted for 2016 dollars using the CPI inflation calculator from the U.S. Bureau of Labor Statistics (www.bls.gov/data/inflation_calculator.htm).

Internal Communications

Corporations, unions, and membership organizations can communicate express advocacy messages to their restricted classes. Interest groups use internal communications because information is more credible coming from a connected organization than from an unknown group or candidate. Table 3-3 shows the cost of internal communications in presidential elections from 1980 to 2016. Expenditures on such internal communications increased from $25 million in the 2000 presidential election cycle to $37 million in 2004 and then decreased to $24 million in 2008 and $21 million in 2012 (adjusted for inflation). In 2016, internal communications continued to decrease, to $18 million.[7] In midterm cycles, internal communications peaked at $25 million in 2010 and dropped to $5 million in 2014.

The PAC that spent the most on internal communications in the 2015–16 election cycle was the American Federation of Teachers labor union, spending $5.3 million. Another teachers' union in the top ten, the National Education Association, spent $1.5 million. Five other labor unions are also in the top ten, as are two ideological PACs, the NRA and NARAL Pro-Choice America. Only one business organization, the NAR, is in the top ten spenders on internal communications.

Expenditures on internal communications are a small percentage of what interest groups spend in elections. In 2016, internal communications accounted for about 1 percent of interest group expenditures. For example, the NAR spent over $36 million contributing to candidates but only $1.4 million communicating with its members.

Conventional Independent Expenditures

Individuals acting on their own and political groups (PACs) have long been able to make independent expenditures, subject to contribution limits for standard PACs. Independent expenditures by individuals and PACs are unlimited. For two decades, political party committees have also been able to make unlimited independent expenditures with limited and disclosed contributions. (Party independent expenditures are discussed in chapter 7.) After soft money was banned by the Bipartisan Campaign Reform Act (BCRA) in 2002, conventional independent expenditures increased. The *Citizens United* and *SpeechNow.org* court decisions and FEC administrative rulings have dramatically expanded independent spending. A new variation on how PACs may organize was recognized in 2011 by the U.S. District Court for the District of Columbia, which ruled that a conventional PAC could create a second bank account for unlimited contributions to the PAC and that this separate part of the PAC could make unlimited contributions just as Super PACs may do. This mode of PAC organization is known as a hybrid PAC or Carey PAC, named after the person who brought the case, Rear Admiral James Carey.[8] Table 3-4 compares independent expenditures made by PACs, party committees, Super PACs, hybrid PACs, and individuals not acting through a political committee in 2010–16.

By 2016, aggregate independent expenditures had increased to well above what the outside spending levels were at the peak of the soft-money and issue advocacy period in 2000 and 2002, when party soft money rose to nearly $500 million in each cycle.[9] In 2016, there was a 78 percent increase in outside spending by Super PACs and hybrid PACs compared to the 2012 presidential election cycle. Independent spending by parties did not change noticeably between 2012 and 2016. Conventional independent expenditures by PACs were at near parity in 2012 and 2016, with both presidential cycles higher than in the 2010 and 2014 midterm cycles. Only independent expenditures by individuals other than political committees declined, by about $100 million from the $300 million spent in this way in 2012.

Table 3-4. *Independent Expenditure Totals and Percentages by Committee and Filer Type*
Dollars

	2010		2012		2014		2016	
Standard PAC independent expenditures[a]	55,017,388	14%	78,044,150	6%	48,829,678	7%	76,176,918	5%
Party independent expenditures	191,149,935	49%	252,361,301	20%	228,993,297	33%	254,502,794	16%
Independent-expenditure-only political committees (Super PACs)	62,549,345	16%	606,808,037	49%	339,402,611	49%	1,056,466,148	65%
Political committees with noncontribution accounts (hybrid PACs)	n.a.		12,915,159	1%	2,573,469	0%	46,661,972	3%
Independent expenditures reported by persons other than political committees	79,927,800	21%	300,393,644	24%	68,045,226	10%	197,194,244	12%
Total independent expenditures	388,644,468		1,250,522,291		687,844,281		1,631,002,075	

Source: Federal Election Commission, "Independent Expenditure Summary Totals by Committee and Filer Type" (www.fec.gov/press/campaign_finance_statistics.shtml). Includes activity through December 31, 2016.

a. The standard political action committee (PAC) total excludes amounts for independent-expenditure-only political committees (Super PACs) and political committees with noncontribution accounts (Hybrid PACs). These committee types are represented in this table as separate line items.

While conventional independent expenditures are now in the aggregate much less than spending by Super PACs, some groups continue to make independent expenditures, with contributions subject to FECA PAC contribution limits. Many of these groups had been making independent expenditures for several elections before Super PACs came into existence. Table 3-5 presents conventional independent expenditures made by groups in 2016.

Three of the most active conventional independent-expenditure groups in 2016 have been active in the last three presidential election cycles, spending nearly $10 million or more per group independently in each cycle. The three groups are the Service Employees International Union (SEIU), the NRA, and the American Federation of State, County, and Municipal Employees (AFSCME). The NRA has been the most consistent in its level of independent spending, with more spending in 2016 than in 2012 or 2008. When all election-related spending by the NRA is combined, one source estimated it spent at least $55 million in 2016.[10] Of these three groups, two are unions (SEIU and AFSCME) and the NRA is a membership organization. For organizations like these, much of the money they raise is from individual contributions, which must not exceed the contribution limits. Sometimes a new group arises in a particular election cycle and makes substantial conventional independent expenditures. That was the case in 2016 with End Citizens United, a progressive reform group supporting candidates who favor overturning *Citizens United* and that spent $13 million in PAC contributions and independent expenditures in support of Democrats.

When the courts interpreted the U.S. Constitution to permit independent-expenditure-only PACs and to allow unlimited individual contributions as well as allow unions and corporations to make contributions from their general funds, it was unknown how many of the groups that had been making conventional independent expenditures paid for with limited contributions would switch to Super PACs. Those uncertainties grew when the court permitted existing standard PACs to create separate independent-expenditure-only accounts within the same overall PAC, a hybrid or Carey PAC.

Table 3-5 permits tracking of standard PACs that had made independent expenditures and seeing which ones substantially reduced or abandoned their conventional independent-expenditure activity. It shows which ones started up as new groups, which ones stopped making conventional independent expenditures and switched to Super PACs, and

Table 3-5. *Interest Group Conventional Independent Expenditures Paid for with Donor Limited Funds, 2008, 2012, 2016*[a]

Dollars

Organization	2007–08	2011–12	2015–16	Total
Service Employees International Union	43,132,219	16,374,940	9,616,480	69,123,639
National Rifle Association	17,711,357	16,554,005	19,296,995	53,562,357
American Federation of State, County, and Municipal Employees	10,585,015	12,449,381	15,259,972	38,294,368
End Citizens United			13,683,017	13,683,017
National Association of Realtors	6,746,234	3,391,843		10,138,077
National Republican Trust PAC	9,496,369			9,496,369
MoveOn.org	6,649,335	1,169,542		7,818,877
National Right to Life	3,658,461	2,642,497	458,074	6,759,032
Republican Majority Campaign	3,089,333	2,360,392		5,449,725
Our Country Deserves Better PAC	4,463,507	704,073		5,167,580
United Auto Workers	4,878,930			4,878,930
Conservative Majority Fund		3,024,846	1,549,180	4,574,026
Senate Conservatives Fund	22,397	3,546,738	942,805	4,511,940
Club for Growth	3,557,934	716,310	203,730	4,477,974
American Federation of Teachers	3,876,056	53,436	411,480	4,340,972
International Association of Firefighters	2,177,895	1,830,327	25,782	4,034,004
American Hospital Association	589,663	1,981,184	1,278,070	3,848,917
Tea Party Majority Fund		134,327	3,375,747	3,510,074
National Federation of Independent Business	1,350,193	1,411,930	665,700	3,427,823
National Education Association	531,901	2,677,430	5,000	3,214,331
EMILY's List	3,202,786			3,202,786
Credit Union National Association	530,415	816,464	1,813,271	3,160,150
National Campaign	1,573,445		1,470,000	3,043,445
American Medical Association	1,554,895	1,136,912	141,612	2,833,419
Freedom's Defense Fund	50,628	385,617	2,005,227	2,441,472
Government Integrity Fund		2,431,748		2,431,748
Life and Liberty PAC	1,475,955	800,000	3,000	2,278,955
Conservative Campaign Committee		1,614,947	53,465	1,668,412
Reform Wisconsin Fund			1,375,057	1,375,057
Legacy Committee PAC	1,171,236			1,171,236
Montana Hunters and Anglers Leadership Fund		1,161,693		1,161,693

Source: Compiled from Federal Election Commission data (ftp://ftp.fec.gov/FEC), as of July 25, 2017.

a. Table represents interest groups that spent more than $1 million in independent expenditures with traditional PAC funds in at least one of the included election cycles. Totals include independent expenditures made by local affiliates of each organization.

which ones were little changed. Conventional independent expenditures dropped between 2008 and 2012 for some groups, as Super PACs became an alternative way to spend independently. The NAR, for example, spent over $6.7 million in conventional independent expenditures in 2008, $3.4 million in 2012, and nothing in 2016. However, the NAR spent $10.9 million in independent expenditures through its Super PAC in 2016 and a similar amount in 2014. The United Auto Workers (UAW) and EMILY's List also did not make conventional independent expenditures in 2012 or 2016 but did make them in 2008. The UAW spent $3.7 million through the union's Super PAC in 2016.

Super PACs

The most significant recent development in federal campaign finance is the creation and growth of independent-expenditure-only committees, or Super PACs. The U.S. Supreme Court made clear in its *Buckley* v. *Valeo* ruling on FECA that individuals and groups have a constitutional right to spend money independently in federal election campaigns.[11] Independent expenditures have grown in importance, with subsequent court decisions recognizing that political parties are allowed to make independent expenditures[12] and that independent-expenditure-only committees (i.e., Super PACs), which facilitate making independent expenditures, are allowed.[13] Super PACs can raise unlimited amounts from individuals, corporations, and unions, including their general treasury funds. Figure 3-3 presents the money contributed to Super PACs by individuals, corporations, and unions since 2010.

While *Citizens United* v. *Federal Election Commission* and *Speech-Now.org* v. *Federal Election Commission* recognized spending by unions and corporations from their general treasuries on independent expenditures as legal, most of the money raised by Super PACs has been given by individuals. The share of funds given by individuals, rather than unions and corporations, ranged from 87 percent in 2010 to 97 percent in 2016. Unions made most of the remaining contributions, and corporations contributed 1 percent of Super PAC funds in 2014 and 2016. Corporations donate little in comparison to trade unions and individuals.

Some individuals had made their own independent expenditures before the *Citizens United* and *SpeechNow.org* decisions, but the amount spent by individuals through Super PACs far exceeded individuals' spending between the 1976 *Buckley* decision and 2010, the first election year

Figure 3-3. *Super PAC Receipts from Individuals, Corporations, and Unions, 2010–16*

Millions of dollars

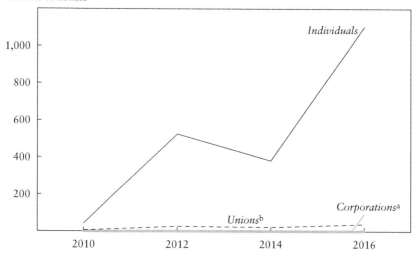

Source: Federal Election Commission (ftp://ftp.fec.gov/FEC), as of August 16, 2017.
a. Totals include PACs designated as corporations, corporations without capital stock, and trade associations.
b. Totals include labor organizations.

after *Citizens United* and *SpeechNow.org.* It is much easier for an individual wanting to make an independent expenditure to do so through a Super PAC than to do it personally. The Super PAC has staff to manage the required reporting to the FEC and provides the legal representation to ensure the group is in compliance with the law. The Super PAC presumably has expertise in hiring political consultants and negotiating with pollsters, media firms, and television stations to maximize the impact of the expenditure, and the Super PAC's leadership is trusted by the candidate or congressional party leaders, reinforcing the donor's future ability to have greater access to the candidate the Super PAC is supporting. The courts' decisions recognizing Super PACs as legal also removed any uncertainty about the constitutionality of spending unlimited amounts of money on elections in this way.

Contributions to Super PACs can come in relatively large amounts, often well beyond the standard BCRA PAC contribution limits. Table 3-6 provides the largest individual donors to Super PACs in 2016.

Table 3-6. *Top Individual Contributors to Super PACs, 2015–16*
Dollars

Name	Aggregate amount donated to Super PACs	Number of Super PACs donated to	Aggregate amount given to other committees/candidates	Committee receiving most other funds
Thomas F. Steyer	89,544,744	3	1,029,240	Hillary Victory Fund
Sheldon and Miriam Adelson	77,900,000	6	4,324,600	Cleveland 2016 Host Committee Inc.
S. Donald Sussman	38,645,000	8	3,655,000	Hillary Victory Fund
Fred Eychaner	35,250,000	4	2,679,304	Hillary Victory Fund
James H. and Marilyn Simons	25,025,000	6	1,275,108	DCCC
Paul E. Singer	24,095,153	17	2,024,325	RNC
Michael R. Bloomberg	23,679,624	3	58,600	Leaders in Education
Robert L. Mercer	22,551,000	17	1,674,250	RNC
George Soros	20,789,693	9	1,674,318	Color of Change PAC
Dustin Moskovitz and Cari Tuna	19,915,000	7	5,151,236	MoveOn.org
Richard Uihlein	18,228,500	22	1,531,700	Madison Project Inc.
Jay R. and Mary K. Pritzker	17,950,848	4	2,351,525	Correct the Record
Diane Hendricks	16,970,900	3	1,252,590	Cleveland 2016 Host Committee Inc.
John Joe and Marlene Ricketts	14,473,829	10	864,959	RNC
Haim and Cheryl Saban	13,780,000	4	2,693,400	Hillary Victory Fund
Ronald M. Cameron	13,246,000	8	1,073,697	Trump Victory
Warren A. Stephens	11,842,613	17	1,669,495	NRCC
Kenneth C. Griffin	11,688,290	10	2,054,153	RNC
Bernard Marcus	11,457,900	10	1,105,194	RNC
Linda E. McMahon	10,010,000	10	965,725	RNC

Source: Compiled from Federal Election Commission records of donations linked and aggregated by donors in excess of $10 million (ftp://ftp.fec.gov/FEC), as of June 3, 2017.
Note: Table includes individuals who donated in excess of $10 million where data were aggregated using all name variations of donors.

In 2016, the largest individual donor to Super PACs was Thomas F. Steyer, a hedge-fund founder and environmentalist, who gave $89.5 million to Super PACs. He was not a Super PAC donor in 2012. In 2016, Steyer was followed by Sheldon and Miriam Adelson, who gave $79.9 million to Super PACs, $10.5 million less than in 2012. Some Super PAC donors gave more in 2016 than they did in 2012, including Fred Eychaner, who gave $21.4 million more, and Michael Bloomberg, whose $11.6 million increase nearly doubled his Super PAC donations over this same period. All of these major Super PAC donors also made contributions to candidate campaign committees, party committees, or both, with the mean for this group an additional nine contributions beyond Super PAC contributions. These campaign and party committee contributions generally went to one party. For example, Thomas Steyer donated to the Hillary Victory Fund, while the Adelsons donated to the RNC's Convention Fund.

Total spending by Super PACs in 2015–16 exceeded $1 billion, and if expenditures by hybrid PACs are included, the total climbs to over $1.1 billion. However, most of the spending by Super PACs was by the largest ones. Table 3-7 presents the spending by the top twenty-five Super PACs in 2016.

The top twenty-five Super PACs in 2016 spent about $830 million, and the party division in how the money was spent was remarkably close ($408 million for Democrats and $422 million for Republicans). Super PACs often spend most of their money attacking opponents, but a distinct element in 2016 was the two Super PACs that were funded in whole or in part to stop Donald Trump's candidacy—America Leads, which spent $18.6 million, and United We Can, which spent $13 million.

As table 3-4 shows, combined Super PAC spending in 2016 was much higher than in 2012. The growth in combined Super PAC spending is especially noteworthy because Donald Trump had less Super PAC support in 2016 than Mitt Romney did in 2012. In 2012, Romney had a total of $251,178,045 spent on his behalf by his Super PAC (Restore Our Future) and by American Crossroads.[14] In 2016, Trump had a total of $83,652,776 spent on his behalf by Super PACs not associated with interest groups, plus another $10,625,444 in Super PAC spending by the NRA, $7,832,399 in independent spending by the Republican National Committee, and $1,008,982 in independent spending by one individual, Steven Adams.[15] Super PAC spending in support of Romney's candidacy in 2012 was about 2.5 times greater than Super PAC spending in support of Trump's candidacy in 2016. Much of Trump's spending came

Table 3-7. *Independent Expenditures by the Top Twenty-Five Super PACs, 2015–16*
Dollars

Organization	Candidate supported	Grand total	For Democrats / against Republicans	For Republicans / against Democrats
Priorities USA Action	Clinton	133,407,972	133,407,972	0
Right to Rise USA	Bush	86,817,138	3,140,677	83,676,461
Senate Leadership Fund	Party (R)	85,994,270	482,330	85,511,940
Senate Majority PAC	Party (D)	75,389,818	75,389,818	0
Conservative Solutions PAC	Rubio	55,443,483	16,489,407	38,954,076
Get Our Jobs Back[a]	Trump	50,010,166	0	50,010,166
House Majority PAC	Party (D)	47,470,121	46,560,636	909,485
Congressional Leadership Fund	Party (R)	40,125,691	0	40,125,691
Women Vote!	Issue	33,167,285	31,166,517	2,000,768
Freedom Partners Action Fund	Issue	29,728,798	0	29,728,798
Granite State Solutions	Party (R)	24,267,135	0	24,267,135
Future45	Trump	24,264,009	0	24,264,009
Rebuilding America Now	Trump	21,194,739	81,000	21,113,739
Club for Growth Action	Bush	19,181,962	10,704,006	8,477,956
America Leads	Christie	18,578,852	634,880	17,943,972
Our Principles PAC	Anti-Trump	18,327,047	18,323,577	3,470
League of Conservation Voters	Issue group	15,689,081	15,689,081	0
Ending Spending Action Fund	Issue group	14,849,164	3,594,268	11,254,896
Make America Number 1	Cruz/Trump	13,454,894	3,115,611	10,339,283
Independence USA PAC		13,387,635	7,404,395	5,983,240
NextGen California Action	Issue group	13,130,014	13,130,014	0
United We Can	Anti-Trump	13,048,275	12,823,414	224,861
Planned Parenthood Votes	Issue group	12,108,113	12,106,385	1,728
New Day for America		11,189,297	175,434	11,013,863
National Association of Realtors	Issue group	10,225,968	3,863,571	6,362,397
Totals		830,450,927	408,282,993	422,157,768[a]

Source: Center for Responsive Politics, "Super PACs" (www.opensecrets.org/pacs/superpacs.php?cycle=2016), as of June 3, 2017.
a. Get Our Jobs Back did not make any contributions to a single campaign or other political entity during the 2016 cycle. It received a single $50 million donation, which it immediately returned to the donor. The two other donations were much smaller. One was immediately returned to the donor and the other, a $15,477 donation, was given in part to an organization owned by the treasurer of Get Our Jobs Back. This figure removes the $50,010,166 reported by Get Our Jobs Back.

late, including spending by Super PACs and a 501(c)(4) group supporting him (see chapter 5).

What explains the $483 million increase in Super PAC fundraising from 2012 to 2016? Part of the answer is that the Republican presidential primary field, aside from Trump, had some very active Super PACs. Those supporting Jeb Bush, Ted Cruz, and Marco Rubio alone account for $171 million of outside money receipts. In 2012, Super PACs supporting

Romney, Santorum, Gingrich, Paul, Cain, Huntsman, and Perry spent $103.7 in the nomination phase, with Romney's Restore Our Future spending another $33.1 million in the bridge period after he secured the nomination but before the convention.[16] Spending by the party-centered congressional Super PACs was also higher in 2016, totaling $257 million, compared to $243.7 million in 2012.[17] Interest groups also were often more active in Super PAC and other outside activity in 2016, including unions, pro-choice and environmental groups, the NRA, the Club for Growth, and the Koch brothers–affiliated Freedom Partners. In short, the growth was widespread and could have been even higher had Trump been a more conventional candidate.

Super PACs can be classified into three broad types: candidate-specific, party centered, and issue or ideology based.[18] In the 2012 and 2016 presidential contests, the candidate-specific Super PACs were the most active in both the intraparty and interparty competitions. Candidate-specific Super PACs provide an easy way for candidates to secure campaign resources that will be spent to advance their electoral success while avoiding contribution limitations. Moreover, candidates have found ways to reap electoral benefits from a Super PAC without directly controlling it.[19]

Candidate-specific Super PACs have been less common in congressional campaigns, but are beginning to emerge. An example of a candidate-specific Super PAC at the congressional level in 2016 was Granite State Solutions, which supported New Hampshire Republican incumbent senator Kelly Ayotte and opposed Maggie Hassan. This Super PAC raised $25.5 million, and the largest contributor was Sheldon Adelson.[20] It formed late, and its first filings with the FEC came August 31, 2016. In a second example, incumbent Republican senator Rob Portman also formed a candidate-specific Super PAC, the Fighting for Ohio Fund; in February 2015, he named his longtime political adviser Barry Bennett to head it.[21] This Super PAC raised $9.9 million, and the largest contributor was Peter Thiel, who gave $1 million.[22] In 2014, the most active candidate-specific Super PACs spent in races in Kentucky, West Virginia, North Carolina, Louisiana, and Alaska.[23]

A second type of Super PAC focusing on congressional contests is party centered. These can be an extension of party leaders in either the House or the Senate or more broadly serving the party at the presidential and congressional levels. Senate Democrats, with the support of Senate Democratic leader Harry Reid, formed a Super PAC in 2010, the Majority PAC (formerly Commonsense Ten and later Senate Majority PAC),[24] and

House Democrats, with the support of their leader, Nancy Pelosi, launched the House Majority PAC in 2011.[25] The House Majority PAC and Senate Majority PAC remain prominent in spending in competitive contests. In 2011, House Republicans, under the leadership of John Boehner, formed the Congressional Leadership Fund,[26] and formed the Young Guns Action Fund, identified with Majority Leader Eric Cantor.[27] American Crossroads was started by Karl Rove and Steven Law soon after the court decisions in 2010 and was the most active Republican party-centered Super PAC in 2010, 2012, and 2014, spending in congressional races in 2010 and 2014 and in the presidential and congressional races in 2012. The Senate Leadership Fund was formed following the 2014 election cycle and was prominent in spending to assist Republicans in 2016.[28] Steven Law, who leads the Senate Leadership Fund, explains its success as follows:

> One of the reasons why the number of the creation of—a number of these candidate-specific groups on the Republican side has started to decline is I think they have got track record now of if we get involved in a race, we stick with it. We're not out to drive the debate. We're out to amplify and support. We don't run ads that have to be pulled. There is sort of a sense of relative certainty about our execution.[29]

In 2016, spending by Super PACs closely linked to the party leadership in each chamber rose dramatically. Together, the four congressional party leadership Super PACs spent nearly $250 million in 2016. As table 3-4 reports, party-committee independent expenditures were another $254 million in 2016. Taken together, these expenditures mean the party leadership in 2016 was able to direct about the same amount of resources to competitive districts in 2016 as they were in the era of party soft money in 2000 and 2002, when the party committees spent nearly $500 million in soft money.[30] The success of the party leaders in raising money for party-independent expenditures and party-aligned Super PAC spending prompted the Campaign Finance Institute to conclude, "Perhaps it is time to stop bemoaning the weakness of political parties in financing federal elections."[31]

Given that spending occurs in congressional campaigns beyond the candidate's own campaign committee, and that this can come from conventional independent expenditures by groups as well as from Super PACs

Table 3-8. *Top Outside Spending in Senate and House Races, 2015–16*
Dollars

Senate race	Total	For Democrats / against Republicans	For Republicans / against Democrats
Pennsylvania Senate	102,523,073	52,098,497	50,424,576
Nevada Senate	74,265,195	32,031,193	42,234,002
New Hampshire Senate	73,857,946	40,213,557	33,644,389
Ohio Senate	46,680,675	16,281,068	30,399,607
North Carolina Senate	45,858,860	19,036,843	26,822,017
Florida Senate	40,795,144	11,754,899	29,040,245
Indiana Senate	33,227,315	10,001,311	23,226,004
Missouri Senate	32,482,367	13,318,147	19,164,220
Wisconsin Senate	26,641,100	9,679,322	16,961,778
Arizona Senate	6,987,021	2,241,196	4,745,825

House race	Total	For Democrats / against Republicans	For Republicans / against Democrats
Minnesota District 8	8,604,166	3,733,942	4,870,224
Nevada District 3	8,330,063	3,534,838	4,795,225
Virginia District 10	6,243,145	2,446,243	3,796,902
Pennsylvania District 8	6,227,769	2,818,809	3,408,960
New York District 19	5,624,804	1,532,318	4,092,486
New Jersey District 5	5,146,426	4,780,389	366,037
Florida District 26	5,132,656	1,725,214	3,407,442
Maine District 2	5,108,354	3,899,961	1,208,393
Colorado District 6	4,814,546	2,229,964	2,584,582
California District 10	4,671,275	1,020,424	3,650,851

Source: Center for Responsive Politics, "2016 Outside Spending, by Race" (www.opensecrets.org/outsidespending /summ.php?cycle=2016&disp=R&pty=N&type=S and www.opensecrets.org/outsidespending/summ.php?cycle=2016 &disp=R&pty=N&type=H), as of June 4, 2017.

Note: Does not include party-committee spending.

and 501(c) committees, it is useful to aggregate how much outside money was spent in what races. Table 3-8 lists congressional contests that had the most outside spending (not including party committees) in U.S. Senate and U.S. House races in 2016 and how much was spent in efforts to elect a Democrat or Republican. Spending against a candidate in this case would be counted as money spent to help elect the opponent.

Super PACs have concentrated their spending on competitive races, especially U.S. Senate races. Examples of contests in which Super PACs were active in 2014 include those in Kentucky, West Virginia, North Carolina, Louisiana, and Alaska,[32] but not all Senate candidates in 2014 had great success in raising funds for their Super PAC.[33] In 2016, outside groups outspent the candidate campaign they were affiliated with in twenty-seven congressional races. Outside groups outspent candidate campaign organizations in one-fifth of all eligible Senate races. The 2016 Nevada Senate race featured some of the highest spending rates for any Senate race during the cycle—Democrat Catherine Cortez Masto spent $19 million, while Republican challenger Joe Heck spent $12 million—but this was eclipsed by nearly $88 million of outside spending on behalf of the two candidates.[34] Much of the Republican spending came late. Steven Law of the Senate Leadership Fund explained the perceived need for more spending late in the cycle as follows: "About two weeks in October, put out an APB to all of our donors and indicated that as generous as they've been, we really needed them to help further to try to even out the financial spending gap. We ended up raising about $38 million in the states in about 10, 11 days. We were able to deploy that to equalize what was on the air."[35]

A third type of Super PAC is more ideological, focusing on issues and investing in races where candidate choices are related to these issues. Some of these groups are extensions of the activities of groups that were active in campaign finance before there were Super PACs (such as Freedom Partners, Club for Growth, SEIU, Planned Parenthood), and others were new in 2012 (such as Now or Never PAC or Ending Spending Action Fund). Steven Law of the Senate Leadership Fund contrasted his party-centered Super PAC with others as follows:

> Our value proposition in their [donors'] minds is that we're technicians who execute high quality political activity at a very low cost. There are other groups that offer a more ideological—the Kochs, for example, they have a much more ideological policy or direction than we do. So, that's if you're largely directed by the ideology, you might support that effort or you can support that exclusively, but there are a lot of donors who just want to win races and those are the ones who tend to find their place here.[36]

One strategic advantage of Super PACs is their ability to form very quickly. If their mode of spending is advertising on television, radio, or through social media, Super PACs can also start to deliver messages very quickly. This was the case with some Super PACs supporting Donald Trump in 2016. The Future 45 Super PAC was initially an anti-Hillary Super PAC funded by Republicans who appeared to want to help Clinton's

Democratic opponent Bernie Sanders by attacking Clinton.[37] The group ran an ad on Clinton's "inaction" before the attack on the U.S. consulate in Benghazi, Libya, and her connections to Wall Street.[38] Future 45 was later repurposed to be a late-spending Super PAC, again attacking Clinton and seeking to elect Donald Trump, by describing Clinton as "scandal plagued."[39] In this phase of the campaign, it was funded mostly by Sheldon and Miriam Adelson ($20 million of the $24 million raised).[40] The Adelsons, along with Todd Ricketts, are also reported to have funded the 45Committee, a 501(c)(4) committee that reported spending $21 million in 2016.[41] Late funding can bolster the activities of existing Super PACs, as with the contributions late in the process to the Senate Leadership Fund and Congressional Leadership Fund. Here again, the Adelsons gave $35 million to the Senate Leadership Fund and $20 million to the Congressional Leadership Fund, with some of their contributions coming in the final weeks of the campaign.

The tone of Super PAC ads has most often been negative, and some have characterized outside groups as doing the "dirty work" in campaigns.[42] In 2014, for example, the proportion of negative ads was double the proportion of positive ads (52 percent to 26 percent, with pro-Democratic spending more negative than pro-Republican spending), but outside group and party independent-expenditure ads were almost universally negative (90 and 98 percent, respectively, for Democrats and 70 and 92 percent, respectively, for Republicans). The Wesleyan Media Project, the successor to the Wisconsin Media Project, has been tracking and coding television ads since 1998. In addition to "negative," the other coding categories used by Wesleyan are "contrast" and "positive."[43] Advertising in the 2016 presidential race was less negative than in 2012 but more negative than in 2000, 2004, and 2008. The Wesleyan scholars found that Clinton's ads were negative more often than Trump's ads (48 percent compared to 28 percent). Outside group ads in 2016 were more negative than candidate ads, especially those by outside groups supporting Clinton (96 percent were negative) compared to those by outside groups supporting Trump (60 percent negative). Figures for House and Senate ads were comparable to those of other election cycles since 2008, when negativity became more common.[44]

Given the negative focus of much Super PAC advertising, it is not surprising that specialized Super PACs have been created to assist in the opposition research needed for this kind of communication. Democrats created a Super PAC named American Bridge 21st Century to do this, and Republicans now have their own media-tracking Super PAC, America Rising. Candidates have also created specialized media-response Super PACs. In 2016, Democrats building on American Bridge started a new Super PAC, Correct the Record, a Super PAC aligned with Hillary Clinton that served as a rapid-response messenger for Clinton through social media. Correct the Record broke new ground in 2015–16 by announcing it would "work in coordination" with the Clinton campaign. The group claimed that since the material it produced was directed to the web and social media, it was not subject to the standard Super PAC prohibitions on coordination.[45]

Consistent with independent expenditures before BCRA, most outside spending since BCRA, including the very large amounts spent by Super PACs, is done in competitive contests. Groups can hedge their bets by giving to incumbents while participating in outside money groups for partisan or ideological reasons. After the Democratic Party took control of Congress in 2006, the proportion of corporate PAC money going to Republican members of the House fell from its 2004 level of 69 percent to 49 percent in 2008.[46] Going into the 2010 House elections, when Democrats controlled the House, corporate giving and independent expenditures for Democrats and Republicans in the House were nearly equal ($58.8 million for Democrats compared to $57 million for Republicans). Two years later, when Republicans controlled the House, corporate PAC contributions for Republicans were nearly double the contributions for Democrats ($89 million and $45.1 million, respectively).[47]

Groups sometimes use an approach called "access strategy," in which they contribute to an incumbent's campaign through a PAC and then also make an independent expenditure or give to a Super PAC or a 501(c) group. This permits them to preserve a relationship with senior incumbents in both parties, which will be important to their policy agenda, but they can also spend independently to try to ensure that the majority party is their preferred party.

Candidate campaigns, party committees, and outside groups are all tapping the same pool of pollsters, media consultants, managers, and other campaign professionals. One polling firm may be working for a candidate in one Senate race but for the party-committee independent-expenditure operation in another and for a Super PAC in a third. In 2012, about one-third of spending went to a small number of media groups.[48] Multiple campaigns and allied Super PACs pay or use the same private vendors (such as e-mail lists, political strategy consultants, and so on).

For example, in 2016 Marco Rubio's campaign committee, the Rubio Victory Committee; his 501(c)(4) group, the Conservative Solutions Project; and his leadership PAC all employed the same fundraiser at the same time, Anna Rogers, Inc.[49]

The involvement of Super PACs in making and placing advertisements on television and radio, staging events, managing campaign activities on the ground, and developing databases and data-driven campaign efforts calls into question just how independent the independent expenditures by Super PACs really are. Some prior research found that Super PACs and candidates "lacked foreknowledge of each other's behavior."[50] These same scholars found that Super PACs and candidates spent in complementary ways.[51]

Super PACs also have a broader impact on campaigns and elections in the United States. The possibility that an opponent might have a well-funded aligned Super PAC increases candidate uncertainty, leading to more fundraising and prompting more candidates to want their own Super PAC. It is now commonplace for presidential candidates to have their own Super PACs, and this phenomenon is spreading to the U.S. Senate and U.S. House.

Section 501(c) Groups

The 2016 cycle saw growth in the role of interest groups and individuals funding election activity beyond contributions to candidates, party committees, and standard PACs. This was in the form of spending by section 501(c) groups, named after section 501(c) of the Internal Revenue Code (IRC). These groups have existed for decades but have risen in importance as an alternative way for interested money to be spent defeating or electing particular candidates. As with Super PACs, some 501(c) groups have become extensions of particular candidate campaigns, and candidates are using them for multiple campaign functions (see chapters 1, 5, and 6).

Organized interests have an ongoing relationship with the Internal Revenue Service. Contributions to 501(c)(4), 501(c)(5), and 501(c)(6) organizations are not tax deductible, but contributions to section 501(c)(3) groups are. These 501(c)(3) groups include churches, foundations, and charitable organizations. 501(c)(3) groups are exempt from sales and property taxes and are eligible for discounted postage rates. Some nonprofit social welfare groups seeking anonymity for their donors and to be exempt from income taxes are organized under section 501(c)(4) of the Internal Revenue Code.[52] Examples of such organizations include volunteer fire departments, and civic groups like Rotary International and the League of Women Voters. Similarly, unions are organized under section 501(c)(5) and trade associations under section 501(c)(6) of the IRC.

501(c)(3) Organizations

In part because contributions to 501(c)(3) groups are tax deductible, such organizations have for more than eighty years been banned from political campaign activities.[53] This prohibition includes the use of the organization's resources (computers, offices, staff work hours, and other resources). Possible penalties include excise taxes on responsible individuals, revocation of the organization's tax-exempt status, and payment of back taxes by the organization. Because groups have other organizing options under the code, courts have little reason to be lenient on 501(c)(3) groups that engage in partisan political involvement.[54]

Section 501(c)(3) groups largely continued their past patterns of not becoming involved in the financing of the 2016 elections. Some campaigns and groups appear to have benefited from research and fundraising relationships with foundations in 2016. Critics of candidates closely associated with foundations claim that contributions to foundations may purchase greater access to candidates. As the weekly magazine *The Economist* summarized, "The problem is that a foundation, which is led by an ex-president and someone who hopes to be elected president by the end of the year, can appear vulnerable to conflicts of interest. One of the reasons the Clinton Foundation has become such a formidable fundraising machine is that donors appear to hope to gain access to the corridors of political power with their gifts."[55] A second foundation linked to a presidential candidate that was also scrutinized in 2016 was the Foundation for Excellence in Education, which promoted school reform. Jeb Bush had founded that foundation years before he announced his candidacy, and he had also been its leader. The foundation was the subject of questions about Bush's ongoing role and his relationship with large donors to the foundation.[56]

The limitations on churches becoming involved in electoral politics include an amendment to what became the Internal Revenue Code of 1954. The amendment, known as the Johnson Amendment, was introduced by then Senate Minority Leader Lyndon B. Johnson in 1954 and prohibits 501(c)(3) organizations from endorsing or opposing political candidates. However, the degree to which churches can become involved in candidate elections has been contested. There were increased reports of 501(c)(3) candidate advocacy activity in the 2004 election. The IRS investigated 107 cases and found that 62 of the 501(c)(3) groups, including 47 churches, had violated the ban. Five 501(c)(3) groups had their status revoked. The IRS found that the violations by the others were anomalous or that steps had been taken to prevent them from happening again.[57] Some churches protested the IRS decisions and openly violated the ban because they saw that political issues such as presidential choices impacted moral and religious issues such as gay marriage. In 2008 and again in 2012, hundreds of pastors joined together for "Pulpit Freedom Sunday," in which they delivered sermons with political messages. In 2012, news accounts of Pulpit Freedom Sunday stated that the IRS is not investigating churches for political activity even though there is overwhelming evidence that churches are engaging in it.[58] Data from the Pew Forum Survey are consistent with this reporting; the survey found that "40 percent of black Protestants who attend worship services regularly said their clergy have discussed a specific candidate in church."[59] Pulpit Freedom Sunday and the Alliance Defending Freedom organizations were active during both 2014[60] and 2016.[61] The IRS has not released clarifications about what type of speech violates the ban.

The prohibition on religious group involvement became a campaign issue in 2016 as some called for the abolition of the Johnson Amendment, which prohibited all representatives of 501(c)(3) groups from political campaign activity for or against any candidate. Although the IRS has not revoked the tax-exempt status of churches that have spoken out on political issues from the pulpit, some religious groups were concerned that the Johnson Amendment could be used in the future to curtail religious speech that also touched on political issues or candidates. In 2017, President Trump signed an executive order aimed at "making it easier for churches to participate in politics."[62] Congress is also considering legislation to remove the Johnson Amendment.[63]

501(c)(4) Organizations

The prohibition on candidate campaign activity for 501(c)(3) organizations does not extend to other nonprofits. According to the IRC, groups organizing under section 501(c)(4) are "social welfare" organizations "not organized for profit but operated exclusively for the promotion of social welfare."[64] In 1959, the Treasury Department issued a regulation that redefined the "exclusive" requirement to mean that "an organization is operated exclusively for the promotion of social welfare if it is *primarily* engaged in promoting in some way the common good and general welfare of the people of the community."[65] Since "primarily" has not been defined by the Treasury Department or IRS, the requirement remains vague. Presently the IRS uses a "facts and circumstances test" to determine whether the activity of a section 501(c)(4) organization is primarily used for social welfare.[66] In 2013, the IRS released proposed "guidance" on what constituted a social welfare organization, with the proposal providing a set of definitions of "candidate-related political activity," including express advocacy for or against a candidate, grants and contributions to candidates, and activities closely related to elections and candidates (voter registration, get out the vote, voter guides, literature, holding an event, and others).[67] The IRS has not taken further action on the proposed guidelines. Some argue that "as long as a group's political activity is forty-nine percent or less of its total activity, then that group has not jeopardized its (c)(4) status."[68]

501(c)(4) groups are required to report to the IRS annually using Form 990. This form is due on the May 15 after the close of the organization's fiscal year. Groups can obtain a three-month extension and, with a successful appeal, another three-month extension. This reporting cycle effectively means many 501(c)(4)s are not reporting on a timetable that makes their disclosure available to the public before an election. They report their direct and indirect campaign activities, the amount of money spent conducting these activities, the volunteer hours given, the amounts of money the organization has given to other organizations, the names and taxpayer identification numbers of other section 527 groups to whom payment was made, and the amount of the payment.[69]

A major advantage of section 501(c)(4) organizations is that they are not required to disclose their donors' identities unless the donation was made with the express intent that the money be used to influence an election. Substantial donors, those who contribute $5,000 or more, are reported on Form 990, Schedule B, without any identifying information.[70]

501(c)(4)s are regulated under both the Internal Revenue Code and FECA. FECA regulations include that 501(c)(4) groups may not make direct contributions to candidates or parties and are required to report independent expenditures and election communications that fall within the definition of express advocacy. While 501(c)(4) groups are exempt from income tax, donations made to them are not tax deductible, and they are ineligible for sales tax exemptions or special mailing rates. The income-tax exemption applies to investment income, and if a 501(c)(4) group has little or no investment income, then they effectively pay no taxes.[71]

In 2016, there was a proliferation in the number of 501(c)(4) organizations. As shown in table 1-5, at least ten presidential candidates in 2015–16 had a candidate-specific 501(c)(4) group supporting their candidacy that was at least indirectly endorsed by the candidate. Some were parallel to Super PACs and have a name that varies only slightly from that of the aligned Super PAC. An example would be Marco Rubio's Conservative Solutions Project, which was active in the 2016 presidential campaign. Tax filings filed months after the campaign indicate that 93 percent of the funds for the Conservative Solutions Project came from two anonymous donations.[72] Some 501(c) groups mask the source of funds by giving grants of funds to other 501(c) groups. Examples of this in 2016 were Majority Forward, a 501(c)(4) group that transferred funds to Women's Vote, a Super PAC, and on the Republican side, the American Action Network, a 501(c)(4) group, transferred funds into the Senate Leadership Fund Super PAC.[73] A well-documented case arose in California, where a web of 501(c)(4) organizations transferred funds, making it difficult to follow the money as it passed from organization to organization.[74]

There has been a substantial increase in the amount spent by 501(c)(4) groups since 2006, when they spent a combined $5 million. In 2008, 501(c)(4) groups spent $69.1 million, in 2010 a combined $136 million, and in 2012 spending rose to $309 million.[75] In 2016, spending by 501(c)(4) groups fell to $147 million.[76] In recent cycles, conservative and Republican groups have been much more active as 501(c)(4) groups than Democrats have. For example, the Center for Responsive Politics reports that 501(c)(4) groups spent $266 million for conservatives, $34 million for liberals, and $10 million for others in 2012.[77] Much of the spending by 501(c) groups is by a small number of groups. For example, American Crossroads, Americans for Prosperity, and American Future Fund together spent $129 million in 2012, according to the Center for Responsive Politics.[78] The largest 501(c) groups in 2016 were the NRA ($33.7 million), the U.S. Chamber of Commerce ($29 million), and 45Committee, a late-forming pro-Trump group ($21.3 million).[79]

As noted, because 501(c)(4) groups do not disclose their donors publicly, and because their reporting schedules do not align with the campaign season and FEC reporting periods, it is hard to know much about how they are funded. Super PACs are reportedly using 501(c)(4) groups as a means of keeping donors' identities undisclosed. Donors can contribute anonymously to a 501(c)(4) group, which can then contribute to the Super PAC.[80] Other observers contend that corporations are reportedly using 501(c)(4) groups to disburse anonymous political expenditures.[81] The annual reporting for 501(c)(4) groups along with reporting extensions means that "a group can 'pop up' right before an election, self-declare as a (c)(4), spend large amounts on activities that influence the outcome of an election, and by the time the IRS receives that group's Form 990 tax return, the group could already have disbanded."[82] Carolina Rising, the section 501(c)(4) group supporting successful 2014 Republican challenger Thom Tillis against Kay Hagan in North Carolina, spent nearly all of its funds ($4.7 million) on that one race.[83] The funds for this group came from one donor, Crossroads GPS.[84]

Section 501(c)(4) groups were active on both TV and radio in 2016. Florida senator Marco Rubio's 501(c)(4) Conservative Solutions Project was the second most active among GOP presidential advertisers in 2015, with nearly 5,000 airings, trailing only Right to Rise (Bush's Super PAC), with three times as many airings.[85] Use of a 501(c)(4) group in this way is unusual. It has been reported that Conservative Solutions Project said it is not devoted to a particular candidate. However, its name and top staff (or spouses of top staff) were shared by a Super PAC, Conservative Solutions PAC, which supported Rubio's campaign.[86] The 501(c)(4) group's ads mentioned Rubio by name and included excerpts from his speeches. They were primarily targeted to states with early primaries and caucuses.[87] At one point, Conservative Solutions PAC submitted filings with the FEC indicating that it was engaged in political advertising for Rubio. The campaign later said the forms were incorrectly filled out.[88] A second 501(c)(4) supporting Rubio, American Encore, ran ads in Iowa attacking Cruz for his stance on electronic surveillance issues.[89]

Because section 501(c)(4) organizations report on a different schedule and to the IRS in addition to the FEC, any assessment of their campaign activity is likely incomplete. Some preliminary data on expenditures reported to the FEC indicate that some groups ramped up their activity through their 501(c)(4) groups. These groups include the NRA, the Club for Growth, and the League of Conservation Voters. Several groups active in outside money campaigning have a Super PAC as well as a

501(c)(4) organization. Additional research will be needed to estimate the total outside spending of these groups.

501(c)(5) Organizations

Section 501(c)(5) organizations have remained active in the period since BCRA took effect. There has been little research using the reports labor unions filed with the U.S. Department of Labor. We know of their activity because of expenditures reported to the IRS and because of their activity in competitive races. Reporting to the FEC appears uneven over time for 501(c)(5) groups. The Center for Responsive Politics reports that aggregate spending by these groups was $21.6 million in 2016, compared to $3.1 million in 2014 and $24 million in 2012.[90]

Unions continue to participate through get-out-the-vote efforts such as door-to-door visits and workplace encouragement to vote.[91] They are also participants with other interest groups in the America Votes coalition, an organization formed to facilitate coordination and communication between groups actively supporting Democrats.[92] Looking only at one union, two *Wall Street Journal* reporters examined Department of Labor filings for the UAW in 2016 and found that the union spent $13.2 million, a substantial drop from the $29.9 million it spent in 2012.[93] For the 1998 Senate race between Harry Reid and John Ensign, "Ninety full-time shop stewards went door-to-door visiting the homes of 40,000 labor union members."[94]

Section 501(c)(6) Organizations

Trade associations are organized under section 501(c)(6) of the IRC and, like section 501(c)(4) and 501(c)(5) organizations, cannot have electioneering as their primary purpose. The most visible and important of these "business leagues" in terms of campaign finance has been the U.S. Chamber of Commerce. It has become more active in intraparty competition, such as the 2014 U.S. Senate primary in Mississippi between Republican incumbent Thad Cochran and challenger Chris McDaniel.[95] In 2016, the only contested primary where the U.S. Chamber of Commerce was active was the Republican primary in the first congressional district in Kansas between incumbent Tim Huelskamp and challenger Roger Marshall. It spent a combined $400,000 against Huelskamp and for Marshall. Marshall won the primary and went on to win the general election.[96]

While the U.S. Chamber of Commerce is the most recognized and among the most active of the 501(c)(6) organizations, there are many other active 501(c)(6) organizations. Examples include the National Federation of Independent Business and the NAR. Also included as 501(c)(6) organizations is Freedom Partners, a group associated with the Koch brothers. The Center for Responsive Politics reports that section 501(c)(6) group spending in 2016 was $33,912,224, down from $41 million in 2014 and $55 million in 2012.[97] Because section 501(c)(6) groups are not required to disclose their donors, there is some question about the extent to which corporations mask donors' identities while helping fund campaigns against or for particular candidates.[98]

501(c) Groups Taken Together

Spending reported to the FEC by 501(c) groups can be substantial, and not all of the activity of 501(c) groups must be reported to the FEC. As noted, reporting to the IRS by 501(c) groups is on a different schedule and therefore is often unknown through Election Day of the cycle in which the spending was done; it is also not as detailed as the FEC reporting. Table 3-9 presents the spending for express advocacy reported to the FEC in the 2012, 2014, and 2016 election cycles.

Some 501(c) groups have been active in each of the last three election cycles, while others formed for one election only. Some groups, including the NRA and the Club for Growth, have increased their reported activity. The surge in spending by the NRA in 2016 is noteworthy. It spent $8.6 million through its 501(c)(4) group in 2012, then $12.6 million in 2014, and then nearly tripled that amount in 2016, spending $35.2 million. As noted earlier in this chapter, when all independent expenditures are included, the NRA spent at least $55 million.[99] The amounts spent by the Club for Growth are smaller, but the increase in spending by their 501(c)(4) group is also large, rising from under $700,000 in 2012 to over $4 million in 2016. As with the NRA, the Club for Growth was also active in making conventional independent expenditures (see table 3-5).

Some groups have reported spending less through their 501(c) in 2016 than in previous cycles. These groups included conservative groups such as Americans for Prosperity (AFP), founded in 2004 by David and Charles Koch; American Future Fund, which, like AFP, benefited from some Koch network funding;[100] American Action Network; and Patriot Majority. Liberal groups included the League of Conservation Voters and Planned Parenthood. Some groups, such as the League of Conservation Voters and Planned Parenthood, opted to spend much more through affiliated Super PACs than through 501(c) groups in 2016. The League of Conser-

Table 3-9. *Top-Spending 501(c) Organizations in the 2012, 2014, and 2016 Elections*[a]

Dollars

Organization	2011–12	2013–14	2015–16	Total
American Crossroads/Crossroads GPS/One Nation	71,181,940	26,015,713	3,405,180	100,602,833
U.S. Chamber of Commerce	35,657,029	35,464,243	29,106,034	100,227,306
National Rifle Association	8,607,876	12,675,153	35,157,585	56,440,614
Americans for Prosperity	36,637,579	2,763,318	13,628,734	53,029,631
American Future Fund	25,415,969	2,447,719	12,735,724	40,599,412
American Action Network	11,689,399	8,958,129	5,559,198	26,206,726
League of Conservation Voters	11,229,498	9,563,129	4,162,118	24,954,745
45Committee			21,339,017	21,339,017
Patriot Majority USA	7,013,886	10,652,282	214,622	17,880,790
National Association of Realtors	4,606,898	11,693,182	1,373,941	17,674,021
Americans for Tax Reform	15,794,552	122,500	4,500	15,921,552
Americans for Job Security	15,872,864			15,872,864
Planned Parenthood	6,858,077	1,586,593	2,237,207	10,681,877
Majority Forward			10,116,977	10,116,977
Americans for Responsible Leadership	9,793,014			9,793,014
Ending Spending		6,420,885	2,636,359	9,057,244
VoteVets.org	2,119,985	4,804,373	1,195,208	8,119,566
Kentucky Opportunity Coalition		7,573,748		7,573,748
Environmental Defense Action Fund		2,905,996	4,285,793	7,191,789
AFL-CIO			6,463,202	6,463,202
Club for Growth	660,220	481,773	4,061,719	5,203,712
60 Plus Association	4,615,892	347,399	121,897	5,085,188
Republican Jewish Coalition	4,595,666		486,320	5,081,986
YG Network	2,874,481	1,597,680		4,472,161
NARAL Pro-Choice America	1,710,358	1,101,122	1,325,556	4,137,036
Humane Society Legislative Fund	1,490,762	1,153,670	1,030,809	3,675,241
Susan B. Anthony List	1,961,223	943,362	756,139	3,660,724
American Chemistry Council	648,600	2,382,566	291,600	3,322,766
Carolina Rising		3,279,626		3,279,626
Center Forward	2,057,089	663,518	257,607	2,978,214
Citizens for Responsible Energy Solutions		1,512,165	1,443,122	2,955,287
Focus on the Family	2,574,666	749,382	45,000	3,369,048
National Federation of Independent Business	2,143,878			2,143,878
American Commitment	1,858,765	196,204		2,054,969
Center for Individual Freedom	1,864,735			1,864,735
Citizens for a Working America	1,555,051		147,622	1,702,673
Emergency Committee for Israel	356,095	1,277,187	56,800	1,690,082
American Energy Alliance	1,361,500			1,361,500
National Association of Home Builders			1,309,822	1,309,822
Oklahomans for a Conservative Future		1,296,459		1,296,459
Associated Builders and Contractors			1,274,000	1,274,000
Libre Initiative			1,227,098	1,227,098
Sierra Club	20,677	1,081,949		1,102,626

Sources: Center for Responsive Politics, "2012 Outside Spending, by Group" (www.opensecrets.org/outsidespending/summ.php?cycle=2012&chrt=V&disp=O&type=U), as of July 10, 2017; Center for Responsive Politics, "2014 Outside Spending, by Group" (www.opensecrets.org/outsidespending/summ.php?cycle=2014&chrt=V&disp=O&type=U), as of July 10, 2017; Center for Responsive Politics, "2016 Outside Spending, by Group" (www.opensecrets.org/outsidespending/summ.php?cycle=2016&chrt=V&disp=O&type=U), as of July 10, 2017).

a. Dollar amounts as reported to the Federal Election Commission, excluding 501(c)(5) groups.

vation Voters spent more than $15 million through its Super PAC, and
Planned Parenthood Votes spent over $12.1 million on federal elections
in 2016 (see table 3-7).

The two most active 501(c) groups in combined spending since 2012
have each spent more than $100 million through their 501(c) organ-
ization. They are American Crossroads (which also included American
Crossroads GPS and One Nation in 2016) and the U.S. Chamber of Commerce. The latter has been more consistent across cycles, with spending
ranging between $29 million and $35.7 million. American Crossroads
in its multiple forms, in contrast, spent very heavily in 2012 ($71 mil-
lion), but then its spending dropped to $26 million in 2014 and dropped
further in 2016, to $3.4 million.

Some 501(c) groups were election specific. For example, 45Commit-
tee in 2016 was reportedly funded by some of the same people who funded
the Future 45 Committee, a Super PAC that started out as an anti–Hillary
Clinton Super PAC but later became a pro-Trump Super PAC.[101]

Given the array of ways in which groups can organize to spend money
to influence elections, what are the advantages and disadvantages of forming a 501(c)(4) group? The primary advantage is donor anonymity. Donors can give unlimited amounts to either a Super PAC or a 501(c)(4)
group, but in the former, the donor is disclosed. The primary disadvantage is that presumably some of a contribution to a 501(c)(4) group may
not be spent on electioneering activity. As noted in chapter 2, it is uncertain what the IRS standard is for "primary purpose" of a social welfare
organization, a 510(c)(4) group, but the fact that the purpose cannot involve all of the money raised and spent by the organization means less of
a contribution goes directly to influencing the outcome of an election.

Section 527 Groups

A different section of the Internal Revenue Code, section 527, provides a
broad designation for tax-exempt political organizations at the federal,
state, and local levels. Groups formed under this section are sometimes
called 527 groups. A 527 group does not need to be an incorporated
entity; it could simply be a single individual. A primary motivation for
forming a 527 group is that such organizations do not need to pay taxes
on anything except investment income.[102] Section 527 groups tend to be
affiliated with interest groups.

The IRS definition of the types of groups eligible for tax-exempt, non-profit status as political committees is more expansive than the FEC's definition. This allowed some groups to gain political committee status under tax law while avoiding regulation under federal election law:

> This mismatch between the Internal Revenue Code and campaign finance laws has spurred the creation of certain types of 527 organizations (sometimes registered as political committees at the state level) that raise unlimited soft money donations and spend them on candidate-specific issue advocacy ads clearly designed to affect federal races. Prominent and well-funded 527s were active at both ends of the ideological spectrum during the 2004 election cycle, from America Coming Together and the Media Fund on the left to Progress for America and the Swift Boat Veterans and POWs for Truth on the right.[103]

There are no amount or source limits on contributions to a 527 group, nor do they have spending limits. However, they must operate independently of candidates. If they engage in express advocacy, they become a political committee and must report to the FEC, and, before BCRA, would have fallen under the same contribution and expenditure rules as other political committees. Since BCRA, a group wanting to make express advocacy communications could form a 527 committee and report to the FEC and IRS.

Electioneering communications fitting the BCRA definition must be reported to the FEC. The definition refers to TV or radio broadcast ads that air thirty days before a primary or sixty days before a general election, mention or refer to a federal candidate, and are aimed at 50,000 or more members of the electorate for the office the candidate is seeking. Note that this does not include cable television, mail, phone banks, get-out-the-vote drives, or other "ground war" expenditures.

The FEC reported $98.9 million in such electioneering communications in 2004. Groups active in this cycle included the Media Fund, Planned Parenthood, and Swift Boat Veterans and POWs for Truth.[104] These groups failed to register with the Federal Election Commission as political committees, failed to report contributions and expenditures to the commission, and knowingly accepted contributions in excess of the corresponding $5,000 limit. Swift Boat Veterans also accepted corporate contributions. In 2006, the FEC collected $630,000 in civil penalties from three 527 organizations: The League of Conservation Voters ($180,000), MoveOn.org ($150,000), and Swift Boat Veterans and POWs for Truth ($299,500).[105]

In 2008, 527 groups' electioneering communications rose to $131 million, but they have since declined with the advent of Super PACs. In 2012, $15.4 million was spent on electioneering communications, and "most of the 527 groups that were active in 2012 were formed in previous election cycles." They endured because "they can make contributions and because they can participate in nonfederal elections." Group preference has a lot to do with determining whether groups register with the FEC as federally recognized Super PACs or whether they remain 527 groups and register only with the IRS.[106]

In the 2016 election cycle, candidates Bobby Jindal and Scott Walker used 527 committees to raise and spend funds. As a 527, the committee could raise unlimited funds and otherwise comply with rules pertaining to 527 groups. Walker used the 527 committee during the "exploratory period." However, in December 2015, the FEC ruled unanimously that this kind of use of 527 groups was not permissible if the person exploring the candidacy became a candidate.[107]

State laws often allow 527 groups to operate more freely, even to the point of giving money to state and local candidates. For example, the Republican Governors Association, the largest 527 group in 2014 both in terms of receipts and in terms of expenditures, gave $7 million directly to Bruce Rauner, the Republican candidate for governor of Illinois.[108] Many times, 527 groups contribute to other groups that support their causes with names that mask their identity, such as Making Colorado Great, which one local news organization characterized as playing "good cop/bad cop" with voters.[109] 527 organizations spent a total of $251 million on federal contests in 2016, while in 2004 they spent $550 million. While 527 groups were less active at the federal level in 2014 and 2016 than in 2004, at the state and local levels the opposite was the case.[110]

Conclusion

Interest groups expanded the scope of their fundraising and campaign activity in 2016. They continued their conventional approaches of contributing to candidates and parties through PACs, and they also continued to make conventional independent expenditures through limited and disclosed contributions to standard PACs. The interest groups that were most likely to continue to engage in conventional independent expenditures were membership organizations where small contributions have long been the norm and provide the funds that can be used for conventional independent expenditures.

Interest groups are also active through Super PACs, but with most of the funding for these campaign participants coming from individuals. It is important to underscore that the individuals giving to Super PACs often have issue agendas and that many of them achieved their wealth through corporate activity. At the presidential level, 2016 saw a substantial expansion of the kinds of activities undertaken on behalf of candidates by Super PACs and 501(c)(4) groups. Donors to 501(c) groups are not disclosed, but often they are connected to interest groups or Super PACs. The extent to which Super PACs and 501(c)(4) groups are independent of candidates is unclear, but what became clear in 2016 was that they now play roles well beyond television advertising for or against federal candidates.

Notes

1. Irving Bernstein, *The Turbulent Years: A History of the American Worker, 1933–1941* (Chicago: Haymart Books, 1969).

2. John R. Wright, *Interest Groups and Congress: Lobbying, Contributions, and Influence* (New York: Longman, 1995), pp. 116–121.

3. We combine corporations without stock PACs with corporate PACs. In addition, there were 237 membership PACs and 42 cooperative PACs, which have both business-oriented and non-business-oriented PACs. Compiled from Federal Election Commission data (transition.fec.gov/press/summaries/2016/tables/pac /PAC1_2016_24m.pdf).

4. Compiled from Federal Election Commission data (transition.fec.gov/press /summaries/2016/tables/pac/PAC1_2016_24m.pdf).

5. Federal Election Commission data (transition.fec.gov/press/summaries /2012/tables/pac/PAC1_2012_24m.pdf).

6. Federal Election Commission, "Top 50 PACs by Contributions to Candidates" (www.fec.gov/press/campaign_finance_statistics.shtml). Includes activity through December 31, 2016.

7. Center for Responsive Politics, "Total Outside Spending by Election Cycle, Excluding Party Committees," 2017 (www.opensecrets.org/outsidespending /cycle_tots.php).

8. *Carey* v. *Federal Election Commission*, Civil Action 2011-0259 (D.C. 2012).

9. Robin Kolodny and Diana Dwyre, "A New Rulebook: Party Money after BCRA," in *Financing the 2004 Election*, edited by David B. Magleby, Anthony Corrado, and Kelly D. Patterson (Brookings, 2006), p. 186.

10. Peter Stone and Ben Weider, "NRA Spent More than Reported during 2016 Election," McClatchy, October 5, 2017.

11. *Buckley* v. *Valeo*, 424 U.S. 45 (1976).

12. *Colorado Republican Federal Committee* v. *Federal Election Commission*, 518 U.S. 604 (1996).

13. *Citizens United* v. *Federal Election Commission*, 558 U.S. 310 (2010), permitted the building of infrastructure, which has facilitated Super PAC formation and activity. *SpeechNow.org* v. *Federal Election Commission*, 599 F.3d 686 (D.C. Cir. 2010) (en banc).

14. David B. Magleby, ed., *Financing the 2012 Election* (Brookings, 2014), p. 22.

15. Center for Responsive Politics, "2016 Outside Spending, by Candidate" (www.opensecrets.org/outsidespending/summ.php?cycle=2016&disp=C&type =R). This equals a total of $103,119,546. For purposes of this comparison, Super PACs spending less than $1 million in support of Trump were excluded.

16. John C. Green, Michael E. Kohler, and Ian P. Schwarber, "Financing the 2012 Presidential Nomination Campaigns," in *Financing the 2012 Election*, edited by Magleby, p. 98.

17. Paul S. Herrnson, Kelly D. Patterson, and Stephanie Perry Curtis, "Financing the 2012 Congressional Elections," in *Financing the 2012 Election*, edited by Magleby, p. 161.

18. David B. Magleby, "Classifying Super PACs," in *The State of the Parties*, 7th ed., edited by John Green, Daniel Coffey, and David Cohen (Lanham, Md.: Rowman and Littlefield 2014), pp. 231–50. See also David B. Magleby, "Super PACS and 510(c) Groups in the 2016 Election," paper presented at the State of the Parties Conference, University of Akron, November 9–10, 2016.

19. Richard Briffault, "Coordination Reconsidered," *Columbia Law Review* 113 (May 2013), pp. 88–101. See also Robert Boatright, Michael Malbin, and Brendan Glavin, "Independent Expenditures in Congressional Primaries after Citizens United: Implications for Interest Groups, Incumbents, and Political Parties," *Interest Groups and Advocacy* 5, no. 2 (May 9, 2016), pp. 119–40.

20. See Center for Responsive Politics, "Super PAC Donors," 2017 (www .opensecrets.org/pacs/pacgave2.php?cycle=2016&cmte=C00574533).

21. See Deirdre Shesgreen, "Portman Confidant to Form Super PAC for 2016 Race," Cincinnati.com, 2015.

22. Center for Responsive Politics, "Fighting for Ohio Fund, Top Donors, 2016 Cycle" (www.opensecrets.org/outsidespending/contrib.php?cmte=C005 73014&cycle=2016).

23. Scott Bland and Alex Roarty, "Small Super PACs Playing Outsize Role in Senate Races," *National Journal*, February 3, 2014.

24. See Manu Raju, "Senate Dems Launch 'Super PAC,'" *Politico*, February 23, 2011.

25. See John Bresnahan and Alex Isenstadt, "Pelosi, Reid Raise Super PAC Cash," *Politico*, June 27, 2011.

26. See Ken Vogel, "Get to Know a Super PAC: Congressional Leadership Fund," *Politico*, July 23, 2012.

27. See Jake Sherman and Alex Isenstadt, "Cantor PAC Backs Rookie over Veteran," *Politico*, March 16, 2012.

28. See Politico, "Q&A with Senate Leadership Fund," 2016 (www.politico .com/tipsheets/morning-score/2016/05/q-a-with-senate-leadership-fund-unions -aim-to-take-on-trump-with-new-super-pac-reid-to-grayson-i-want-you-to-lose -214253).

29. Steven Law, president and CEO of the Senate Leadership Fund, interview by David Magleby, March 15, 2017.

30. Kolodny and Dwyre, "A New Rulebook," p. 186.

31. See Campaign Finance Institute, "Political Parties and Candidates Dominated the 2016 House Elections While Holding Their Own in the Senate," 2017 (www.cfinst.org/Press/PReleases/17-04-13/POLITICAL_PARTIES_AND _CANDIDATES_DOMINATED_THE_2016_HOUSE_ELECTIONS_WHILE _HOLDING_THEIR_OWN_IN_THE_SENATE.aspx).

32. Bland and Roarty, "Small Super PACs Playing Outsize Role in Senate Races."

33. See Morning Consult, "The Year of the Senate Super PAC?" 2015 (morning consult.com/2015/06/the-year-of-the-senate-super-pac/).

34. The $88 million includes party-committee expenditures. The $74 million in table 3-8 does not include party-committee expenditures. See Center for Responsive Politics, "Outside Groups Spent More than Candidates in 27 Races, Often by Huge Margins," 2017 (www.opensecrets.org/news/2017/02/outside -groups-spent-more-than-candidates-in-27-races-often-by-huge-amounts/).

35. Law, interview.

36. Ibid.

37. Quoted in Sam Stein, "The New Anti-Sanders Super PAC Is Funded by Anti-Clinton Donors," *Huffington Post*, January 31, 2016.

38. Eugene Kiely, "PAC Attack on Clinton's Benghazi Record," FactCheck .org, November 3, 2016; Lauren Carroll, "Hedge Fund–Backed PAC Attacks Clinton's Wall Street Ties," *Politifact*, March 9, 2016.

39. Associated Press, "Donald Trump Is Getting a $10 Million TV Ad Boost from This Super PAC," *Fortune*, November 2, 2016.

40. See Center for Responsive Politics, "Super PAC Donors," 2017.

41. See Center for Responsive Politics, "Outside Spending, Total by Spender," 2017 (www.opensecrets.org/outsidespending/fes_summ.php?cycle=2016).

42. Daniel P. Tokaji and Renata E. B. Strause, *The New Soft Money: Outside Spending in Congressional Elections* (Election Law @ Moritz and The Ohio State University, Moritz College of Law, 2014).

43. See Wesleyan Media Project, "2014 General Election Advertising Opens Even More Negative than 2010 or 2012," 2014 (www.mediaproject.wesleyan.edu/releases/2014-general-election-advertising-opens-even-more-negative-than-2010-or-2012/). On the coding of ads, Erika Franklin Fowler, Travis N. Ridout, and Michael M. Franz have written: "The Wesleyan Media Project (consistent with the Wisconsin Advertising Project before it) classifies negative as those that solely mention an opponent, positive ads as those solely mentioning the sponsor, and contrast ad as those mentioning both." See Erika Franklin Fowler, Travis N. Ridout, and Michael M. Franz, "Political Advertising in 2016: The Presidential Election as Outlier?" *The Forum* 14, no. 4 (2016), pp. 457–59.

44. Fowler, Ridout, and Franz, "Political Advertising in 2016," pp. 445–69.

45. Quoted in Nicholas Confessore and Eric Lichtblau, "'Campaigns' Aren't Necessarily Campaigns in the Age of 'Super PACs,'" *New York Times*, May 17, 2015.

46. Allan Cigler, "Interest Groups and Financing of the 2008 Elections," in *Financing the 2008 Election*, edited by David B. Magleby and Anthony Corrado (Brookings, 2011), p. 259.

47. FEC data compiled by the authors.

48. See Center for Media and Democracy, "Where Did All Those Super PAC Dollars Go? 1/3 of All Outside Money Moved through Handful of Media Firms," 2012 (www.prwatch.org/news/2012/12/11868/where-did-all-those-super-pac-dollars-go-13-all-outside-money-moved-through-handf).

49. See Center for Responsive Politics, "New Tax Forms Show Strong Ties between Pro-Rubio Group and Campaign," 2016 (www.opensecrets.org/news/2016/05/new-tax-forms-rubio-dark-money-legacy-even-darker/).

50. Dino P. Christenson and Corwin D. Smidt, "Following the Money: Super PACs and the 2012 Presidential Nomination," *Presidential Studies Quarterly* 44, no. 3 (September 2014), pp. 410–30.

51. Ibid.

52. See I.R.C. § 501(c)(4)(a) (www.irs.gov/Charities-&-Non-Profits/Charitable-Organizations/The-Restriction-of-Political-Campaign-Intervention-by-Section-501(c)(3)-Tax-Exempt-Organizations).

53. Daniel C. Willingham, "Are You Ready for Some (Political) Football: How Section 501(c)(3) Organizations Get Their Playing Time during Campaign Seasons," *Akron Tax Journal* 28, no. 1 (2013), pp. 83–122.

54. Ibid.

55. "Why the Clinton Foundation Is so Controversial," *The Economist*, February 8, 2016.

56. On Bush, see Lyndsey Layton, "Jeb Bush Education Foundation Played a Leading Role in Mixing Politics, Policy," *Washington Post*, January 6, 2015. On Clinton, see Amy Chozick and Steve Eder, "Foundation Ties Bedevil Hillary Clinton's Presidential Campaign," *New York Times*, August 20, 2016.

57. Nanette Byrnes, "As Churches Get Political, IRS Stays Quiet," Reuters, June 21, 2012.

58. Ibid.

59. See "IRS Not Enforcing Rules on Churches and Politics," MPR News, 2012 (www.mprnews.org/story/2012/11/03/politics/irs-churches-activism).

60. Anugrah Kumar, "Over 1,800 Pastors Take Part in Pulpit Freedom Sunday," *Christian Post*, October 11, 2014.

61. Quoted in Eugene Scott, "Pastors Take to Pulpit to Protest IRS Limits on Political Endorsements," CNN, October 1, 2016.

62. John Wagner and Sarah Pulliam Bailey, "Trump Signs Order Seeking to Allow Churches to Engage in More Political Activity," *Washington Post*, May 4, 2017.

63. Sarah Pulliam Bailey, "Trump Promised to Destroy the Johnson Amendment. Congress Is Targeting It Now," *Washington Post*, June 30, 2017.

64. I.R.C. § 501(c)(4)(a) (www.irs.gov/Charities-&-Non-Profits/Charitable -Organizations/The-Restriction-of-Political-Campaign-Intervention-by -Section-501(c)(3)-Tax-Exempt-Organizations).

65. Treasury Regulation § 1.501(c)(4)-1(a)(2)(i) (1960).

66. Jennifer Mueller, "Defending Nuance in an Era of Tea Party Politics: An Argument for the Continued Use of Standards to Evaluate the Campaign Activities of 501(c)(4) Organizations," *George Mason Law Review* 22, no. 1 (2014), pp. 103–58.

67. U.S. Treasury, Internal Revenue Service, "IRS Will Issue Proposed Guidance for Tax-Exempt Social Welfare Organizations," November 26, 2013 (www .irs.gov/newsroom/treasury-irs-will-issue-proposed-guidance-for-tax-exempt -social-welfare-organizations).

68. Lindsey McPherson, *EO Training Materials Suggest 51 Percent Threshold for Social Welfare Activity*, 73 Exempt Org. Tax Rev. 122 (2014).

69. Erika K. Lunder and L. Paige Whitaker, "501(c)(4)s and Campaign Activity: Analysis under Tax and Campaign Finance Laws," Congressional Research Service, May 17, 2013 (fas.org/sgp/crs/misc/R40183.pdf).

70. Ibid.

71. Ibid.

72. See Robert Maguire, "Two (at Most) Secret Donors Funded 93% of Pro-Rubio Nonprofit," Center for Responsive Politics, May 3, 2017.

73. Robert Maguire, political nonprofits investigator for the Center for Responsive Politics, interview by David Magleby, April 14, 2017.

74. Matea Gold, "Koch-Backed Political Network, Built to Shield Donors, Raised $400 Million in 2012 Elections," *Washington Post*, January 5, 2014.

75. Center for Responsive Politics, "Outside Spending, Total by Spender."

76. Maguire, interview.

77. See Center for Responsive Politics, "2012 Outside Spending, by Group," (www.opensecrets.org/outsidespending/summ.php?cycle=2012&chrt=V&disp =O&type=).

78. Ibid.

79. Maguire, interview.

80. See Sunlight Foundation, "Nine Things You Need to Know about Super PACs," 2012 (sunlightfoundation.com/blog/2012/01/31/nine-things-you-need -know-about-super-pacs/).

81. Daniel C. Kirby, "Legal Quagmire of IRC Sec. 501(c)(4) Organizations and the Consequential Rise of Dark Money in Elections," *Chicago-Kent Law Review* 90, no. 1 (2015), pp. 223–46.

82. Kim Barker, "How Nonprofits Spend Millions on Elections and Call It Public Welfare," *ProPublica*, August 18, 2012.

83. Ann M. Ravel and Ellen L. Weintraub, "Statement of Reasons of Commissioners Ann M. Ravel and Ellen L. Weintraub in the Matter of Carolina Rising," MUR 6880, 2016 (eqs.fec.gov/eqsdocsMUR/16044403093.pdf).

84. Robert Maguire, "Pro-Tillis Nonprofit Goes Dark after Tillis Victory, but Keeps Paying Former President," Center for Responsive Politics, December 14, 2016.

85. Wesleyan Media Project, "Super PACs Dominate Airwaves," December 15, 2015 (www.mediaproject.wesleyan.edu/releases/super-pacs-airwaves/).

86. Nicholas Confessore, "Nonprofit Group to Marco Rubio Raises Millions While Shielding Donors," *New York Times*, July 7, 2015, p. A12. See also Mark Murray and Leigh Caldwell, "Campaign Watchdogs: Pro-Rubio TV Ads Are Breaking the Law," *NBC News*, November 24, 2015.

87. Andrew Prokop, "Marco Rubio's Operation Is Relying on Unprecedented Dark Money Spending," *Vox*, November 24, 2015.

88. Murray and Caldwell, "Campaign Watchdogs."

89. Richard Skinner, "Marco Rubio Breaks New Ground in Dark Money," Sunlight Foundation, November 24, 2015.

90. Center for Responsive Politics, "Total Outside Spending by Election Cycle, Excluding Party Committees," 2017.

91. David B. Magleby, J. Quin Monson, and Kelly D. Patterson, *Dancing without Partners: How Candidates, Parties, and Interest Groups Interact in the Presidential Campaign* (Lanham, Md.: Rowman and Littlefield, 2007).

92. Magleby, "Classifying Super PACs," pp. 231–50.

93. Christina Rogers and John D. Stoll, "UAW Political Spending Way Down in 2016," *Wall Street Journal*, April 4, 2017.

94. David B. Magleby, ed., *Outside Money: Soft Money and Issue Advocacy in 1998 Congressional Elections* (Lanham, Md.: Rowman and Littlefield, 2000).

95. Nick Corasaniti and Jonathan Martin, "Incumbent in Mississippi Runoff Aims for More than Just GOP Votes," *New York Times*, June 4, 2014.

96. See Elena Schneider, "Huelskamp Loses GOP Primary after Ideological Battle," *Politico*, August 2, 2016.

97. Center for Responsive Politics, "Outside Spending, Total by Spender," 2017.

98. Robert G. Boatright, Michael J. Malbin, Mark J. Rozell, and Clyde Wilcox, "Interest Groups and Advocacy Organizations after BCRA," in *The Election after Reform: Money, Politics and the Bipartisan Campaign Reform Act*, edited by Michael J. Malbin (Oxford: Rowman and Littlefield, 2006), pp. 112–40.

99. Stone and Weider, "NRA Spent More than Reported during 2016 Election."

100. Jane Mayer, *Dark Money: The Hidden History of the Billionaires behind the Rise of the Radical Right* (New York: Doubleday, 2016), p. 241.

101. On donors to the Future 45 Super PAC, see Center for Responsive Politics, "Super PAC Donors, Future 45," 2016 (www.opensecrets.org/pacs/pacgave2 .php?cycle=2016&cmte=C00574533); Stein, "The New Anti-Sanders Super PAC Is Funded by Anti-Clinton Donors." On donors to 45Committee, see Kenneth P. Vogel, "Secret Money to Boost Trump: A Former Anti-Trump Financier Offers GOP Mega-donors Who Are Embarrassed by Trump the Chance to Help Him Anonymously," *Politico*, September 28, 2016.

102. Anthony Corrado, Thomas E. Mann, Daniel R. Ortiz, and Trevor Potter, *The New Campaign Finance Sourcebook* (Brookings, 2005).

103. Ibid.

104. *Financing the 2004 Election*, edited by Magleby, Corrado, and Patterson.

105. Peter Overby, "FEC Fines '527' Groups, Including Swift Boat Vets," NPR, December 14, 2006.

106. David B. Magleby and Jay Goodliffe, "Interest Groups," in *Financing the 2012 Election*, edited by Magleby, pp. 215–61.

107. Federal Election Commission, "Advisory Opinion 2015-09" (www.fec .gov/pages/fecrecord/2015/december/ao2015-09.shtml).

108. Monique Garcia, "Quinn, Rauner Line Up New Endorsements," *Chicago Tribune*, September 12, 2014.

109. Brandon Rittiman, "Truth Test," *9News*, September 15, 2014.

110. Center for Responsive Politics, "527s: Advocacy Group Spending" (www .opensecrets.org/527s/index.php).

FOUR

Financing the 2016 Presidential Nomination Campaigns

JOHN C. GREEN

Although the 2016 election set new federal campaign finance records in some respects (see chapter 1), candidate spending for the presidential nomination declined for the second election cycle in a row—to the surprise of many observers. Indeed, aggregate candidate fundraising and spending were lower in 2016 than in 2008, the most recent contest for an open seat in the White House. Major-party candidates in 2016 raised $1 billion for the nomination campaign and spent $911 million; the comparable figures for 2008 and 2012 in constant dollars were $1.4 billion and $1.3 billion, respectively.[1]

One reason for this decline was the relatively small number of Democratic presidential candidates in 2016. Another reason was the unusual campaign of Republican Donald Trump. His largely self-financed nomination campaign spent less than those of other GOP nominees in recent times, and his unconventional campaigning short-circuited the efforts of many of his rivals, limiting the aggregate level of spending despite the very large number of candidates. Yet another factor was changes in the election calendar in 2016, shortening the length of the nomination campaign.

However, the decline in candidate fundraising was offset by a dramatic increase in spending by groups other than candidate committees. This "outside money" includes financial activities of candidate-linked Super PACs. In 2016, such Super PACs raised $489 million and spent $443 million; a comparable list of Super PACs in 2012 raised $167 million and spent $137 million. Other kinds of outside spending for or against candidates during the nomination campaign also increased: in 2016, the amount was at least $370 million; in 2012, it was at least $248 million; and in 2008, it was at least $92 million.

The financing of the 2016 presidential nomination phase expanded the new focus on "private cash and Super PACs" that began in 2012. The 2016 campaign witnessed a raft of organizational innovations by candidates but also revealed some limitations in the effectiveness of such money in winning nomination contests.

Rules, Rivals, and Resources

Federal campaign finance laws, the structure of competition, and the availability of resources have long had a bearing on presidential nomination finance, and 2016 was no exception. On the first count, previous changes in the law influenced the pattern of funds raised and spent by and on behalf of candidates, especially the continued development of Super PACs. On the second count, President Obama was term limited in 2016, creating likely competitive contests for the Democratic and Republican presidential nominations to fill the open seat in the White House. On the third count, the candidates deployed a wide variety of strategies to prepare for and finance their nomination campaigns.

Rules

Federal campaign law creates two sets of rules in presidential campaigns: contingent regulations, which apply to candidates who voluntarily accept public financing, and mandatory regulations, which apply to all federal candidates. In 2016, the contingent regulations had little impact, because only one candidate accepted matching funds in the primary season, continuing a twenty-year retreat from the public financing system.[2] This retreat was highlighted when Congress eliminated public financing for the major-party national conventions in 2014 (see chapter 2).[3] Nonparticipation in public financing has reduced restraints on campaign spending and allowed candidates to deploy financial strategies that were more comprehensive.

The legislation that ended the public financing for conventions also allowed each party's national committee to establish a separate account to fund the nominating conventions, along with similar new accounts for the costs of election recounts and litigation and the funding of national party headquarters (see chapter 2). For these accounts, the national committees were allowed to raise funds in amounts larger than the standard limits for individual and PAC donations to party committees: $100,200 per year to each of these committees. These changes may have had an indirect impact on candidate fundraising strategies because of the 2014 U.S. Supreme Court decision in *McCutcheon* v. *Federal Election Commission*, which abolished the aggregate limit on individual donations to federal campaigns.[4] Wealthy donors could now give larger amounts to the national parties as part of "jumbo" fundraising events.[5]

A key element of mandatory campaign finance regulations is the limit on contributions to candidate committees. In 2016, for example, the maximum individual donation to a presidential candidate was $2,700 per election (for a total of $5,400 in a contest including a primary and a general election). These limits help define a division in the election calendar: the *nomination campaign* (including the primary season and a bridge period) and the *general election campaign*.

The primary season is the first part of the nomination campaign. It begins in the calendar year preceding primaries and caucuses, and it concludes when active competition for the nomination ceases. The 2016 primary season officially began January 1, 2015, and ended in May 2016. Traditionally, observers have identified an "invisible primary" early in the primary season: the competition to raise funds in the calendar year before the actual contests begin.[6] In 2016, winning the invisible primary was less important than in other recent elections. Among the Democrats, Hillary Clinton's fundraising success did not prevent a contested primary season, and neither did Donald Trump's lower level of fundraising preclude his being competitive and ultimately successful.

The second part of the nomination campaign, the bridge period, occurs between the end of the competitive primary season and the official nomination of the presidential candidates at the national conventions. During the bridge period, the nomination campaign fundraising limits still apply to candidates, but the general election campaign is effectively under way. Indeed, the presumptive nominees have often used the bridge period to raise funds for the general election campaign. Because contested nominations have varied in length, the bridge period is less precisely defined. In 2016, it was roughly from June 1 to July 31.[7] Because of its shorter duration, the bridge period had less of an impact on the candidates' finances in 2016 than in previous years: both Clinton and Trump left their respective party conventions with ample opportunities to raise funds for the general election campaign.

As its name implies, the general election campaign begins after the national conventions and lasts until Election Day. Although candidates operate under primary election contribution limits during the nomination campaign, they may also solicit funds for the general election. However, such funds cannot be spent until after the candidate is officially nominated at the convention. In addition, primary and general election contributions to a candidate can be raised along with party contributions via joint fundraising committees. Joint fundraising committee contribution limits are annual limits rather than two-year election cycle limits. Hillary Clinton exploited this by starting her joint fundraising committee, the Hillary Victory Fund, in September 2015, allowing donors to give to the committee in both 2015 and 2016. The contributions to the candidates are transferred to the candidate's campaign committee, while the party donations are transferred to party committees to be used for partisan activities in the general election campaign. As in 2012, the eventual major-party nominees participated in joint fundraising committees during the 2016 nomination campaign. The increased sophistication of joint fundraising committees led some analysts to warn about the return of a form of "soft money" to major-party finance.[8]

Spending outside the candidate committees can occur throughout the nomination campaign and is often part of a team effort to support presidential candidates.[9] The deregulation of such outside money has encouraged the growth of independent expenditures during the nomination campaign. Of particular importance was the U.S. Supreme Court decision *Citizens United* v. *Federal Election Commission*,[10] the D.C. Circuit Court of Appeals case *SpeechNow.org* v. *Federal Election Commission*,[11] and the subsequent recognition of "independent-expenditure-only political action committees" by the Federal Election Commission (see chapter 2).[12] These "Super PACs" can raise and spend unlimited amounts of money as long as their activity remains independent of candidate campaigns (see table 3-7).

Such organizations were an avenue for political entrepreneurship in 2016, and the number of Super PACs expanded substantially.[13] As part of this trend, Super PACs linked to presidential candidates became commonplace. Another innovation was the creation of "hybrid" or "Carey" committees. Based on a 2011 federal court ruling, *Carey et al.* v. *Federal Election Commission* [Civil Action 2011-0259 (D.C. 2011)], a hybrid PAC is an umbrella committee with separate accounts for direct and independent expenditures.[14] Hybrid committees established by candidates were often linked to 501(c)(4) tax-exempt organizations.[15]

The Brennan Center for Justice identified several innovations in candidate-linked Super PACs and related organizations in 2016:[16]

- Candidates delayed the formal announcement of their candidacies so that they could directly raise funds for favorable Super PACs without being constrained by the $5,400 per person limit on candidate fundraising.
- Candidates' top associates and aides were more fully involved in organizing and directing candidate-linked Super PACs. It was also true that some Super PACs were organized without the candidate's consent.
- Many candidates engaged in extensive fundraising for Super PACs and other allied outside groups.
- Some candidates used Super PACs for basic campaign functions and not just to engage in advertising via independent expenditures (see table 1-6).
- Candidates found new and clever ways to coordinate campaign activities with Super PAC activities.
- Alongside the organization of Super PACs, some candidates also formed 527 and 501(c)(4) tax-exempt organizations to conduct educational activities related to the campaign (see table 1-5).

In part because of such innovations, other sources of outside money were less prominent in the 2016 nomination campaign than in 2012, including independent expenditures and partisan communication expenditures by other kinds of political committees, and electioneering communication by tax-exempt groups (see chapter 3).

Rivals

In addition to being influenced by campaign finance regulations, nomination finance is influenced by the structure of competition among rival candidates. This structure has two basic elements: the number of candidates running and the schedule of the nomination contests. The interaction of these factors helps account for the financial patterns in 2016.

As in the past, the absence of an incumbent president seeking reelection generated competition for each of the major-party nominations in 2016. A partial exception has been a candidate closely associated with the previous incumbent, such as a sitting vice president. In 2016, Hillary Clinton had such an advantage, having served as secretary of state in the Obama administration. This status plus the long-standing prominence of the Clinton family in Democratic Party circles made her a strong front-runner for the 2016 nomination. This reality had the effect of largely clearing the field of prominent rivals—including the sitting vice president, Joe Biden—and producing a small field by the standards of previous open-seat contests. This pattern was exacerbated by the depletion of the Democratic bench during the Obama administration.

In contrast, the Republicans had a large field of candidates by such standards, fueled by the perception that after eight years of Democratic control of the White House, 2016 would be a good year for Republicans.[17] The GOP also had a strong front-running candidate in former Florida governor Jeb Bush, the son and brother of recent Republican presidents. However, the Republican bench expanded during the Obama administration, including U.S. senators Marco Rubio (2010), Ted Cruz (2012), and Rand Paul (2010), plus governors Scott Walker (2010), John Kasich (2010), and Chris Christie (2009).

In 2016, the Democratic and Republican national committees achieved the long-sought goal of reducing "front loading" of nomination contests— the tendency of states to move their primaries or caucuses earlier in the election year to influence the outcome. The 2016 calendar protected the four traditional early events (the Iowa caucuses, New Hampshire and South Carolina primaries, and Nevada caucuses) and spread them fairly evenly throughout February 2016. The Republicans joined the Democrats in requiring that delegates be distributed on a proportional basis in the four early contests, but they still allowed winner-take-all primaries beginning March 1. Consequently, the primaries and caucuses started later than in recent elections, with a different distribution of contests by size and the number of delegates across the calendar.[18]

Another adjustment to the calendar was to schedule the national conventions in July 2016, with the Republicans first (July 18–21), followed the next week by the Democrats (July 25–28). Yet another change by the national committees was to sponsor debates among the primary candidates in partnership with news organizations. The Republicans scheduled twelve debates, down from the twenty debates Republicans had in 2012 and twenty-one in 2008. The Democrats eventually scheduled ten, beginning in the second half of 2015 and continuing into the spring of 2016.[19] In 2008, the Democrats had twenty-five debates.[20]

Resources

Campaign finance laws and the structure of competition set the basic parameters for candidates' finances, with each candidate calculating how best to raise and spend the funds necessary to be successful. In this regard, there are now three commonly recognized general fundraising approaches: a high-dollar insider strategy, a small-dollar outsider strategy, and a mixed strategy employing elements of the high-dollar and small-dollar approaches. While particular candidates may have a preference for one strategy over another, many candidates are forced to adopt a particular strategy by their political circumstances.

A high-dollar fundraising strategy relies on national prominence and strong connections with established fundraising networks to raise funds in large amounts. One common tactic is to form a leadership PAC or other kind of organization to finance activities before the election cycle and secure allies by contributing to their campaigns. Another tactic is to recruit a cadre of high-dollar fundraisers, known as "bundlers," and hold extensive fundraising events.

If successful, a high-dollar fundraising strategy reinforces candidate prominence, dissuades potentially strong rivals from entering the race, secures a resource advantage in the initial contests, and provides financial resilience if the candidate encounters setbacks. The goal is a decisive victory early in the primary campaign, at which point the strategy can be applied to preparing for the general election campaign during the bridge period. Republican George W. Bush used this approach in 2000, as did Democrat Hillary Clinton in 2008 and again in 2016.

A small-dollar strategy depends on candidate novelty and clear issue positions to raise money from beyond established financial networks. A common tactic is to solicit multiple small donations via social media, e-mail, telephone calls, and direct mail.[21] If successful, such a strategy establishes credibility, undermines better-financed opponents, and produces sufficient funds to compete in the initial contests. The goal is to secure early victories to establish "momentum" that will translate to success by the end of the primary season. Then the strategy can be applied to preparing for the general election campaign during the bridge period. Republican John McCain in 2000, Democrat Howard Dean in 2004, and Republican Ron Paul in 2008 are good examples of this approach, as was Bernie Sanders in 2016.

Some candidates deployed mixed strategies, using elements of high-dollar and small-dollar fundraising, such as Democrat Barack Obama and Republican John McCain in 2008. Another approach is the self-financing of nomination campaigns, in whole or in part, a strategy used by Republicans Steve Forbes in 1996 and Mitt Romney in 2008. In 2016, Donald Trump substantially paid for his nomination campaign, but his novel appeal also attracted small donations, especially during the bridge period.

In some respects, Super PACs organized to support a candidate fit with a high-dollar fundraising strategy, especially when funded by a few very large donations from well-connected donors. In 2012, both Barack Obama and Mitt Romney benefited from Super PACs in this fashion; by 2016, most candidates in both parties used this approach with Super PACs. But Super PACs can also assist insurgent candidates, by providing a high level of spending for poorly financed campaigns that otherwise rely on the limited contributions candidates can raise. Such wealthy candidate patrons have long been a staple of presidential nomination campaigns, but typically by means of personal independent expenditures or the activities of tax-exempt organizations. In 2012, Republicans Newt Gingrich and Rick Santorum benefited from such patrons via their candidate-aligned Super PACs. This practice is not entirely new: in the 2000 campaign, before there were Super PACs, some wealthy individuals funded "issue ads," often opposing a candidate. One notable example was a group named Republicans for Clean Air, which attacked John McCain in the 2000 primaries.[22]

Likewise, joint fundraising committees can be linked with high-dollar fundraising when well-connected donors give large donations that are then divided between a candidate and political parties. However, joint fundraising committees can also solicit small donations via direct appeals to regular party donors once there is a presumptive nominee. Both patterns occurred for the major-party nominees in 2016.

Candidate Campaign Receipts and Disbursements in 2016

Table 4-1 lists total adjusted receipts and disbursements for all presidential candidates in the nomination campaign (January 1, 2015, to July 31, 2016). For the eventual major-party nominees, Clinton and Trump, these totals are also divided into the primary season (January 1, 2015, to May 30, 2016) and bridge period (June 1 to July 31, 2016).

Table 4-1. *Receipts and Disbursements, 2016 Presidential Nomination Campaigns*[a]

Millions of dollars

Candidate	Receipts[b]	Disbursements[c]
Democratic Party		
Hillary for America	326.8	268.4
Primary season[d]	238.2	195.7
Bridge period[e]	88.7	72.6
Sanders	236.6	230.5
O'Malley	6.4	6.2
Webb	0.8	0.8
Republican Party		
Trump for President	128.0	89.5
Primary season[d]	64.6	63.3
Bridge period[e]	63.4	26.3
Cruz	92.9	92.3
Carson	64.4	62.6
Rubio	47.5	50.8
Bush	35.4	35.4
Kasich	19.5	19.3
Paul	12.3	12.3
Fiorina	12.1	11.3
Walker	8.8	8.7
Christie	8.7	8.7
Graham	5.9	5.8
Huckabee	4.3	4.3
Santorum	1.4	1.4
Perry	1.4	1.8
Jindal	0.6	0.1
Pataki	0.5	0.5
Gilmore	0.4	0.4
Libertarian Party		
Johnson	3	1.8
Green Party		
Stein	1.9	1.5

Source: Based on disclosure filings reported to the Federal Election Commission (www.fec.gov/finance/disclosure/candcmte_info.shtml), as of May 7, 2017.

a. Receipts and disbursements are from January 1, 2015, through July 31, 2016, except for Webb, Rubio, Bush, Kasich, Christie, Santorum, Perry, Jindal, Pataki, and Gilmore, which are through June 30, 2016.

b. Transfers to affiliated committees and total contribution refunds are deducted from the joint fundraising committee receipt totals to avoid double counting.

c. Transfers to affiliated committees and offsets to operating expenditures are deducted from the joint fundraising committee disbursement totals to avoid double counting.

d. Primary period data are from January 1, 2015, through May 31, 2016.

e. Bridge period data are from June 1, 2016, through July 31, 2016.

Presidential candidate committees raised a combined total of $1 billion during the 2016 nomination campaign. This figure is substantially less than the $1.4 billion raised by all candidates in 2008, the most recent contest for an open seat in the White House. In 2016, major-party candidate committees spent a combined total of $911 million during the nomination campaign—also substantially less than the $1.3 billion spent in 2008.

Democratic Candidate Committees

In 2016, Democratic presidential candidates raised a total of $571 million during the nomination period and spent $506 million. These figures are much lower than comparable Democratic candidate financial activity in 2008, when a total of $892 million was raised and $785 million spent.

Hillary Clinton's successful 2016 nomination campaign raised and spent $327 and $268 million, respectively. These figures were substantially more than the $252 million raised and $243 million spent in her unsuccessful 2008 bid for the nomination. However, Clinton's 2016 finances were lower than Barack Obama's successful 2008 primary campaign, where he raised and spent $520 million and $431 million, respectively. During the 2016 primary season, Clinton raised $238 million (including $13 million in general election funds)[23] and spent $196 million. She then raised $89 million and spent $73 million during the bridge period (27 percent of the total). Thus, Clinton ended the 2016 nomination campaign with a surplus of $59 million in cash on hand, the amount often taken to assess the future financial well-being of the campaign.

In addition, the Clinton campaign participated in two joint fundraising committees during the 2016 nomination campaign: Hillary Victory Fund (with the Democratic National Committee and thirty-two state Democratic parties) and Hillary Action Fund (with the Democratic National Committee). The Hillary Victory Fund was organized in September 2015 and the Hillary Action Fund in June 2016.[24]

During the nomination campaign, these committees raised $56 million in individual donations that were transferred to the Clinton campaign (included under Hillary for America in table 4-1). By starting her joint fundraising committee with the DNC in 2015, Clinton took advantage of the fact that contribution limits to party committees are annual limits and not cycle limits. During 2015, the Clinton/DNC joint committee raised $26.9 million.[25] Beyond contributions to Clinton, the joint fundraising committees raised about $50 million for Democratic Party organization during the nomination campaign, ostensibly for general election activities such as voter registration and "get out the vote" (GOTV). Overall, Clinton's 2016 joint fundraising committee activity was larger than that of Obama during the 2012 nomination campaign.[26]

In 2016, three other Democratic presidential candidates raised $244 million and spent $238 million. The vast majority of this financial activity was by Bernie Sanders. It is worth noting that Sanders's fundraising total was comparable to Clinton's during the primary season ($236 million and $238 million, respectively). However, because there were fewer candidates in 2016, this total was considerably smaller than in 2008, when unsuccessful Democratic candidates raised and spent $372 million and $353 million, respectively. During the 2016 primary season, Sanders spent $231 million, about $35 million more than Clinton's spending of $196 million. In November 2015, Sanders formed a joint fundraising committee with the Democratic National Committee, the Bernie Victory Fund, but it remained inactive.[27] Writing well after the election, interim DNC chair Donna Brazile, who just before the national convention replaced former DNC chair Debbie Wasserman Schultz, described a conversation she had with Bernie Sanders after the election, in which she discussed the terms of the Hillary for America/DNC joint fundraising agreement. She described the agreement as "a cancer" and defined that as meaning "that she [Hillary Clinton] had exerted this control [joint fundraising] of the party long before she became the nominee."[28]

Republican Candidate Committees

In 2016, Republican presidential candidates raised a total of $444 million during the nomination campaign and spent $405 million. These figures are also markedly lower than Republican candidate financial activity in 2008, when a total of $532 million was raised and $490 million spent, despite the larger number of candidates in 2016.[29]

Donald Trump's successful 2016 nomination campaign raised and spent $128 million and $90 million, respectively, including his own funds. These figures are very low compared to those of successful Republican candidates in other recent nomination campaigns. For example, 2012 GOP nominee Mitt Romney raised more than twice as much ($306 million) and spent almost three times as much ($250 million) as Trump did.

Trump's finances are even more impressively low if one considers only the primary period, where he raised $65 million (including $2 million in general election funds)[30] and spent $63 million. Trump matched his primary season fundraising during the bridge period, ending the nomination campaign with a surplus of $38 million, or $21 million less than Clinton had in cash on hand. During the nomination campaign, Clinton raised roughly two and a half times as much as Trump and spent almost three times as much.

It is worth noting that 2000 Republican nominee George W. Bush, in a campaign waged sixteen years earlier than Trump's, had nomination campaign receipt and expenditure figures comparable to Trump's (respectively $133 million and $122 million in constant dollars). Bush declined the public matching funds, establishing a practice followed by others in 2004 and since.[31]

Like the Clinton campaign, the Trump campaign also participated in two joint fundraising committees during the 2016 nomination period: Trump Victory Committee (with the Republican National Committee and eleven state Republican parties) and Trump Make America Great Again Committee (with the Republican National Committee). These committees were organized in May 2016.[32] During the nomination campaign, these committees raised $17 million in individual donations that was transferred to the Trump campaign committee (included under Trump for President in table 4-1). Beyond contributions to Trump, the joint fundraising committees raised about $28 million for Republican Party organizations during the nomination campaign, ostensibly for general election activities such as voter registration and GOTV. Overall, Trump's 2016 joint fundraising committee activity was markedly smaller than that for Romney during the 2012 nomination campaign.[33]

Trump's rivals for the Republican presidential nomination raised and spent $316 million, a figure modestly higher than the financial activity of unsuccessful Republican candidates in 2008 ($291 million raised and $233 million spent). Ted Cruz was the most successful fundraiser, raising $93 million and spending $92 million (one-third more than Trump during the primary season). Ben Carson was second best, raising $64 million and spending $63 million (matching Trump's performance). Marco Rubio came in third, raising $48 million and spending $51 million (about four-fifths as much as Trump). Jeb Bush was fourth, raising and spending $35 million (a bit more than half as much as Trump). John Kasich was fifth, raising and spending about $19 million (less than one-third as much as Trump). Rand Paul and Carly Fiorina raised and spent about $12 million each. The remaining nine candidates each raised less than $10 million, for a total of $32 million. In addition, Cruz, Rubio, and Paul had joint fundraising committees.[34]

For the sake of completeness, it is worth noting that minor-party primary candidate fundraising during the 2016 nomination campaign was $4.9 million, about the same as in 2012 ($4.7 million) but higher than in 2008 ($3.4 million).

Sources of Candidate Funds in 2016

Table 4-2 reports the amounts given by individual donors to the major candidates' nomination campaigns by size of contribution.[35] For Clinton and Trump, the figures are once again divided into the primary season and the bridge period. For nearly all the candidates, donations from individuals accounted for the vast majority of funds raised during the nomination campaign; other sources of funds will be discussed where relevant.

Democratic Candidates

Table 4-2 illustrates Hillary Clinton's high-dollar fundraising strategy. Overall, 36 percent of Clinton's donations were the maximum amount of $2,700 ($118 million), and 50 percent were $1,000 or more ($166 million). At the same time, only 29 percent were less than $200 ($96 million). This high-dollar pattern is even clearer during the primary season, with 58 percent of Clinton's donations totaling $1,000 or more ($133 million) and just 19 percent ($44 million) in amounts less than $200.[36] However, small donations to the Clinton campaign increased during the bridge period, when donations of $200 or less accounted for 50 percent of the funds raised ($52 million).

Clinton participated in nearly 300 fundraising events during the nomination campaign, many with celebrities, well-connected businesspeople, and prominent political leaders.[37] Indeed, fundraising often took precedence over campaigning—such as when Clinton left Iowa three days before the caucuses to attend a fundraiser in Philadelphia.[38] In this respect, her 2016 campaign reflected Republican Mitt Romney's high-dollar strategy more than Obama's mixed strategy in 2012.[39] In addition, Clinton raised

Table 4-2. *Individual Contributions to Major-Party Nomination Campaigns*[a] (Includes all Contributions from Joint Fundraising Committees Attributed to the Campaigns)
Millions of dollars

Party and candidate	Amount of individual donations				
	$200 or less	$201–$999	$1,000–$2,699	$2,700	Total under $2,700
Democrats					
Clinton	136.8 (22.0%)	159.0 (25.6%)	109.3 (17.6%)	215.9 (34.8%)	621
Primary season[b]	*63.6 (33.0%)*	*57.8 (29.9%)*	*31.5 (16.3%)*	*40.1 (20.8%)*	*193*
Bridge period[c]	*73.2 (17.1%)*	*101.2 (23.6%)*	*77.8 (18.2%)*	*175.8 (41.1%)*	*428*
Sanders	99.7 (44.1%)	86.2 (38.1%)	31.5 (13.9%)	8.6 (3.8%)	226
O'Malley	0.5 (11.1%)	0.6 (13.3%)	1.0 (22.2%)	2.4 (53.3%)	4.5
Republicans					
Trump	238.6 (69.3%)	44.7 (13.0%)	28.9 (8.4%)	31.9 (9.3%)	344.1
Primary season[b]	*23.1 (62.3%)*	*7.0 (18.9%)*	*3.5 (9.4%)*	*3.5 (9.4%)*	*37.1*
Bridge period[c]	*215.5 (70.1%)*	*37.7 (12.3%)*	*25.4 (8.3%)*	*28.4 (9.3%)*	*307*
Cruz	25.4 (29.3%)	31.3 (36.1%)	16.1 (18.6%)	13.9 (16.0%)	86.7
Carson	30.8 (50.3%)	19.4 (31.7%)	8.2 (13.4%)	2.8 (4.6%)	61.2
Rubio	9.9 (24.5%)	8.4 (20.8%)	9.7 (24.0%)	12.4 (30.7%)	40.4
Bush	1.7 (5.2%)	2.0 (6.2%)	4.9 (15.1%)	23.9 (73.5%)	32.5
Kasich	3.7 (20.2%)	3.0 (16.4%)	3.7 (20.2%)	7.9 (43.2%)	18.3
Fiorina	5.1 (42.9%)	2.8 (23.5%)	2.0 (16.8%)	2.0 (16.8%)	11.9
Paul	4.6 (42.6%)	2.9 (26.9%)	1.7 (15.7%)	1.6 (14.8%)	10.8
Walker	2.8 (37.8%)	1.1 (14.9%)	1.1 (14.9%)	2.4 (32.4%)	7.4
Christie	0.4 (4.7%)	0.5 (6.0%)	1.5 (17.9%)	6.0 (71.4%)	8.4

Sources: Campaign Finance Institute, "President Trump, with RNC Help, Raised More Small Donor Money than President Obama; as Much as Clinton and Sanders Combined," table 2 (http://www.cfinst.org/Press/PReleases/17-02-21/President_Trump _with_RNC_Help_Raised_More_Small_Donor_Money_than_President_Obama_As_Much_As_Clinton_and_Sanders _Combined.aspx). See also Campaign Finance Institute, "Table 1-4A: Individual Contributions to 2016 Presidential Candidates, Aggregated by Donors, Cumulative through June 30, 2016" (http://www.cfinst.org/pdf/federal/2016Report/pdf/CFI_Federal-CF _16_Table1-04a.pdf).

Note: In these data, all the itemized donations from each individual are combined into a single figure, so multiple donations from a single person are taken into account.

a. Individual contributions are from January 1, 2015, through July 31, 2016, for Clinton and Trump. For all others, they are from January 1, 2015, through June 30, 2016.

b. Primary season data are from January 1, 2015, through June 30, 2016.

c. Bridge period data are from June 30, 2016, through July 31, 2016.

$2.3 million from other sources during the primary campaign, including almost $1 million of her own funds.

In contrast, Bernie Sanders ran a classic outsider campaign focused on small-dollar fundraising. Overall, 44 percent of his donations were of $200 or less ($100 million), and just 4 percent were of the maximum amount of $2,700 ($9 million). Like Obama's campaigns in 2008 and

2012, many of Sanders's donors were repeat givers, allowing the campaign to match Clinton's funds during the primary season. The Sanders campaign made a number of innovations in small-dollar fundraising, building on techniques used by previous campaigns and organizations. Tim Tagaris of the Sanders campaign described these innovations:

> You asked what we were building upon to get here. There are two pieces: the first is the one-click donating. Something that the president [Obama] pioneered in his reelection campaign, ActBlue built shortly after that, but what was really helpful, and in a sense . . . we were building on every previous Democratic campaign organization that had ever used ActBlue because of the pool of one-click donors that they had been able to build over the years since it was put into place. I think we built upon Dean and Obama in the sense that the way that they empowered people to organize themselves, whether it was through meetup or mybarackobama.com, trained thousands upon thousands of people across the country, Democratic activists, to successfully pull off organizing themselves in their own communities in a way that made it easier for Bernie to get to scale more quickly because of people who had this experience beforehand.[40]

According to Tagaris, 95 percent of Sanders's individual donations were raised online.

Despite this success, Sanders's donations of $200 or less were slightly more than half of what Obama raised in 2008 ($181.3 million). Another weakness was the high cost of online fundraising. According to Sanders campaign manager Jeff Weaver: "Despite what people think about campaigning on the Internet, it actually is an expensive place to campaign."[41] Thus, Sanders's fundraising netted fewer dollars for campaign purposes than a high-dollar strategy. In addition, Sanders transferred $1.5 million to his presidential committee from his U.S. Senate campaign committee.[42]

Martin O'Malley's unsuccessful campaign also relied on large donors—with more than one-half of his individual contributions totaling $2,700 ($2.4 million). O'Malley was the only major-party candidate to apply for matching funds in the primary season (a dollar-for-dollar match up to $250 donated), receiving over $1 million in public financing.[43] Green Party candidate Jill Stein, the only other candidate to qualify for and accept matching funds, received $456,000 in matching funds in 2016.[44]

Republican Candidates

Donald Trump largely self-funded his 2016 nomination campaign, contributing approximately $50 million of his own funds (including $48 million in loans, which he eventually forgave).[45] These funds accounted for nearly three-fourths of his funds during the primary season. The amount of this self-funding was of about the same magnitude as Mitt Romney's contribution to his own campaign in 2008 ($51 million) but somewhat smaller than Steve Forbes's self-contribution in 1996 ($57 million). Beyond his own funds, Trump received $15 million in individual contributions during the primary season, with 62 percent in amounts of $200 or less ($9 million) and just 10 percent at the maximum donation amount of $2,700. This pattern largely persisted during the bridge period, with 58 percent of his donations totaling $200 or less ($36 million) and 13 percent totaling $2,700 ($9 million). The proportion of Trump's small donations was greater than for Sanders (at 44 percent), but Sanders raised $63 million more than Trump from small donors.

Some of Trump's Republican rivals deployed a high-dollar fundraising strategy. For example, Jeb Bush raised 73 percent ($24 million) and Chris Christie raised 71 percent ($6 million) in maximum donations (Bush gave nearly $800,000 of his own funds to his campaign as well). Other rivals pursued a small-dollar strategy, such as Ben Carson, with 50 percent of his individual donations totaling $200 or less ($31 million), and Carly Fiorina and Rand Paul, with 42 percent of donations to their campaigns being of $200 or less (about $5 million for each). Still others tried a mixed strategy with individual donations: Ted Cruz (27 percent and $25 million in small donations; 20 percent and $19 million in maximum allowed donations), Marco Rubio (24 percent and $10 million in small donations; 33 percent and $14 million in maximum allowed donations), and John Kasich (20 percent and $4 million in small donations and 43 percent and $8 million in maximum allowed donations).

Candidate Support Organizations

In addition to presidential campaign committees, many major-party candidates established special organizations to help finance political activities before announcing a nomination bid. The most common was the long-standing practice of establishing a leadership PAC under the mandatory campaign finance regulations.[46] However, there were also some organizational innovations for this purpose in 2016, including the tax-exempt groups and Super PACs. Many of these efforts persisted in one form or another once the formal nomination campaigns began.[47]

On the Democratic side, Bernie Sanders (Progressive Voters of America), Jim Webb (Born Fighting), and Martin O'Malley (O'Say Can You See) benefited from leadership PACs; O'Malley also established a tax-exempt 527 committee with the same name.[48]

In contrast, Hillary Clinton benefited from the establishment of Ready for Hillary (a hybrid committee) to "draft" Clinton for the 2016 Democratic presidential nomination. It raised $17 million to create a campaign organization for Clinton in advance of the formal announcement of her candidacy:

> For over two years, inside a fifth-floor suite on North Kent Street in the dress-shirt-and-slacks Washington suburb of Rosslyn, Virginia, the thirty staffers of the Ready for Hillary super PAC had worked to lure Hillary into the presidential race. They built a list they boasted had three million Hillary supporters, identified nearly two hundred thousand donors, and raised $15 million to lay a foundation for the Clinton campaign and give Hillary a much-needed head start.[49]

Ready for Hillary was terminated in 2015, shortly after the formal announcement of Clinton's candidacy.[50] Clinton also benefited from a 501(c)(4) committee, American Bridge 21st Century Foundation, and perhaps other tax-exempt organizations managed by allies.[51]

On the Republican side, Jeb Bush (Right to Rise PAC),[52] Marco Rubio (Reclaim America), Ted Cruz (Jobs, Growth and Freedom Fund), Chris Christie (Leadership Matters for America), Ben Carson (USA First PAC), Rand Paul (RAND PAC), Rick Santorum (Patriot Voices PAC, a Carey PAC), Mike Huckabee (HuckPAC), Bobby Jindal (Stand Up to Washington), Rick Perry (RickPAC), and Lindsey Graham (Fund for America's Future) all had leadership PACs, raising a total of $27 million through these PACs ahead of their official announcement of candidacy. In addition, Carson, Huckabee, Santorum, Jindal, Graham, Pataki, and Walker—plus Trump—established presidential exploratory campaigns in 2015.

Meanwhile, Pataki (Americans for Real Change) and Perry (Americans for Economic Freedom) established 501(c)(4) committees, while Huckabee (America Takes Action, Prosperity for All Fund), Bobby Jindal (America Next, American Future Project), and John Kasich (Balanced Budget Forever, New Day for America) formed both 501(c)4 and 527 committees, and Scott Walker formed just a 527 committee (Our American Revival).[53] Carly Fiorina was associated with a Super PAC (Unlocking Potential Project) ostensibly to help female candidates, raising $1.8 million.[54]

A major innovation in 2016 was the near ubiquity of candidate-linked Super PACs. Indeed, such organizations were an element of campaign strategy for all the candidates except Sanders and initially Trump. Table 4-3 reports the finances of the major Super PACs linked to candidates. To put Super PAC spending in context, the expenditure figures are then expressed as a percentage of expenditures from the candidates' own campaign committees.

Overall, Super PACs listed here raised $489 million and spent $443 million during the nomination campaign. All such spending equaled 41 percent of total expenditures by candidate committees. These figures represent dramatic growth over 2012, when a comparable list of candidate-linked Super PACs raised $169 million and spent $137 million; such spending equaled 17 percent of total expenditures by candidate committees.[55]

With just a few exceptions, these Super PACs were funded by very large donations that would have been illegal if given directly to a candidate—a pattern allowed because the Super PAC's spending is meant to be independent of any campaign. A study by the Campaign Finance Institute found that by the end of April 2016, 82 percent of donations to candidate-linked Super PACs totaled $100,000 or more (from 549 individuals) and 56 percent totaled $1 million or more (from 101 individuals).[56] This pattern is a continuation from the 2012 election, the first presidential election with Super PACs.

Democratic Super PACs

Super PACs were a centerpiece of Hillary Clinton's high-dollar fundraising strategy. Priorities USA Action was the second largest of the candidate-linked Super PACs in the 2016 nomination campaign and supported Hillary Clinton. Originally established in April 2011 by two former Obama aides and other prominent Democratic operatives, it supported Obama's

Table 4-3. *Super PACs Linked with Candidates, 2016 Presidential Nomination Campaigns*[a]
Millions of dollars (unless otherwise indicated)

Name	Linked to	Receipts	Expenditures	% Candidate expenditures
Democrats				
Priorities USA Action,	Clinton	116.6	76.8	29
Correct the Record	*Primary season*[b]	94.8	41.7	21
	Bridge period[c]	21.8	35.1	48
Generation Forward	O'Malley	0.8	0.8	13
Republicans				
Multiple Super PACs	Trump	7.7	5.9	7
	Primary season[b]	2.5	2.0	3
	Bridge period[c]	5.2	3.9	15
Right to Rise USA	Bush	121.3	118.2	334
Keep the Promise PACs	Cruz	66.4	64.5	70
Conservative Solutions PAC	Rubio	60.6	59.8	118
Unintimidated PAC	Walker	24.1	24.1	277
America Leads PAC	Christie	20.3	20.2	232
New Day for America PAC	Kasich	17.7	25.8	134
CARLY for America Committee	Fiorina	14.3	14.3	127
2016 Committee	Carson	13.0	12.5	20
Other candidate Super PACs	(eight candidates)[d]	26.2	25.8	112

Source: Compiled from Federal Election Commission data.
a. This does not include all Super PACs.
b. Primary season data are from January 1, 2015, through May 31, 2016.
c. Bridge period data are from June 1, 2016, through July 31, 2016.
d. Gilmore, Graham, Huckabee, Jindal, Paul, Pataki, Perry, and Santorum.

2012 nomination and general election campaigns. In 2014, Priorities USA Action began backing Clinton's 2016 nomination campaign. Its chairman was Guy Cecil, the political director for Clinton's 2008 presidential bid; other Clinton confidants served in leadership capacities.

A hybrid Super PAC, Correct the Record, was established in May 2015. Headed by Clinton associate David Brock, it spent its funds exclusively on digital media to exploit a loophole in campaign finance laws (see chapter 2). In July 2015, Priorities USA Action and Correct the Record formed a joint fundraising effort to minimize confusion among potential donors.

The Clinton campaign developed complex procedures for interacting with these Super PACs, including a high level of coordination with Correct the Record (see chapter 3).[57]

During the nomination campaign, these pro-Clinton Super PACs raised $117 million. The fundraising was concentrated during the primary season ($95 million). A total of twenty-nine individuals gave these Super PACs donations of over $1 million (accounting for 80 percent of funds raised to date); top donors included financier Donald Sussman ($11 million), investor George Soros ($7 million), and venture funders Jay and Mary Pritzker ($9.2 million).[58]

These pro-Clinton Super PACs spent $77 million during the nomination campaign, fairly evenly divided between the primary season ($42 million) and the bridge period ($35 million). This spending equaled 29 percent of the Clinton campaign committee's expenditures (21 percent during the primary season and 48 percent during the bridge period). Priorities USA Action's financial activity was considerably larger in 2016 than in 2012, when it raised $27 million and spent $23 million in support of Obama's nomination campaign (this 2012 spending equaled 6 percent of the Obama campaign committee's expenditures). One observer noted: "Unlike Obama, Clinton fully embraced super PACs from the very beginning of her race, helping pull in larger cheques from donors than the president did."[59] These efforts dwarfed the Super PAC activity of Clinton's Democratic rivals, such as Generation Forward, a Super PAC supporting Martin O'Malley (raising and spending some $831,000).[60] In contrast, Bernie Sanders was the only major-party candidate without a supportive Super PAC during the nomination campaign, despite the desire of some supporters to organize such efforts. He actively discouraged such efforts as part of his small-dollar fundraising strategy, proclaiming, "I do not have a super PAC, and I do not want a super PAC."[61]

Republican Super PACs

Like Sanders, Donald Trump was initially opposed to Super PACs as part of his self-financing strategy. He also actively discouraged such efforts early in the nomination campaign, such as the Make America Great Again PAC, founded by former Trump campaign aide Roger Stone.[62] In February 2016, Republican operative Ed Rollins and Tea Party activists founded TrumPAC, which, after a protest from the Trump campaign, was renamed the Great America PAC (a hybrid committee).[63] It persisted in supporting Trump, however, raising $2.5 million and spending $2.0 million during the primary season.

Near the end of the nomination campaign, a number of Super PACs supporting Trump were established, often with the active participation of former Trump campaign officials.[64] An example is the Rebuilding America Now PAC, led in part by Trump's former campaign manager Paul Manafort.[65] Several of these groups had originally supported rival candidates for the Republican nomination. For example, Make America Number 1 was originally named "Keep the Promise I" and supported the Ted Cruz campaign. Following Trump's victory in the nominating contests, it was renamed in June 2016 and began backing the presumptive nominee.[66] Future 45 was formed in March 2015 to back a GOP candidate who could defeat Hillary Clinton. It became dormant as Trump advanced in the primary season, but was eventually reorganized to back him.[67] These efforts were aided when Trump changed his position on Super PACs and endorsed such efforts on behalf of his campaign in July 2016.[68] Nevertheless, soon afterward, the Trump campaign was described as having a "Super PAC problem," with limited means divided among competing organizations.[69] One problem with this mix of Super PACs is that the Trump campaign had less control over its message than the campaigns of many of his rivals did.

All told, these pro-Trump Super PACs raised a total of $8 million during the nomination campaign ($2.5 million in the primary season and $5.2 million during the bridge period) and spent $5.9 million ($2 million in the primary season and $3.9 million during the bridge period). This spending equaled just 7 percent of the Trump campaign committee's expenditures during the nomination campaign. Trump's Super PAC activities were modest compared to those of many other Republican candidates and Priorities USA Action in the 2016 nomination campaign. They were also smaller than the spending by Mitt Romney's Super PAC in 2012 (which raised $96 million and spent $74 million, spending that equaled 29 percent of Romney's campaign committee expenditures).[70]

The largest Super PAC in 2016 was Right to Rise USA, organized to support Jeb Bush's nomination bid. It was one of three organizations established for this purpose, including a leadership PAC (with the same name) to prepare for the campaign (see note 52) and Right to Rise Policy Solutions, a 501(c)(4) organization, to develop and disseminate Bush's policy proposals.[71] Initially organized by allies of Bush with his direct assistance, it was later led by Mike Murphy, a key Bush operative. Thereafter, Right to

Rise USA handled all advertising and digital media, while Bush's campaign committee handled candidate activities and voter outreach.[72]

Right to Rise USA was a fundraising success, raising $121 million; twenty-six donors made contributions of $1 million or more, accounting for 35 percent of the funds raised. Top donors included health care executive Mike Fernandez ($3.2 million), former U.S. ambassador to the Vatican Francis Rooney ($2.6 million), and Home Depot cofounder Bernard Marcus ($1.7 million). Right to Rise USA spent $118 million, equal to more than triple (334 percent) the spending by the Bush campaign committee.

Super PACs like Right to Rise USA supported most of the remaining Republican presidential candidates. Many of these candidates never achieved any traction during the primary season, but several of the more promising campaigns were hampered by the legal limits of Super PACs. A good example is Wisconsin governor Scott Walker. The Unintimidated PAC, created to back his campaign, raised $24 million and was expected to reach $40 million by the end of 2015. Meanwhile, Walker's campaign committee was unable to raise enough money to stay in operation, and he quickly ended his campaign.[73] Indeed, Unintimidated PAC's spending equaled 277 percent of the Walker campaign committee's expenditures. Still, the Super PACs linked to the ten GOP candidates who were least successful at the polls raised a total of $53 million—not an inconsequential sum.

Ted Cruz's allies took a different route with Super PACs.[74] They established a set of related groups to accommodate the wishes of individual donors, including Keep the Promise ($1 million and $500,000, respectively, from executives Richard Uihlein and Robert McNair), Keep the Promise I ($11 million from hedge fund manager Robert Mercer), Keep the Promise II ($10 million from private equity manager Toby Neugebauer),[75] and Keep the Promise III ($15 million from entrepreneurs Farris and Daniel Wilks). Organized in one way or another by Dathan Voelter, a friend of Cruz, most of these committees were eventually combined into a single committee, Trusted Leadership PAC. The total raised by these organizations was an impressive $66 million, with ten contributors giving more than $1 million each (accounting for 74 percent of the funds raised). These PACs spent $64 million during the primary season, equaling about 70 percent of the Cruz campaign committee's expenditures. As with the Trump campaign, the multiple Super PACs reduced the Cruz campaign's ability to control its message.

Other candidates found creative solutions to the problem of Super PAC independence. Marco Rubio's supporters also created dual organizations: Conservative Solutions PAC, a Super PAC, and Conservative Solutions Project, a 501(c)(4) group. Although the groups remained separate from the Rubio campaign committee, they worked closely with each other, sharing key staff and vendors.[76] Both organizations engaged in campaign activity, with the Super PAC spending on traditional attacks on Rubio's opponents, while the nonprofit advertised policies supported by Rubio. The Conservative Solutions Super PAC raised $60 million, with fifteen donors making donations of $1 million or more, accounting for 75 percent of the funds raised. Top donors included businessman Norman Braman ($6 million), technology executive Larry Ellison ($3 million), and hedge fund manager Kenneth Griffin ($2.8 million). The Super PAC spent $60 million, equaling 118 percent of the Rubio campaign committee's expenditures. Although not reported in table 4-3, the 501(c)(4) Conservative Solutions Project raised an additional $22 million and spent at least $8 million on television ads during the primary season.[77]

When John Kasich announced his presidential bid, he converted his 527 committee, New Day for America, into a Super PAC by the same name and created a second Super PAC, New Day Independent Media. The pro-Kasich Super PACs had a broader range of activities than those of most other candidates, including extensive field operations to mobilize voters alongside Kasich's regular campaign committee.[78] The New Day committees raised $18 million and spent $26 million, equaling 134 percent of the Kasich campaign committee's expenditures.

In a similar fashion, Carly Fiorina's campaign outsourced nearly all traditional campaigning to a supportive Super PAC, CARLY for America (an acronym for Conservative, Authentic, Responsive Leadership for You; the capital letters were required to avoid violating federal law, which the FEC interprets as prohibiting Super PACs from using a candidate's name).[79] The Fiorina campaign made its plans and schedules public, allowing the Super PAC to actually organize the activities and events. CARLY for America raised and spent $14 million, accounting for 127 percent of the Fiorina campaign committee's expenditures.[80]

Super PACs supporting Ben Carson provide a sharp contrast to those of the other candidates. An effort to draft Ben Carson to run for president began in 2013, when the National Draft Ben Carson Super PAC was founded by John Philip Sousa IV (a great-grandson of the composer). In the 2014 election cycle, the Super PAC raised almost $14 million,

three-fifths of which was in donations of $200 or less. When Carson an-
nounced his candidacy in May 2015, the committee changed its name to
the 2016 Committee but was known as the "Run, Ben, Run" committee. In November 2015, it merged with Our Children's Future, a Super
PAC founded by a former Carson campaign operative. During the nomination campaign, the 2016 Committee raised and spent about $13 million,
equaling 20 percent of the Carson campaign committee's expenditures.
The 2016 Committee engaged in extensive grassroots campaigning in
support of Carson during the primary season.[81]

Outside Spending in 2016

How did activities of candidate-linked Super PACs fit into the broader
pattern of outside spending in the 2016 nomination campaign? Table 4-4
helps put such spending in context, reporting four kinds of outside money
reportedly spent for and against the candidates: independent expenditures
by Super PACs, independent expenditures and partisan communication
costs by 501(c)(4) and other groups, and electioneering communication costs reported by 527 committees. Here again, the figures for the
Clinton and Trump campaigns are separated into the primary season and
the bridge period. Given the limitations of reporting requirements, especially for tax-exempt groups, these figures may well understate the level
of outside money.

These data indicate that spending by groups not directly controlled
by or linked to the candidates but that spent to advance or defeat a particular candidate during the nomination campaign totaled at least $371
million in 2016, equaling 41 percent of total candidate spending. This
spending was almost 50 percent higher than a comparable estimate in
2012 ($248 million, or 30 percent of total candidate spending). There-
fore, outside spending was larger in absolute and relative terms in the
2016 presidential nomination campaigns.

The largest source of outside money listed in table 4-4 was independent expenditures from Super PACs. The 2016 figure was $323 million
(which accounted for 87 percent of all outside spending during the nomination campaign), almost twice the size of comparable estimates in 2012
($169 million, which accounted for 68 percent of all outside spending).
Therefore, independent expenditures by Super PACs increased in both absolute and relative terms in 2016. A glance back at table 4-3 reveals that

Table 4-4. *Outside Money Spent in 2016 Presidential Nomination Campaigns*[a]
Dollars

Party and candidate	Super PAC independent expenditures		Other group independent expenditures		Partisan communication costs		Electioneering communication costs	
	For	Against	For	Against	For	Against	For	Against
Democrat								
Clinton	11,309,441	9,593,403	4,552,278	9,204,551	5,962,521	0	276,550	0
Primary season[b]	8,236,741	2,773,967	3,704,458	5,391,329	4,933,810		276,550	
Bridge period[c]	3,072,700	6,819,436	847,820	3,813,222	1,028,711			
Sanders	4,934,472	859,314	374,054	23	304,153	0	0	0
O'Malley	362,912	0	11,909	0	0	0	0	0
Republicans								
Trump	2,541,469	69,303,057	7,967,231	12,432,178	0	85,851	326,550	0
Primary season[b]	353,671	38,094,178	2,099,825	11,019,213	0	83,512	326,550	0
Bridge period[c]	2,187,798	31,208,879	5,867,406	1,412,965	0	2,339	0	0
Cruz	21,687,259	5,700,068	762,601	2,196,649	0	97,175	98,665	0
Carson	5,233,233	1,634	78,447	7,404	0	0		0
Rubio	39,797,124	8,372,946	39,080	154,829	0	108,525	0	0
Bush	83,761,601	3,147,145	8,453	107,267	0	45,264	0	0
Kasich	14,851,130	4,543,505	16,260	1,807,799	0	0	0	0
Paul	5,334,433	0	0	14,282	0	96,980	0	0
Fiorina	3,837,155	12	22,896	163	0	0	0	0
Walker	2,259,623	7,016	0	11,205	0	90,682	0	0
Christie	19,724,250	3,603,065	8,362	18,987	0	0	0	0
Perry	2,373,876	0	0	4,681	0	3,968	0	0

Source: Compiled from Federal Election Commission data.

a. Expenditures reported as for or against a candidate are self-reported by the groups making the expenditures. Amounts are from January 1, 2015, through July 31, 2016.

b. Primary season data are from January 1, 2015, through May 31, 2016.

c. Bridge period data are from June 1, 2016, through July 31, 2016.

candidate-linked Super PACs spent far more than other Super PACs during the nomination campaign, $449 million to $329 million.

In 2016, a total of $217 million was self-reported independent expenditures *for* candidates (67 percent of these independent expenditures), while $106 million was *against* candidates (33 percent). This two-to-one advantage in support of candidates represents a reversal of the patterns in 2012, when spending was two to one in opposition to candidates ($51 million for and $110 million against). Therefore, the nature of reported Super PAC independent expenditures shifted in 2016 as well.[82]

A total of $27 million in Super PAC independent expenditures were directed for or against Democratic candidates in 2016. Hillary Clinton was the most common target, with $11 million for and $9 million against. The bulk of this spending was during the primary season ($8 million for and $3 million against), but in the bridge period, the pattern reversed itself ($3 million for and $7 million against). Bernie Sanders was the target of $6 million in Super PAC independent expenditures ($5 million for and less than $1 million against). These figures were lower than in 2012, largely because of $43 million in Super PAC independent expenditures against Obama during the bridge period.

A total of $296 million in Super PAC independent expenditures were directed for or against Republican candidates in 2016. Donald Trump was the target of $71 million, with $2.5 million for him (mostly in the bridge period) and $69 million against him ($38 million in the primary season and $31 million in the bridge period; for details on the sources of this spending, see figure 4-4). These figures are much larger than those for Mitt Romney in 2012 ($47 million) but with similar direction ($15 million for and $32 million against) and timing (more opposition in the bridge period).[83]

All of the other Republican candidates showed a different pattern than Trump: the independent expenditures for the candidates were larger than the expenditures against them. Jeb Bush is a good example, with $84 million in expenditures for and just $3 million against. All told, Trump's GOP rivals were supported by $199 million in Super PAC independent expenditures and were opposed by $25 million. These figures are much larger than comparable figures for 2012, when candidates who did not win the nomination were targets of $77 million in Super PAC spending, with $34 million for and $43 million against. Therefore, with the exception of Trump, 2016 Super PAC independent expenditures shifted toward supporting candidates and away from opposing them.

Independent expenditures reported by political organizations other than Super PACs were $39 million in 2016, accounting for 11 percent of all outside spending. These figures are smaller than in 2012 ($69 million and 28 percent of all outside spending), showing both an absolute and a relative decline in this source of independent expenditures. However, the direction of the expenditures was similar: in 2016, $14 million was for candidates and $25 million was against them. In 2012, the comparable figures were $2.5 million for and $67 million against. Here, too, the major factor was $57 million in expenditures against Obama during the 2012 bridge period.

Among Democrats in 2016, Clinton was the primary target of independent expenditures by other groups, with $5 million for and $9 million against. On the Republican side, Trump was the primary target, with $8 million for and $12 million against. For the 2016 presumptive nominees, spending in opposition was concentrated in the primary season.

In 2016, $6 million was spent on partisan communication costs, up from $2.6 million in 2012. These expenditures were for Clinton in 2016 ($6 million) and against Republican candidates ($500,000). In 2016, a little more than half a million dollars was spent on electioneering communication costs by 527 committees, down from $5 million in 2012. These funds were about evenly divided between those supporting Clinton and those favoring Trump in the 2016 primary season, but in 2012 such funds were largely spent against Obama in the primary season.[84]

The Dynamics of the Primary Season in 2016

As President Obama's second term passed its midpoint, political observers anticipated expensive contests to replace him. Based on recent history, a clear front-runner was recognized for the major-party presidential nominations: Hillary Clinton for the Democrats and Jeb Bush for the Republicans. There was considerable speculation about which and how many candidates would challenge the presumptive front-runners.

Unanticipated by nearly all analysts was that the public's deep distrust of the party establishments would dominate the nomination campaigns. According to pollster Geoff Garin, "People's sense of corruption of the political system was quite powerful and, I think, fueled both Sanders and Trump."[85] These two unexpectedly strong candidates dominated the nomination campaigns.

The Democratic Contest

On April 12, 2015, Hillary Clinton formally announced her candidacy for the Democratic presidential nomination. The announcement from the former First Lady, U.S. senator from New York, and secretary of state in the Obama administration had long been anticipated. Clinton and her allies were well prepared: a campaign organization in waiting, extensive fundraising plans in place (including the backing of a sophisticated Super PAC), and numerous endorsements from Democratic officeholders, party leaders, and liberal interest groups. In many respects, Clinton embodied the recent leadership experience of the Democratic Party as well as its future aspirations, including the election of the first female president of the United States. Her campaign slogans, "Forward Together" and "Stronger Together," implied a continuation of the changes under the Obama administration. In financial terms, her strategy bore a close resemblance to her effort in 2008.[86] The goal of the primary campaign was clear, according to campaign manager Robby Mook: "The mission of the campaign in the primary was to get a majority of delegates."[87]

On April 30, 2015, U.S. senator Bernie Sanders announced he would challenge Clinton for the nomination. Elected as an independent from Vermont, he unabashedly described himself as a "democratic socialist." Although he caucused with the Democrats in the Senate, he had a history of tension with the party. Indeed, the initial goal of the Sanders campaign was to push the party platform toward more liberal policies and not necessarily to win the nomination.[88] To many analysts, the seventy-four-year-old with an eccentric style and quixotic reputation seemed well suited to achieve his initial goal.[89]

Other prominent Democrats eventually decided not to run in 2016, including U.S. senator Elizabeth Warren of Massachusetts, New York governor Andrew Cuomo, and Vice President Joe Biden. Lesser-known candidates tried to fill the vacuum. Martin O'Malley, former Baltimore mayor and Maryland governor, joined the contest on May 30, 2015, followed on June 15, 2015, by former U.S. senator and Rhode Island governor Lincoln Chafee, and then on July 2, 2015, by former U.S. senator Jim Webb of Virginia. Both Chafee and Webb began their political careers as Republicans.[90]

Sanders's major campaign theme was a critique of "millionaires and billionaires." His message focused on policies to reduce economic inequality, such as a single-payer health care system, free college tuition, and higher taxes on the rich, but the campaign also included a sharp attack on "big money" in politics, including within the Democratic Party. For example, Sanders criticized Clinton for her well-known connections with the wealthy, such as controversial gifts to the Clinton Foundation while she was secretary of state, her well-paid speeches to Wall Street groups, and her high-dollar fundraising strategy. On the last point, Sanders drew a contrast between his campaign finances and Clinton's: he would only accept individual donations within the mandatory limits, with a focus on small donors, and, as noted, he rejected the backing of Super PACs. "I am very proud to be the only candidate up here," Sanders said in debate, "who does not have a super PAC, who's not raising huge sums of money from Wall Street and special interests."

As the campaign progressed, Sanders accused Clinton and the Democratic Party of violating election rules, a charge for which some evidence eventually emerged.[91] A particular point of contention was the impact of Clinton's joint fundraising agreements with the DNC. As Mark Longabaugh, a senior adviser to the Sanders campaign, said:

> One of the most extraordinary things that—I can't ever think of a Democratic primary candidate suing the DNC in my life until now. . . . I mean, it's just unconscionable . . . there should be nobody operating a joint fundraising agreement in the midst of a competitive primary with the Dem financial committee. It just shouldn't happen and it certainly shouldn't happen when one candidate is making use of it and the other candidate is not.[92]

Almost a year after the 2016 general election, Donna Brazile, the interim DNC chair during the campaign, offered a similar analysis:

> The Joint Fund-Raising Agreement between the DNC, the Hillary Victory Fund, and Hillary for America . . . specified that in exchange for raising money and investing in the DNC, Hillary would control the party's finances, strategy, and all the money raised . . . This victory fund agreement . . . had been signed in August 2015, just four months after Hillary announced her candidacy and nearly a year before she officially had the nomination. . . . The funding arrangement with HFA and the victory fund agreement was not illegal, but it sure looked unethical. If the fight had been fair, one campaign would not have control of the party before the voters

had decided which one they wanted to lead. This was not a criminal act, but as I saw it, it compromised the party's integrity.[93]

The Sanders campaign was well aware of Clinton's financial advantages, according to manager Jeff Weaver:

In terms of money, Secretary Clinton was an excellent fundraiser. She had a Super PAC, multiple Super PACs, a 501(c)(4) that was doing turnout, and our early estimates were that we were going to raise between $30 and $50 million, total. What came as a complete surprise in this campaign that really allowed this campaign to go toe-to-toe was that we ended up raising over $230 million, primarily from small donors online.[94]

The Sanders "revolution" started dramatically, with 100,000 people signing up to endorse his campaign within the first twenty-four hours, according to Keegan Goudiss of the Sanders campaign.[95] The initial financial results were impressive: by the end of June 2015, he had raised $15 million, about one-third of Clinton's $47 million.

The Clinton campaign took Sanders's insurgency seriously, having learned some lessons from the 2008 nomination campaign. "We were afraid of Bernie very early on, particularly when we saw that he raised $15 million in his first quarter," said Clinton's campaign manager, Robby Mook.[96] Clinton's allies quickly set up a special Super PAC, Correct the Record, to provide a rapid response to Sanders's criticism via digital media,[97] and soon established joint fundraising committees with Democratic Party committees, in part to cement her relationship with party leaders. In this vein, the campaign began touting support for Clinton among the unelected "super delegates" to the Democratic National Convention[98] and continued building campaign infrastructure for the upcoming nomination events.[99]

By the time the Democratic candidates met for the first debate, on October 13, 2015, the contest had become a two-way race between Clinton and Sanders. Consequently, Webb and Chafee soon ended their candidacies; O'Malley continued until his poor third-place finish in the Iowa caucuses.[100] Indeed, the October financial report showed that Sanders had raised nearly as much money as Clinton, $26 million to $29 million, a pattern that continued with the year-end report, with Sanders at $33 million and Clinton at $38 million. In January 2016, Sanders surpassed

Figure 4-1. *Democratic Cumulative Primary Receipts, 2016*

Millions of dollars

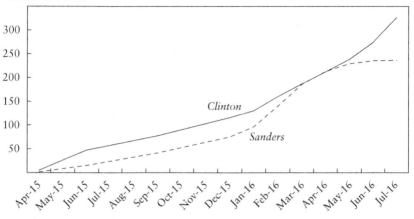

Source: Compiled from the Federal Election Commission.

Clinton's fundraising, $21 million to $15 million. He would match her fundraising total by the end of the primary season (see figure 4-1).

In some ways, the Sanders campaign resembled the Obama campaign in late 2007. Like Obama, Sanders raised a significant amount of money in small donations, attracted strong support among young voters, and appealed to liberal activists eager for change. But, unlike Obama, Sanders had less potential appeal among minorities, offered a narrower message to Democratic voters, and campaigned for change from a Democratic White House. Also, Sanders did not add a high-dollar element into his fundraising effort.[101]

Clinton made winning the Iowa caucuses a top priority, hoping to avoid an early loss as in 2008. At the beginning of 2016, she led Sanders in public opinion polls and grassroots organization in the Hawkeye State and had much more cash on hand than her rival ($33 million to $14 million). However, Clinton prevailed in Iowa by the smallest of margins.[102] One reason for the virtual tie was that Sanders spent heavily in Iowa, nearly matching Clinton in television ads.[103] The next contest was the New Hampshire primary. Although the Granite State was regarded as a "home game" for Vermonter Sanders, Clinton and Sanders committed extensive resources. Sanders outspent Clinton and won by a large margin.[104] Buoyed by this success, Sanders's fundraising and cash on hand expanded (see figure 4-2).

Figure 4-2. *Democratic Cash on Hand and Independent
Expenditures, 2016*

Millions of dollars

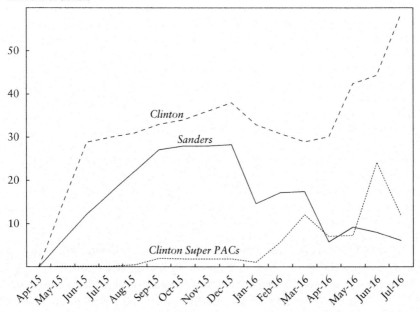

Source: Compiled from the Federal Election Commission.

The electoral tide was about to turn, however, in the Nevada caucuses
and South Carolina primary. Although Sanders was able to match Clinton's television buys in these contests,[105] he could not match her appeal
to minority voters. Clinton won a solid victory in the Silver State and a
lopsided one in the Palmetto State.[106] In retrospect, Sanders might have
used his funds more effectively in these contests, but as Mark Longabaugh
said, "If we knew we were going to have the money that we ultimately
had, I think we'd have approached Nevada in a much different manner.
We would have staffed it earlier, built it much more robust."[107]

The momentum of these wins carried Clinton into the March 1 "Super
Tuesday" states, with twelve primaries and caucuses. Clinton won across
the south, including Alabama, Arkansas, Georgia, Tennessee, Texas, and
Virginia. Although Clinton outspent Sanders in these Dixie primaries,
neither campaign invested heavily, given Clinton's strength among
minority voters. Likewise, next to nothing was spent in Vermont, which

Sanders won handily. There was more action in the Massachusetts and Oklahoma primaries as well as the Minnesota and Colorado caucuses. Sanders outspent Clinton in all four—and won all but Massachusetts.[108]

After Super Tuesday, Clinton was clearly ahead in the elected delegate count, but because of the proportional distribution of delegates, it would take many more contests to secure the nomination. Sanders certainly had the finances to continue the campaign. Through mid-March, Sanders outspent Clinton on television buys in eleven contests.[109] Sanders won the Maine, Kansas, and Nebraska caucuses as well as a surprise victory in the Michigan primary. Meanwhile, Clinton won the Louisiana, Mississippi, North Carolina, and Florida primaries by large margins, and prevailed in Illinois, Missouri, and Ohio by smaller ones. Sanders continued to match Clinton's ad buys and enjoyed a string of victories in late March and early April, including caucuses in Alaska, Hawaii, Washington State, and Wyoming, and primaries in Idaho, Utah, and Wisconsin. Clinton countered with a win in the Arizona primary. Despite these mixed results, Sanders raised $46 million in March.[110]

The hard-fought campaign had affected fundraising in both camps. For Clinton, the unexpectedly strong challenge from Sanders made high-dollar fundraising more difficult: "With regard to the donors, 'It was harder to get them to take action when things were going well,' said one person familiar with her fund-raising operation. 'The times that people thought she was losing or something challenging happened, that's when people would rally behind her.' That was the opposite of the experience of many political candidates, including Obama, who could raise cash off their successes."[111] But looked at another way, Clinton's high-dollar strategy nonetheless allowed her to raise funds in reaction to electoral setbacks—a pattern that resembles the ability of threatened incumbent congressional candidates to raise more funds than strong challengers can. In contrast, Sanders faced the opposite problem—and opportunity: "We had to win every week to keep funding the campaign."[112]

Given the competitive nature of the 2016 contest between Clinton and Sanders, it is perhaps surprising that Priorities USA Action chose not to attack Sanders in the way candidate-specific Super PACs did in the GOP nomination contests in 2012 and 2016. There were two reasons for this pattern. First, the Clinton campaign had the assistance of another Super PAC, Correct the Record, which was engaged in tough criticism of Sanders via digital media. Second, the campaign was concerned about alienating Sanders's supporters. Clinton later said: "My team kept reminding me that we didn't want to alienate Bernie's supporters. President Obama urged me to grit my teeth and lay off Bernie as much as I could. I felt like I was in a straitjacket."[113] As figure 4-2 reveals, Clinton Super PAC spending did not peak until the bridge period, when ads were directed against the presumptive GOP nominee, Donald Trump.

Campaign spending was high in the New York primary—the state where Sanders was a native born and Clinton was a resident—and both candidates were closely matched in television spending as Election Day approached.[114] However, Clinton prevailed in the Empire State, in large part thanks to minority voters in New York City. A week later, Sanders outspent Clinton in the "Acela" primaries (a set of contests named for the states that are along the high-speed Amtrak train line that runs from Boston to Washington, D.C.), but Sanders won only Rhode Island, while Clinton carried Connecticut, Delaware, Maryland, and Pennsylvania.[115]

As Clinton's lead among elected delegates continued to grow, Sanders's fundraising began to decline and his cash on hand dwindled.[116] Still, Sanders had enough money to remain competitive in May, winning the Indiana, Oregon, and West Virginia primaries and holding Clinton to a very narrow victory in Kentucky.[117] In a last-ditch effort, Sanders spent heavily in delegate-rich California,[118] but on June 7, Clinton won the California, New Jersey, New Mexico, and South Dakota primaries, collecting enough delegates to ensure the nomination. Although Sanders said on June 24 that he would vote for Clinton, he took his campaign all the way to the Democratic convention.

According to Mark Longabaugh, Sanders stayed in the race until the end because they "were building a movement inside of the party, and that all of those people who were funding and powering this campaign from the beginning, millions of dollars, $230 million, came at 27 bucks a pop. . . . They wanted to be able to cast their ballot for Bernie and that was really important for him and, I would argue, for them."[119]

During the primary season, Sanders raised nearly as much money as Clinton and spent $35 million more. Outside money, including the Super PACs allied with Clinton, accounted for only about one-sixth of total candidate spending during this period. Thus, it seems unlikely that the amount of money spent was the central factor in the results. Instead, it may have been how effectively the funds were expended and ultimately the strengths and weaknesses of the candidates. In the end, Clinton had a better strategy for winning the nomination, and Sanders's insurgency had its limitations. Some analysts argued that the hard-fought primary season created financing headaches for the Clinton campaign going into the general election.[120] Clinton and her allies turned to raising funds for the general election and attacking the presumptive Republican nominee during the bridge period.

The Republican Nomination Contest

On March 23, 2015, U.S. senator Ted Cruz of Texas announced his candidacy for the Republican presidential nomination. He was quickly followed on April 7 by U.S. senator Rand Paul of Kentucky and on April 13 by U.S. senator Marco Rubio of Florida. In May, the field continued to grow: Ben Carson, a retired neurosurgeon and conservative author, and Carly Fiorina, former CEO of Hewlett-Packard, joined on May 4; former Arkansas governor Mike Huckabee (a prominent candidate in 2008) declared his candidacy on May 5; former U.S. senator Rick Santorum of Pennsylvania (a prominent candidate in 2012) entered the race on May 27; and former New York governor George Pataki joined the race on May 28.

June was an even busier month: U.S. senator Lindsey Graham of South Carolina entered the race on June 1; former Texas governor Rick Perry (a candidate in 2012) on June 4; real estate developer and reality TV star Donald Trump on June 6; Wisconsin governor Scott Walker on June 13; former Florida governor Jeb Bush on June 15; Louisiana governor Bobby Jindal on June 24; and New Jersey governor Chris Christie on June 30. The field of seventeen contenders was completed in July with the addition of Ohio governor John Kasich on July 21 and former Virginia governor Jim Gilmore on July 30.[121]

For the presumed front-runner, Jeb Bush, the late entry reflected the development of outside organizations supporting the candidate:

> [Jeb Bush] was legitimately holding off to see what kind of support he'd get, if it made sense to run. . . . [O]ne advantage of that process taking a while was that he had the bandwidth to be involved as a special guest at Super PAC events. . . . [W]e took the position that he would not solicit money for Super PAC events. That's using the FEC's definition of "Solicit," which means, "to directly ask for it." . . . [O]ther candidates like John Kasich and others did solicit for their Super PAC.[122]

The unexpectedly large number of candidates suggested intense competition for campaign funds, but despite—or perhaps because of—this list of accomplished candidates, Donald Trump immediately dominated all aspects of the race. He was well known to the public from his multiple business and entertainment enterprises as well as his ostentatious lifestyle, brash personality, and contentious rhetoric. Although he had toyed with running for president since 1988, his political activities were largely instrumental and his partisanship mercurial. Few observers took his campaign seriously, including perhaps Trump himself,[123] but it fascinated everyone. Conventional wisdom saw his campaign as a series of disasters from the beginning, with a steady stream of gaffs, quarrels, and controversies forecasting a quick end (a view Trump may also have shared).[124] The campaign did, however, make for great reading, listening, and viewing in all forms of media all across the political spectrum.

Like Sanders, Trump's main theme was a critique of wealth and power, but without Sanders's clear ideological focus. Promising to "Make America Great Again," he attacked economic and political elites who had presided over the nation's decline. A trifecta of issues—international trade, illegal immigration, and security threats—was at the center of his "post-ideological" agenda. For many voters, Trump's complaints were validated by his unorthodox business success, disrespect for "political correctness," and admitted engagement with political corruption. "So I will tell you," Trump said, "I understand the game, I've been on the other side all of my life. And they have a lot of control over our politicians. And I don't say that favorably, and I'm not sure if there's another system, but I say this. I am not accepting any money from anybody. Nobody has control of me other than the people of this country."[125] Indeed, a mantra of his campaign was that the system was "rigged" by the establishment, including Republican leaders. Trump emphasized this point by declaring he would self-finance his campaign and reject the backing of Super PACs.[126]

By the time the Republican contenders met for the first televised debate, in August 2015, Trump led the field in opinion polls. A common worry among GOP officials was that after performing poorly against his more accomplished rivals, Trump would use his wealth to run as an independent candidate in the general election and harm the GOP nominee (a threat Trump returned to often).[127]

The format of the debates worked in Trump's favor. First, the candidates were arrayed onstage according to their poll standings, which put Trump at center stage, flanked by his rivals in order of declining popularity (and the seven least popular candidates on a separate undercard, televised before the main event). Trump's harsh and personal attacks took his opponents off stride.[128] He often repeated himself, speaking in short, catchy phrases, an approach that was effective against his rivals' respectful and polished statements. And no one knew how to handle Trump: some attacked, some praised, and others ignored the front-runner—often to the detriment of their own prospects. The remaining televised debates generally followed this pattern throughout the fall of 2015, and Trump remained ahead in the polls.[129] By the end of the year, if not before, Trump believed he could be a "winner" rather than a "loser."

The winnowing of the large field soon began, in part because of poor finances, especially in hard-dollar fundraising. Rick Perry and Scott Walker exited in September, Bobby Jindal in November, Lindsey Graham and George Pataki in December. Others continued weak campaigns into the early contests in 2016: Mike Huckabee, Rick Santorum, and Rand Paul left after the Iowa caucuses, while Chris Christie, Carly Fiorina, and Jim Gilmore withdrew after the New Hampshire primary; Ben Carson soldiered on until after Super Tuesday.

Many of these candidacies were undermined in part by extensive fundraising by the most prominent candidates, especially Jeb Bush. Mike DuHaime, chief strategist for Chris Christie, reported that once Bush became a candidate "it fundamentally changed the race for everyone from the establishment side that needed to raise money and couldn't self-fund. Jeb being in was a huge obstacle for everyone. Any time any one of us got any oxygen and started to shoot up—for Christie, it was after the Union Leader endorsement—Jeb's Super PAC hammered whoever got oxygen." This was because "there is no donor network close to the Bush donor network. . . . I'm sure a lot of other people around the table heard the exact same thing. 'I'd be with you but I've been with Bush since 1979, so I'm going to be with Jeb.' . . . From a donor point of view, it was really problematic."[130]

Ironically, many candidates were hurt by their own early fundraising success. According to Larry Noble, "Because what you had is a very large Republican field that lasted probably much longer than it would have lasted if it didn't have all that money. . . . Trump benefited tremendously by the fact that there were people staying in the race probably longer than they would have without all of the private funding."[131]

Another factor was heavy early spending by the better-funded candidates, who jockeyed with one another to become Trump's main opponent. For example, Team Bush (his campaign and allied Super PAC) spent $36 million and Team Rubio $16 million on advertising in 2015, focused

Figure 4-3. *GOP Cumulative Primary Receipts, 2016*

Millions of dollars

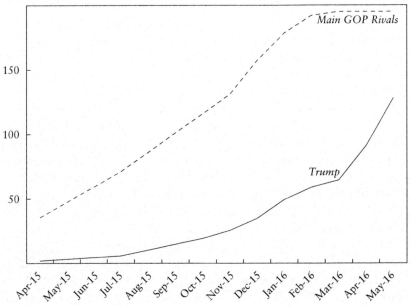

Source: Compiled from the Federal Election Commission.

heavily on Iowa and New Hampshire.[132] Here the conventional wisdom benefited Trump, according to Michael Glassner of the Trump campaign: "This concept of the primary candidates being in particular lanes . . . was probably a tremendous advantage to us because we weren't in any lane, and Trump could go and cross over into lanes as he chose and did so regularly."[133] In all these regards, the large number of Trump rivals prevented the emergence of a single strong alternative candidate—a pattern found in some previous nomination campaigns, such as for Republicans in 2012.

Meanwhile, Trump's "penny pinching" campaign raised and spent very little money by comparison.[134] Through December 2015, Trump had raised less than one-fifth as much as his top four rivals combined (Bush, Rubio, Cruz, and Kasich)—and most of it from his own funds (see figure 4-3). In the fall of 2015, Trump spent just $200,000 on television advertising.[135] This spending disparity continued throughout the primary season.

Trump's campaign style also differed dramatically from his rivals. James Ceaser and his colleagues described it this way:

While [the other candidates] prepared, Trump broke all the rules. He forswore fundraising and spent little on the army of pollsters and consultants that traditionally surrounds every major campaign. He relied on rallies, Twitter, and free media to spread his message; by one estimate, he eventually received nearly $2 billion worth of free media coverage through mid-March 2016. . . . Trump eschewed endorsements as a matter of necessity—there were few Republican officeholders willing to back him—though lack of endorsements also made him a more authentic outsider. He largely eschewed organization, relying instead on his ephemeral charisma. . . . [H]e kept his opponents off balance by simply refusing to play by the rules of civility; he "punched down" at trailing contenders more than any other candidate.[136]

In this regard, Trump effectively branded his rivals—"low energy Jeb," "little Marco," and "lying Ted." One of the campaign's innovations was the use of social media. Trump campaign manager Corey Lewandowski said: "Donald Trump also has the ability to bypass the mainstream media by going directly to social media and using it more effectively than anybody has. Not just his Twitter account and his Facebook account but also his Instagram account, which now, among those three mediums, have 30 million followers."[137] Michael Glassner concurred: "With social media and on Twitter, Mr. Trump would say that it was like owning the New York Times without the overhead or the debt. . . . He could directly communicate his message and it was widely disseminated for zero money."[138]

According to consultant Mark Mellman, Trump was effective on Facebook as well:

They were able to look at a certain ad and say, "People with this kind of psychological—or this kind of profile based on their likes or other things about them on Facebook—people with this profile will respond to this ad and will likely click on it, the more likely will engage with it, so on and so forth. So let's direct more of this ad to these types of people and these other types of people are not engaging with this ad so let's stop directing it to them and give them something else. . . . [T]here are tools that a lot of people have not been using, tools that are pretty cutting edge for the most part."[139]

Overall, "One thing that Trump did very successfully was use the social media to drive the earned media, and he did that very effectively."[140]

Another Trump tactic—campaign rallies—was also low cost and quite effective. Michael Glassner reported: "Those people that came to the Trump rallies early in the campaign were people who had been disaffected by the process. They hadn't voted in a long time, or they had never voted, and I think that his message of a positive economic future for them personally was extremely powerful."[141]

Corey Lewandowski recalled, "We didn't poll test things. We didn't go out and focus group things like every other campaign did. We just did it. Because it was such a small team and because Donald Trump has such an instinct to do things, we relied on his ability to read the American people."[142] But in terms of campaign strategy, Trump followed the conventional wisdom. According to Lewandowski, "We put together a three-state strategy, like many other campaigns did, and looked at Iowa, New Hampshire and South Carolina."[143]

These patterns continued when the nomination contests began in February 2016. Trump finished a strong second in Iowa and first in New Hampshire, South Carolina, and Nevada. In February, Trump spent some $9 million on advertising. By comparison, Team Bush spent $55 million, Team Rubio $26 million, and Team Cruz $14 million.[144] This level of spending steadily depleted these candidates' hard-dollar cash on hand (see figure 4-4) and put a dent in the accounts of supporting Super PACs and 501(c)(4) organizations.

After a poor finish in South Carolina, Bush ended his campaign. It was an ignominious end for the financial juggernaut of the GOP field. The organization of the Bush effort may have been a fundamental problem: a strict division of labor between the campaign committee, allied Super PAC, and related 501(c)(4), with most of the campaign's finances resting with the Super PAC.[145] Michael Beckel of the Center for Public Integrity noted:

> One of the more fascinating studies of this election would be looking at Right to Rise USA and their $100 million war chest. I believe that they spent over 80% of their money touting Jeb Bush, who comes from a family that's very well known and has a name brand that's very well known. So, they know how much bang for their buck did they get with positive ads about Jeb Bush, versus instead maybe spending $80 million taking out one of the other candidates?[146]

Figure 4-4. *GOP Cash on Hand and Anti-Trump Independent Expenditures, 2016*

Millions of dollars

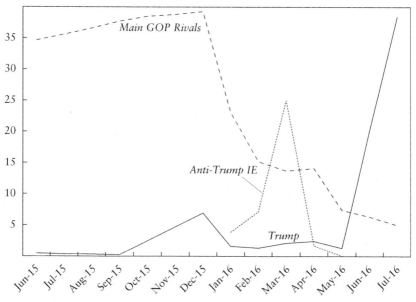

Source: Compiled from the Federal Election Commission.

Meanwhile, Trump's success provoked a dramatic increase in independent expenditures against him—a total of $37 million from January 2016 through May 2016 (see figure 4-4). These figures included Super PACs allied with rival candidates as well as explicitly anti-Trump Super PACs.[147] These attacks were reinforced by extensive criticism of Trump by a wide range of Republican and conservative leaders.[148] Much of this effort was designed to drive votes away from Trump—in the hope that other GOP candidates would be able to attract such voters.[149] This did not happen. Mike Lux observed, "TV ads just don't have the punch at least in presidential politics . . . 90, say, percent of it was wasted."[150]

In March, the Republican primary rules allowed winner-take-all primaries, and some states had changed their rules to help "favorite son" candidates. This strategy failed for Rubio, who lost the Florida primary to Trump and ended his campaign on March 15. According to pollster Whit Ayres, "Then the money would stop coming in when [Rubio] started losing. And that's ultimately what drives candidates out of the race."[151]

As with Bush, Rubio's sophisticated fundraising organizations made for an inefficient campaign.[152]

The "favorite son" strategy worked for Cruz in the Texas primary (building on his first-place finish in Iowa) and Kasich in the Ohio primary (adding to his second-place finish in New Hampshire). Cruz soon became Trump's main opponent, winning seven contests to Trump's five. In March, the Trump campaign spent about $6 million on advertising, while Team Rubio spent $12 million and Team Cruz spent $8 million.[153]

On April 5, Cruz scored a victory over Trump in the Wisconsin primary. To some of Trump's critics, the Texas senator appeared to be the clear alternative for the nomination. However, Republican activists did not rally behind Cruz, and Kasich remained in the race, potentially dividing the anti-Trump vote. Cruz's campaign had long needed other candidates to exit the race, but as his campaign manager, Jeff Roe, noted, "when you need people to get out of the race, they don't always comply in the time that you need them to."[154] Roe also observed that a key to Trump's success was effective campaigns in caucus states:

> From an organizational principle, particularly in caucus states, it helps if you're able to, in person, in the last 72 hours, go touch a voter with an issue—whether you're swatting it down or whether you're pushing it on another candidate. . . . But particularly in caucus states and, I would argue, even primary states, you cannot do it if you can't execute on the ground because you don't know if people are seeing your ads. That's why I think the ground is more important today than it ever has been.[155]

However, the campaign was turning to expensive primary states: Trump's home state of New York and the "Acela" primary states of the northeast. Here Trump crushed his remaining rivals, securing enough delegates to win the nomination. Cruz made a last stand in the Indiana primary on May 3, but Trump won the Hoosier State. Cruz withdrew from the race, followed by Kasich, ending the contest. From the Wisconsin primary to the Indiana primary, the Trump campaign spent some $5 million on advertising and Team Cruz spent a bit over $4 million.[156] Anti-Trump Republicans waged an effort to defeat Trump at the Republican convention, but to no avail.

Trump spent a total of $63 million (aided by $2 million in unauthorized Super PAC spending) to secure the Republican presidential nomination.

These figures are roughly one-tenth of the funds spent by his Republican rivals. Funds spent specifically against Trump may well have exceeded his own spending, an indication of how unusual this nomination contest was.[157] As in the Democratic contests, it seems unlikely that the amount of money spent by the candidates was the central factor in the results. A case can be made that Trump spent more wisely than his many opponents, but one can also make the case that he did not need to spend as much, given his high name recognition and extensive earned media coverage. The Trump campaign had little money left at the end of the primary season, however.[158] Trump and his allies used the bridge period to raise general election funds and attack the presumptive Democratic nominee.

The National Conventions

The nomination contests ended with the national party conventions in July 2016. For the first time since 1976, there were no public financing moneys allocated to help pay for the conventions (see chapter 2). However, as in 2012, the federal government did allocate $50 million to the host cities, Cleveland and Philadelphia, to defray the costs of security.

The Cleveland host committee raised $66 million to stage the event beyond the federal dollars, and the Republican National Committee raised an additional $24 million to conduct the convention.[159] The GOP party funds included $14.7 million from the new convention account, with $6.5 million in the maximum amount of $100,200. Likewise, the Philadelphia host committee raised $70 million, and the Democratic National Committee raised an additional $15 million.[160] The Democratic Party funds included $3.5 million from the new convention account, with $701,000 in the maximum amount of $100,200. The host committee funds included in-kind contributions from state and local governments as well as gifts from corporations, interest groups, and wealthy donors.[161] Federal funds aside, the conventions cost $175 million, up 22 percent from the $143 million spent in 2012.

Innovations and Limitations

The 2016 presidential election will long be remembered for the extraordinary nomination victory of Donald Trump and, perhaps to a lesser degree, for Bernie Sanders's remarkable campaign. Of course, much will depend on how much the 2016 campaign and its aftermath reflect long-term changes in American politics rather than short-term perturbations. Certainly both were preludes to the general election—winning the White House for Trump and, for Sanders, revealing Hillary Clinton's weaknesses. For example, "the whole bought-and-paid-for thing came from Bernie," according to Clinton campaign staff, "lamenting that it hadn't really been a knock against her among Democrats coming into the campaign." This theme of Clinton being "owned" by special interests was picked up by Trump in the general election campaign.[162]

Winning a presidential nomination is about more than having raised the most money. The failure of Jeb Bush in 2016 makes this point clearly. The unusually low cost of Trump's largely self-financed nomination campaign may presage future candidacies by celebrities—rich in fame (or infamy), communication finesse, and personal funds. But with the lesson of Trump in mind, career politicians may find a way to counter such candidacies. Perhaps a more likely effect is the success of the Sanders campaign: it is clearly possible to adequately fund an insurgent campaign with small, online donations. Mark Mellman, a highly regarded Democratic pollster, observed of the Sanders campaign, "He was really raising it from small donations online, and that is a route that's available for people who capture the imagination of a constituency that's willing to open their wallets online, and the technology makes that possible in a way that it really wasn't before."[163]

One of the ironies of contemporary presidential campaign finance is that the opportunity to raise money in small amounts coexists with the expansion of very large donations from Super PACs and tax-exempt groups to party and convention financing. What all these techniques have in common is the efficient raising of large war chests by tapping the extensive resources of wealthy donors. While this made sense for many candidates seeking to win an expensive race, in 2016 such "big money" options became a major issue, adroitly exploited by Trump and Sanders. Indeed, the prominence of big money increases the possibility of a major scandal involving donors—one of the major factors in the reform of campaign finance laws (see chapter 8). Indeed, Clinton's influence over the Democratic National Committee via joint fundraising committees may be an early example. Self-financing by wealthy candidates can raise similar issues—as the complex relationship between President Trump and his family businesses reveals.

Potential scandals aside, the extensive innovations in campaign fundraising may generate pressure for reform as well. As anticipated by many observers, the Super PAC phenomenon expanded in 2016. Some candidates, such as Clinton and Bush, created a set of organizations to exploit a full range of fundraising options—including efforts to encourage donations to Super PACs. Clinton used a Super PAC to set up her campaign under the guise of a "draft Hillary" effort. Bush almost completely outsourced his advertising effort to a Super PAC; Kasich and Fiorina outsourced much of their voter contact operations (see chapter 1). Super PACs also became an opportunity for political entrepreneurship, sometimes inspired by candidates and sometimes in the hopes of attracting the attention of a particular candidate.

Other Republican candidates founded and allowed tax-exempt organizations to conduct portions of their campaign activities, ranging from policy development, to positive advocacy, to grassroots campaigning. Such forays into groups providing little disclosure resemble the activities of some large interest groups that have established an array of organizations for different tasks, ranging from hard-dollar PACs to different kinds of tax-exempt organizations. This area is likely to expand in the 2020 election cycle.

All of these innovations have put further strains on the "independence" of such spending. Few observers believe that funds spent by organizations that are part of the team dedicated to electing a candidate are really separate entities—no matter how closely strict legal definitions of independence are followed. This disjunction clearly reduces the legitimacy of campaign finance. At the same time, the legal independence of Super PACs and related groups can hinder efficient and effective campaign spending. In 2016, as in 2012, many candidacies were hindered by the lack of coordination among team members. The Bush and Rubio campaigns are good examples.

Furthermore, in 2016, candidates experimented with different ways of solving this coordination problem. First, they became more adept at infiltrating the leadership of Super PACs and allied organizations with operatives closely linked to the candidates. Second, they found loopholes in the law that allowed coordination, such as for digital media, and housed tax-exempt organizations together. Still another approach was to make campaign operations transparent and public, so that other organizations could easily adjust their activities accordingly. In this regard, it is significant that many Super PACs spent more on positive advertising for their favorite candidate in 2016 than on negative advertising against rival candidates—or outside groups.

Finally, the 2016 nomination contests point to the limitations of money in winning elections. "The mantra about money buying elections has been demonstrated to be so 100 percent false," said Republican attorney Jim Bopp, adding, "Money buys speech."[164] Such purchased speech can affect elections by providing voters with new, useful, and persuasive information, but in 2016, much of the speech purchased for or against candidates may not have provided this kind of information—a high volume of ineffective speech is unlikely to improve the impact of money. Once speech can be purchased, its quality is what matters. The massive attacks on Trump appear to be a good example of this phenomenon—and appear to have had little impact, despite uniting major GOP donors against him.

By the same token, Trump's and Sanders's more economical spending may have had a greater impact because of the quality of the information conveyed. As Bush's campaign manager, Danny Diaz, commented: "A presidential campaign is an earned media campaign."[165] In this regard, pollster Geoff Garin may have captured the heart of the 2016 nomination campaigns: "If we analogize Trump and Sanders . . . we watched people attracted by Sanders' position as an outsider who did not look or act like a traditional politician. That was important for Trump as well."[166]

Notes

1. Unless otherwise noted, all 2016 finance figures come from the FEC. All 2012 and 2008 figures in this chapter are in 2016 dollars. On the 2012 nomination campaign, see John C. Green, Michael E. Kohler, and Ian P. Schwarber, "Financing the 2012 Presidential Nomination Campaigns," in *Financing the 2012 Election*, edited by David B. Magleby (Brookings, 2014), pp. 77–122. On the 2008 campaign, see John C. Green and Diana Kingsbury, "Financing the 2008 Presidential Nomination Campaigns: A Requiem for the Public Financing System?" in *Financing the 2008 Election*, edited by David B. Magleby (Brookings, 2011), pp. 86–126. For 2004, see John C. Green, "Financing the 2004 Presidential Nomination Campaigns," in *Financing the 2004 Election*, edited by David B. Magleby, Anthony Corrado, and Kelly D. Patterson (Brookings, 2006), pp. 93–125.

2. The trend toward candidate nonparticipation in public financing began in 1996 with Republican Steve Forbes's self-financed nomination campaign. On the impact of contingent public finance regulations, see Green and Kingsbury, "Financing the 2008 Presidential Nomination Campaigns," 2008 being the most recent presidential campaign where public financing was an important factor.

3. Peter Overby, "Say Goodbye to the Taxpayer-Funded Political Convention," NPR, March 26, 2014.

4. *McCutcheon* v. *Federal Election Commission*, 572 U.S. ___ (2014).

5. Michael Beckel, "The 'McCutcheon' Decision Explained—More Money to Pour into Political Process," Center for Public Integrity, April 22, 2014.

6. On the invisible primary in 2008, see Arthur C. Paulson, "The 'Invisible Primary' Becomes Visible: The Importance of the 2008 Presidential Nominations, Start to Finish," in *Winning the Presidency, 2008*, edited by William J. Crotty (Boulder, Colo.: Paradigm Publishing, 2009), pp. 87–109.

7. The bridge period was shorter than in 2016 partly because both national party conventions were held in July rather than in late August and early September as in 2012.

8. Carrie Levine, "Soft Money Is Back—and Both Parties Are Cashing In," *Politico*, August 4, 2017.

9. David B. Magleby, "Electoral Politics as Team Sport: Advantage the Democrats," in *The State of the Parties: The Changing Role of Contemporary American Parties*, 6th ed., edited by John C. Green and Daniel J. Coffey (Lanham, Md.: Rowman and Littlefield, 2011), pp. 81–101.

10. *Citizens United* v. *Federal Election Commission*, 558 U.S. 310 (2010).

11. *SpeechNow.org* v. *Federal Election Commission*, 599 F.3d 686 (D.C. Cir. 2010).

12. See Advisory Opinion 2010-09 Club for Growth, which permitted Club for Growth, a section 501(c)(4) group, to pay the administrative and solicitation costs of its independent-expenditure-only PAC. See Advisory Opinion 2010-11 Commonsense Ten, which established Super PACs.

13. On the broader phenomenon, see David B. Magleby, "Super PACs and 501(c) Groups in the 2016 Election," paper presented at "State of the Parties: 2016 and Beyond," Ray C. Bliss Institute of Applied Politics, University of Akron, November 9–10, 2017.

14. Bryan F. Jacoutot, "The 2016 PAC Problem: To Go Super or Hybrid?" *Public Interest Advocacy*, July 18, 2015.

15. Hybrid committees allow for the efficient administration of funds from different sources, such as limited hard-dollar donations as well as unlimited donations for independent expenditures.

16. Brent Ferguson, "Candidates and Super PACs: The New Model in 2016," Brennan Center for Justice, 2015 (www.brennancenter.org/sites/default/files /analysis/Super_PACs_2016.pdf).

17. The 2008 campaign is a good standard for the number of candidates seeking a major-party presidential nomination. See Green and Kingsbury, "Financing the 2008 Presidential Nomination Campaigns," pp. 86–126.

18. For the 2016 primary calendar, see www.uspresidentialelectionnews.com /2016-presidential-primary-schedule-calendar/.

19. On the debate schedule, see www.uspresidentialelectionnews.com/2016 -debate-schedule/.

20. Harry Enten, "Is Six Democratic Debates Too Few?" *FiveThirtyEight*, May 6, 2015.

21. The matching funds provision of the public financing system was beneficial to small-dollar strategies because donations of $250 or less were doubled in size. Since 2000, few candidates have sought matching funds—even those following a small-dollar strategy—because of the limits on campaign spending tied to matching funds.

22. The ads were funded by Sam Wyly, a supporter of George W. Bush. See David B. Magleby, "A High Stakes Election," in *Financing the 2000 Election*, edited by David B. Magleby (Brookings, 2002), p. 9.

23. In 2012, Obama raised $41.3 million in general election funds during the nomination contest. See Green, Kohler, and Schwarber, "Financing the 2012 Presidential Nomination Campaigns," p. 84.

24. Matea Gold and Tom Hamburger, "Democratic Party Fundraising Effort Helps Clinton Find New Donors, Too," *Washington Post*, February 20, 2016; Dan Merica, "First on CNN: Hillary Clinton to Start Fundraising for the General Election, Democratic National Convention," CNN, June 9, 2016.

25. Individual Contributions and Receipts, Hillary Clinton, 2015

Dollars

	Total individual contributions	Total receipts
Hillary for America	108,932,228	115,569,138
Hillary Victory Fund	25,514,960	26,921,629
Hillary Action Fund	0	0
DNC	51,999,387	64,250,717

Source: Based on disclosure filings reported to the Federal Election Commission (www.fec .gov/finance/disclosure/candcmte_info.shtml).

26. Green, Kohler, and Schwarber, "Financing the 2012 Presidential Nomination Campaigns," p. 85.

27. Gabriel Debenedetti, "Sanders Campaign Inks Joint Fundraising Pact with DNC," *Politico*, November 5, 2016.

28. Donna Brazile, *Hacks: The Inside Story of the Break-ins and Breakdowns That Put Donald Trump in the White House* (New York: Hachette Books, 2017), p. 102.

29. The exact number of candidates depends on how one defines a candidacy. For example, CNN counted nineteen in 2016 and seven in 2008. See www.cnn .com/interactive/2015/05/politics/2016-election-candidates/ and www.cnn.com /ELECTION/2008/primaries/results/scorecard/#R.

30. In 2012, Romney raised $43.4 million in general election funds during the nomination contest. See Green, Kohler, and Schwarber, "Financing the 2012 Presidential Nomination Campaigns," p. 86.

31. See John C. Green and Nathan S. Bigelow, "Financing the 2000 Presidential Nomination Campaigns: The Costs of Innovation," in *Financing the 2000 Election*, edited by Magleby, pp. 49–78.

32. See Reena Flores, "Donald Trump, RNC Sign Fundraising Deal," *CBS News*, May 18, 2016; Gabby Morrongiello, "RNC Makes Small-Dollar Pitch for Its 'Make America Great Again' Fund," *Washington Examiner*, May 31, 2016.

33. Green, Kohler, and Schwarber, "Financing the 2012 Presidential Nomination Campaigns," p. 87.

34. Cruz Victory Committee raised $491,000, Rubio Victory Committee, $4,732,000, and the Paul Victory Committees, $1,791,000. See Center for Responsive Politics (www.opensecrets.org/jfc/top.php?type=C).

35. The figures in table 4-2 come from the Campaign Finance Institute. The author is grateful for the assistance of Brendan Glavin in assembling the table. See Campaign Finance Institute, "President Trump, with RNC Help, Raised More Small Donor Money than President Obama; as Much as Clinton and Sanders Combined," table 2 (www.cfinst.org/Press/PReleases/17-02-21/President_Trump _with_RNC_Help_Raised_More_Small_Donor_Money_than_President _Obama_As_Much_As_Clinton_and_Sanders_Combined.aspx). In these data, all the itemized donations from each individual are combined into a single figure, so multiple donations from a single person are taken into account.

36. The lack of small donations may reflect a failing of the Ready for Hillary Super PAC to develop good lists of potential donors: "Ready for Hillary had grossly . . . exaggerated the group's lists. After accounting for bad email addresses, one official later groused, 'It wasn't half a million names.'" See Jonathan Allen and Amie Parnes, *Shattered: Inside Hillary Clinton's Doomed Campaign* (New York: Crown, 2017), p. 28.

37. For estimates of the number of Clinton fundraising events, see http:// politicalpartytime.org/search/Beneficiary/Hillary%2520Victory%2520Fund/. On the nature of the events, see Gabriel Debenedetti, "Exclusive: Hillary's Jam-Packed Fundraising Schedule," *Politico*, June 2, 2015.

38. Tim Tagaris, digital fundraising director for Sanders 2016 campaign and partner for Revolution Messaging, interview by David Magleby, March 15, 2017.

39. Green, Kohler, and Schwarber, "Financing the 2012 Presidential Nomination Campaigns," pp. 89–93.

40. Tagaris, interview.

41. Jeff Weaver, campaign manager, Bernie Sanders for President, quoted in Institute of Politics, *Campaign for President: The Managers Look at 2016* (Lanham, Md.: Rowman and Littlefield, 2017), p. 39.

42. Betsy Woodruff, "Bernie Sanders's Millions Raised Sans Moneymen," *Daily Beast*, January 11, 2016; Clare Foran, "Bernie Sanders's Big Money," *The Atlantic*, March 1, 2016.

43. John Fritze, "O'Malley Campaign Secures Public Cash before Dropping Out," *Baltimore Sun*, February 6, 2016.

44. Marilyn W. Thompson, "Green Party's Jill Stein Gets a Financial Boost, Thanks to Taxpayers," *Washington Post*, September 20, 2016.

45. Ari Melber, "Forgiving Campaign Loans, Trump Fulfills His Pledge to Self-Fund Primary," *NBC News*, July 21, 2016.

46. Kurtis Lee, "Campaign Cash: 'Leadership PACs' Becoming Vehicle of Choice for Presidential Candidates," *Los Angeles Times*, March 11, 2015.

47. See Ian Vandewalker, "Shadow Campaigns: The Shift in Presidential Campaign Funding to Outside Groups," Brennan Center for Justice, August 4, 2015; Democracy in Action, "Building Campaign Organizations," 2015 (www.p2016.org/chrnprep/organization2015.html); Center for Responsive Politics, "Behind the Candidates: Campaign Committees and Outside Groups" (www.opensecrets.org/pres16/outside-groups?type=A).

48. Andrew Perez and David Sirota, "Bernie Sanders PAC Funded the Democratic Party Establishment," *IBTimes*, February 11, 2016.

49. Allen and Parnes, *Shattered*, p. 27.

50. Seth Bringman, *Ready for Hillary: The Official, Inside Story of the Campaign before the Campaign* (Self-published by author, 2015).

51. Ibid.; Dave Levinthal, "Inside Hillary Clinton's Big-Money Cavalry," Center for Public Integrity, April 7, 2016.

52. Bush formed both a leadership PAC and a Super PAC simultaneously, with the same name, Right to Rise. See Jeremy Diamond, "Jeb Bush Launches Leadership PAC," CNN, January 6, 2015.

53. Many of these committees raised no funds in the prenomination period. The exceptions were Kasich (see www.factcheck.org/2016/01/new-day-for-america/) and Walker (see www.opensecrets.org/527s/527cmtedetail.php?ein=472796803).

54. Katie Day, "Carly Fiorina on Leadership and Unlocking Human Potential," HUFFPOST, October 29, 2014.

55. This figure was calculated from the data in table 4-1 and table 4-3.

56. Campaign Finance Institute, "Million-Dollar Donors Dominate Presidential Super PAC Giving," June 17, 2016 (www.cfinst.org/Press/PReleases/16-06-17/Million-Dollar_Donors_Dominate_Presidential_Super_PAC_Giving.aspx).

57. Branko Marcetic, "A Newly Leaked Hillary Clinton Memo Shows How Campaigns Get Around Super PAC Rules," *In These Times*, June 20, 2016. See also Matea Gold, "How a Super PAC Plans to Coordinate Directly with Hillary Clinton's Campaign," *Washington Post*, May 12, 2015.

58. See Center for Public Integrity, "Top Donors to Priorities USA Action," 2016 (www.publicintegrity.org/2016/08/24/20140/top-donors-priorities-usa-action).

59. Matea Gold and Anu Narayanswamy, "How Mega-donors Bankrolled Hillary Clinton's Campaign to the Tune of $1 Billion," *Sydney Morning Herald*, October 24, 2018.

60. Gabriel Debenedetti, "O'Malley Super PAC Nets Disappointing Haul," *Politico*, July 31, 2015.

61. Linda Qiu, "Is Bernie Sanders the Only Presidential Candidate without a Super PAC?" *PolitiFact*, September 20, 2015.

62. Jenna Johnson, "Donald Trump Tells Super PACs Supporting His Candidacy to Return All Money to Donors," *Washington Post*, October 23, 2015.

63. Ballotpedia, "Great America PAC" (https://ballotpedia.org/Great_America_PAC).

64. Perhaps the oddest of these organizations was Get Our Jobs Back PAC, which claimed to have provided $50 million in in-kind public relations assistance to the Trump campaign. However, the donations were returned to the original donors. See Hanna Trudo and Kenneth P. Vogel, "Convicted Ponzi Schemer: I'll Conduct $50 Million Marketing Campaign for Trump," *Politico*, June 14, 2016.

65. Zachary Gross, "Rebuilding America Now," FactCheck.org, June 10, 2016.

66. Ballotpedia, "Make America Number 1" (https://ballotpedia.org/Make_America_Number_1).

67. D'Angelo Gore, "Future 45/45 Committee," FactCheck.org, November 3, 2016.

68. Alex Isenstadt and Kenneth P. Vogel, "Trump Blesses Major Super PAC Effort," *Politico*, July 20, 2016.

69. Alex Altman and Zeke J. Miller, "The War among the Donald Trump Super PACs," *Time*, June 2, 2016; Kelly Riddell, "Donald Trump's Super PAC Problem," *Washington Times*, September 23, 2016. It is worth noting that Trump also benefited from a 501(c)(4) group organized during the fall campaign. See Kenneth P. Vogel, "Secret Money to Boost Trump," *Politico*, September 28, 2016.

70. Green, Kohler, and Schwarber, "Financing the 2012 Presidential Nomination Campaigns," pp. 97–98.

71. Robert Costa, "Jeb Bush and His Allies Form Leadership PAC and Super PAC, Both Dubbed Right to Rise," *Washington Post*, January 6, 2015.

72. The Bush campaign also created an LLC, "BHAG," to trademark the campaign's logo "JEB!" with a view toward future merchandizing opportunities. See Russ Choma, "Why Does Jeb Bush Have a Mysterious Shell Company?" *Mother Jones*, June 29, 2015.

73. Kenneth P. Vogel, "Scott Walker, Rick Perry Show Limits of Super PACs," *Politico*, September 22, 2015.

74. Libby Watson, "The Super PACs behind Ted Cruz's Fundraising Juggernaut," Sunlight Foundation, February 23, 2016.

75. Keep the Promise II spent only $1 million of the $10 million he gave. See www.dallasnews.com/news/politics/2016/05/18/20-million-left-to-spend-what -will-the-super-pacs-who-backed-ted-cruz-do-with-it; Nathan Gianni, "Major Ted Cruz Donor Is Taking Back $9 million," *AOL News*, May 5, 2016; Alex Daugherty, "Texas Billionaire and GOP Fundraiser Considered for Mexico Ambassador, Report Says," McClatchey DC Bureau, December 19, 2016.

76. Shane Goldmacher, "Marco Rubio's Secret (Money) Legacy," *Politico*, March 28, 2016; Robert Maguire, "Two (At Most) Secret Donors Funded 93% of Pro-Rubio Nonprofit," Center for Responsive Politics, May 3, 2017.

77. For a summary of spending by nonprofits over time, see Center for Responsive Politics, "Political Nonprofits (Dark Money)" (www.opensecrets.org /outsidespending/nonprof_summ.php?cycle=2018&type=type&range=tot).

78. Dan Tuohy, "Presidential Hopeful Kasich Combines Data Mining with Traditional Campaigning," *Government Technology*, December 28, 2015.

79. Hunter Schwarz, "Carly for America Has to Change Its Name to CARLY for America, Because the FEC is LOL," *Washington Post*, June 17, 2015.

80. Nick Corasaniti, "Carly Fiorina's 'Super PAC' Aids Her Campaign, in Plain Sight," *New York Times*, September 30, 2015.

81. Jane C. Timm, "Exclusive: Ben Carson Super PACs Plan to Form 'Massive Army,'" MSNBC, October 20, 2015; Ballotpedia, "The 2016 Committee" (https://ballotpedia.org/The_2016_Committee); Betsy Klein, "Turf Grass to Grassroots: The Unlikely Force behind Ben Carson's Iowa Campaign," CNN, September 25, 2015.

82. These data must be viewed with caution since the groups define for themselves whether a particular expenditure is "for" or "against" a candidate. Hence, these reports are subjective.

83. Green, Kohler, and Schwarber, "Financing the 2012 Presidential Nomination Campaigns," pp. 95–96.

84. The following accounts draw heavily on James W. Ceaser, Andrew E. Busch, and John J. Pitney, *Defying the Odds: The 2016 Elections and American Politics* (Lanham, Md.: Rowman and Littlefield, 2017), especially chapters 2 and 3.

85. Geoff Garin, president of Hart Research Associates, interview by David Magleby, June 1, 2017.

86. Green and Kingsbury, "Financing the 2008 Presidential Nomination Campaigns," pp. 106–111.

87. Robby Mook, campaign manager, Hillary for America, quoted in Institute of Politics, *Campaign for President*, p. 33.

88. Bernie Sanders, *Our Revolution: A Future to Believe In* (New York: Thomas Dunne, 2016), pp. 52–54.

89. Jonathan Martin, "What Bernie Sanders Would Need to Do to Win," *New York Times*, April 30, 2015.

90. Ceaser, Busch, and Pitney, *Defying the Odds*, pp. 41–49.

91. Aaron Blake, "Here Are the Latest, Most Damaging Things in the DNC's Leaked Emails," *Washington Post*, July 25, 2016.

92. Mark Longabaugh, senior Sanders 2016 campaign adviser, interview by David Magleby, February 8, 2017.

93. Brazile, *Hacks*, pp. 97–98.

94. Weaver, quoted in Institute of Politics, *Campaign for President*, p. 37.

95. Keegan Goudiss, director of digital advertising for Sanders 2016 campaign and partner for Revolution Messaging, interview by David Magleby, March 15, 2017.

96. Mook, quoted in Institute of Politics, *Campaign for President*, p. 36.

97. Chloe Nurik, "Correct the Record," FactCheck.org, January 22, 2016.

98. Stephen Ollemacher and Hope Yen, "Big Nomination Lead for Clinton: Pocketing 'Superdelegates,'" Associated Press, November 13, 2015.

99. "How Bernie Sanders and Hillary Clinton Differ in Campaign Spending," Associated Press, October 16, 2015 (www.cbsnews.com/news/how-bernie -sanders-and-hillary-clinton-differ-in-campaign-spending/).

100. Ceaser, Busch, and Pitney, *Defying the Odds*, pp. 48–49.

101. See Associated Press, "How Bernie Sanders and Hillary Clinton Differ in Campaign Spending."

102. Glenn Thrush and Annie Karni, "How Iowa Went Wrong for Hillary Clinton," *Politico*, February 2, 2016.

103. Mark Murray, "And the Total Amount Spent on Campaign Ads in Iowa Is . . . ," *NBC News*, February 2, 2016.

104. Gabriel Debenedetti, "Bernie's Bucks Bury Clinton in New Hampshire," *Politico*, February 7, 2016.

105. Reid Wilson, "Who Spent the Most in S.C. and Nevada," *Morning Consult*, February 19, 2016.

106. About this time, if not before, Sanders concluded he could win the nomination. See Allan Smith, "BERNIE: My Close Loss in Nevada Shows I 'Can Win Anywhere,'" *Business Insider*, February 20, 2016.

107. Mark Longabaugh, senior adviser, Bernie Sanders for President, quoted in Institute of Politics, *Campaign for President*, p. 93.

108. Laura Woods, "Super Saturday 2016 Election Results: Presidential Candidates' Ad Spending per Vote," *Go Banking Rates*, March 7, 2016.

109. Mark Murray, "Sanders Narrowly Outspends Clinton in Ads in March 15 States," *NBC News*, March 15, 2016.

110. Isaac Arnsdorf, "Sanders Outraises Clinton for Third Month in a Row," *Politico*, April 20, 2016.

111. Allen and Parnes, *Shattered*, p. 305.

112. Longabaugh, interview.

113. Hillary Rodham Clinton, *What Happened* (New York: Simon and Schuster, 2017), p. 230.

114. Jonathan Chew, "This Is How Much Super PACs and Candidates Have Spent to Win New York," *Fortune*, April 19, 2016.

115. Mark Murray, "Sanders Outspends Clinton in April 26 Primary States," *NBC News*, April 26, 2016.

116. John Wagner, "Bernie Sanders's Fundraising Drops Off Sharply in April," *Washington Post*, May 1, 2016.

117. Chris Frates, "Clinton, Sanders Square Off in Tight Indiana Primary," CNN, May 3, 2016; Mark Murray, "Clinton Outspends Sanders in Kentucky," *NBC News*, May 17, 2016.

118. Cady Zuvich, "Defiant Bernie Sanders Pours Remaining Cash into Last-Ditch Ad Blitz; Hillary Clinton Still Poised to Win Democratic Nomination," Center for Public Integrity, June 7, 2016.

119. Longabaugh, quoted in Institute of Politics, *Campaign for President*, p. 95.

120. Nicholas Confessore and Sarah Cohen, "Long Primary Carries Costs for Hillary Clinton: Money and Time," *New York Times*, April 21, 2016.

121. Potential Republican candidates who did not enter the race included the 2012 presidential nominee, Mitt Romney, and vice presidential nominee, Paul Ryan, as well as Indiana governor Mike Pence.

122. Charlie Spies, leader for Clark Hill's national political law practice, interview by David Magleby, February 10, 2017.

123. See Stephanie Cegielski, "An Open Letter to Trump Voters from His Top Strategist-Turned-Defector," *XO Jane,* March 28, 2016.

124. Theodore Schleifer, "CNN's 'Unprecedented': Trump Told Christie He Didn't Think He'd Last Past October 2015," CNN, November 15, 2016.

125. Donald Trump, "Wednesday's GOP Debate Transcript, Annotated," *Washington Post*, September 16, 2015.

126. Ceaser, Busch, and Pitney, *Defying the Odds*, pp. 71–74.

127. Nolan D. McCaskill, "Trump Again Threatens Independent Bid," *Politico*, March 3, 2016.

128. Brett LoGiurato, "TRUMP: Here's the Backstory on My 'Low Energy' Takedown of Jeb Bush," *Business Insider*, November 19, 2015; Aaron Blake, "9 Truly Awful Things Ted Cruz and Donald Trump Said about Each Other," *Washington Post*, September 23, 2016.

129. "Iowa Caucus Results," *New York Times*, February 1, 2016; Nate Cohn, "Why This Is the Iowa Poll That Everyone Was Waiting For," *New York Times*, January 30, 2016.

130. Mike DuHaime, chief strategist, Chris Christie for President, Inc., quoted in Institute of Politics, *Campaign for President*, p. 138.

131. Larry Noble, senior director for ethics and general counsel of Campaign Legal Center, interview by David Magleby, March 9, 2016.

132. Philip Bump, "Team Jeb Bush Has Spent $6.4 Million on Ads for Every 1 Point He Has Lost in the Polls," *Washington Post*, December 15, 2015.

133. Michael Glassner, deputy campaign manager, Donald J. Trump for President, quoted in Institute of Politics, *Campaign for President*, p. 32.

134. David A. Graham, "Is Trump Finally Willing to Spend Big?" *The Atlantic*, December 29, 2015.

135. Bump, "Team Jeb Bush Has Spent $6.4 Million."

136. Ceaser, Busch, and Pitney, *Defying the Odds*, p. 75.

137. Corey Lewandowski, primary campaign manager, Donald J. Trump for President, quoted in Institute of Politics, *Campaign for President*, p. 146.

138. Glassner, quoted in Institute of Politics, *Campaign for President*, p. 32.

139. Mark Mellman, CEO of The Mellman Group, interview by David Magleby, May 30, 2017.

140. Ibid.

141. Glassner, quoted in Institute of Politics, *Campaign for President*, p. 33.

142. Lewandowski, quoted in Institute of Politics, *Campaign for President*, p. 140.

143. Ibid., p. 29.

144. These figures are summed from the sources listed in notes 102 through 105.

145. Mary Jordan, "Mike Murphy Plots a Win for Jeb Bush in the Land of Hollywood Liberals," *Washington Post*, June 12, 2015; Ashley Parker and Maggie Haberman, "As Jeb Bush Struggles, Some Allies Blame His 'Super PAC,'" *New York Times*, January 22, 2016.

146. Michael Beckel, reporter for the Center for Public Integrity, interview by David Magleby, March 9, 2016.

147. Jason Russell, "Anti-Trump Super PAC Spending Passes New Milestone," *Washington Examiner*, May 31, 2016.

148. Ceaser, Busch, and Pitney, *Defying the Odds*, p. 85.

149. See, for example, the comments of consultant Ed Goeas at www.bloomberg.com/news/videos/2016-03-18/gop-strategist-ed-goeas-trump-s-doing-damage-to-himself.

150. Mike Lux, cofounder and president of Progressive Strategies, LLC, and senior adviser for progressive outreach for the Democratic National Committee, interview by David Magleby, January 6, 2017.

151. Whit Ayres, founder and president of North Star Opinion Research, interview by David Magleby, April 25, 2016.

152. Russell Berman, "The Rubio Campaign Ends Where It Began," *The Atlantic*, March 15, 2016.

153. These figures are summed from the sources listed in notes 108 and 109.

154. Jeff Roe, campaign manager, Cruz for President, quoted in Institute of Politics, *Campaign for President*, p. 24.

155. Ibid., p. 56.

156. These figures are summed from the sources listed in notes 114, 115, and 117.

157. Abigail Abrams, "How Much Money Have Republicans Spent to Stop Donald Trump? After $67 Million in Attack Ads, Trump Is Still Voters' Pick," *International Business Times,* April 26, 2016.

158. "Donald Trump Acknowledges He Needs GOP Help to Raise Campaign Funds," *Chicago Tribune*, June 21, 2016.

159. Ashley Balcerzak, "RNC Covered Its Convention Costs, but Some Who Gave in 2012 Stayed Away," Center for Responsive Politics, September 20, 2016.

160. Ashley Balcerzak, "And the Good Times Rolled: 17 Donors Gave Three-Quarters of Dems' Convention Money," Center for Responsive Politics, September 28, 2016.

161. For example, for donors to the Cleveland host committee, see Center for Responsive Politics (www.opensecrets.org/pres16/conventions).

162. Allen and Parnes, *Shattered*, pp. 217–18.

163. Mellman, interview.

164. Michael Beckel, "Ted Cruz and Pals Spent $10 a Vote in Indiana. Trump Won Anyway," *NBC News*, May 4, 2016.

165. Danny Diaz, campaign manager, Jeb 2016, quoted in Institute of Politics, *Campaign for President*, p. 43,

166. Garin, interview.

FIVE   *Financing the 2016*
            Presidential General Election

DAVID A. HOPKINS

The presidential election of 2016 produced the biggest upset in American politics since 1948, when Harry S. Truman unexpectedly defeated Thomas E. Dewey to win a second term in the White House. Pundits, politicians, and political professionals in both parties judged Donald Trump to have little chance of victory against Hillary Clinton from the moment that he became the presumptive Republican presidential nominee in late spring. When videotaped evidence of Trump making lewd comments about women during a 2005 interview for TV's *Access Hollywood* surfaced in the news media roughly a month before the election, many analysts and even some top Republicans concluded that Trump was a certain loser who could potentially drag the GOP's congressional candidates to defeat as well.[1] House Speaker Paul Ryan responded to the release of the *Access Hollywood* footage by privately telling Republican members of the House of Representatives to distance themselves from Trump if they felt it necessary to salvage their own campaigns, while Republican National Committee chair Reince Priebus personally suggested to Trump that he drop out of the race for the greater good of the party.[2] Yet Trump ultimately shocked the nation—and the world—on election night by carrying enough battleground states to win an Electoral College majority despite losing the national popular vote to Clinton by a margin of 2.1 percentage points and 2.8 million votes.

Before the election, most political analysts had viewed Clinton as holding a prohibitive advantage over Trump for a number of reasons, including her superior debate performances (as measured by national surveys),

Trump's personal unpopularity, and the steady growth of Democratic-leaning minority groups within the American electorate. But a major element of the supposed competitive mismatch between the candidates was the widely claimed financial and organizational superiority of the Clinton campaign. During the final weeks of the race, many pundits assumed that Clinton and her aides were running a generously funded and mechanically sharp operation—especially compared to a Trump campaign that superficially appeared to be in constant crisis and suffering from damaging rifts with other centers of power within the Republican Party. Media accounts describing Clinton as overseeing an "efficient" and "mathematical" campaign with the power to "dwarf" her opponent in campaign spending and analytical firepower[3] contrasted with press headlines that routinely used terms like "turmoil" and "chaos" to refer to the apparent state of affairs within Trump's campaign organization.[4]

These impressions were reinforced by opinion polls that consistently found Clinton to be leading Trump not only in the national popular vote but also in enough states to represent a majority in the Electoral College. None of the visible tactics of the Clinton campaign—such as the state-level targeting of paid advertisements or personal visits by the candidate—indicated that the private data analysis conducted by Clinton's advisers produced a less favorable forecast of her chances than the publicly available surveys sponsored by media organizations. Indeed, Clinton and her staff were apparently as shocked as the rest of the political world by her defeat, to the extent that she declined to make the traditional public appearance in front of her supporters on the night of the election and waited until the following day to personally concede the race. From the moment that Trump's stunning victory became apparent, retrospective analysis of the 2016 general election largely focused on attempts to account for the methodological failures that had produced incorrect polling results in several pivotal states, as well as rampant second-guessing of Clinton's strategy and message. Much less attention has been paid to the unforeseen effectiveness of Trump's professional campaign staff, along with the Republican National Committee (RNC) and groups operating outside the control of the campaign, reflecting the consensus view of the political community in Washington that Trump did not win the presidency so much as Clinton lost it.

The review of the financial landscape of the 2016 general election presented in this chapter reveals a more complex picture. As it will show, the conventional wisdom that took hold during the campaign itself was not wholly inaccurate. Clinton indeed held an edge over Trump in both direct contributions and expenditures on her behalf by independent groups, and her campaign built a more extensive infrastructure to contact voters than the Trump campaign did.

However, the discrepancy between the relative financial and organizational positions of the two candidates was much less pronounced in reality than had been widely assumed in the heat of the race. The evidence demonstrates that Clinton failed to build a resource advantage that matched those enjoyed by fellow Democrat Barack Obama in 2008 and 2012, while the Republican opposition, for all the visible day-to-day foibles of the Trump candidacy, nevertheless attracted sufficient monetary support to construct an effective voter persuasion and mobilization operation led by the Republican National Committee. This effort was mostly ignored by a skeptical news media prone to view Trump and the orbit around him as hopelessly undisciplined and politically inept, perhaps even "the worst campaign in modern history."[5] Like her first-place finish in the national popular vote, Clinton's lead in the 2016 money race was real but, in the end, insufficiently strong to prevent Trump from narrowly achieving an unexpected triumph in the Electoral College.

An Overview of Spending in the 2016 General Election

While many other attributes of the 2016 election represented dramatic departures from the usual precedent, the decision of both major candidates to decline public financing of their campaigns was fully consistent with recent trends. As discussed in chapter 4, this included the rejection of public matching funds by all leading candidates for the nominations of both parties. In every general election between 1976 and 2004, the Democratic and Republican nominees had each accepted full public funding of their postconvention campaigns, which provided each candidate with $20 million in 1974 dollars from the federal treasury but prohibited additional donations or expenditures beyond this amount except to pay the costs of legal compliance. Barack Obama calculated in 2008 that he would gain an advantage by declining the public money and associated spending cap, instead financing his campaign entirely through private contributions.[6] Obama's fundraising success allowed him to outspend his general election opponent John McCain, who accepted the public funds, by a rate of more than three-to-one (see table 5-1), signaling

Table 5-1. *Campaign Expenditures, 2004, 2008, 2012, and 2016 Presidential General Elections*
Millions of 2016 dollars

	2004 Election		2008 Election		2012 Election		2016 Election	
	Bush	Kerry	Obama	McCain	Obama	Romney	Trump	Clinton
Candidate								
Candidate/public	94.8	94.8	n.a.	93.8	n.a.	n.a.	n.a.	n.a.
Candidate/private	n.a.	n.a.	375.6	n.a.	399.9	261.1	253.5	317.0
Candidate/GELAC[a]	15.5	11.3	n.a.	51.7	n.a.	n.a.	n.a.	n.a.
Candidate subtotal	110.3	106.1	375.6	145.5	399.9	261.1	253.5	317.0
Party								
Coordinated expenditures	20.5	20.3	7.1	21.1	2.9	1.0	20.3	22.9
Independent expenditures[b]	23.1	152.9	1.2	59.7	0.0	20.8	0.5	7.7
Hybrid advertising expenditures[c]	29.1	15.3	0.0	32.2	0.0	20.9	n.a.	n.a.
Victory funds[d]	0.1	0.4	20.6	17.9	56.8	83.1	108.7	110.3
Party subtotal	72.8	188.9	29.0	130.8	59.8	125.8	129.5	140.9
Groups and political committees								
Independent expenditures[e]	9.7	44.7	42.9	29.9	84.6	291.0	115.1	207.6
Electioneering communications[f]	46.8	22.9	6.7	10.3	0.0	0.0	0.0	0.0
Communication costs	1.7	29.2	33.2	1.1	7.6	0.7	0.8	5.1
Group subtotal	58.1	96.9	82.8	41.3	92.3	291.8	115.9	212.7
Total	241.2	391.8	487.5	317.6	552.0	678.7	498.9	670.6

Source: Based on data reported to the FEC and CMAG. Unless noted otherwise, figures represent funds spent in the period from the date of the national nominating convention through the end of the election. Data adjusted for 2016 dollars using CPI inflation calculator from the U.S. Bureau of Labor Statistics (www.bls.gov/data/inflation_calculator.htm).

a. The amount reported for McCain includes the total amount deposited in his GELAC account. Of this amount, $16.9 million had been spent by the end of the election year.

b. Includes all party independent expenditures (IEs), including DNC and RNC IEs made before the national nominating conventions. The total for each candidate includes expenditures in support of the candidate and against his or her opponent.

c. Figures only include the share of hybrid spending that can be attributed to the party, since the moneys spent by the candidate are included in the candidate's funds. In 2004, Bush and the RNC spent a total of $45.8 million on hybrid advertising, while Kerry and the DNC spent $24 million. In 2008, McCain and the RNC spent a total of $57.9 million. In 2012, the RNC and Romney spent $20 million on hybrid advertising (Rick Wiley, political director of the Republican National Committee, interview by David Magleby, February 11, 2013) and the DNC and Obama spent nothing (see Emily Miller, "Obama's Cash Crunch; RNC has the Edge in a Key Monetary Battle," *Washington Times*, October 26, 2012, p. B2).

d. Transfers to affiliated committees and offsets to operating expenditures are deducted from the joint fundraising committee disbursement totals to avoid double counting.

e. Totals for each candidate include expenditures in support of the candidate and against his or her opponent. Spending by Super PACs is included for the 2012 and 2016 elections.

f. Totals for 2008 do not include the $2.6 million spent by The One Campaign on advertisements that referenced both Obama and McCain.

to future candidates that opting out of the federal system could prove to be a smart tactical decision.

For the first time since its creation nearly forty years earlier, neither major-party nominee participated in the public financing system during the 2012 election, and this pattern held once again in 2016. Rather than accept the available $96 million apiece in federal funding, both Clinton and Trump chose to seek private donations and remain free of the corresponding limit on campaign expenditures. The Clinton campaign spent more than three times, and the Trump campaign more than two and a half times, the maximum amount available to them had they participated in the public financing program, which now seems to have thoroughly exhausted its usefulness in the eyes of major-party nominees (see chapter 2).

Most media coverage of the two candidates' financial resources in 2016 portrayed Clinton as swamping Trump in the money race. For example, a representative October story from NBC reported that "Hillary Clinton and the Democrats have a massive fundraising advantage," while "throughout his campaign Trump has struggled to raise money."[7] Even after Trump's upset victory, *Time* characterized the Republican as having "defeated big money" because he was "wildly outspent" by "a candidate [Clinton] with a fundraising operation unparalleled in politics."[8]

As table 5-1 and figure 5-1 indicate, however, these accounts overstated the magnitude of the financial imbalance between the two sides in the general election, even when spending by Super PACs is included. With respect to expenditures made directly by the candidates' own campaign organizations, Clinton indeed outspent Trump by a margin of $317 million to $253.5 million between the July national conventions and Election Day, but this $63.5 million gap was substantially narrower than the $139 million advantage enjoyed by Barack Obama over Mitt Romney in 2012 and paled in comparison to the $230 million head start that Obama established against John McCain in 2008. Even without adjusting for inflation, the Clinton campaign spent less in 2016 than Obama had in either of the two previous elections—despite a general election period that was a month longer because of changes in the scheduling of the national conventions. Notwithstanding press accounts that characterized the Trump campaign as a shoestring operation, Trump's general election expenditures roughly matched those of Romney four years earlier and substantially exceeded the budgets of McCain in 2008 and George W. Bush in 2004.

Figure 5-1. *Receipts and Disbursements, 2016 Presidential
General Election*

Millions of dollars

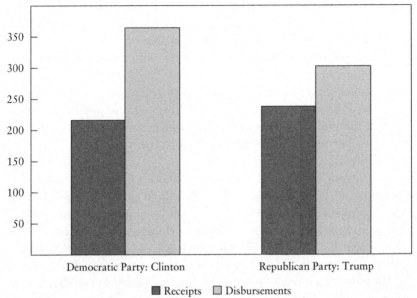

Democratic Party: Clinton   Republican Party: Trump

■ Receipts   □ Disbursements

Source: Based on disclosure filings reported to the Federal Election Commission (www.fec.gov/finance/disclosure
/candcmte_info.shtml), as of May 21, 2017.
Note: Receipts and disbursements include totals from candidate committees and joint fundraising committees.
Data are from August 2016 through December 2016 for the candidate committees and October 2016 through December 2016 for the joint fundraising committees. Transfers to affiliated committees and total contribution refunds
are deducted from the joint fundraising committee receipt totals to avoid double counting. Transfers to affiliated
committees and offsets to operating expenditures are deducted from the joint fundraising committee disbursement
totals to avoid double counting.

Widening the lens to encompass spending by party organizations and
outside groups as well as by the candidates themselves does not appreciably
change the overall picture. In the 2016 general election phase, Democratic
Party committees modestly outspent Republican committees on behalf
of the presidential candidates. However, both sides were well funded by
historical comparison, roughly matching or exceeding their expenditures
in the previous two presidential elections.

Democrats established a more significant edge over Republicans in outside expenditures by party-aligned Super PACs and other independent
entities, though this spending is of less strategic value to the candidates
than direct contributions, because it cannot be coordinated with the

campaigns under federal law (and because outside groups, unlike candidates, are not legally guaranteed the lowest available rates for television advertising). In combination, the Clinton campaign and Democratic-affiliated groups (including Super PACs) outspent the Trump campaign and Republican-associated organizations, but the two parties were not dramatically mismatched. Clinton and Democratic groups spent $395 million after October 1, compared to $300 million for Trump and Republican-affiliated groups. The victorious Republican side collectively spent about $499 million in 2016, or about $53 million less (in 2016 dollars) than the Democrats had spent en route to victory in 2012, while the losing Democratic side spent a total of $671 million in 2016—about $8 million less (in 2016 dollars) than the unsuccessful Republicans four years earlier.

The overall amount of disclosed money spent on the general election for president by the two major candidates, parties, and outside groups reached a plateau in 2016 after years of steady growth. The collective price tag for the 2016 general election totaled $1.17 billion, nearly identical to the $1.18 billion spent in 2012 ($1.23 billion in 2016 dollars). While the party organizations experienced a rise in expenditures between 2012 and 2016 (especially on the Democratic side), this increase was offset by the Clinton campaign's inability to match Obama's previous fundraising success and a lower amount of support for Trump by pro-Republican Super PACs in comparison to Romney four years earlier.

In retrospect, it is possible to identify four main reasons why news media coverage exaggerated the extent of the Democratic Party's financial edge in 2016. First, these analyses commonly included expenditures from the prenomination phase of the election when calculating the relative amount of money disbursed by the two candidates' campaign organizations. Because Clinton spent much more to defeat Bernie Sanders in the Democratic primaries than it cost Trump to capture the Republican nomination (see chapter 4), counting this money when making head-to-head comparisons between the two general election candidates overstated the magnitude of Clinton's advantage once the fall campaign began.

Second, a narrow focus on the candidates' own expenditures ignored the differentially effective role played by the national party committees in preparing for the 2016 race. Immediately after its narrow defeat in 2012, the Republican National Committee had made significant internal investments in its voter targeting and turnout infrastructure—a resource that paid dividends for the party four years later when the slow-to-organize

Trump campaign was able to rely on the RNC to mobilize voters in battleground states instead of spending money to build its own separate field operation.[9] The Democratic National Committee, in contrast, was hampered by years of relative neglect during the presidency of Barack Obama and encumbered by $24 million of debt and unpaid vendors from Obama's 2012 election.[10] The party also faced an unprecedented series of leaked controversial e-mails from WikiLeaks, which led to the abrupt midsummer departure of its national chairwoman.[11]

Third, premature declarations of overwhelming Democratic dominance in spending and television advertising during the early fall of 2016 did not account for a disproportionate growth in expenditures on the Republican side over the final few weeks of the campaign. After an initial wariness to weigh in on Trump's behalf, Republican-aligned Super PACs and 501(c)(4) groups became more active as Election Day approached. Trump's own campaign organization also followed a strategy of husbanding its financial resources until the last stage of the race. "We really backloaded all our media buys . . . in the last 12 or 14 days," recalled Trump digital director Brad Parscale.[12] From mid-October onward, Trump even pulled ahead of Clinton in weekly television ad expenditures.[13]

Finally, it seems likely that the real-time analysis of journalists and pundits was colored to some degree by their contemporary impressions of the relative strategic and tactical acumen of the two nominees and their top advisers. Because the Clinton campaign team was widely viewed as even keeled, professional, and risk averse, while the Trump side was judged as tempestuous and incompetent, analysts may have been predisposed to resolve any ambiguous evidence within the campaign finance data in Clinton's favor and to Trump's detriment. Clinton's lead in the polls throughout the duration of the race seemed only to confirm the (ultimately inaccurate) consensus view that she was not only far outpacing Trump in the crucial political task of fundraising but also surpassing him in the act of translating dollars into votes in battleground states.

The next three sections of the chapter provide a closer examination of spending in the 2016 general election by the major- and minor-party presidential candidates, by the major-party committees, and by Super PACs and 501(c)(4) organizations. It then concludes by considering whether the 2016 campaign is a unique case in modern American politics and what lessons will likely be drawn from the election by the leaders of both parties as they look ahead to 2020.

Fundraising and Spending by the Candidates

The widespread expectation that Hillary Clinton would be a far more successful fundraiser than Donald Trump was based on several assumptions. Clinton benefited from the existence of a donor network inherited from her 2008 presidential campaign, as well as from her husband, Bill Clinton—who was known as a particularly successful fundraiser during his two successful presidential bids in the 1990s. Both the Republican opposition and much of the political press suspected the Clintons of using the Clinton Foundation, a nonprofit organization founded by the family in 2001, to make contacts with wealthy interests that could provide her campaign with generous financial backing.[14] Her strongest supporters in the American electorate were thought to be middle-aged professionals with ample disposable income, and her predecessor Barack Obama had also built a large base of financial contributors within the Democratic Party during the 2008 and 2012 elections, attracting record-breaking donation levels that contradicted the traditional reputation of the party as habitually trailing its wealthier Republican opposition in the money race.

Trump, in contrast, was an outsider candidate who received little enthusiastic support from the normal Republican donor class that had funded the more conventional candidacies of Romney, McCain, and George W. Bush. Some commentators openly wondered if many citizens would be motivated to contribute funds to a famously moneyed businessman who had even suggested on several occasions that he would underwrite his campaign out of his own pocket. Despite these claims, Trump ultimately contributed $16.1 million of his own money to his campaign during the general election—representing about 6 percent of his total campaign expenditures after the national party conventions.[15] Moreover, the supposedly skeletal and amateurish Trump campaign organization, in combination with his multiple personal controversies and lagging position in the polls for most of the race, was widely thought to further depress his fundraising efforts.

Though Clinton outraised Trump over the postconvention period, Trump was able to fund what turned out to be a competitive campaign. He was especially adept at attracting small donations, raising more than $50 million in direct contributions from small donors via such strategies as using his website to sell his signature red baseball cap with the campaign's slogan, "Make America Great Again," printed above the brim. In total, 65 percent of Trump's total receipts from direct individual donations

Figure 5-2. *Individual Donors, 2016 Presidential General Election*

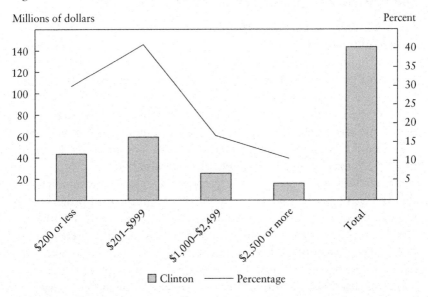

Millions of dollars

Percent

☐ Clinton ——— Percentage

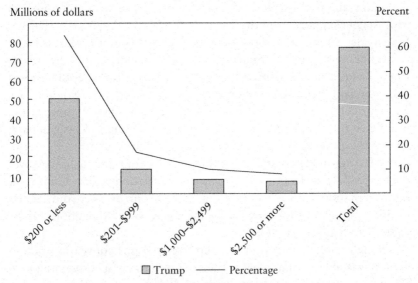

Millions of dollars

Percent

☐ Trump ——— Percentage

Source: Unitemized contributions based on disclosure filings reported to the Federal Election Commission (www.fec.gov/finance/disclosure/candcmte_info.shtml), as of May 7, 2017, and itemized contributions compiled from Federal Election Commission data (ftp://ftp.fec.gov/FEC/).

Note: Individual contributions are from August 2016 through December 2016.

during the general election came from contributions of $200 or less (see figure 5-2). When the primary and general election campaigns are combined and donations routed through joint fundraising committees are included, Trump's financial haul from donors giving $200 or less totaled $238.6 million—representing 58 percent of his campaign's total receipts and 69 percent of its individual contributions.[16]

In addition, Clinton was unable to replicate Obama's previous success in attracting small-dollar donations; while Obama had raised a total of nearly $300 million in contributions of under $200 in the 2012 general election, Clinton received just $43 million—representing only 30 percent of her total war chest. The large population of casual citizen donors who had previously helped to fuel Obama's two presidential bids, often by making multiple contributions of $10, $25, or $50 each, did not transfer their affections en masse to the Clinton campaign. This element of Obama's fundraising strategy was much better employed by Bernie Sanders, Clinton's chief rival in the Democratic primaries, who unexpectedly raised enough cash—including $218 million in online contributions alone—to compete with her during a long nomination battle despite little institutional backing from the traditional Democratic Party network.[17]

The extended Clinton-Sanders nomination race left both candidates and their most fervent supporters with hard feelings by the summer of 2016. Sanders waited a full month after the primary calendar ended before formally endorsing Clinton on July 12—a delay that signaled a reluctant, if not grudging, attitude on his part—and did not devote much energy during the general election campaign toward mobilizing his large bloc of enthusiastic backers on her behalf. Unlike Clinton in 2008 after losing the Democratic nomination race to Obama, Sanders chose not to share his valuable electronic list of financial contributors with his primary opponent or with a Democratic National Committee that he blamed for procedurally "rigging" the nomination process to Clinton's advantage.[18]

One of the most valuable benefits of fundraising by aggregating small-dollar donations is the low marginal cost. Most of these contributions are made online via credit card transactions, often in response to bulk e-mail communications or social media targeting of previous donors and other identified supporters. Internet-based fundraising requires resource investments from the campaign that, while substantial, are usually less than those required for fundraising strategies that are more traditional. In comparison, high-dollar donations are more likely to necessitate relatively intensive personal solicitation from campaign staff or even the candidate, as well as the organization of formal receptions and other fundraising events with sizable associated expenses.

Without an enthusiastic base of small donors, Clinton decided to spend much of the month after the Democratic convention courting support from wealthy contributors. "August represented her last, best chance to collect six-figure checks from 'high touch' donors—the kind of contributors who expected real face time for real money," reported Jonathan Allen and Amie Parnes, adding, "Hillary didn't love fundraising, but she understood that she relied more on the wealthiest donors than did the passion candidates like Sanders and Obama, who could use digital and grassroots fund-raising techniques to fill their coffers. And she knew that her contributors, in particular, needed a lot of hand-holding."[19]

Clinton's aggressive wooing of deep-pocketed donors allowed her to outraise Trump substantially in contributions at or near the maximum legally permitted amount of $2,700 but also cost her precious days away from the campaign trail as she devoted her attention to the personal courting of wealthy supporters in private settings. Clinton's fundraising schedule also inspired unfavorable media coverage portraying her as preferring the company of the rich to ordinary Americans, suggesting that she would be particularly sympathetic to the policy priorities of her upper-class contributors.[20] "People didn't think that she cared that much about small donors," explained Democratic consultant Mike Lux, adding, "Everyone sort of tied her to the big donors."[21]

The Trump campaign faced a very different set of challenges. Many of the Republican Party's top contributors and fundraisers did not back Trump during the primary campaign and remained resistant to his candidacy even after he captured the nomination—whether because they disagreed with his positions on issues like international trade, because they had no personal relationship with him or his top aides, or because they viewed him as a near-certain loser in the general election.[22] "People are very concerned about what a Trump presidency would mean," observed one top Republican fundraiser in May 2016, while another decried Trump's rhetorical attacks on wealthy donors as influence seekers: "Why would I give to someone who claims that the only reason I give is to get something?"[23] Some traditional Republican funders warmed to Trump as the general election campaign progressed, while others remained on the sidelines or even crossed party lines to support Clinton (this last group included Boston financier Seth Klarman and tech sector

CEO Meg Whitman, the 2010 Republican nominee for governor of California).[24]

But Trump was able to partially compensate for this lack of enthusiasm within established fundraising networks by attracting a level of small-dollar donations that was unprecedented for a presidential candidate of his party. The $50.3 million that Trump raised in contributions of $200 or less during the general election period easily surpassed the $33 million raised by Mitt Romney in 2012 and even bested Clinton's $43 million small-donor total. Though one Republican consultant's quip that Trump was "the Republican Obama in terms of online fundraising" was hyperbolic (Obama had raised $178 million in small-dollar donations during the 2008 general election and over $193 million in 2012),[25] Trump benefited from a committed set of individual supporters who provided his campaign with nearly two-thirds of its direct contributions.[26] Trump was especially buoyed by small-dollar donors during periods of the election season when he was struggling to be taken seriously as a candidate by political professionals and the news media. His campaign organization attracted over $12 million in unitemized (under $200) direct contributions during an otherwise rough August 2016, the month following the Republican convention, which was filled with multiple public controversies and culminated with the replacement of campaign manager Paul Manafort.[27] He also took in more than $8.5 million during a three-week period in October that coincided with the televised debates, all won by Clinton according to most pundits, as well as the release of the *Access Hollywood* video (see table 5-2).

Reflecting the historically exceptional personal unpopularity of both Clinton and Trump, minor-party presidential candidates proved more successful than usual at attracting financial contributions in 2016 (see table 5-3). Gary Johnson, the former Republican governor of New Mexico who was making his second consecutive bid for the presidency as the nominee of the Libertarian Party, raised more than $12 million in total—a significant increase from the $2.7 million in donations received by his campaign in 2012. Jill Stein of the Green Party, also a repeat candidate, increased her own fundraising totals by a factor of ten between 2012 and 2016—from $1.1 million to $11 million—while independent Evan McMullin, a former Republican congressional staffer and CIA officer running as an anti-Trump conservative, attracted $1.6 million in donations despite appearing on the presidential ballot in only eleven states.

Table 5-2. *Itemized and Unitemized Individual Contributions to Presidential Candidates, 2016 General Election*
Dollars

Candidates	August 1–31, 2016	September 1–30, 2016	October 1–19, 2016	October 20– November 28, 2016	November 29– December 31, 2016
Clinton					
Itemized	18,434,758	28,854,340	19,343,723	33,342,757	0
Unitemized	8,463,833	12,146,089	8,662,459	14,031,593	0
Total	26,898,591	41,000,429	28,006,182	47,374,350	0
Trump					
Itemized	6,251,140	7,648,802	4,923,306	7,715,292	187,996
Unitemized	12,105,618	9,705,600	8,559,015	18,507,721	1,412,120
Total	18,356,758	17,354,402	13,482,321	26,223,013	1,600,116

Source: Based on disclosure filings reported to the Federal Election Commission (www.fec.gov/finance/disclosure/candcmte _info.shtml), as of May 21, 2017.

Table 5-3. *Total Expenditures of Minor-Party Presidential Candidates, 2008–16*
Dollars

Year	Candidate	Party	Expenditures
2016	Gary Johnson	Libertarian	12,287,912
	Jill Stein	Green	11,090,196
	Evan McMullin	Independent	1,642,165
2012	Gary Johnson	Libertarian	2,752,658
	Jill Stein	Green	1,122,027
	Randall Terry	Independent	502,083
	Virgil Goode	Constitution	202,253
2008	Ralph Nader	Independent	4,490,579
	Bob Barr	Libertarian	1,405,825
	Chuck Baldwin	Constitution	244,115
	Cynthia McKinney	Green	240,463

Source: Federal Election Commission (http://classic.fec.gov/fecviewer/CandidateCommitteeDetail.do), as of October 9, 2017.

Fundraising and Spending by the Parties

The Democratic and Republican parties raise and spend substantial sums on behalf of the presidential nominees in every general election campaign. Between 1976 and 2004, when candidates participated in the federal public funding program and were thus barred from accepting individual contributions in the period between the national conventions and the

November election, citizens who wished to provide financial support to one side or the other were directed instead to the national party committees. Unlike the candidates, these committees could accept limited private donations to fund advertising or voter mobilization efforts on behalf of their nominees. Yet the decision by recent candidates to eschew the public financing system has not resulted in a corresponding decline in the ability of party organizations to attract significant direct donations of their own.

The 2016 election furthered a recent trend toward the increasing centrality of joint fundraising committees in the financing of presidential elections. Joint fundraising committees—often known colloquially as "victory funds"—allow candidates and party organizations to divide a single set of contributions among themselves according to a specific formula formalized by a written agreement between the participating candidates and party committees. These joint fundraising committees can accept donations from individuals above the legal ceiling that applies to direct contributions to candidates' own campaign organizations (which stood at $2,700 in the 2016 general election), with the excess amount collected by national and state party organizations up to the limits for individual contributions to party committees divided according to the agreed formula.

As table 5-1 demonstrates, joint fundraising committees had already become important components of presidential campaign finance by the 2012 election. But they were given a further boost before 2016 when the U.S. Supreme Court's 2014 decision in *McCutcheon* v. *Federal Election Commission* struck down the statutory limit on the aggregate amount of money that an individual contributor could donate to federal candidates and parties per two-year election cycle.[28] Before the Court's ruling, a single donor was prohibited from giving more than $48,600 in total to candidates for federal office, and more than $74,600 collectively to party organizations, during a single presidential or congressional election. The *McCutcheon* ruling affected joint fundraising committees by substantially increasing the size of the contributions that they could legally accept. A donor to the Hillary Victory Fund, a committee formed by the Clinton campaign in collaboration with the Democratic National Committee and forty state Democratic Party organizations, could write a single check for more than $400,000—with the bulk of the money winding up in the hands of the national party (since most of the funds ostensibly donated to the state parties were subsequently rerouted back to the DNC). The participation of state party committees in joint fundraising agreements is often criticized by campaign finance watchdogs for circumventing the extant limits on direct contributions to national party organizations, though the national parties also transfer funds to state parties in electoral battlegrounds such as Ohio and Florida to help finance voter mobilization efforts.[29] Former DNC chair Donna Brazile reported that the 2016 Clinton/DNC joint fundraising agreement required nearly all of the Hillary Victory Fund money to be transferred to the Clinton campaign.[30]

The fundraising success of the party organizations in 2016 was especially critical for the fortunes of the Trump campaign, which began the election at a severe disadvantage in the "ground game" of personally contacting and motivating supporters. Rather than build an extensive independent field operation, Trump largely relied on the existing infrastructure supplied by the Republican National Committee, which had invested heavily in improving its voter mobilization tools in the period leading up to the 2016 election. After the disappointing losses of 2012, RNC chair Reince Priebus initiated an internal postmortem analysis called the Growth and Opportunity Project (GOP). A well-publicized "autopsy report" produced and released publicly by the RNC included suggestions that party leaders moderate their positions on issues such as immigration reform in order to attract more minority and young voters (recommendations that were ultimately ignored once Trump captured the party nomination on an anti-immigration platform), as well as enumerating what turned out to be much more consequential plans to improve the party's data analysis and voter targeting capacity.

After the election was over, Trump deputy campaign manager David Bossie argued that "the RNC did an amazing job . . . they kept the same field staff . . . from the 2014 cycle, which is a huge advantage. Instead of having to . . . relearn the area . . . you had the same people organizing the same volunteers over again, and it was a tremendous asset. . . . The lengths [to] which we were [organized] in every one of these [battleground] states [were] more . . . than anybody understands." Brad Parscale, the Trump campaign's digital director, agreed, observing that, "The press was saying that we don't have a ground game because we don't have as many [campaign field] offices [as Clinton]. That was a dumb argument and one thing that the media got wrong about the ground game."[31]

The news media routinely focused on what appeared to be the limited tactical sophistication of Trump's own campaign, while ignoring the ways in which the RNC was well equipped to compensate for these deficiencies. At the same time, national Democrats' much-celebrated reputation for organizational effectiveness—earned during the Obama victories of

2008 and 2012, when the party combined noteworthy fundraising success with the application of innovative data analysis techniques to the task of voter mobilization—remained intact in 2016 despite growing signs of danger. Obama had not made the Democratic National Committee an institutional priority while he was president, preferring to focus on building his own personal organization, Organizing for America, and declining to engineer the removal of DNC chair Debbie Wasserman Schultz after the party suffered significant losses in the 2014 midterm elections. "Literally, no one [in the White House] cares enough [about the DNC] to get her out of there," observed one former Obama official in 2015.[32]

Even before the 2016 campaign began, Wasserman Schultz was accused by many Democratic critics of having failed to maintain the party's fundraising needs and organizational infrastructure.[33] She ultimately departed the DNC in July 2016 amid a controversy over whether the national party had favored Clinton over Sanders in the Democratic primaries—an internal fight that was further inflamed after the website WikiLeaks released illegally obtained electronic messages from DNC officials that were privately critical of Sanders and his staff.[34]

Both the midcampaign leadership turnover at the top of the DNC and the belief by many Sanders supporters that the nomination process had been unfairly stacked against their candidate undoubtedly damaged party fundraising efforts that were already hampered by Obama's years of inattention and Wasserman Schultz's difficulties. Clinton herself was sharply critical of the DNC after her loss in the election, claiming that upon being nominated she "inherit[ed] nothing from the Democratic Party. . . . It was bankrupt, it was on the verge of insolvency, its data was mediocre to poor, non-existent, wrong."[35]

While such remarks can appear to reflect a candidate's desire to deflect responsibility for a painful defeat, Clinton was not the only observer who found the national party apparatus to be inadequately prepared for the 2016 election. Democratic consultant Mike Lux later argued that "first Obama and then the Clinton campaign basically used the DNC as a bank rather than trying to build it as an institution, and that was a huge mistake. It left us without a genuine political or field operation that was independent."[36] The DNC continued to face serious fundraising difficulties in 2017 and 2018 despite the presence of an unpopular Trump presidency as a motivating force to encourage Democratic contributions, further confirming the existence of serious and enduring institutional deficiencies.[37] What looked to many outside observers during the 2016

campaign like a decided Democratic advantage in the relative organizational strength of the two partisan sides was thus at the very least a
much more evenly matched battle in reality.

Fundraising and Spending by Outside Groups

Super PACs and other outside groups legally prohibited from coordinating with candidate and party organizations had become key elements of
the campaign finance universe in the 2012 general election, and they
maintained this role in 2016 as well. As table 5-1 indicates, however, the
overall partisan tilt of these sources shifted substantially between the two
elections. In 2012, most outside spending favored Republican nominee
Mitt Romney, while in 2016 it was the Democratic side that achieved
greater fundraising success. Democrat-aligned Super PACs spent a total
of nearly $190 million promoting Clinton or attacking Trump in the
period after August 1, while pro-Republican Super PACs only spent about
$60 million in comparison (see table 5-4). Other independent groups,
such as 501(c)(4) organizations, only partially made up this difference,
spending another $55 million on Trump's behalf (or against Clinton) and
$25 million in support of Clinton (or against Trump). In sum, Clinton
enjoyed a net advantage of $78 million in outside spending after Octo-
ber 1, 2016. While substantial, this amount is much less than her advantage over the full cycle and does not account for Trump's countervailing
dominance in earned media coverage (see chapter 1).

As in 2012, the single most dominant independent group on the Democratic side was Priorities USA Action, a Super PAC founded in 2011 by
former aides to then president Obama to support his reelection bid. In
early 2014, Priorities USA Action publicly signaled its endorsement of
Hillary Clinton before Clinton herself had officially announced that she
would seek the presidency in 2016, proceeding to advocate her candidacy
in both the Democratic primaries and the general election.[38] Priorities
USA Action ultimately spent more than $95 million between August 1
and the November election, dwarfing the total expenditures of any other
single independent organization on either side (see table 5-5).

In contrast to the Democrats, the universe of Republican independent
groups evolved considerably between 2012 and 2016. American Crossroads, a Super PAC founded by former aides to George W. Bush, and its
associated 501(c)(4) organization Crossroads GPS, spent a combined $103
million on behalf of Mitt Romney in the 2012 general election, while the

Table 5-4. *Outside Money, 2016 Presidential General Election*[a]
Dollars

	Super PAC independent expenditures		Other group independent expenditures		Internal communication costs		Electioneering communication costs	
	For	Against	For	Against	For	Against	For	Against
Candidates								
Trump	4,089,460	91,116,030	22,601,393	15,014,755	787,171	101,199	0	0
Clinton	25,457,923	36,386,068	4,587,953	14,057,918	3,794,244	0	0	0

Source: Compiled from Federal Election Commission data.

a. Figures represent funds spent from October 1, 2016, through the end of the election. Expenditures reported as for or against a candidate are self-reported by the groups making the expenditures.

Super PAC Restore Our Future, organized by three former Romney staffers, spent over $60 million in total.[39] By 2016, however, neither group remained active in presidential politics. Restore Our Future became moribund after Romney's defeat, while American Crossroads devoted its attention in 2016 to U.S. Senate races (largely via its sister organizations One Nation and the Senate Leadership Fund) while ignoring the Trump-Clinton battle.[40]

Trump's distant relationship with most of the existing Republican big-donor network—especially brothers Charles and David Koch, normally generous funders of conservative political causes—prevented him from benefiting from Super PAC support to the degree that Romney had in 2012. However, he still received substantial and well-timed assistance from outside groups funded by large donations. Future 45, a Super PAC backed by businessmen Joe and Todd Ricketts and well-known Las Vegas magnates Sheldon and Miriam Adelson, spent nearly $25 million on an aggressive anti-Clinton television ad campaign across a number of battleground states.[41] The Ricketts family also created a parallel 501(c)(4) organization, 45Committee, which spent an additional $21.3 million on Trump's behalf; under federal law, the donors to this organization do not need to be publicly disclosed. The Super PAC Rebuilding America Now received $6 million in contributions from former World Wrestling Entertainment CEO and two-time U.S. Senate candidate Linda McMahon, who was later appointed by Trump to lead the federal Small Business Administration.[42] In addition, the Super PAC affiliated with the National Rifle Association allocated nearly $27 million on Trump's behalf (see table 5-5), surpassing the $18 million that it spent in favor of Romney in

Table 5-5. *Independent Expenditures by Top Groups, 2016 Presidential General Election*[a]

Dollars

Group	Total expenditures	Partisan classification[b]
Priorities USA Action	95,937,696	Democrat
National Rifle Association	26,939,632	Republican
Future 45	23,532,500	Republican
Great America PAC	17,724,650	Republican
NextGen Action Committee	15,592,484	Democrat
Rebuilding America Now	14,562,005	Republican
Women Vote!	10,755,162	Democrat
Lift Leading Illinois for Tomorrow	9,922,027	Democrat
United We Can	9,145,081	Democrat
League of Conservation Voters	8,293,560	Democrat
For Our Future	7,203,318	Democrat
Planned Parenthood Votes	4,901,170	Democrat
Working America / AFL-CIO / AFSCME	4,302,202	Democrat
Reform America Fund	4,058,735	Republican
Make America Number 1	4,033,799	Republican
RGA Right Direction PAC	3,957,491	Republican
Immigrant Voters Win PAC	3,524,722	Democrat
Black PAC	3,497,235	Democrat
Save America from Its Government	3,415,286	Republican
Stop Hillary PAC	3,133,127	Republican
iAmerica Action	2,995,005	Democrat
Fair Share Action	2,956,774	Democrat
House Majority PAC	2,761,357	Democrat
Service Employees International Union	2,222,147	Democrat
Purple PAC Inc.	2,066,513	Libertarian
Senate Majority PAC	2,051,868	Democrat
National Campaign	1,470,000	Republican
Local Voices	1,412,852	Democrat
El Super PAC Voto Latino	1,388,786	Democrat
Future in America Inc.	1,180,648	Republican
Alternative PAC	1,117,028	Libertarian

Source: Compiled from Federal Election Commission data (ftp://ftp.fec.gov/FEC), as of May 22, 2017.

a. Expenditures made in support of or in opposition to presidential candidates in excess of $1 million during the general election period beginning August 1, 2016. Expenditures for all national affiliates of an organization are combined, but expenditures for the state affiliates are excluded.

b. The partisan classifications were determined by the author based on each group's stated intent, the partisan orientation of their contributors (if data were available), and/or newspaper accounts of the group's activity.

Table 5-6. *Total Expenditures by Key Super PACs and 501(c)(4) Group Supporting Trump and Clinton, Pre-general to Year End, 2016*
Dollars

Organization	Support	October 1–December 31, 2016	Election total	% of Election total
Priorities USA Action	Clinton	54,347,583	190,710,175	28%
Future 45	Trump	21,209,614	24,970,329	85%
Rebuilding America Now	Trump	5,680,804	22,763,915	25%
Make America Number 1	Trump	4,098,197	19,659,532	21%
45Committee	Trump	21,339,015	21,339,015	100%

Note: All listed organizations are Super PACs except 45Committee, a 501(c)(4) group.

2012.[43] Republican consultant Michael Meyers recalled that the NRA was "huge," crediting them as " the most consistent . . . spenders for Trump that probably helped keep his [poll] numbers up through the spring and summer."[44]

Outside spending on the Republican side increased considerably in the final weeks of the campaign—after Washington conventional wisdom had prematurely declared Trump persona non grata in Republican donor circles and a sure loser in the presidential race. As table 5-6 shows, the Ricketts-controlled Super PAC Future 45 and 501(c)(4) group 45Committee heavily concentrated their spending in the last month before the election. When combined with nearly $10 million spent after October 1 by the pro-Trump Super PACs Rebuilding America Now and Make America Number 1, these expenditures nearly matched the $54 million spent over the same period by Priorities USA Action, the main pro-Clinton Super PAC. "There is a direct correlation between Trump's comeback in the closing month of the campaign and the money spent by Future 45 and 45Committee," noted Republican election attorney Charlie Spies, adding, "That [independent spending] really filled in the gap for the lack of television advertising on the [Trump] campaign side."[45]

Super PAC funding was dominated by large donations on both sides in 2016. As figure 5-3 illustrates, 73 percent of the total funds received by Priorities USA Action, and 76 percent of the funds raised by the four most prominent Trump-aligned Super PACs, came from benefactors contributing at least $1 million. Besides those already mentioned, these "megadonors" included financier Donald Sussman, television distributor Haim Saban, and investor George Soros in support of Clinton, and

Figure 5-3. *Individual Contributions to Super PACs, 2016 Presidential General Election*

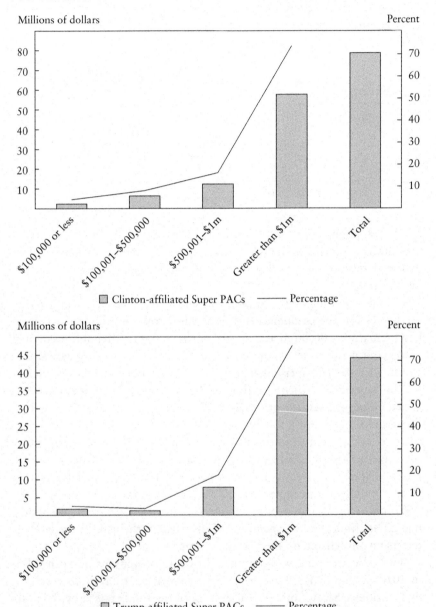

Millions of dollars   Percent

☐ Clinton-affiliated Super PACs   ——— Percentage

Millions of dollars   Percent

☐ Trump-affiliated Super PACs   ——— Percentage

Source: Compiled from Federal Election Commission data.

Note: Data from August 2016 through December 2016 included only major Super PACs directly affiliated with each candidate. Beginning January 1, 2015, the FEC categorized contributions from individuals using the calendar year-to-date amount for PACs. An individual who gave five separate $1,000 contributions would not be included in the $2,500 or less column because of the separate contributions being under that threshold but would instead be placed in the $2,501 to $5,000 column because of the aggregate amount (assuming the same calendar year).

venture capitalist Peter Thiel, poultry magnate Ron Cameron, and Home Depot cofounder Bernard Marcus on behalf of Trump.[46]

Was 2016 Unique?

The distinctive, and in some important respects unprecedented, nature of the Trump candidacy raises the question of whether the 2016 presidential election represents a unique deviation from historical norms. Trump's initial independence from most of the elected officials, interest group leaders, and high-dollar fundraisers who collectively constitute the extended Republican Party network was often interpreted during the campaign as a fatal disadvantage in an era of close-fought national elections that require each nominee to attract near-universal support from his or her own partisan team. But many Republican voters who expressed serious misgivings to pollsters about Trump's fitness for the presidency ultimately voted for him anyway, in part because their views of Clinton were even less favorable.[47] Moreover, the Republican National Committee and Republican-affiliated Super PACs contributed critical financial and organizational assets that not only represented a key example of cooperation between the institutional party and the Trump campaign but also effectively compensated for one of Trump's most notable weaknesses: a data analysis and field staff operation that was inferior to that of his Democratic opponent.

The money raised by candidates, parties, and outside groups that is not spent on the "ground game" mobilization of voters is overwhelmingly devoted to paid advertisements on television, radio, and—increasingly— the internet, but presidential elections receive so much attention from the news media that campaign ads are not the primary source of information about the candidates for most voters.[48] This was especially true in 2016, when perpetual fascination with the Trump candidacy dominated national affairs reporting for the entire length of the campaign. According to one estimate, the attention that Trump attracted from the national media across the full election cycle gave him the same visibility as $5 billion in paid advertising, compared to $3 billion for Clinton.[49]

Echoing similar complaints by Trump's opponents in the Republican primaries, Clinton advisers lamented their inability to attract press coverage for their own daily activities, criticizing the media for devoting attention to Trump-related controversies rather than their own candidate's substantive proposals. "There was a fundamental challenge when you are about to give a policy speech on the economy and, on MSNBC, CNN, and Fox News, there is an empty podium waiting for Donald Trump to come and speak. Or when the latest tweet [from Trump] changes what we're talking about on a given day," argued Clinton adviser Karen Finney after the election, to which another Clinton aide, Jennifer Palmieri, agreed, saying Trump "gets all the coverage and you [reporters] only covered her when she was talking about him."[50]

Despite these protestations, however, the Clinton campaign itself also spent much of the race discussing Trump's personal qualities. One frequently aired Clinton television spot portrayed Trump's character as representing a poor role model for the nation's children, while others compiled footage of his derogatory comments about women and suggested that he lacked the proper temperament to serve as commander-in-chief of the military. A postelection study by the Wesleyan Media Project found that Clinton's advertisements contained by far the lowest level of policy content of any general election presidential campaign since at least 2000, with only 25 percent of her paid spots focusing on policy (compared to 70 percent of Trump's ads).[51]

Concentrating her attacks on what appeared to be Trump's most vulnerable—though not ultimately disqualifying—attributes, Clinton largely abandoned the traditional Democratic appeal to middle-class economic interests that had been the primary theme of Barack Obama's victorious campaigns in 2008 and 2012, as well as her husband's successful candidacies in the 1990s. It is possible that this shift in emphasis cost the Democratic ticket crucial votes among white working-class residents of crucial battleground states such as Pennsylvania, Michigan, and Wisconsin, who proved highly receptive to the populist message of the Trump campaign. "The Democrats, as you look at them from a spending perspective in terms of overall spending and also how money was spent, simply didn't do a good enough job in making the persuasion case to persuadable voters," concluded Democratic consultant Guy Cecil.[52] Mike Podhorzer of the AFL-CIO also attributed Trump's victory to "a lot of white working-class voters who sat out 2012 [but who] voted for Trump in 2016."[53]

At the same time, retrospective analyses that present the outcome as reflecting Clinton's faults and strategic errors—though popular in the days and weeks after the election[54]—risk overlooking the ultimate effectiveness of a Trump campaign whose political competence was too readily dismissed during the race itself. For example, a Trump initiative code-named Project Alamo synthesized user data on social media platforms to target individualized messages to specific voting blocs. The project not only identified pro-Trump voters to mobilize on its own behalf but also directed content questioning Clinton's liberal credentials to key elements of the Democratic base, such as racial minorities and young women, in order to discourage them from supporting her.[55] Trump "was spending more on social media compared to us," observed Democratic consultant Mike Lux, while "we were spending most of our dollars on TV per usual."[56]

The Trump campaign's particular emphasis on reaching voters online may prove in retrospect to be a watershed moment in the evolution of campaign tactics. "We spent 50 percent of our money on digital and 50 percent on TV," recalled Trump's digital media director Brad Parscale after the election. "That's a groundbreaking thing for a presidential campaign. . . . Previously, most people spent 15 or 20 percent. We spent $100 million on digital and $100 million on TV. That's a pretty big change. . . . Facebook and Twitter helped us win this."[57]

But Trump received help from other sources as well. Over the course of the 2016 campaign, it became increasingly clear that foreign actors with ties to the Russian government were intervening in the American presidential election on behalf of the Trump-Pence ticket and Republican congressional candidates.[58] This activity included the theft and strategic public release of internal electronic communications of the Clinton campaign and Democratic National Committee (as mentioned earlier) as well as an ambitious social media offensive that encompassed false Twitter accounts and Facebook posts dedicated to the promotion of Trump and sharp attacks against Clinton.[59] Facebook acknowledged in October 2017 that it had identified 80,000 items of campaign content linked to Russian-operated accounts or targeted advertising placements, to which at least 126 million users had been exposed.[60] Whether and to what extent Trump campaign officials were aware of, or participated in, the clandestine foreign operations favoring their candidate in 2016 was the subject of serious investigations by several congressional committees and the U.S. Justice Department in the aftermath of the election.

Many of the mistakes made by the Clinton campaign arose from misplaced faith in the accuracy and potency of its technological and analytical tools, which led to such blunders as the misallocation of campaign resources to nonpivotal states such as Arizona and North Carolina rather than investing more heavily in Michigan and Wisconsin. It is possible that the Democratic side had become overconfident after the elections of 2008 and 2012, in which the party's supposed methodological advantage over its Republican opponents had been widely credited with contributing to Obama's two national victories.[61] In any event, neither party can count on maintaining a consistent edge in the technological arms race that characterizes contemporary campaigns, and the effectiveness of these tactics is often unclear except in retrospect.

Some of the changes that occurred in the campaign finance landscape between 2012 and 2016 may not endure in future elections. With Trump having proven his ability to win a national campaign, and with his administration pursuing a more ideologically conservative path than many observers had expected, it is likely that a potential Trump reelection bid in 2020 will receive more support from established Republican donor networks and party-aligned Super PACs than his 2016 candidacy did. At the same time, grassroots enthusiasm among Democrats for recapturing the White House after (presumably) four years of the Trump presidency will probably allow the next Democratic nominee to attract small-dollar donations much more easily than Hillary Clinton did in 2016. However, any future opponent will need to grapple with the same challenge that vexed the Clinton campaign: Trump's unmatched ability to capture and hold popular attention. For that reason, the money race in the next election may hold limited power to sway the behavior of voters who have already developed strong opinions—whether positive or negative—about the current resident of the White House.

Notes

1. Jonathan Martin, Maggie Haberman, and Alexander Burns, "Lewd Trump Tape Is Breaking Point for Many in G.O.P.," *New York Times*, October 9, 2016, p. A1.

2. Lindsey McPherson, "Ryan on Trump: Members Should 'Do What's Best for You,'" *Roll Call*, October 10, 2016; Glenn Thrush and Maggie Haberman, "G.O.P. Hopes a Chief of Staff Brings Stability," *New York Times*, January 18, 2017, p. A1.

3. Shane Goldmacher, "Hillary Clinton's 'Invisible Guiding Hand,'" *Politico*, September 7, 2016; Jake Miller, "Hillary Clinton Dwarfs Donald Trump in TV Ad Spending," *CBS News*, August 24, 2016.

4. Cathleen Decker, "Amid Trump Chaos, Republicans Seek a Path to Survival," *Los Angeles Times*, October 8, 2016; Alex Isenstadt and Glenn Thrush, "Turmoil Reigns Inside Trump Tower," *Politico*, October 8, 2016.

5. Fareed Zakaria, "Donald Trump Has Run the Worst Campaign in Modern History," *Washington Post*, October 27, 2016. See also, for example, David A. Graham, "There Is No Trump Campaign," *The Atlantic*, June 9, 2016; Marcus Wohlsen, "Trump's Ground Game Gamble Could Be a Fatal Mistake," *Wired*, October 9, 2016.

6. Anthony Corrado, "Financing the 2008 Presidential General Election," in *Financing the 2008 Election*, edited by David B. Magleby and Anthony Corrado (Brookings Institution, 2011), pp. 130–31, 159.

7. Leigh Ann Caldwell, "Clinton and Democrats Have Major Fundraising Advantage over Trump," *NBC News*, October 16, 2016.

8. Carrie Levine, Michael Beckel, and Dave Levinthal, "Donald Trump Dismantles Hillary Clinton's Big Money Machine," *Time*, November 8, 2016.

9. Ellen Bredenkoetter, chief data officer at the Republican National Committee, interview by David Magleby, May 30, 2017.

10. Donna Brazile, *Hacks: The Inside Story of the Break-ins and Breakdowns That Put Donald Trump in the White House* (New York: Crown, 2017), p. 33.

11. Jonathan Martin and Alan Rappeport, "Debbie Wasserman Schultz to Resign D.N.C. Post," *New York Times*, July 24, 2016.

12. Quoted in Institute of Politics, *Campaign for President: The Managers Look at 2016* (Lanham, Md.: Rowman and Littlefield, 2017), p. 237.

13. David Sherfinski, "Donald Trump Finally Outspending Hillary Clinton on TV Advertising," *Washington Times*, October 27, 2016.

14. Jennifer Rubin, "Foreign Donations to Foundation Raise Major Ethical Questions for Hillary Clinton," *Washington Post*, February 18, 2015.

15. Campaign Finance Institute, "President Trump, with RNC Help, Raised More Small Donor Money than President Obama," press release, February 21, 2017 (www.cfinst.org/Press/PReleases/17-02-21/President_Trump_with_RNC _Help_Raised_More_Small_Donor_Money_than_President_Obama_As _Much_As_Clinton_and_Sanders_Combined.aspx).

16. Ibid.

17. Revolution Messaging, "Bernie 2016" (https://revolutionmessaging.com /cases/bernie-2016).

18. Andrew McGill, "Will Bernie Sanders Give Away His Supporters' Data?" *The Atlantic*, June 10, 2016.

19. Jonathan Allen and Amie Parnes, *Shattered: Inside Hillary Clinton's Doomed Campaign* (New York: Crown, 2017), p. 303.

20. See, for example, Amy Chozick and Jonathan Martin, "Clinton Uses Access to Woo the Ultrarich," *New York Times*, September 4, 2016, p. A1; Joseph Weber, "Where's Hillary? Clinton off Campaign Trail as Trump Seeks

Comeback," *Fox News*, August 24, 2016; Courtney Weaver, "Fundraising Drive Underlines Clinton's Reliance on Wealthy Backers," *Financial Times*, August 31, 2016.

21. Mike Lux, cofounder and president of Progressive Strategies, LLC, and senior adviser for progressive outreach for the Democratic National Committee, interview by David Magleby, January 6, 2017.

22. Jonathan Martin and Alexander Burns, "Donors' Aversion to Trump Clouds Big Funding Goal," *New York Times*, May 22, 2016, p. A1.

23. David M. Drucker, "GOP Donors: Not a Dime for Trump," *Washington Examiner*, May 4, 2016.

24. Nicholas Confessore, "Trump Allies Seek Out Once-Scorned G.O.P. Donors," *New York Times*, August 8, 2016, p. A14.

25. Estimates of amounts raised from small donors vary, and some small donors became large donors as the election cycle unfolded. The estimates provided here for Obama in 2008 and 2012 are drawn from the Obama campaign. See David B. Magleby, Jay Goodliffe, and Joseph A. Olsen, *Who Donates in Campaigns? The Importance of Message, Messenger, Medium and Structure* (Cambridge University Press, 2018).

26. Shane Goldmacher, "Trump Shatters GOP Records with Small Donors," *Politico*, September 19, 2016.

27. Gregory Krieg, "Donald Trump's 27-Day Spiral: From Convention Bounce to Campaign Overhaul," CNN, August 18, 2016.

28. *McCutcheon* v. *Federal Election Commission*, 572 U.S. ___ (2014).

29. See Libby Watson, "How Political Megadonors Can Give Almost $500,000 with a Single Check," Sunlight Foundation, June 1, 2016; Kenneth P. Vogel and Isaac Arnsdorf, "DNC Sought to Hide Details of Clinton Funding Deal," *Politico*, July 26, 2016.

30. Brazile, *Hacks*, p. 96.

31. Quoted in Institute of Politics, *Campaign for President*, p. 235.

32. Sam Stein and Amanda Terkel, "The Hardest-Working Scapegoat in Washington," *Huffington Post*, September 29, 2015.

33. Edward-Isaac Devore, "Dems Turn on Wasserman Schultz," *Politico*, September 17, 2014.

34. Maquita Peters, "Leaked Democrat Emails Show Members Tried to Undercut Sanders," NPR, July 23, 2016. See also Donna Brazile, "Inside Hillary Clinton's Secret Takeover of the DNC," *Politico Magazine*, November 2, 2017.

35. MJ Lee, "Clinton Slams *New York Times*, DNC, Comey for Her Loss," CNN, May 31, 2017.

36. Lux, interview.

37. Gabriel Debenedetti, "DNC Fires Its Top Fundraiser," *Politico*, November 2, 2017.

38. Nicholas Confessore, "Huge 'Super PAC' Is Moving Early to Back Clinton," *New York Times*, January 24, 2014, p. A1.

39. Candice Nelson, "Financing the 2012 Presidential General Election," in *Financing the 2012 Election*, edited by David B. Magleby (Brookings, 2014), p. 136.

40. Matea Gold, "Here Comes the Republican Senate Super PAC Blitz," *Washington Post*, September 30, 2016; Josh Israel, "Karl Rove's Outside Spending Groups Migrate to New Dark Money Outfit," *ThinkProgress*, August 11, 2016.

41. Theodoric Meyer, "Ricketts, Adelson Super PAC Plans $25M Clinton Attack," *Politico*, November 4, 2016.

42. Matea Gold and Anu Narayanswamy, "Linda McMahon, Who Once Called Trump's Comments about Women 'Deplorable,' Gave $6 Million to Support His Bid," *Washington Post*, October 16, 2016.

43. Nelson, "Financing the 2012 Presidential General Election," p. 136.

44. Michael Meyers, president of TargetPoint, interview by David Magleby, June 1, 2017.

45. Charlie Spies, leader of Clark Hill's national political law practice, interview by David Magleby, February 10, 2017.

46. See Center for Responsive Politics, "2016 Top Donors to Outside Spending Groups" (www.opensecrets.org/outsidespending/summ.php?cycle=2016&disp=D&type=V&superonly=N).

47. See Tami Luhby, "Americans Held Their Noses to Vote for Trump," CNN, November 9, 2016.

48. Nelson W. Polsby, Aaron Wildavsky, Steven E. Schier, and David A. Hopkins, *Presidential Elections: Strategies and Structures of American Politics*, 14th ed. (Lanham, Md.: Rowman and Littlefield, 2016), chapter 3.

49. MediaQuant, "A Media Post-Mortem on the 2016 Presidential Election," November 14, 2016 (www.mediaquant.net/2016/11/a-media-post-mortem-on-the-2016-presidential-election/).

50. Quoted in Institute of Politics, *Campaign for President*, p. 181.

51. Erika Franklin Fowler, Travis N. Ridout, and Michael M. Franz, "Political Advertising in 2016: The Presidential Election as Outlier?" *The Forum* 14, no. 4 (2016).

52. Guy Cecil, chief strategist at Priorities USA Action, interview by David Magleby, March 15, 2017.

53. Mike Podhorzer, political director at AFL-CIO, interview by David Magleby, March 17, 2017.

54. For example, Allen and Parnes, *Shattered*.

55. Joshua Green and Sasha Issenberg, "Inside the Trump Bunker, with Days to Go," Bloomberg, October 27, 2016.

56. Lux, interview.

57. Quoted in Institute of Politics, *Campaign for President*, p. 228.

58. VICE, "US Officials Say They Have Proof Russia Provided WikiLeaks with Hacked DNC Emails," VICE, January 5, 2017 (www.vice.com/en_nz /article/vvdwb4/us-officials-say-they-have-proof-russia-provided-wikileaks -with-hacked-dnc-emails-vgtrn).

59. Mike Isaac and Daisuke Wakabayashi, "Russian Influence Reached 126 Million through Facebook Alone," *New York Times*, October 30, 2017.

60. Issie Lapowsky, "Eight Revealing Moments from the Second Day of Russia Hearings," *Wired*, November 1, 2017.

61. See, for example, Sasha Issenberg, *The Victory Lab: The Secret Science of Winning Campaigns* (New York: Crown, 2012).

SIX

Financing the 2016 Congressional Election

MOLLY E. REYNOLDS AND
RICHARD L. HALL

Congress may be the first branch of government, but in presidential election years, it can be overshadowed by what is happening at the top of the ticket. In the era of the "perpetual campaign," where both parties reasonably believe they might control one or both chambers of the institution after the next election, the stakes for congressional elections are high.[1] Investments by individuals, parties, and outside groups reflect this attitude, and 2016 was no exception. The 2016 contest saw the parties navigating a continually changing legal architecture of the campaign finance system; new legal developments were not, however, as sizable as the emergence of Super PACs immediately after the U.S. Supreme Court's decision in *Citizens United* v. *Federal Election Commission*.[2] In many other ways, patterns in raising funds and spending them followed recent trends, including spending gaps that favored incumbents over challengers, growing levels of outside spending in congressional races, and strategic allocations of funds both by members of Congress and by party congressional campaign committees as both parties pursued the ultimate goal of majority control of the House and Senate.

2016: The Broader Political Context

In the Senate, the distribution of seats being contested in 2016 was favorable to the Democrats. Of the thirty-four seats up for reelection, Democrats held only ten, with the remaining twenty-four in Republican hands. Only two of the Democratic seats—those held by Senator Michael Bennet (D-Colo.) and by retiring senator Harry Reid (D-Nev.)—were thought to be potentially competitive at the start of the cycle. On the Republican side, meanwhile, seven seats were in states (Florida, Illinois, Iowa, New Hampshire, Ohio, Pennsylvania, and Wisconsin) won by President Barack Obama in both 2008 and 2012. As early as 2015, a narrative about the favorability of the 2016 Senate map began to emerge in the national press. In January, the *Washington Post* called the Senate map "the Democrats' friend in the 2016 cycle,"[3] and other outlets followed suit, pronouncing the Democrats' chances of taking back the Senate majority "great"[4] and referring to Republicans' task as "daunting."[5] Of the eleven competitive Senate races, nine were in states with at least one of the nation's top twenty-five media markets, and eight were in presidential swing states. Given this distribution of seats across media markets, party-connected groups were faced with trade-offs. Democrats, for example, decided that investing in Indiana, North Carolina, and Missouri instead of Florida, with its expensive media markets, was a better allocation of resources.[6] Republicans also faced a similar dilemma, referring to Florida, with its eleven media markets, as "like its own country."[7] In addition, Democrats, according to 2016 Democratic Senatorial Campaign Committee (DSCC) deputy executive director Preston Elliot, "went into this cycle knowing that we were going to play in more states where the presidential [race] was going to be competitive."[8] This overlap had both advantages and disadvantages. On the plus side, the common areas of focus meant that much of the party's field operation needs could be met by the presidential campaign, leaving the DSCC with more money to spend on television ads. At the same time, the presence of the Clinton campaign on the airwaves in those states drove up the cost of buying time for the Senate campaigns and the DSCC's independent TV ads.[9]

In the House, meanwhile, the probability of Democrats retaking control was thought to be small at the outset, with the party needing to pick up thirty seats to gain a majority. Certainly, the large losses the party had sustained in both 2010 and 2014 had left them with room for improvement.[10] Republican-leaning voters, however, with their tendency to live in suburbs and rural areas, are distributed more evenly across congressional districts than Democratic voters are. These patterns, when combined with redistricting decisions made following the 2000 and 2010 censuses, have advantaged Republican House candidates in recent congressional elections.[11] As with Senate races, the geographic distribution of these seats forced the parties to make strategic choices about where to send their resources. Roughly 45 percent of competitive House races (twenty-six of fifty-seven) were in the nation's top twenty-five media markets, and approximately the same share (twenty-three of fifty-seven) were in presidential swing states. In many cases, these categories did not overlap. There were fifteen races, for example, in expensive media markets that, according to political analyst Nathan Gonzales, "weren't in presidential battlegrounds . . . you had a half dozen races in New York, you had three in Minnesota."[12] Indeed, 2016 National Republican Congressional Committee (NRCC) executive director Rob Simms identified the existence of closely contested races in New York and California— two solidly Democratic states with virtually no presidential campaign activity—as a consideration in party decision making.[13]

While these structural dynamics certainly shape expectations about what will happen in a given year's congressional races, the increasing nationalization of House and Senate contests means that, in presidential years, what is happening at the top of the ticket also matters a great deal. By 2012, for example, party loyalty rates—that is, the share of voters supporting their party's candidate for president, House, and Senate—were at their highest levels since 1956; ticket splitting, meanwhile, was at near record lows in 2012.[14] Entering the 2016 cycle, many observers were bullish on Democrats' chances of retaining control of the White House.[15] At the same time, the fundamentals of the presidential contest as identified by a long literature in political science—including national economic performance, the incumbent president's approval rating, and the fact that Democrats were seeking a third consecutive term in the White House—did not strongly favor the party and perhaps weakly advantaged Republicans.[16]

It was in this environment that both parties began to recruit candidates to run in 2016. Research by Jason Roberts, Jacob Smith, and Sarah Treul suggests that, even in an era of increased partisan competition for control of the House, most potentially competitive seats do not attract high-quality challengers.[17] In mid-2015, Democrats were still without strong candidates in many competitive districts,[18] and while the party did eventually draw a more experienced set of candidates in open seat races than the Republicans did, a majority of these candidates lacked previous elected office experience. According to the Brookings Institution's Primaries Project data, there were forty-three open House seats with primaries in at least one of the major parties in 2016,[19] and approximately 48 percent of the winning Democratic candidates in these races had previously held office as compared to roughly 37 percent of winning Republicans.[20]

The emergence of Donald Trump as a serious, and eventually successful, contender for the Republican presidential nomination also affected expectations about congressional races. By February 2016, Democrats began to express optimism that "Republicans will scare away moderate and independent voters if Donald Trump . . . tops the ticket,"[21] and as the year wore on, congressional campaigns in both parties began to prepare explicitly for the possibility that voters would split their tickets for Clinton and Republican congressional candidates. In Ohio, for example, Senator Rob Portman's campaign distributed literature touting his union endorsements at Clinton rallies.[22] Research by Robert Erickson suggests that well-informed voters do engage in such voting behavior, casting their ballots for congressional candidates of the opposite party that they expect to win the presidency in an act of "anticipatory balancing."[23]

A Three-Legged Stool: The Infrastructure of Congressional Campaign Finance

Alongside this broader political context in 2016 sat the basic infrastructure of the campaign finance system, which one interview subject referred to as a "three-legged stool" comprised of candidate-raised funds, party money, and resources from outside groups.[24] The first category represents money collected by individual candidates into their principal campaign committees (PCCs) from a variety of sources. In the House, the average general election candidate in a majority-party contested race for an open seat drew more funds than either incumbents or challengers; in the Senate, however, the average raised by an incumbent exceeded both challengers and open seat candidates. (This likely reflects the fact that of the eleven competitive Senate races, only two were open seats.) In terms of the source of funds, for the average candidate in either chamber, a majority of these funds still come from individual contributors. As table 6-1 shows, the only exception is for House incumbents, who receive, on average, roughly the same amount from individuals and from political action committees (PACs). This pattern does not hold in the Senate, where the average incumbent received roughly 2.5 times more from individuals than from PACs. In both chambers, candidates in open seat

Table 6-1. *Average Source of House and Senate Candidates' Receipts, 2016 Congressional Elections*[a]

Hundreds of thousands of dollars

	House			Senate		
	Incumbents	Challengers	Open	Incumbents	Challengers	Open
Party committees	0.1	0.1	0.3	5.6	3.0	5.2
Candidates	0.1	0.5	4.1	0.2	2.9	1.1
PACs	8.0	0.7	2.8	23.5	3.6	10.1
Individuals	7.9	3.1	9.8	61.8	48.0	71.4
Total	16.1	4.4	17.0	91.1	57.5	87.8

Sources: Compiled from Federal Election Commission data (ftp://ftp.fec.gov/FEC/2016/); Politico, "2016 House Election Results" (www.politico.com/2016-election/results/map/house); Politico, "2016 Senate Election Results" (www.politico.com/2016-election/results/map/senate).

a. Figures represent average receipts for general election candidates in major-party contested races. Party-committee contributions include coordinated expenditures. Candidate contributions include loans candidates made to their own campaigns.

races drew more individual contributions than either incumbents or challengers did.

While individuals make up the majority of contributors for most candidates, other sources of funds to PCCs are also important. The first row of table 6-1 reflects the average contribution from the parties' congressional campaign committees (CCCs): the Democratic Congressional Campaign Committee (DCCC), the National Republican Congressional Committee (NRCC), the Democratic Senatorial Campaign Committee (DSCC), and the National Republican Senatorial Committee (NRSC). There are limits, however, on the amount that these entities can contribute directly to candidates' campaigns.

Row three also demonstrates that political action committees (PACs) represent a significant source of funds, especially for House incumbents. As in previous election cycles, a majority of these funds came from PACs associated with either corporate entities or trade or membership groups.[25] This figure includes contributions from leadership PACs, which are established by individual House members and senators to raise funds and then reallocate them to their colleagues. While originally associated primarily with members of the House and Senate leadership, an increasing number of rank-and-file legislators also now sponsor leadership PACs, seeing them as an additional tool to help them achieve both personal and collective party goals.[26] As table 6-2 indicates, in 2016, contributions

Table 6-2. *Party-Connected Contributions, 2016 Congressional Elections*[a]
Dollars

	House		Senate	
	Democrats	*Republicans*	*Democrats*	*Republicans*
Leadership PACs	9,324,462	18,381,224	6,021,626	7,788,055
Candidates	3,422,342	3,912,804	206,193	2,448,326
Congressional retirees and members not up for reelection	425,699	523,741	127,785	194,269
PACS not sponsored by federal politician	25,150	286,288	11,300	180,850
Total	13,197,653	23,104,057	6,366,904	10,611,500

Sources: Compiled from data from Federal Election Commission (ftp://ftp.fec.gov/FEC/2016/) and Center for Responsive Politics (www.opensecrets.org/pacs/industry.php?txt=Q03&cycle=2016).

a. Figures are for contributions from leadership PACs, congressional candidates, retired members, members of Congress not up for reelection in 2016, and PACs sponsored by nonfederal politicians to candidates in all congressional elections, including those in primaries, runoffs, and uncontested races.

from leadership PACs comprised the largest source of non-CCC, party-connected funds amassed by candidates for both Democrats and Republicans and in both the House and Senate.

As in 2012 and 2014, House Republicans gave more than their Democratic colleagues through their leadership PACs; the former's advantage over the latter was slightly larger in 2016 than in 2012. The other patterns in the lower chamber—small GOP advantages in contributions by candidates, retirees, and members not running for reelection, and a large Republican lead in donations from the PACs of nonfederal politicians—are also similar to those present in 2012. On the Senate side, however, there are several notable differences. In 2012, Senate Democrats enjoyed a small advantage in leadership PAC giving over Republicans (approximately $300,000). In 2016, however, the GOP led the Democrats, with an advantage of roughly $1.8 million. A similar difference across the two cycles is also present for contributions from retirees and from members not running for reelection. In 2012, Senate Democrats received roughly three times as many of these contributions as their Republican peers, but in 2016, Republicans garnered approximately one and a half times as many. Together, these shifts gave congressional Republicans a roughly $14 million advantage over Democrats across the two chambers in 2016, as compared to their $10 million lead in 2012,[27] but this gap is erased by party-committee independent expenditures, as discussed later in this chapter.

Figure 6-1. *Party Contributions, Coordinated Expenditures, and Independent Expenditures, 2016 Congressional Elections*

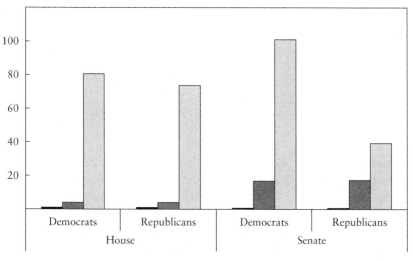

Millions of dollars

■ Contributions   ■ Coordinated expenditures   ☐ Independent expenditures

Source: Compiled from Federal Election Commission data (www.fec.gov/files/bulk-downloads/index.html).
Note: Includes expenditures by national, state, and local political parties.

While the CCCs can and do give directly to campaigns, a sizable majority of their activity comes in a different form, which comprises the second leg of the stool: party independent expenditures, or spending on things such as TV ads and direct mail that advocate for the election or defeat of a specific candidate but are done independently of his or her campaign. Unlike contributions and coordinated expenditures, CCCs can engage in unlimited expenditures on behalf of a candidate. As figure 6-1 shows, these kinds of independent expenditures make up a sizable majority of spending by parties in congressional elections. There were thirty-two House races that saw more than $1 million in party independent expenditures. In the Senate, meanwhile, there were eight such races—Florida, Indiana, Missouri, Nevada, New Hampshire, North Carolina, Ohio, and Pennsylvania—with an average of $17.3 million spent in each.

The third and final leg of the stool is nonparty outside money, which, as table 6-3 shows and as discussed in chapters 1 and 2, takes a number of forms. Within each of these groups, there are several important

Table 6-3. *Outside Spending in Congressional Races, Including Party Independent Expenditures, 2015–16*

Dollars

Super PACs—independent expenditures	487,708,485
501(c)—independent expenditures	83,248,606
Conventional PACs—independent expenditures	54,780,384
Hybrid PACs—independent expenditures	13,396,550
Internal communications	5,332,841
Party committees—independent expenditures	294,330,169
Total	938,797,035

Source: Compiled from Federal Election Commission data (ftp://ftp.fec.gov/FEC/2016/).

distinctions to note. Some Super PACs—which can raise unlimited sums but engage only in independent expenditures—are affiliated with existing interest groups; a super PAC associated with the Club for Growth, a conservative advocacy group, for example, raised approximately $20 million in the 2016 cycle.[28] Since their emergence in 2010, Super PAC involvement in congressional elections has continued to grow; 2016 saw roughly 40 percent more Super PAC spending than 2014. Money from these groups also represented a greater share of outside spending in 2016 than ever before. In 2012—the first full cycle in which Super PACs were involved—approximately half of all outside spending in congressional races came from Super PACs. By 2014, that share had increased to roughly two-thirds, and in 2016, it grew again, to approximately three-quarters.

For congressional races, however, two other types of Super PACs are particularly important. First are a set of Super PACs closely aligned with each of the parties in the House and Senate. On the Democratic side, these groups are the Senate Majority PAC (SMP) and the House Majority PAC (HMP), while on the Republican side they are the Senate Leadership Fund (SLF) and the Congressional Leadership Fund (CLF). Just as overall Super PAC spending in congressional races has increased since 2012, investments by these types of groups have grown over time—though not necessarily at rates comparable to the aggregate growth in Super PAC expenditures (see chapter 3). Between 2012 and 2016, the total spent by Super PACs on congressional elections roughly doubled, as did spending by the SMP. Expenditures by the HMP grew more slowly, by approximately 60 percent, while spending by the CLF increased more sharply; it was roughly three times higher in 2016 than in 2012.

Table 6-4. *Major Party-Aligned Super PACs, 2015–16 Congressional Elections*

Dollars

Super PAC	Party	Independent expenditures
Senate Leadership Fund	Republican	85,994,270
Senate Majority PAC	Democrat	75,413,426
House Majority PAC	Democrat	47,420,121
Congressional Leadership Fund	Republican	40,125,691

Source: Compiled from Federal Election Commission data (ftp://ftp.fec.gov/FEC/2016/).

In contrast to these unified, party-aligned groups sit candidate-specific Super PACs that focus on a single race. Since the emergence of Super PACs following the Supreme Court's decision in *Citizens United* v. *Federal Election Committee*, Democrats have tended to focus on a single party Super PAC for their efforts, especially in the Senate. Doing so increases message discipline, allows the party to take advantage of economies of scale,[29] eliminates the possibility of organizational redundancies,[30] and reduces the chances that the candidate engages in illegal coordination with his or her candidate-specific Super PAC.[31] Senate Republicans, meanwhile, having not had an aligned Super PAC as recently as the end of the 2014 cycle,[32] entered the 2016 cycle attempting to change course in their use of the tool. Indeed, Senate Majority Leader Mitch McConnell (R-Ky.) asked his members not to set up their own groups.[33] While some Republican Senate candidates maintained their own Super PACs in 2016—Super PACs supporting Senators Rob Portman (R-Ohio) and Marco Rubio (R-Fla.) raised roughly $10 million and $5 million, respectively.[34] More broadly, the Super PACs aligned with Senate Republicans ultimately outraised their Democratic counterparts by $11 million in 2016, but with much of the spending coming late in the cycle (see chapter 3). The emergence of the SLF in 2016, moreover, also helped shift the center of gravity in congressional Super PAC spending toward resources over which congressional party leaders had substantial control. As table 6-4 indicates, these groups were responsible for roughly half of all Super PAC congressional election independent expenditures in the 2016 cycle. In 2014, the SMP, HMP, and CLF accounted for approximately a quarter of the total, while in 2012 it was nearly one-third.

Now that Senate Republicans have established a leadership-connected Super PAC, the parties are relatively similar in their approaches to the tool. There are, however, important differences in the types of outside groups that tend to ally themselves with each party. On the Democratic side, for example, the coalition of outside groups includes a number of membership groups with large bases of mass supporters. This is often seen as an advantage for the party, but as Democrats have worked to unite their allied outside groups together under a single umbrella, a group named America Votes, since 2003, the party has had to determine which parts of the coalition are most helpful to which candidates (see chapter 3).[35] Strong support from unions and groups like the League of Conservation Voters may be more helpful for centrist Democrats such as Senators Jon Tester (D-Mont.) and Heidi Heitkamp (D-N.Dak.), for example, while Democrats who are more liberal may benefit more from outside spending by groups such as EMILY's List.[36]

Each leg of the stool had the potential to change or to continue an existing evolution in important ways between 2012 and 2016. First, 2016 was the second presidential contest conducted after the *Citizens United* decision, which led to a notable increase in outside spending by nonparty entities in congressional races.[37] In addition, the 2016 election was the first presidential contest after the Supreme Court's decision in *McCutcheon* v. *Federal Election Committee*, which abolished aggregate individual limits on federal political giving.[38] Post-*McCutcheon*, the amount an individual donor may give to a single candidate's committee, party, or PAC remains restricted, but the total an individual can donate is no longer capped. Joint fundraising committees (JFCs), or entities that allow contributors to write a single check that then gets disbursed to a number of different individual committees representing candidates and/or the party, were one major area of focus during the Supreme Court's oral arguments.[39] The change made by *McCutcheon* allows JFCs to represent many more individual candidate or party committees, since aggregate limits are no longer in place, allowing them to function as tools for party leaders to amass a significant pool of resources separate from those collected by outside groups in the form of Super PACs.[40] Speaker of the House Paul Ryan (R-Wis.), for example, has a JFC that funnels contributions to his PCC, the NRCC, and his leadership PAC.[41] Senate Minority Leader Chuck Schumer (D-N.Y.), meanwhile, sponsored a JFC in 2016 that benefited not only his PCC, his leadership PAC, and the DSCC but also fourteen individual Democratic Senate candidates across the country.[42] JFCs are hardly a new phenomenon; one Republican interviewee described their use in 2016 as "more a continuation of what we've been doing."[43] In addition, on the Democratic side, 2016

DSCC executive director Tom Lopach explained that the number of individual donors who participate at a level such that their behavior would be changed by the advent of more JFCs is relatively small.[44] At the same time, 2016 NRCC executive director Rob Simms explained that JFCs did make it easier to attract large donors who prioritize the Republican National Committee (RNC) or the NRSC by giving them opportunities to facilitate giving to multiple entities at once.[45]

In addition to changes ushered in by the Supreme Court, legislation passed by Congress in December 2014 (known as the CRomnibus because it contained elements of a continuing resolution and those of an omnibus appropriations bill) also created new opportunities for giving to the parties in 2016 (see chapter 2 and 7). The provision created three new kinds of party accounts: a convention committee, a building committee, and a recount/legal committee. The first could only be set up by the Democratic and Republican national committees (to pay for presidential nominating conventions), but the latter two new entities could be established by the party committees as well as by their House and Senate campaign arms. As a result, a donor looking to give to a particular party now had up to seven additional outlets for doing so.[46] While these new vehicles for giving had the potential to increase the power of the parties relative to outside groups,[47] the parties entered the 2016 cycle needing to educate their donors about these new accounts and to learn exactly how they would operate.[48]

For House Republicans, meanwhile, much of the 2016 campaign was contested under different party leadership in the chamber than the previous four elections had been. Then Speaker of the House John Boehner (R-Ohio) announced in September 2015 that he would be resigning his post, with current Speaker Paul Ryan (R-Wis.) elected to succeed him. This change had implications for the party's fundraising operation. Boehner's donor base reflected his career in the chamber, having been built over time as Boehner himself rose through the ranks to become Speaker, explained 2016 NRCC executive director Rob Simms. Ryan, meanwhile, had access to a different kind of donor base thanks to his appearance on the Republican presidential ticket in 2012. This included high-dollar donors who had not traditionally given to House races, perhaps because of the lack of a personal connection to the lower chamber. With Ryan at the helm, however, Simms explained, "he was able to tap into a Romney-Ryan presidential fundraising network that until that time had not been engaged in House races relatively speaking."[49]

Money in 2016: Where Did It Come From?

As shown in table 6-1, on average, House challengers and open seat candidates received the majority of their funds in 2016 from individual contributors. Incumbents, meanwhile, garnered roughly equivalent shares on average from individual donations and from PACs. This distribution is similar to that for various types of House candidates in 2012.[50] The only exception to this trend is that the average contribution by an open seat House candidate to his or her own campaign was roughly three times larger in 2016 than in 2012, a growth driven by the presence of four open seat candidates who gave more than $3 million to their own campaigns.[51] In the Senate, meanwhile, the average 2016 candidate also received the majority of their funds from individuals, with incumbents again garnering more support from PACs than challengers or open seat candidates did. Senate challengers and candidates in open seat contests similarly relied heavily on individual contributions in 2012, but in 2016 incumbents saw more contributions from the party committees. In 2012, CCC contributions to Senate incumbents were negligible, while in 2016 the typical incumbent saw $560,000 from the DSCC or the NRSC. There are a number of possible explanations for this difference, including two factors related to coordinated expenditures. First, the NRSC has historically favored incumbents in its coordinated expenditures,[52] and, as discussed, there were nine vulnerable Republican incumbents in 2016 as opposed to just two in 2012; there were simply more races in which the NRSC would be expected to get involved in 2016. Second, the Senate-coordinated party expenditure limits vary across states, based, in part, on the size of the state's voting-age population. The states in which incumbents faced competitive races in 2016 were generally more populous than those with similar contests in 2012, allowing for greater levels of party spending under the law.[53]

When the CCCs are allocating these funds in the form of direct contributions and coordinated expenditures, they would be expected to do so in a way that maximizes the chances that their party gains or holds the majority in their respective chambers; this has traditionally meant a focus on competitive races and on potentially vulnerable incumbents.[54] For most of the CCCs in 2016, this pattern held true. The NRCC made direct contributions to twenty-two candidates, eighteen of whom were in competitive races; for the DSCC and the NRSC, the comparable figures were ten of thirteen and eleven of thirteen, respectively. The DCCC, meanwhile, took a slightly different approach, contributing some amount directly to 108 candidates, only 45 of whom were in competitive races. The Democratic House candidates in competitive races did receive more, on average, from the DCCC than their peers in safer seats (approximately $6,900 vs. roughly $1,000), and all five candidates to whom the DCCC gave the maximum ($10,000) were in competitive races. Of the candidates in safe districts to which the DCCC gave, nearly all—58 of 63—were incumbents, suggesting that the Democrats' House arm also saw value in rewarding some of its nonvulnerable incumbents.

In many cases, these funds that the CCCs are allocating to campaigns are raised by incumbent members themselves. Candidates may transfer unlimited amounts from their PCCs to the party campaign arms, though leadership PAC contributions are limited (to $15,000 per year in 2015–16).[55] On the House side, this practice dates to the 1990s, when both the DCCC and NRCC began formal programs to raise funds from their members;[56] both committees continue to have a dues structure, where members are expected to contribute certain amounts based on their position within the party.[57] On the Republican side, 165 of the conference's 247 members contributed to the NRCC, giving an average of $200,735. Democrats had a higher participation rate—160 of the caucus's 188 members—but a lower average contribution, $180,149.

On the Senate side, meanwhile, Democrats have traditionally been more successful at getting incumbent party members to give directly to the DSCC than Republicans have to the NRSC; in 2008, for example, Democrats gave $20.6 million, while Republicans gave only $2.8 million.[58] In 2016, twenty-four of the forty-six Democratic incumbents gave an average of $404,000 to the DSCC from their PCCs, while eighteen of fifty-four Republican incumbents contributed an average of $196,000 to the NRSC from their PCCs.[59] In both parties, the largest contributions were from party leaders. On the Democratic side, now minority leader Schumer ($3 million) and Conference Secretary Patty Murray (D-Wash.) ($1.3 million) led the way. On the Republican side, Conference Chair John Thune (R-S.Dak.) topped the Republicans' list—thanks, in part, to a personal appeal from McConnell that elicited some unusually generous behavior from his colleagues. As the *Cook Political Report*'s Jennifer Duffy explained:

McConnell got up at lunch on a Tuesday and said, "This matters. This is where we are. This is how far behind Democrats we are with money. These are the races we need to spend in." So he went around the room. There's an article about this and I loved it because I think even Ted Cruz gave out money. I think Mike Lee probably held out. Because if you were in cycle, I don't think he leaned on you as hard as he did if you were out of cycle. . . . So he went through two or three people who gave him $100,000 apiece. He got to John Thune, who said, "I will give you two." McConnell said, "$200,000. Thank you. That's very nice." He said, "No, I will give you $2 million."[60]

Contributions from their PCCs to the party campaign committees are not the only way that incumbent members of Congress can engage in party-connected giving; indeed, on the Republican side, the NRCC emphasizes joint events that benefit both a member and the committee, as well as having members give directly to candidates in addition to contributions directly to the NRCC.[61] Members can also give to other candidates directly, either from their own PCCs or from their leadership PACs. Approximately 65 percent of House members did the former, while roughly 70 percent did the latter. The maximum size of a donation from one member's PCC to another's is lower ($2,000) than the largest possible contribution from a member's leadership PAC to a candidate's PCC ($5,000), and the average member-to-member giving of each type reflects this difference. Of members who gave from their own PCC to another candidate's, the average total contribution was roughly $24,000; for leadership PACs, it was approximately $76,000.

In an era of close competition for party control of the chamber,[62] it is in the interest of the party leadership to ensure that these contributions from incumbent officeholders are directed in a way that increases the party's chances of gaining or holding the majority.[63] There is reason to believe, however, that *Citizens United* may have made that goal more difficult, as incumbent House members became more concerned about the possibility of large influxes of outside spending into their own races. Indeed, between 2008 and 2012, House incumbents gave a smaller share of their own PCC funds to their parties' campaign committees and other candidates. In some cases, members compensated for this shift by giving more from their leadership PACs, since those funds cannot be used in their own races.[64] This trend appears to have continued in 2016, at least for contributions to other individual candidates. Of the incumbent members who gave from both their PCCs and their leadership PACs to other candidates, the distribution of funds was roughly one-third from the former and two-thirds from the latter.

Citizens United also appears to have prompted a shift in where incumbents were giving their funds between 2008 and 2012, with a greater share in 2012 after *Citizens United* going to safe incumbents at the expense of nonincumbents.[65] In 2016, there were only five vulnerable Democratic incumbents, so it is not surprising that a relatively small share of House Democrats' contributions—approximately 8 percent—were directed to those campaigns.[66] Republicans, meanwhile, were defending a larger number of at-risk seats in 2016, which was reflected in their contribution patterns; roughly 46 percent of House Republicans' donations went to their colleagues in competitive races, compared to 35 percent in 2012.[67]

If Democrats had relatively few vulnerable incumbents to prop up in 2016, where did they send their resources instead? Largely to their safe incumbent colleagues. House Democrats directed roughly a third of their contributions in 2016 to other House Democrats running in safe districts; that was up from 18 percent in 2012.[68] While they also gave a greater share to nonincumbents between 2012 and 2016, the size of that increase was much smaller—only 3 percent, from 57 percent to 60 percent. House Republicans, meanwhile, actually gave less to nonincumbents in 2016 than in 2012, 25 percent versus 35 percent, respectively, while contributing similar shares to safe incumbents in both years (roughly 29 percent in both 2012 and 2016). Republicans' increased giving to their vulnerable peers in 2016, then, came at the expense of nonincumbents rather than their safe colleagues. In both cases, these patterns are consistent with a concern since *Citizens United* on the part of House incumbents—even ones in safe districts—about the possibility of large influxes of outside money in their contests.

In addition, there may be reasons to expect that intraparty divisions that plagued the Republican Party heading into the 2016 elections may have affected party-connected giving. The payment of party dues has periodically been a source of conflict within both party caucuses in the House,[69] but in 2016, some members of the House Freedom Caucus withheld their contributions to the NRCC out of frustration that party leaders were favoring the more establishment wing of the party.[70] This phenomenon is not necessarily new. Eric Heberlig and Bruce Larson document a broader trend of members opting out of party giving when they do not need the formal party apparatus to achieve their personal political or policy goals.[71] Recent work by John Aldrich, Andrew Ballard, Joshua

Lerner, and David Rohde also suggests that concerns about ideological cohesion within the majority party can affect intraparty giving.[72] In 2016, the typical rank-and-file Republican member who gave to the NRCC was no different ideologically than the typical member who did not give,[73] but rank-and-file members of the House Freedom Caucus gave, on average, smaller amounts than their noncaucus peers. The average donation to the NRCC from a rank-and-file GOP House member not in the Freedom Caucus in the 2016 cycle was $80,418, while for Freedom Caucus members it was only $38,640.[74] Importantly, there is no statistically significant difference in the average amount given by Freedom Caucus members from their PCCs and leadership PACs to other candidates versus such giving by other rank-and-file House Republicans.[75] Freedom Caucus members, then, were still active in making contributions to Republicans' campaign efforts; they simply chose to direct more of their resources to specific campaigns rather than to the party's collective pool.

On the Democratic side, meanwhile, rank-and-file members who gave to the DCCC were more liberal than their nondonating counterparts.[76] This result holds even if the small number of Democratic districts (five) in which incumbents were facing competitive races in 2016 are omitted, suggesting that the difference is not necessarily driven by members in vulnerable seats—who might also be more moderate—withholding funds.

Fundraising and Spending in 2016: Incumbents versus Challengers

While congressional incumbents may be concerned about the possible influx of outside money into their reelection races and adjust their contributions to other candidates accordingly, consistent with prior cycles these incumbents overwhelmingly won reelection. In 2016, 97 percent of the House members and 93 percent of the senators who sought reelection won another term. More than one wag has observed that reelection rates in Congress compare to those in the old Soviet Politburo, which had only one party and negligible competition,[77] and many observers have noted the contrast between congressional reelection rates and Congress's public approval rating, which has averaged less than 20 percent over the last ten years and was at 18 percent shortly before the 2016 election.[78]

As this section will show, incumbents also raise and spend much more money on their campaigns than challengers do. In contests where no incumbent is running, there are also substantial inequalities in spending. But does campaign spending influence who wins? To what extent does spending by outside groups affect the incumbency advantage? Data from the 2016 elections provide some clues, but for reasons to be discussed, these questions are difficult to answer. Many of the popular claims about money and congressional elections rest on somewhat thin evidence.

Little more than a decade ago, incumbents rarely faced significant challenges from within their own party. According to a 2017 Brookings study, as recently as 2006, only about 20 percent of House incumbents faced primary challengers.[79] In the 2016 election, the rate was more than twice that. The intervening period was marked by the emergence of the Tea Party movement, which was responsible for some high-profile challenges from the far right targeting Republican incumbents. In one stunning upset, the Tea Party backed Dave Brat, who defeated Eric Cantor, the House majority leader, in the 2014 Virginia Republican primary. That Cantor could be successfully challenged provided a new warning shot to 2016 incumbents. Even well-established incumbents must worry about getting "primaried."

Noteworthy cases like this one remind incumbents that, if possible, it is better to preempt a strong challenger than to face one—a principle that holds for general elections as well. Challengers who have previously run for office, for instance, are more significant threats than political newcomers are.[80] Political scientists have shown that, generally speaking, incumbents' ability to avoid quality challengers is an important source of their advantage.[81]

One way that incumbents try to deter strong challengers is by building up a campaign "war chest" well in advance of their party's primary. Some war chests are very large. For instance, in June 2015—a date far in advance of all primary filing deadlines for 2016 and nine months before the first primaries would take place—more than seventy-five House incumbents had more than $1 million in cash on hand.[82] The June 2015 average cash on hand for incumbent senators running for reelection was almost $5 million. Individuals thinking about challenging an incumbent must ponder those sums. How much of my life do I want to use up raising enough money just to get in the game?

But do incumbent war chests actually deter challengers from entering the race? Close observers of electoral politics have long thought so,[83] but the social scientific evidence on this point is weak. Identifying the deterrent effect of large war chests is complicated by the fact that incumbents typically enjoy many advantages other than money that might intimidate potential candidates, such as name recognition, constituency service and casework, and well-developed political networks. A war chest, in other words, is only one factor that might deter challengers from entering. Research that attempts to disentangle these factors has found little evidence of a war chest deterrent effect,[84] though it is also easy to underestimate the relationship.[85]

Even if quality challengers remain undeterred by incumbents' large war chests, they still face an uphill battle in fundraising. Challenging an incumbent of one's own party is especially risky, though the spending by candidates in congressional primaries is difficult to calculate. The FEC does not require candidates to assign their spending to primary and general election categories, and one cannot assume that money spent before primary voting ends is primary related. Spending on campaign infrastructure early in the year serves general election purposes, for instance, and some spending after a primary is necessary to retire prior election debts. However, serious primary challenges are uncommon. Outside spending in primaries in the form of nonparty independent expenditures has increased over the last several cycles, but relatively few challengers to incumbents in primaries actually attract large amounts of outside spending; in 2014, for example, only nine House primary challengers drew more than $100,000 in independent expenditures.[86]

Looking at spending over the entire 2016 campaign cycle, incumbent campaign committees spent far more than challengers did, as they have every year since reporting began. Table 6-5 reports spending per candidate by House and Senate general election candidates during 2015–16. Averaging across all campaigns, House incumbents spent over $1.5 million on their campaigns, but in those races where they faced a challenger, the gap alone was almost $1.3 million—a ratio of incumbent-to-challenger spending of nearly 4 to 1. Substantial inequalities occurred in Senate races as well. Again, it is not surprising that the Senate magnitudes are greater than those in the House, but the balance is better in Senate campaigns. The ratio of Senate incumbent-to-challenger spending was lower but still very large, 1.8 to 1.

There are substantial spending inequities in open seat races as well. The three columns at the right of table 6-5 compare the high and low spending by the two best-financed general election contenders. Here, "high" designates the candidate who spent more than the "low"-spending opponent, regardless of the actual levels spent by either candidate.[87] Because they are more competitive, open seat contests see greater aggregate spending, but it is not evenly distributed. In the forty-three House

Table 6-5. *Average House and Senate General Election Candidate Campaign Expenditures, 2015–16*
Dollars

	Incumbent (I)	Challenger (C)	Gap (I–C)	Open seat—high (H)	Open seat—low (L)	Open seat gap (H–L)
House	1,511,885	404,258	1,294,696	2,058,279	695,375	1,472,637
	(386)	(266)	(266)	(49)	(43)	(43)
Senate	9,936,687	5,575,988	4,360,699	12,967,312	6,869,674	6,097,638
	(29)	(29)	(29)	(5)	(5)	(5)

Source: Compiled from Federal Election Commission data (ftp://ftp.fec.gov/FEC/2016/).
Notes: Entries are the average spending by candidates' campaigns, with the number of candidates in the category listed in parentheses. Note that the gaps are calculated only for races where two candidates were running. If there was no major-party challenger, the challenger is defined as the third-party candidate with the greatest spending.

Table 6-6. *Average Outside Spending on Behalf of Candidate, 2015–16*
Dollars

	Incumbent (I)	Challenger (C)	Gap (I–C)	Open seat—high (H)	Open seat—low (L)	Open seat gap (H–L)
House	248,157	397,523	–42,665	1,181,752	764,820	567,879
	(386)	(266)	(266)	(49)	(43)	(43)
Senate	8,169,489	8,963,585	–794,096	16,094,359	13,556,145	2,538,214
	(29)	(29)	(29)	(5)	(5)	(5)

Source: Compiled from Federal Election Commission data (ftp://ftp.fec.gov/FEC/2016/).
Notes: Entries are the average outside spending amounts for a candidate or against his or her opponent, with the number of candidates in the category in parentheses. (See table 6-5 for the definition of challenger.) Note that the gaps are calculated only for races where two candidates were running. Outside spending amounts include independent expenditures, coordinated expenditures, internal communications, and electioneering communications by interest groups and political parties.

races where there were two candidates running, the ratio of spending by the richer candidate's campaign committee to that of the poorer candidate's committee was almost 3 to 1. In the five Senate open seat races, the ratio of high to low was almost 2 to 1.

As noted, of course, a candidate's own campaign spending is not the whole story. As shown in figure 6-1, independent expenditures make up roughly 87 percent of party involvement in congressional races, and table 6-3 summarizes other types of outside spending. Taken together, independent expenditures by political parties and outside groups exceed what candidates themselves spend. Table 6-6 shows this dynamic for incumbents and challengers, displaying the average spending in the 2016 cycle on behalf of House and Senate candidates by other organizations that spend for a candidate or against their opponent. The contrast of in-dependent spending to candidate spending reported in table 6-5 is strik-ing. In both the House and the Senate races, outside groups actually spent more on the campaigns of challengers than on incumbents; in the House, the challenger advantage was roughly $43,000 per race, while in the Senate it was approximately $794,000. Importantly, this dy-namic is driven by large amounts of outside spending in favor of chal-lengers in a small number of competitive races. In the House, there were ten races in which outside spending on behalf of the challenger exceeded that on behalf of the incumbent by more than $1 million. Of these, nine were closely competitive, rated either as toss-ups or as leaning for one candidate in the final *Cook Political Report* race ratings before the election.[88]

In the Senate, meanwhile, there were three competitive races—New Hampshire, North Carolina, and Pennsylvania—in which the challeng-ers enjoyed a greater than $10 million advantage over their opponents in terms of outside spending. These large disparities skew the results not just for Senate candidates as a whole but also for the subset of competi-tive races; there, challengers in competitive races averaged a $3 million advantage (roughly $28.5 million to $25.5 million) in total outside spending on their behalf. When this set of races with exceptionally large advan-tages for challengers is excluded, outside groups do have a better propor-tional balance in spending than is evident in candidates' own campaign spending in the House (roughly 1.25 to 1). In the Senate, however, the figures are approximately the same (2 to 1).

The degree to which noncandidate spending redresses the proportion-ate imbalance in candidate spending is apparent in table 6-7, which combines a candidate's own campaign spending and the outside spend-ing on their behalf. (Here, "outside spending" is defined as independent expenditures, coordinated expenditures, electioneering communica-tions, and internal communications by parties and interest groups, in-cluding party-connected super PACs.) House incumbents retain a sub-stantial advantage in spending overall, but independent expenditures have equalized the ratio. Recall that incumbents' own campaigns out-spent those of challengers by 3.7 to 1. When noncandidate spending is added in, their advantage is reduced to about 2 to 1. In Senate races, the equalizing effect of outside spending in 2016 was also significant. In-cumbents' own campaigns outspent those of challengers by 1.8 to 1, but the advantage in combined spending was less than 1.25 to 1. Spending

Table 6-7. *Average Combined Spending by Candidate and on Behalf of Candidate, 2015–16*

Dollars

	Incumbent (I)	Challenger (C)	Gap (I–C)	Open seat—high (H)	Open seat—low (L)	Open seat gap (H–L)
House	1,760,042	801,781	1,252,031	2,980,115	1,756,379	1,448,148
	(386)	(266)	(266)	(49)	(43)	(43)
Senate	18,106,176	14,539,574	3,566,602	28,450,872	21,036,618	7,414,254
	(29)	(29)	(29)	(5)	(5)	(5)

Source: Compiled from Federal Election Commission data (ftp://ftp.fec.gov/FEC/2016/).

Notes: Entries are the average of combined candidate and outside spending amounts, with the number of candidates in the category in parentheses. (See table 6-5 for the definition of challenger.) Note that the gaps are calculated only for races where two candidates were running. Outside spending amounts include independent expenditures, coordinated expenditures, internal communications, and electioneering communications by interest groups and political parties.

not under the control of the candidate is concentrated in competitive contests, and this spending is less skewed than candidate campaign spending for both competitive and noncompetitive races.

In open seat races, the addition of independent spending has slightly increased inequality in dollar terms, in both the House and the Senate, but again not in proportional terms. The 3 to 1 advantage in candidate spending in House races is cut nearly in half when noncandidate spending is factored in. In Senate races, the ratio changes from about 2 to 1 to 1.4 to 1.

To summarize, while the growth of outside spending over the last decade has been much maligned, in 2016 it did not exacerbate the large fundraising advantage of incumbents and rich open seat candidates. In proportional terms, it has equalized it.

Spending and Winning: Does Money Matter?

Close observers and critics of the campaign finance process often point to the high correlation between spending and winning.[89] Most citizens think that elections, if not bought and sold, depend heavily on which candidate spends the most money. Indeed, this is one of the few issues on which Republicans and Democrats agree. A *New York Times* poll found that 84 percent of respondents said that money has too much influence on election campaigns.[90] With the rapid rise in independent expenditures, the concern about big money in elections has only gone up. Democratic presidential candidate Bernie Sanders was not the first to emphasize this theme in a presidential campaign, but in 2016 it got considerably more traction.

Figure 6-2. *Relationship between Challenger Advantage or Disadvantage in All Spending and Challenger Vote Share in House Races, 2016*

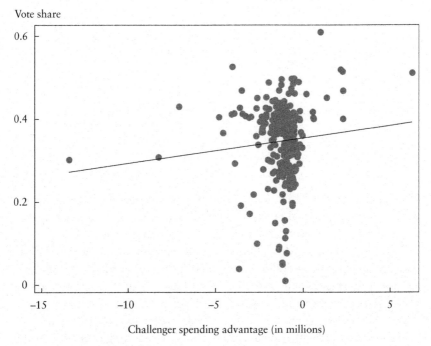

Vote share

Challenger spending advantage (in millions)

Note: The vertical axis is the challenger vote share in the 2016 House election where an incumbent was running. The horizontal axis is the combined candidate spending and outside spending for the challenger minus the same sum for the incumbent. (See table 6-7 note.)

In fact, the correlation between spending advantage and winning is positive. In 2016, the candidate who spent more won in over 90 percent of the races, but such statistics are often misinterpreted. Figure 6-2 plots the relationship between the challenger's spending disadvantage or advantage vis-à-vis the incumbent and their vote share in House races. Note that in these figures spending includes all money spent by the candidate and outside spending on their behalf. Figure 6-3 plots the same relationship for Senate challengers. The graphs show considerable case-by-case variation—some big spenders do poorly, and some small spenders do well—but the relationship in both the House and Senate graphs is positive, if modest. As challengers spend more, their vote share tends to go up.

But can one infer from this pattern that spending more money buys challengers more votes? Put differently, do the financially advantaged can-

Figure 6-3. *Relationship between Challenger Advantage or Disadvantage in All Spending and Challenger Vote Share in Senate Races, 2016*

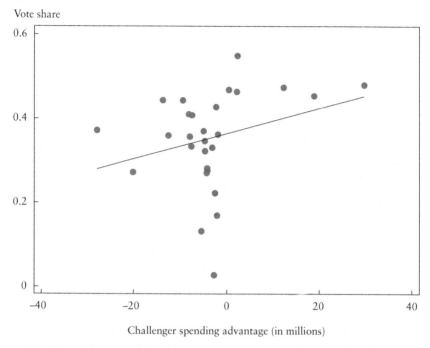

Vote share

Challenger spending advantage (in millions)

Note: The vertical axis is the challenger vote share in the 2016 Senate elections where an incumbent was running. The horizontal axis is the combined candidate spending and outside spending for the challenger minus the same sum for the incumbent.

didates do better *because of* their financial advantage? Critics of the campaign finance system assume that the answer is yes, but that conclusion involves a dangerous leap. The first principle of statistics is that correlation does not imply causation, and that is certainly true here. Challengers are able to raise and spend more money when they have a good chance of winning for other reasons (e.g., prior campaign experience, a weak economy, an incumbent involved in a scandal). In contrast, individual donors and PACs have little incentive to give to challengers almost certain to lose, and challengers often lose for reasons other than lack of money.[91]

Figure 6-4 shows the relationship in House open seat races between spending advantage and vote share for out-party candidates, meaning candidates who are challenging the party that currently holds the seat.[92] In these races, the relationship between money and vote share appears

Figure 6-4. *Relationship between All Spending by the Out-Party Candidate and Vote Share in House Open Seat Races, 2016*

Vote share

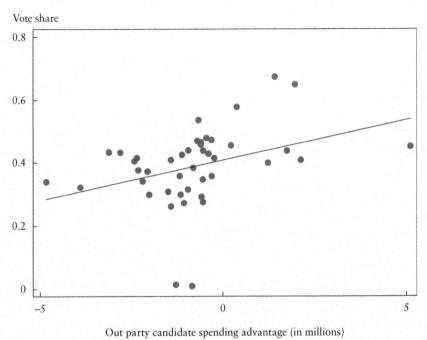

Out party candidate spending advantage (in millions)

Note: The vertical axis is the vote share of the candidate challenging the party holding the seat in 2015–16. The horizontal axis is the combined candidate spending and outside spending for the challenger minus the same sum for the incumbent.

stronger, as indicated by the relatively steep positive slope, but even here, it is not clear how much of the relationship is causal. The qualities that make an open seat candidate strong also make it easier to raise money. Likewise, not even highly partisan outside groups will spend money on behalf of a candidate who is almost certain to lose.

In summary, the correlations between spending advantage and votes in 2016 are consistently positive, but interpreting them is problematic. Political methodologists have tried to sort out the complex causal connections between spending and winning, with limited success.[93] At this point, the evidence of spending effects is mixed.[94] For instance, one early study examined cases where the same two candidates faced each other in two different elections, thus controlling for many of the nonmonetary advantages or disadvantages specific to each. The study found the causal effect of campaign spending on election campaigns was "extremely small regardless of who does the spending."[95] Two more recent studies estimated the effects of corporate spending bans on election outcomes. One found that, insofar as this source of spending is concerned, restricting it had little effect,[96] while the other found that the bans had a significant effect on the party composition of legislatures.[97] The evidence of spending effects in studies of other developed countries likewise is either mixed or weak.[98]

It would be premature to conclude that campaign spending matters little in elections, however. A long list of studies has found at least circumstantial evidence that spending improves one's chances.[99] No doubt, some minimum level of spending is needed to win—it is hard to win over voters if no one knows you are running. More generally, spending may increase a candidate's vote share, but it might hit the point of diminishing marginal returns before it gets very large. Finally, one must be suspicious of strong claims that spending does *not* affect election returns. There are many factors that can conspire to produce a null result in statistical analysis; that there is no actual effect is only one.[100] It is also too soon to tell whether and how much the extraordinary growth in outside spending will change the election equation. In short, there is much about spending and winning that remains unknown.

The Post-election Implications of Election Spending

Even if spending in congressional elections has little influence on their outcomes, should we not care about it? Should populist candidates, good government groups, and democratic reformers quit wasting their breath and instead work on something else?

The answer depends, in part, on the postelection implications of election spending. There is considerable evidence that interest groups consider their campaign spending an investment in what happens after the election is over and the next congress convenes. For example, interest group PACs prefer giving to incumbents not in danger of defeat, a puzzling regularity if their goal is to influence election returns. For this reason, many critics assert that members' "cash constituents" trade on the legislator's gratitude to get a legislative favor or buy a vote, perhaps displacing the interests of their "constitutional constituents."[101] Again, the public agrees with this view. A recent Rasmussen poll found that 60 percent of citizens believe that members of Congress sell their votes,[102] but here, too, the social scientific evidence is thin. Most donors give to candidates who already agree with them, and most members' votes are overdetermined anyway. However, campaign contributions do have an effect on access,[103] and access enables interest groups to mobilize their legislative allies to work on specific issues or agency rules the group cares about.[104] In other words, even if the financiers of congressional campaigns do not influence elections, the money can get them better representation at the stage of the policymaking process where influence matters most.

Finally, the allocation of party-connected money—who gives it and who gets it—can play an important role in intraparty conflicts. Factions within a party, such as the Freedom Caucus in 2016, can and do threaten to withhold resources from their party committees because of various disagreements over party strategy. Those same party committees can also punish individual members by holding back financial support, using the power of money to ensure that legislators hew to the party line.[105] The rise of party-aligned Super PACs has also given party leaders another tool they can use to try to shape the makeup of their caucus, especially by intervening in primaries.[106] The role of money, then, does not begin and end with its potential effect on election outcomes. As the parties compete for control of Congress in a hyperpolarized environment, campaign funds, both from inside and outside the institution, will continue to play an important role in party politics.

Notes

1. Frances E. Lee, *Insecure Majorities: Congress and the Perpetual Campaign* (University of Chicago Press, 2017).

2. *Citizens United* v. *Federal Election Commission*, 558 U.S. 310 (2010).

3. Chris Cillizza and Aaron Blake, "In 2016 Senate Races, Democrats Like the Map and the Math," *Washington Post*, January 19, 2015, p. A2.

4. Jonathan Easley, "Dems Have Clear Edge in 2016 Race for Senate," *The Hill*, May 12, 2015, p. 22.

5. Jennifer Steinhauer, "Some Battle Lines Harden, Others Fade, in 2016 Fight for Senate Control," *New York Times*, September 1, 2015, p. A15.

6. Tom Lopach, executive director of the Democratic Senatorial Campaign Committee, interview by David Magleby, December 13, 2016.

7. Sarah Morgan, political director for the National Republican Senatorial Committee, interview by David Magleby, February 22, 2017.

8. Preston Elliot, deputy executive director for the Democratic Senatorial Campaign Committee, interview by David Magleby, December 13, 2016.

9. Ibid.

10. Stuart Rothenberg, "Can Democrats Win the House in 2016?" *Roll Call*, January 13, 2015.

11. Gary C. Jacobson, "It's Nothing Personal: The Decline of the Incumbency Advantage in U.S. House Elections," *Journal of Politics* 77, no. 3 (July 2015), pp. 861–73.

12. Nathan Gonzales, editor and publisher of *Insider Elections*, interview by David Magleby, November 21, 2016.

13. Rob Simms, executive director for the National Republican Congressional Committee, interview by David Magleby, December 12, 2016.

14. Gary C. Jacobson, "Barack Obama and the Nationalization of Electoral Politics in 2012," *Electoral Studies* 40 (December 2015), pp. 471–81.

15. See, for example, Dan Balz, "The Republican Party's Uphill Path to 270 Electoral Votes in the 2016 Elections," *Washington Post*, January 18, 2014.

16. John Sides, Michael Tesler, and Lynn Vavreck, "The Electoral Landscape of 2016," *Annals of the American Academy of Political and Social Science* 667 (September 2016), pp. 50–71.

17. Jason M. Roberts, Jacob F. H. Smith, and Sarah A. Treul, "Party Committee Targeting and the Evolution of Competition in U.S. House Elections," *Journal of Elections, Public Opinion, and Parties* 26, no. 1 (2016), pp. 96–114.

18. Emily Cahn, "Democrats' Window to Find Strong House Candidates Slowly Closing," *Roll Call*, July 28, 2015.

19. This excludes two races in Louisiana, where the primary occurs on the same day as the general election.

20. Brookings Institution, "The Primaries Project Data (2016)," 2016 (www.brookings.edu/series/the-primaries-project/).

21. Lauren French, "House Democrats Pick Top Republican Targets," *Politico*, February 11, 2016.

22. Eliana Johnson, "Why Rob Portman Is Crushing His Opponent," *National Review*, September 13, 2016.

23. Robert S. Erickson, "Congressional Elections in Presidential Years: Presidential Coattails and Strategic Voting," *Legislative Studies Quarterly* 41, no. 3 (August 2016), pp. 551–74.

24. Elliot, interview.

25. Brookings Institution, "PAC Contributions to Congressional Candidates, 1978–2016," in *Vital Statistics on Congress* (Washington, D.C., 2018), table 2-10.

26. Kristin Kanthak, "Crystal Elephants and Committee Chairs: Campaign Contributions and Leadership Races in the U.S. House of Representatives," *American Politics Research* 35, no. 3 (May 2007), pp. 389–406.

27. For figures from 2012, see Paul S. Herrnson, Kelly D. Patterson, and Stephanie Perry Curtis, "Financing the 2012 Congressional Elections," in *Financing the 2012 Election*, edited by David B. Magleby (Brookings Institution

Press, 2014), pp. 143–74. For data on leadership PACs in 2014, see Alex Lazar, "Leadership PACs: Background," Center for Responsive Politics (https://www.opensecrets.org/industries/background.php?ind=Q03++).

28. Center for Responsive Politics, "Super PACs" (www.opensecrets.org/pacs/superpacs.php).

29. Morgan, interview.

30. Elliot, interview.

31. Lopach, interview.

32. Alex Roarty, "Senate Republicans' Brewing Super PAC Fight," *The Atlantic*, September 1, 2015.

33. Reid Wilson, "Inside the GOP's Effort to Consolidate the Super PAC Universe," *Morning Consult*, March 24, 2016.

34. Center for Responsive Politics, "2016 Outside Spending by Single-Candidate Super PACs" (https://www.opensecrets.org/outsidespending/summ.php?chrt=V&type=C).

35. See the America Votes web page, https://americavotes.org/about/.

36. Elliot, interview.

37. Eric S. Heberlig and Bruce A. Larson, "U.S. House Incumbent Fundraising and Spending in a Post-*Citizens United* and Post-*McCutcheon* World," *Political Science Quarterly* 129, no. 4 (2014–15), pp. 613–42.

38. *McCutcheon v. Federal Election Commission*, 572 U.S. ___ (2014).

39. R. Sam Garrett, "Campaign Contribution Limits: Selected Questions about *McCutcheon* and Policy Issues for Congress," *Congressional Research Service*, April 7, 2014.

40. Heberlig and Larson, "U.S. House Incumbent Fundraising and Spending in a Post-*Citizens United* and Post-*McCutcheon* World."

41. Center for Responsive Politics, "Team Ryan" (www.opensecrets.org/jfc/summary.php?id=C00545947&cycle=2016).

42. Center for Responsive Politics, "Schumer Committee for the Majority" (www.opensecrets.org/jfc/summary.php?id=C00620013&cycle=2016).

43. Simms, interview.

44. Lopach, interview.

45. Simms, interview.

46. R. Sam Garrett, "Increased Campaign Contribution Limits in the FY2015 Omnibus Appropriations Law: Frequently Asked Questions," *Congressional Research Service*, March 17, 2015.

47. Kenneth P. Vogel, "Budget Rider Would Expand Party Cash," *Politico*, December 10, 2014.

48. Amy Dacey, former CEO of the Democratic National Committee, interview by David Magleby, December 13, 2016.

49. Simms, interview.

50. Herrnson, Patterson, and Curtis, "Financing the 2012 Congressional Elections."

51. These candidates were Randy Perkins (Fla.-18), Francis Rooney (Fla.-19), Paul Mitchell (Mich.-10), and Trey Hollingsworth (Ind.-9). See Center for Responsive Politics, "Self-Funding Candidates" (https://www.opensecrets.org /overview/topself.php?cycle=2016).

52. Brian J. Brox, *Back in the Game: Political Party Campaigning in an Era of Reform* (State University of New York Press, 2013).

53. In 2012, incumbent senators in Florida, Massachusetts, Missouri, Montana, Nevada, and Ohio faced competitive contests, with an average coordinated expenditure limit of $559,000. In 2016, incumbent senators in Arizona, Florida, Illinois, Missouri, New Hampshire, North Carolina, Ohio, Pennsylvania, and Wisconsin faced competitive races, with an average coordinated expenditure limit of $730,200. For coordinated expenditure limits by state and year, see Federal Election Commission, "2012 Coordinated Party Expenditure Limits" (http://classic.fec.gov/info/charts_441ad_2012.shtml); Federal Election Commission, "2016 Coordinated Party Expenditure Limits" (http://classic.fec.gov /info/charts_cpe_2016.shtml).

54. Paul S. Herrnson, "The Roles of Party Organizations, Party-Connected Committees, and Party Allies in Elections," *Journal of Politics* 71, no. 4 (October 2009), pp. 1207–24.

55. Garrett, "Increased Campaign Contribution Limits in the FY2015 Omnibus Appropriations Law."

56. Heberlig and Larson, "U.S. House Incumbent Fundraising and Spending in a Post-*Citizens United* and Post-*McCutcheon* World."

57. Deirdre Shesgreen and Christopher Schnaars, "Lawmakers' Dues to Party: 'Extortion' or Team Effort?" *USA Today*, May 25, 2016; Molly K. Hooper, "House Republican Campaign Chief Furious after Leak on Party Dues," *The Hill*, March 17, 2011.

58. Elliott, interview; Morgan, interview. See also David B. Magleby, "Political Parties and the Financing of the 2008 Elections," in *Financing the 2008 Election*, edited by David B. Magleby (Brookings Institution Press, 2011). pp. 210-248.

59. Senator James Lankford (R-Okla.) made a very small ($75) donation to the NRSC, which is excluded here.

60. Jennifer Duffy, senior editor for the *Cook Political Report*, interview by David Magleby, November 21, 2016.

61. Simms, interview.

62. Lee, *Insecure Majorities*.

63. Heberlig and Larson, "U.S. House Incumbent Fundraising and Spending in a Post-*Citizens United* and Post-*McCutcheon* World."

64. Ibid.

65. Ibid.

66. Here, and in all other figures cited in this paragraph, contributions are from incumbent House members' PCCs and leadership PACs to the PCCs of House candidates.

67. Ibid.

68. Ibid.

69. See, for example, Jessica Brady, "DCCC Pushes for Unpaid Dues," *Roll Call*, November 16, 2011; Jackie Kucinich, "Boehner Pleads with Members to Pay NRCC Dues," *Roll Call*, December 16, 2009.

70. Rachael Bade and Heather Caygle, "Freedom Caucus Stiffs GOP on Campaign Cash," *Politico*, September 20, 2016.

71. Heberlig and Larson, "U.S. House Incumbent Fundraising and Spending in a Post-*Citizens United* and Post-*McCutcheon* World."

72. John H. Aldrich, Andrew O. Ballard, Joshua Y. Lerner, and David W. Rohde, "Does the Gift Keep on Giving? House Leadership PAC Donations before and after Majority Status," *Journal of Politics* 79, no. 4 (October 2017), pp. 1449–53.

73. Ideology here and elsewhere in the chapter is measured using first-dimension Common Space DW-NOMINATE scores, which use members' roll call votes to estimate their ideological position on a left-right spectrum. The average score for a Republican House member who donated to the NRCC in 2016 was 0.47, while for nondonors it was 0.49. Here, rank-and-file members are defined as those not holding party leadership posts or committee chairs. The results are similar if subcommittee chairs are also excluded from the rank-and-file category.

74. The House Freedom Caucus does not publish a formal list of its members, but the Pew Research Center was able to confirm the identities of thirty-six members in 2015. See Drew DeSilver, "What Is the House Freedom Caucus, and Who's in It?" *Fact Tank*, October 20, 2015.

75. The average amount contributed from a Freedom Caucus member's PCC and LPAC to other candidates was approximately $36,000. For rank-and-file non–Freedom Caucus members, the average was approximately $48,000, but a difference-of-means test for whether those averages are equal yields a p value of 0.36.

76. The average Common Space DW-NOMINATE score for a Democratic House member who gave to the DCCC was −0.39, while it was −0.33 for non-donating members; a difference-of-means test for whether those averages are equal yields a p value of 0.004.

77. Doug Mataconis, "Americans Still Hate Congress, but Incumbents Don't Have Anything to Worry About," *Outside the Beltway*, August 5, 2014. Note, however, that incumbents are more likely to retire when they are likely to lose.

78. Calculated from data provided by Gallup, "Congress and the Public" (www.gallup.com/poll/1600/congress-public.aspx), as of August 20, 2017.

79. Elaine Kamarck and Alexander R. Podkul with Nick Zeppos, "Political Polarization and Candidates in the 2016 Congressional Primaries," Center for Effective Public Management at Brookings, January 2017.

80. Again, the Cantor case is interesting because it is an exception to this rule—2014 was the first time that Dave Brat faced the voters.

81. Walter J. Stone, L. Sandy Maisel, and Cherie D. Maestas, "Quality Counts: Extending the Strategic Politician Model of Incumbent Deterrence," *American Journal of Political Science* 48, no. 3 (July 2004), pp. 479–95; Daniel Mark Butler, "A Regression Discontinuity Design Analysis of the Incumbency Advantage and Tenure in the U.S. House," *Electoral Studies* 28 (2009), pp. 123–28; Pamela Ban, Elena Liaudet, and James M. Snyder Jr., "Challenger Quality and the Incumbency Advantage," *Legislative Studies Quarterly* 41, no. 1 (February 2016), pp. 153–70.

82. Calculated from data provided by the Federal Election Commission, "Table 7: House Campaign Activity by State and District," 2015–2016 Election Cycle Data Summaries through 6/30/15 (https://transition.fec.gov/press /summaries/2016/ElectionCycle/6m_CongCand.shtml).

83. See, for example, Clifford D. May, "Bulging War Chests Protect Seats in House," *New York Times*, March 6, 1989.

84. Jay Goodliffe, "The Effect of War Chests on Challenger Entry in the U.S. House Elections," *American Journal of Political Science* 45, no. 4 (October 2006), pp. 830–44; Jay Goodliffe, "Campaign War Chests and Challenger Quality in Senate Elections," *Legislative Studies Quarterly* 32, no. 1 (February 2007), pp.135–56.

85. David Epstein and Peter Zemsky, "Money Talks: Deterring Quality Challengers in Congressional Elections," *American Political Science Review* 89, no. 2 (June 1995), pp. 295–308; Jay Goodliffe, "War Chests for Deterrence and Savings," *Quarterly Journal of Political Science* 4, no. 1 (March 2007), pp. 129–50.

86. Robert G. Boatright, Michael J. Malbin, and Brendan Glavin, "Independent Expenditures in Congressional Primaries after Citizens United: Implications for Interest Groups, Incumbents, and Political Parties," *Interest Groups and Advocacy* 5, no. 2 (May 2016), pp. 119–40.

87. Note that these high and low numbers are *not* comparable to the spending gaps between incumbent and challenger, because there are a few House and Senate races where challengers actually spent more than incumbents did.

88. The tenth race, in Maryland's Sixth Congressional District, involved a challenger, Amie Hoeber, whose husband donated more than $3 million to a candidate-specific Super PAC. See Bill Turque, "Hoeber's Husband Donates Additional $1.4 million to Super PAC Backing Her Md. Congressional Campaign,"

Washington Post, October 17, 2016. Of the nine other races, the challenger won three and the incumbent won six.

89. See, for example, Domenico Montanaro, Rachel Wellford, and Simone Pathe, "Money Is Pretty Good Predictor of Who Will Win Elections," *PBS News-Hour*, November 11, 2014.

90. "Americans' Views on Money and Politics," *New York Times*, June 2, 2015.

91. By the same logic, they have less incentive to give to challengers almost certain to win. That condition rarely holds for challengers, however.

92. In the Senate elections, there are too few open seat contests to estimate the relationship.

93. Gary C. Jacobson, *The Politics of Congressional Elections*, 8th ed. (Upper Saddle River, N.J.: Pearson Education Press, 2013), p. 52.

94. See, for example, Thomas A. Stratmann, "Some Talk: Money in Politics. A (Partial) Review of the Literature," *Public Choice* 124 (2005), pp. 135–56; Jeff Milyo, "Campaign Spending and Electoral Competition: Towards More Policy Relevant Research," *The Forum* 11, no. 3 (October 2013), pp. 437–54.

95. Steven D. Levitt, "Using Repeat Challengers to Estimate the Effect of Campaign Spending on Elections Outcomes in the U.S. House," *Journal of Political Economy* 102, no. 4 (August 1994), pp. 777–98.

96. Raymond J. La Raja and Brian F. Schaffner, "The Effects of Campaign Finance Spending Bans on Electoral Outcomes: Evidence from the States about the Potential Impact of *Citizens United* v. *FEC*," *Electoral Studies* 33 (March 2014), pp. 102–14.

97. Andrew B. Hall, "Systemic Effects of Campaign Spending: Evidence from Corporate Contribution Bans in US State Legislatures," *Political Science Research and Methods* 4, no. 2 (May 2016), pp. 343–59.

98. See, for example, Avi Ben-Bassat, Momi Dahan, and Esteban F. Klor, "Does Campaign Spending Affect Electoral Outcomes?" *Electoral Studies* 40 (December 2015), pp. 102–14.

99. Jacobson, *The Politics of Congressional Elections*, p. 52.

100. To restate this often forgotten point: "No evidence of an effect is not evidence of no effect."

101. Brooks Jackson, *Honest Graft* (New York: Knopf, 1988), p. 107.

102. Rasmussen Reports, "Congress: For Sale," June 26, 2017 (www.rasmussenreports.com/public_content/politics/general_politics/june_2017/for_sale_congress).

103. Joshua L. Kalla and David E. Broockman, "Campaign Contributions Facilitate Access to Congressional Officials: A Randomized Field Experiment," *American Journal of Political Science* 60, no. 3 (July 2016), pp. 545–58.

104. Richard L. Hall and Alan Deardorff, "Lobbying as Legislative Subsidy," *American Political Science Review* 100, no. 1 (February 2006), pp. 69–84;

Richard L. Hall and Kristina C. Miler, "What Happens after the Alarm? Interest Group Subsidies to Legislative Overseers," *Journal of Politics* 70, no. 4 (October 2008), pp. 990–1005; R. Kenneth Goodwin, Scott H. Ainsworth, and Erik Goodwin, *Lobbying and Policymaking* (Washington: CQ Press, 2013).

105. Andrew Clarke, "The House Freedom Caucus: Extreme Faction Influence in the U.S. Congress," working paper, 2017.

106. See, for example, Maureen Grope, "McConnell-Linked Groups Back Young in Indiana Senate Primary," *USA Today*, April 19, 2016.

SEVEN

Party Money in the
                  2016 Election

DIANA DWYRE AND ROBIN KOLODNY

For political parties, the 2016 election was unconventional in a number of respects. The internal battles for the presidential
nomination between establishment and outsider candidates challenged
the integrity of both major national parties. The major parties had an
unusual array of competing internal coalitions as they fought for control
of the presidency and both chambers of Congress. When the votes were
counted, Republicans held the winning hand, a flush,[1] controlling all
three institutions up for grabs yet with little party harmony within and
across the House of Representatives, the Senate, and the White House.[2]
Democrats not only lost, but they endured a number of challenges to
their operations and reputation. For instance, Democratic National Committee (DNC) e-mails were hacked by the Russians and later released by
WikiLeaks, intraparty factional battles grew during the contentious primary season, there were allegations and, after the election, admissions
of DNC favoritism toward Hillary Clinton,[3] and a changing of the guard
at the DNC in the middle of the election season, all of which, at the very
least, distracted party leaders and activists as they sought to defeat Trump
and GOP congressional candidates.[4] For example, Mike Lux, who went
to the DNC along with interim chair Donna Brazile, was tasked with
"collecting labor and liberal donor money from folks who had not given
because they didn't like [DNC Chair] Debbie Wasserman Schultz."[5] For
the Republicans, outsider Donald Trump also claimed the Republican
National Committee (RNC) was a "scam" and "disgrace" as he disputed
the mode of delegate selection in Colorado in early April 2016. He also

likened the RNC to the DNC, which he saw as unfair to Bernie Sanders, describing both processes as corrupt, with the Republican side "more corrupt."[6]

Many political scientists have long agreed that party insiders select the parties' presidential nominees via endorsements from their most prominent elected officials.[7] In turn, elite preferences, rather than good early poll numbers or fundraising totals, influence the selection before the voters make their choices in primaries and caucuses.[8] However, in 2016, both parties' presidential nomination contests were, in effect, hijacked by party outsiders, as voters turned out to express their dissatisfaction with the political class. Celebrity businessman Donald Trump, a former Democrat, defeated sixteen mostly conventional GOP hopefuls to take the Republican nomination, and Democratic Socialist senator Bernie Sanders of Vermont siphoned off support from the Democratic Party's front-runner, former senator and secretary of state Hillary Rodham Clinton. Yet, such minimal party influence is not terribly surprising. Both parties have long sought a larger role in the selection of their presidential nominees, and both consistently oppose any efforts to open up primary elections beyond registered party members.[9] Additionally, a number of scholars and other observers agree that parties should be more empowered than they are, and many advocate a system of stronger parties in elections and governing as a way to enhance democracy in the United States.[10] Our single-member district and winner-take-all rules are not likely to change, and neither are parties likely to replace candidates as the primary focus of elections and campaign spending. Thus, parties focus most of their efforts on a relatively small number of competitive candidate contests.

Of course, some aspects of the 2016 elections were more conventional. For instance, 97 percent of House incumbents and 93 percent of Senate incumbents who sought reelection were reelected,[11] and over 90 percent of the House and Senate candidates who spent more money than their opponents won their elections.[12] This chapter considers these and other important elements of contemporary elections in its analysis of the campaign finance activities of the major political parties in the 2016 federal elections. It starts with a discussion of changes in the campaign finance landscape that affected the parties' electoral activities, including changes to the rules, as well as election dynamics such as Donald Trump and his party and group allies' significantly lower spending than Hillary Clinton and her party and group allies' spending in the presidential race (see chapter 5). It then explores the parties' fundraising—how they raised money, the various sources of that money, the relationship between the party committees and their candidates, and national and subnational party fundraising. It also analyzes the various ways the parties spent money and how they distributed their resources to help their candidates. Finally, it considers the parties' role relative to other campaign finance actors and discusses how the parties continue to develop effective extended party networks with allied nonparty groups that complement the activities of the formal party organizations.

Parties in a Changing Campaign Finance Environment

Since the 2012 elections, there have been some notable changes in the rules and regulations that govern how money is raised and spent by political parties in U.S. elections.[13] As discussed in chapter 2, perhaps the most significant was the 2014 U.S. Supreme Court decision in *McCutcheon v. Federal Election Commission,* in which the Court declared the aggregate campaign contribution limit for individuals an unconstitutional violation of free speech.[14] Previously, limits on the donations of individuals both to specific recipients and overall (the absolute dollar amount donated in the election cycle) was a way to ensure that no individual had too much potential influence on elected government officials. The *McCutcheon* decision struck down the overall dollar amount of donations from one individual in an election cycle while preserving the contribution limits to particular candidates and party committees to avoid the appearance of undue influence from any one funding source, significantly increasing the overall amount of money elite donors could contribute (see chapter 2). There were 1,219 individual donors who gave the maximum in 2012, the last presidential election cycle before the decision.[15] In the 2016 cycle, the Center for Responsive Politics reported that 1,845 donors contributed more than the old limit of $123,280 (the limit in 2012 was $123,200).[16] So, in the first post-*McCutcheon* campaign cycle, over 50 percent more individuals made large aggregate contributions, a jump in both the number of big spenders and the amount of money flowing into the campaign finance system.

Will the parties benefit from this increased spending? The *McCutcheon* decision immediately enhanced the parties' *ability* to raise more money from individual contributors by increasing the overall amount each elite donor may give, which may help parties keep pace with nonparty groups such as Super PACs, which have no real restrictions on their fundraising.[17] Wealthy contributors who may have rationed their donations to candidates, parties, and groups in the past because of the *overall* limit may now contribute to as many of these as they wish, and the maximum to all party committees if they want, as long as they stay within the contribution limits for each.

Yet *McCutcheon* opens up more opportunities for undue influence by a single donor on party leaders and officeholders, who in turn might leverage what they can offer to attract wealthy donors seeking access and policy results. While the contributions to each federal committee (candidate, PAC, or party) are limited, in theory the number of federal committees organized to accept these donations is almost limitless (*all* candidates, *all* PACs, *all* party committees, including state parties), and since the Court's conservative majority reasserted its narrow view of what constitutes corruption in its *McCutcheon* ruling (only quid pro quo corruption warrants concern and regulation),[18] many observers wonder whether the decision will encourage donors, candidates, and parties to push the "influence" envelope. For instance, political scientist Michael Malbin suggests "party leaders (or their agents) may pressure donors to extract higher contributions, the donors will gain agenda-setting access and influence, and the leaders will turn around to pressure the members on policy," something "the *McCutcheon* Court's plurality opinion seems to present as a constitutionally protected interplay."[19] Other observers believe that the *McCutcheon* decision is not likely to have major impacts. For example, Republican campaign attorney Robert Kelner argues that the "rising tide of unregulated outside group spending, rather than the Supreme Court's tweaking of contribution limits for regulated funds, is the dominant drama in our campaign finance system. Viewed against the backdrop of the political parties' collapse due to McCain-Feingold, *McCutcheon* looks like a ripple on the campaign finance pond, not a tsunami."[20] Clearly, we require more election cycles to assess how the *McCutcheon* decision will change the influence of political parties.

Another change in campaign finance rules allows the federal party committees to raise more money from individual contributors and PACs for some specified purposes. In April 2014, Congress passed and President Obama signed P.L. 113-94, also known as the Gabriella Miller Kids First Research Act, which repealed the Presidential Election Campaign Fund convention funding that had been used by both major parties since 1976. While Congress maintained the separate appropriation for security costs for the conventions, $100 million for each of the major parties' 2016 conventions in Cleveland and Philadelphia,[21] lawmakers directed the remaining convention public funds to the "10-Year Pediatric Research Initiative Fund" for research on pediatric cancer, autism, fragile X syndrome, and other childhood diseases.[22] As both donations to the public fund (via tax form check-off box) and confidence in the fund's political function have declined, presidential candidates now rarely accept matching funds or grants, primarily because they can raise so much more on their own. Repealing most of the funding for national party conventions reinforces the reality that public funding of federal elections is now largely absent (see chapter 2).

In December 2014, Congress enacted and President Obama signed the Consolidated and Further Continuing Appropriations Act, 2015 (P.L. 113-235). It became known as the controversial "CRomnibus" bill, a combination of a continuing resolution (CR) and an omnibus spending bill (see chapter 2). Among its many other provisions, P.L. 113-235 increased individual contribution limits to the national party committees and permitted all six of the national party committees[23] to establish new specialized accounts, each with separate contribution limits. Each party committee may have a specialized account for "construction, purchase, renovation, operation and furnishing" of its national party headquarters, another account for "the preparation for and the conduct of election recounts and contests and other legal proceedings," and, to compensate the parties for the loss of convention public funding, the RNC and DNC may each have a separate account to "defray expenses incurred with respect to a presidential nominating convention."[24] The convention accounts have a spending limit of no more than $20 million per convention in order to accept the increased contribution limits.[25] After P.L. 113-235, contribution limits to the parties for the 2015–16 election cycle increased substantially over the 2012 and 2014 limits. Table 7-1 shows how the limits have changed for the different types of contributors since 2012.

For example, table 7-1 indicates that for 2016 a single individual could give up to $33,400 to each national party committee per year (to the DNC and RNC, indexed for inflation), an additional contribution of up to $100,200 per year to a party's national committee for its presidential nominating convention, up to $100,200 per year to each of a party's three national committees (their national committee, House campaign committee, and Senate campaign committee) for legal proceedings and election

Table 7-1. *Annual Contribution Limits to National Political Party Committees, 2012–16*
Dollars

	Before Consolidated and Further Continuing Appropriations Act, 2015		After Consolidated and Further Continuing Appropriations Act, 2015 — New additional segregated accounts and associated limits				
Contributor type	Limits 2012 Contributions[a]	Limits 2014 Contributions[a]	Limits 2016 — 2016 Traditional contributions[a]	2016 Convention account	2016 Building account	2016 Recount/legal account	2016 Total possible contributions
Individual to:							
DNC, RNC	30,800	32,400	33,400	100,200	100,200	100,200	334,000
DCCC, NRCC	30,800	32,400	33,400	n.a.	100,200	100,200	233,800
DSCC, NRSC	30,800	32,400	33,400	n.a.	100,200	100,200	233,800
Total	70,800[b] biennial limit	74,600[c] biennial limit	100,200	100,200	300,600	300,600	801,600
Multicandidate PAC[d] to:							
DNC, RNC	15,000	15,000	15,000/year	45,000	45,000	45,000	150,000
DCCC, NRCC	15,000	15,000	15,000/year	n.a.	45,000	45,000	105,000
DSCC, NRSC	15,000	15,000	15,000/year	n.a.	45,000	45,000	105,000
Total	45,000	45,000	45,000	45,000	135,000	135,000	360,000
Non-Multicandidate PAC[d] to:							
DNC, RNC	30,800	32,400	33,400	100,200	100,200	100,200	334,000
DCCC, NRCC	30,800	32,400	33,400	n.a.	100,200	100,200	233,800
DSCC, NRSC	30,800	32,400	33,400	n.a.	100,200	100,200	233,800
Total	92,400	97,200	100,200	100,200	300,600	300,600	801,600

Sources: Various Federal Election Commission files; Sam Garrett, "Increased Campaign Contribution Limits in the FY2015 Omnibus Appropriations Law: Frequently Asked Questions," *Congressional Research Service*, March 17, 2015).

a. Limits are indexed to inflation each election cycle.

b. This is the biennial contribution limit to all PACs and parties, with an overall biennial limit of $117,000.

c. This is the biennial contribution limit to all PACs and parties, with an overall biennial limit of $123,200.

d. A multicandidate PAC, the most common type of PAC, is a PAC registered for at least six months and with fifty or more contributors that has contributed to five or more federal candidates. Non-multicandidate PACs have fewer than fifty contributors and have contributed to fewer than five candidates (most nonmulticandidate PACs become multicandidate PACs fairly quickly).

recounts, and up to $100,200 to each committee for their national party headquarters (all indexed for inflation). So, in 2016, a single donor theoretically could have given up to $801,600 to the three committees of one national political party in a calendar year, $1,603,200 for the two-year election cycle.[26] There is no legal prohibition on an individual giving up to the maximum amount allowed to more than one political party. However, it is rare for individuals to give substantial amounts to more than one of the political parties. Note that both multicandidate PACs, the most common type, and nonmulticandidate PACs also can give more to the party committees and can give to these new party accounts as well (see table 7-1).[27] Interestingly, a single PAC could give the maximum amount ($360,000 for multicandidate PACs and $801,600 for nonmulticandidate PACs) to *both* parties, which, unlike individuals who generally give only to one party, would not be terribly surprising. Some PACs, especially corporate PACs, already contribute to both parties in an effort to ensure access to a broad base of lawmakers. Nonmulticandidate PACs have higher limits on their contributions to political parties, which may be an explanation for their greater activity in recent years.

Technically, the money contributed to these new party accounts is only to be used for the purposes specified in the law. Yet, some good-government groups, such as the Center for Public Integrity, warn that these new party committee accounts with high contribution limits are the new party "soft money" (unlimited soft-money contributions to parties were made illegal by the Bipartisan Campaign Reform Act in 2002). They also have cautioned that without more detailed guidance from the Federal Election Commission (FEC) (which has deadlocked on moving ahead with regulations for the new spending accounts), parties may be able to legally use these funds to "pay for some election-related costs such as opposition research and data mining."[28] As evidence, they report that the RNC did in fact use some of these funds for staff salaries, and both parties have transferred money from these accounts to other party accounts. However, the new law does stipulate that funds contributed to the headquarters accounts may be used for the "operation" of the party headquarters, and a very generous interpretation of "operation" might include opposition research and data mining.

During the debate on the 2015 CRomnibus appropriations, proponents of public funding for the conventions noted that in the 1970s, private funding of conventions raised corruption concerns, which, in part, motivated the move to public funding of presidential nominating conventions.[29] Moreover, the new party convention fund does not reduce the role of local organizing and host committees, where most of the money spent on conventions is raised. Both the convention host committees and the new party convention accounts must fully disclose all of their contributions and spending (see chapter 2). Some scholars, such as Ray La Raja, favor the new sources of money for the national parties, because, he argues, shifting money to the parties will improve transparency and accountability and even possibly combat polarization and gridlock:

> A greater portion of cash, which is now swishing around outside the formal campaign finance system, will flow instead through highly transparent parties. . . . Making parties the central financiers of elections strengthens their vital role in the political process. . . . [T]hey help aggregate diverse interests in the polity, frame electoral choices, and organize governing. Financially strong parties have the wherewithal to diminish the clout of the most extreme interest groups and Members of Congress who don't ever want to compromise.[30]

The Bipartisan Campaign Reform Act (BCRA) banned party soft money (meaning nonfederal money) beginning with the 2004 election cycle. Previously, national party committees raised this money in unlimited amounts from otherwise restricted sources such as corporations and unions, or from PACs or individuals who had otherwise reached their contribution limit, to run their generic party or "noncampaign" operations (such as the "building" fund), which freed up regulated hard-money contributions for electoral expenses. Soft money fueled the candidate-specific issue advocacy campaigns run by parties in competitive states (for presidential and senatorial elections) and U.S. House districts.[31] The soft-money ban had a perceivable impact on how the parties raised money thereafter.[32]

The 2010 Supreme Court decision in *Citizens United* v. *Federal Election Commission*[33] and the D.C. Circuit Court's ruling in *SpeechNow .org* v. *Federal Election Commission* a few months later,[34] along with a pair of FEC Advisory Opinions,[35] led to the creation of what have come to be called Super PACs. These new political committees can raise and spend unlimited amounts of money from virtually any source, including corporations and labor unions, which cannot give contributions to candidates and parties, and wealthy individuals, as long as their spending is done independently and not in coordination with candidates or their parties. Super PAC spending now constitutes the largest share of all noncandidate spending in federal elections (see chapter 1). However, most Super PAC spending mirrors party targeting and donor networks, creating the unexpected result that this organizational format has become yet another party "soft money" work-around.[36]

Political Conditions and the Party Committees in 2016

Both parties endured painfully contentious nomination contests that set the stage for a hard-fought general election. Democratic voters were split, and allegations that the process was rigged in favor of Clinton were more than background music during the primaries. For instance, Democratic presidential candidates Senator Bernie Sanders and former Maryland governor Martin O'Malley both complained in summer 2015 that the DNC had scheduled too few debates (six in total and only four before the first voters cast their ballots) and had banned the candidates from participating in outside debates sponsored by other organizations.[37] They charged that the DNC was trying to protect Clinton's lead in the polls and prevent discussion of the controversy around Clinton's use of a personal e-mail server while she was secretary of state.[38] Moreover, Hillary Clinton had engaged in a joint fundraising agreement with the DNC starting in 2015 to raise money for her own campaign and for the DNC, and a Sanders campaign official, Mark Longabaugh, explained that the DNC wanted Senator Sanders to raise substantial money (at least $400,000) for the party as well in order to get access to the DNC voter database.[39] Sanders refused to raise funds from big donors, and eventually his campaign just wrote the DNC a check to get access to the voter files. Then the DNC accused the Sanders campaign of accessing the Clinton campaign's confidential voter information. Sanders denied the charge and sued the DNC. After an independent investigation cleared the Sanders campaign, Sanders dropped the lawsuit.[40] Needless to say, these events widened the rift among Democratic voters and drove many Sanders supporters to denounce the party and its eventual nominee, Hillary Clinton.

The Republicans also had an unusual primary season. Former Florida governor Jeb Bush was considered the front-runner before the nomination season began, in part because of the $85 million spent on advertising by the pro-Bush Right to Rise Super PAC, which targeted other candidates, especially his one-time protégé Florida senator Marco Rubio, more than Trump. Yet Trump had higher name recognition than most, if not all, of his GOP primary opponents from his many years as the boss on *The Apprentice* reality television show. Despite his successful fundraising, Jeb Bush suspended his campaign before the end of February.[41] Trump's high-pitched rhetoric laced with us versus them themes struck a chord with angry and disaffected voters across the political spectrum, particularly white rural voters (see chapters 1, 4, and 5). Trump's belittling name-calling of his primary opponents, such as "low energy" Jeb Bush, "Little Marco" Rubio, and "Lyin' Ted" Cruz, may have shocked political elites, but many GOP voters ate it up. Donald Trump was an outsider with no previous political experience who had initially rebuffed the Republican Party. As such, he was not supported by many elected Republicans both during the primaries and even after he became the party's presidential nominee.[42] The RNC stayed out of the primary process but stepped up to offer the Trump campaign its assistance when it was clear Trump would be the nominee.[43]

Both parties entered their summer nominating conventions battered and divided, and the two parties' nominees could not have been any more different. The bifurcated landscape of the presidential general election contest impacted each party's approach to the election. The Democratic nominee was an old school party politician, and the Democratic National Committee played a familiar and traditional role in support of Hillary Clinton. The Clinton campaign had an extensive and widely heralded field operation, with over 5,000 staffers in fifteen battleground states. As the Capitol Hill newspaper *The Hill* reported in late October, "Clinton holds [a] huge ground game advantage over Team Trump."[44] The DNC augmented the Clinton campaign's efforts on the ground with funds and personnel through its coordinated campaign with state and local party organizations, with far more staff on the payroll than the Republicans had.[45] Yet the Clinton get-out-the-vote (GOTV) machine may have actually turned out some voters for Trump. Clinton campaign volunteers in Ohio, Pennsylvania, and North Carolina reported that when they were reminding people to vote, "they encountered a significant number of Trump Voters. . . . [A]nywhere from five to 25 percent of contacts were inadvertently targeted to Trump supporters."[46] Indeed, after the election, some Democratic Party strategists did a deep analysis of the voter turn-out data and concluded that Clinton lost in part because she lost voters who had voted for Barack Obama in 2012.[47] Others pointed to inadequate staffing in states like Michigan,[48] while others pointed to an overreli-ance on data and analytics.[49]

Additionally, in late July, a scandal erupted with the WikiLeaks re-lease of hacked e-mails that revealed possible DNC favoritism toward Clinton over her primary challenger, Vermont senator Bernie Sanders. These leaks forced the resignation of the DNC chair, Florida congress-woman Debbie Wasserman Schultz, on the eve of the Democrats' nomi-nation convention.[50] A substantial plurality of party voters were already disappointed that Sanders did not defeat Clinton for the nomination, and the leaked e-mails fueled more anger and more charges that the national party rigged the process. Additionally, FBI director James Comey an-nounced on July 5, 2016 that the investigation of Hillary Clinton's use of a private e-mail server while she was secretary of state was finished. Then, on October 28, eleven days before the election, Comey sent a letter to Congress announcing he was reopening the investigation because of the discovery of new e-mails. However, on November 6, just two days before Election Day but long after early voting had begun, he sent an-other letter to Congress saying that the new e-mails contained no new information.[51] All of this played out in the news media as breaking news with big headlines. In her postelection book, Hillary Clinton commented on the impact of this episode:

> On November 1 and 2, my campaign conducted focus groups with Independent, swing voters in Philadelphia and Tampa, Florida. The undecideds weren't ready to jump to Trump yet, but in retro-spect, the warning signs were blinking red. "I have concerns about this whole Weiner thing. I find it unsettling. I had been leaning toward Hillary but now I just don't know," said one Florida voter. "I was never a fan of either one, but this email thing with Clin-ton has me concerned the past few days. Will they elect her and then impeach her? Was she giving away secret information?" said another.[52]

Other research confirms that a more general concern about Clinton's e-mails was on the minds of voters in the period from early July through the election. The top word mentioned with reference to what respondents had read, seen, or heard about Clinton in the last day or two was "email."[53]

Trump did not have much of a ground operation coming out of the primaries, but the RNC compensated. They scaled up their data and GOTV operations soon after the 2012 elections. John Philleppe, the RNC's general counsel since 2009, observed that the RNC's leadership knew they trailed in data and digital abilities compared to what Obama and the Democrats had created. He noted that the RNC effort "started in the spring of 2013 . . . [which] allowed us to do more testing on things in the field as well. We ended up with a field model that was much more like what Obama had in 2012 than anything the Republicans had had before."[54] The RNC had permanent staff in place in eleven presidential battleground states by summer 2013.[55] In addition, they trained hundreds of volunteers to do phone banking and door-to-door canvassing, developed an extensive voter data and digital program, and "plowed money into voter registration and field staff."[56]

On top of the RNC's impressive voter data program and stepped-up GOTV operation, Trump's son-in-law Jared Kushner created a sophisticated social media operation—headed by Brad Parscale, who had done marketing work for Trump businesses but had not previously worked in politics—in an office building in San Antonio. The Trump social media effort focused on "message tailoring, sentiment manipulation and machine learning," as the Clinton campaign continued to rely more heavily on traditional media.[57] Kushner hired top-notch Silicon Valley digital marketers to sell lots of bright red Make America Great Again caps and other swag to supporters, air policy videos featuring Trump speaking directly into the camera, and raise money in small amounts. Indeed, 69 percent of Trump's individual contributors gave $200 or less, while only 22 percent of Clinton's individual contributors gave $200 or less (either directly to the campaign or through a joint fundraising committee).[58] Of course, Clinton raised far more from individuals—$618.8 million to Trump's $344.1 million—and Trump loaned his campaign $47.5 million, while Clinton made no loans to her campaign.[59]

Virtually every reputable poll predicted Clinton would win the presidential election,[60] and many election forecasters expected the Democrats to take control of the Senate also but not necessarily the House.[61] Of course, neither happened. However, as noted, forecasters also put stock in the presumption that Democrats had a better ground operation and the fact that Clinton spent far more than Trump, that candidates in competitive House and Senate races were fairly evenly matched in fundraising (with heavy spending by outside groups), and that all three of the Democratic national party committees raised more money than the three Republican national party committees.[62]

The consensus that Trump could not win the presidency and that his campaign was actually hurting the Republicans' chances of keeping control of the Senate had everything to do with the candidate's own behavior on the campaign trail. Trump insulted Mexican Americans, the disabled, women, and the media—hardly any group seemed off-limits. Conventional political candidates would likely have suffered grave consequences at the ballot box had they behaved in this way, but Trump was entirely unconventional. The surprise was that even though Republicans across the country felt they had to explain how much (or how little) they agreed with their party nominee's zingers (delivered both live and in Tweets), their Democratic opponents did not garner more votes as a result. Indeed, Democrats had to continuously defend their nominee's persistent e-mail server issues. Postelection analysis of the Gallup daily poll that asked what respondents had "read, seen or heard" about Clinton and Trump revealed that Clinton's e-mail problem was mentioned more from July to November than any other issue for either candidate, and those who mentioned the e-mail issue had negative views of Clinton.[63] There was no single issue that respondents mentioned as much about Trump, "whose multiple scandals produced a changing, and perhaps more easily overcome, narrative during the campaign."[64] CNN's Chris Cillizza suggested that by "throwing so many balls up in the air every day—via his stump speeches, Twitter, etc.—Trump made it impossible for anyone to follow all of them. Everything seemed like a molehill. Even the mountains."[65]

While this strategy worked well for Trump, he did not have a prior relationship with Republican Party organizations, and the Republican congressional party committees found themselves having to "go it alone" in formulating strategy and procuring resources, while Democrats could pursue a more conventional approach in harmony with their nominee and her organization. These nominee-party dynamics may help explain the interesting trends in party fundraising during the 2016 election cycle.

Party Fundraising

Figure 7-1 shows fundraising by each of the party's three national committees (DNC and RNC), House campaign committees (DCCC and
NRCC), and Senate campaign committees (DSCC and NRSC) for election cycles from 1992 to 2016 (adjusted for inflation in 2016 dollars).
Note that party receipts from 1992 to 2002 include both federal and
nonfederal money (both hard and soft money) but hard money only for
election cycles from 2004 to 2016, after BCRA banned soft money in
2002. Figure 7-1 indicates that most of the party committees certainly
raised less money after the BCRA soft-money ban, especially the House
and Senate campaign committees, which all saw sharp declines in receipts from 2002 to 2004. Interestingly, the DNC actually raised more
in 2004 than it had before the soft-money ban, but the DNC struggled
to keep pace with the RNC from 2006 until 2016, when the two parties'
national committees raised about the same amount.

The unconventional nature of Trump and his campaign may help
explain the significant decline in RNC fundraising in 2016. Indeed,
especially after the video surfaced on October 7 of Trump boasting
about sexually assaulting women and the allegations by numerous women
of Trump's unwelcome sexual advances, some major GOP donors refused
to give their usual large contributions to the party and urged the RNC to
cut ties with Trump.[66] Yet the 2016 election cycle also represents a continuation of the post-2008 decline for the RNC. Thus, it is not clear exactly how much Trump contributed to this trend. It is also evident that
the NRCC and NRSC have not recovered as well as the DCCC and DSCC
from the loss of soft money. Meanwhile, 2016 was the best fundraising
year the DNC and DCCC had since 2004.

The two parties have responded differently to BCRA. The NRSC and
DSCC were at near parity before BCRA, but since 2004 the DSCC has
consistently outraised the NRSC. The predictions that BCRA would hurt
the Democrats more than it would hurt the Republicans, with some at
the time calling it the "Democratic Party Suicide Bill," seem not to have
been realized.[67] As discussed later in the chapter, however, BCRA has
made it difficult for the parties to keep pace with *other* campaign finance actors, some of which have no real limits on their fundraising
and spending.

What's behind this big picture of party fundraising? Figure 7-2 shows
the Democratic and Republican national party committees' sources of

Figure 7-1. *Hard- and Soft-Money Receipts of National Party Committees, 1992–2016*

Millions of 2016 dollars

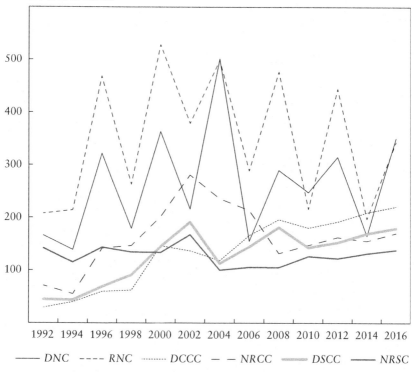

DNC ---- RNC ········ DCCC − − NRCC ▬▬ DSCC ▬▬ NRSC

Source: Compiled by the authors from Federal Election Commission data.
Note: Hard and soft money shown for 1992 to 2002; hard money only for 2004–16.

funds from 2000 to 2016. Both parties went from relying heavily on soft money in the early years post-2000 to relying heavily on limited contributions from individual donors (as they had before the jump in soft-money fundraising in 1996). BCRA pointed parties toward individual donors by increasing the individual contribution limits for money given to party committees from $20,000 per year (1976–2002) to $25,000 per year starting in 2004 and then indexing those higher limits to inflation. Candidates and parties clearly took advantage of this incentive. Recently, the party committees have raised a larger share of their funds from transfers from other party committees at the national, state, and local levels, much of it through joint fundraising committees, especially in presidential

Figure 7-2. *Sources of Party Money, 2000–16*

Millions of 2016 dollars

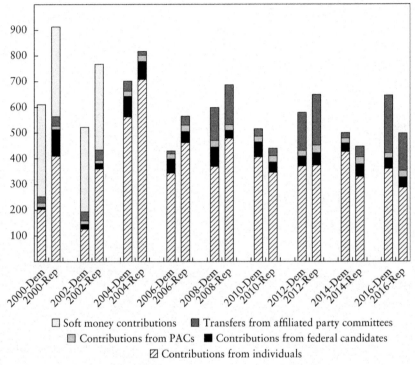

☐ Soft money contributions   ■ Transfers from affiliated party committees
☐ Contributions from PACs   ■ Contributions from federal candidates
▨ Contributions from individuals

Source: Compiled by the authors from Federal Election Commission data.
Note: Figure includes data for all national party committees: the DNC and RNC, DSCC and NRSC, and DCCC and NRCC.

election years. To a lesser extent, the parties have relied on contributions from their own candidates since BCRA.

Party Receipts from Individual Contributors

Both parties continue to raise the vast majority of their money from individual contributors. While BCRA banned party soft money, it also raised the limits on contributions individuals can make to parties and indexed them to inflation. This has helped the national parties compensate somewhat for the loss of unlimited soft-money fundraising. Table 7-2 shows national party committee receipts for the six main national party

Table 7-2. *National Party Committee Receipts from Individual Contributors, 2004–16 Elections*[a]
2016 dollars, except as indicated

	2004	2006	2008	2010	2012	2014	2016
DNC							
Total receipts	513,931,761	155,808,102	290,024,511	247,127,640	303,510,329	165,606,395	350,608,660
Total contributions from individuals	425,113,311	140,476,966	151,146,075	217,056,898	124,586,773	157,658,693	95,852,581
Individual contributions as share of total receipts (%)	82.7	90.2	52.1	87.8	41.1	95.2	27.3
Unitemized	210,250,001	87,180,096	92,237,283	113,764,869	79,273,931	71,342,389	53,145,797
Unitemized as share of total from individuals (%)	49.5	62.1	61	52.4	63.6	45.3	55.4
Contributions at the maximum permitted	55,097,850	4,473,634	46,032,365	24,232,570	6,877,414	20,284,652	8,615,200
Maximum as a share of individual total (%)	13	3.2	30.5	11.2	5.5	12.9	9
DSCC							
Total receipts	112,685,969	144,559,963	181,512,470	142,627,331	152,472,791	170,679,837	179,800,228
Total contributions from individuals	73,428,469	103,893,819	117,038,158	90,922,359	108,871,624	118,730,887	117,479,933
Individual contributions as share of total receipts (%)	65.1	71.9	64.5	63.7	71.4	69.6	65.3
Unitemized	26,919,009	29,187,670	27,445,636	37,696,068	51,848,487	50,888,961	44,131,574
Unitemized as share of total from individuals (%)	36.7	28.1	23.5	41.5	47.6	42.9	37.6
Contributions at the maximum permitted	15,474,425	11,929,890	30,444,518	12,250,166	15,089,097	18,302,193	22,545,700
Maximum as a share of individual total (%)	21.1	11.5	26	13.5	13.9	15.4	19.2

(*continued*)

Table 7-2. *Continued*

2016 dollars, except as indicated

	2004	2006	2008	2010	2012	2014	2016
DCCC							
Total receipts	118,503,181	166,733,303	196,468,156	180,449,553	192,115,976	209,687,081	220,891,388
Total contributions from individuals	64,495,493	99,084,091	101,158,572	98,240,946	137,634,427	150,078,502	147,346,246
Individual contributions as share of total receipts (%)	54.4	59.4	51.5	54.5	71.6	71.6	66.7
Unitemized	32,028,306	37,624,330	34,387,695	41,284,743	73,991,575	76,591,569	66,732,647
Unitemized as share of total from individuals (%)	49.7	38	34	42	53.8	51	45.3
Contributions at the maximum permitted	8,483,925	6,271,746	17,509,403	12,250,166	13,020,896	15,053,532	18,670,600
Maximum as a share of individual total (%)	13.2	6.3	17.3	12.5	9.5	10	12.7
RNC							
Total receipts	498,757,433	289,421,507	476,728,039	216,166,731	407,776,685	197,589,188	343,371,200
Total contributions from individuals	445,318,899	254,222,984	316,589,394	183,358,781	232,699,831	179,221,704	171,288,215
Individual contributions as share of total receipts (%)	89.3	87.8	66.4	84.8	57.1	90.7	49.9
Unitemized	199,663,746	134,403,389	169,716,185	125,326,531	131,071,836	87,939,308	80,288,429
Unitemized as share of total from individuals (%)	44.8	52.9	53.6	68.4	56.3	49.1	46.9
Contributions at the maximum permitted	77,340,350	953,991	41,725,753	4,150,330	29,985,704	32,151,811	32,314,300
Maximum as a share of individual total (%)	17.4	0.4	13.2	2.3	12.9	17.9	18.9

NRSC

Total receipts	100,384,199	105,775,553	105,283,588	123,641,451	122,312,923	130,074,156	138,376,517
Total contributions from individuals	77,291,345	77,670,196	79,204,258	85,279,429	79,652,539	91,076,227	73,342,992
Individual contributions as share of total receipts (%)	77.0	73.4	75.2	69.0	65.1	70.0	53.0
Unitemized	38,128,706	29,209,941	32,267,501	36,447,103	27,466,573	26,619,754	24,061,237
Unitemized as share of total from individuals (%)	49.3	37.6	40.7	42.7	34.5	29.2	32.8
Contributions at the maximum permitted	7,784,875	2,539,927	14,682,320	15,998,851	21,517,010	22,537,975	21,846,009
Maximum as a share of individual total (%)	10.1	3.3	18.5	18.8	27	24.7	29.8

NRCC

Total receipts	236,049,486	209,974,065	131,932,116	147,290,810	162,732,222	155,636,956	170,601,975
Total contributions from individuals	185,385,593	129,607,904	83,533,486	77,731,007	61,826,027	59,958,592	42,927,909
Individual contributions as share of total receipts (%)	78.5	61.7	63.3	52.7	38.0	38.6	25.1
Unitemized	63,282,912	46,598,911	35,802,396	37,513,392	26,076,519	25,382,419	16,906,313
Unitemized as share of total from individuals (%)	34.1	36	42.9	48.3	42.2	42.3	39.4
Contributions at the maximum permitted	4,798,025	222,598	3,130,363	6,091,613	8,966,727	9,120,727	9,183,300
Maximum as a share of individual total (%)	2.6	0.2	3.7	7.8	14.5	15.2	21.4

Sources: Data for 2004 through 2010 from Federal Election Commission (www.fec.gov/press/2010_Full_summary_Data.shtml). Data for 2012 through 2016 compiled from disclosure filings reported to the Federal Election Commission (www.fec.gov/finance/disclosure/candcmte_info.shtml) as of May 29, 2017. Data adjusted for 2016 dollars using the CPI inflation calculator from U.S. Bureau of Labor Statistics (www.bls.gov/data/inflation_calculator.htm).

a. Table includes federal or "hard" money only. Total receipts include other items not listed in table, which include, but are not limited to, offsets to operating expenditures and loans received. Unitemized contributions from individuals are those that total $200 or less in a calendar year from a single person. The maximum contribution from individuals was changed from $20,000 per year to $25,000 per year for the 2004 election cycle, and $26,700 in 2006, $28,500 in 2008, $30,400 in 2010, $30,800 in 2012, $32,400 in 2014, and $33,400 in 2016. Transfers from affiliated committees include transfers from the joint fundraising committees of the presidential campaigns.

campaign committees (excluding the building, recount/legal, and convention accounts, which are considered later in the chapter) from individual donors after BCRA, from 2004 to 2016. These contributions are further broken down by the percentage of total individual receipts from donors contributing $200 or less ("unitemized" contributions, more commonly referred to as small contributions) and the percentage of total individual receipts from contributors giving the maximum allowed in each election cycle (donors could give a maximum of $2,700 per election in 2016). All of the committees, except the DNC and NRCC, relied heavily on individual contributions for the 2016 elections. Only 27 percent of the DNC's receipts and 25 percent of the NRCC's receipts came directly from individual contributors, as both of these party committees raised much more of their money in 2016 through transfers from other party committees of money raised mostly through joint fundraising committees, much of which was originally given by individuals, which is discussed later.

The mix of those making small contributions and those giving the maximum has fluctuated over the years, with all but one of the six national party committees consistently raising more of their funds from small donors each year than from max-out donors, as table 7-2 shows (the exception is the DSCC, which raised 26 percent of its receipts from max-out donors and only 23.5 percent from small donors in 2008). From 2004 to 2016, max-out donors provided the largest share of all individual contributions for Democratic Party committees, while the GOP committees relied most on max-out donors in 2016. For example, almost 30 percent of all individual contributions to the NRSC came from contributors who gave the maximum allowed in the 2016 cycle. It appears that the Republican Party committees in particular were able to benefit from the 2014 *McCutcheon* decision's elimination of the overall contribution limits and, as will be discussed, from the new party accounts allowed under the CRomnibus provisions.

Party Receipts from Other Party Committees and Joint Fundraising Committees

The national party committees received record amounts in transfers from affiliated party committees in 2016. For instance, the DNC and RNC collected $209.3 million and $95.2 million, respectively, from other party committees, with most of that money coming from joint fundraising committees. Table 7-3 shows that the DNC and RNC in particular collect quite a lot of their money from other party committees, especially in presidential election years.

Much of the money the national party committees raise from other party committees comes from joint fundraising committee activity. Joint fundraising committees (JFCs) are committees created by one or more candidates, party committees, and/or PACs, whereby the various participants split the fundraising costs to raise money together and then split the proceeds according to a prearranged formula. Donors can give up to the maximum amount to each candidate(s), party committee(s), and/or PAC(s) in the JFC. For example, in 2016 an individual donor could give no more than $2,700 per election to a specific candidate, $33,400 per year to a national party committee, $10,000 per year to any state party committee, and $5,000 to a PAC. Contributors cannot give any more than they could if the money were given directly to the candidate, party, or PAC, but a donor can write one large check to be distributed to the various members of the JFC according to the prearranged formula (see chapter 2).

Congressional party leaders have long used joint fundraising committees to raise money for themselves, their colleagues, and their parties. In 2000, there were 105 active JFCs. At that time, congressional candidates and party leaders headed up the top JFCs, including then House minority leader Dick Gephardt and New York's Democratic U.S. Senate candidate, Hillary Clinton. The four congressional campaign committees received 40 percent ($14.1 million) of all money raised by all JFCs in 2000 ($35.5 million).[68] State parties also have used JFCs effectively for their national campaign activities, often forming a JFC together with many state party organizations and splitting the proceeds, such as the 1999 State Victory Fund Committee, which raised $5.2 million, distributed to twenty-one state parties.[69] By 2016, there were 616 active JFCs formed by presidential candidates, party leaders, party organizations, dozens of House and Senate candidates, and PACs.[70] Presidential candidates started using JFCs in 2004, when John Kerry Victory raised $42.1 million through a JFC with the Democratic National Committee and allocated $18.1 million of the total to the DNC.[71] Since then, the amount raised by JFCs has been far greater in presidential election years than in midterm years.[72]

In 2016, Hillary Clinton set a new record for joint fundraising, raising $577 million with two JFCs, including her national party committee,

Table 7-3. *National Party Committee Receipts: Transfers from Affiliated Party Committees, 2000–16*
2016 dollars

	2000	2002	2004	2006	2008	2010	2012	2014	2016
DNC	3,391,001	9,113,500	29,009,360	1,326,393	111,035,295	2,993,233	141,204,606	365,529	209,266,979
DSCC	18,578,461	20,370,097	7,747,039	7,147,725	10,633,288	15,730,118	3,559,875	12,655,082	7,930,155
DCCC	2,417,122	5,321,113	1,391,807	2,700,988	6,339,309	10,279,416	2,787,865	8,154,169	6,619,252
RNC	15,695,045	4,697,174	8,808,733	5,477,590	143,819,490	10,030,718	155,789,836	6,176,763	95,202,826
NRSC	14,114,840	17,675,320	3,257,879	8,129,154	7,602,988	10,702,048	17,601,335	10,988,940	14,840,769
NRCC	7,141,030	16,956,141	2,746,416	20,372,055	2,591,109	8,008,316	23,687,851	22,990,585	34,959,873

Sources: Data for 2004 through 2010 from Federal Election Commission (www.fec.gov/press/2010_Full_summary_Data.shtml). Data for 2012 through 2016 compiled from disclosure filings reported to the Federal Election Commission (www.fec.gov/finance/disclosure/candcmte_info.shtml) as of May 29, 2017. Data adjusted for 2016 dollars using the CPI inflation calculator from U.S. Bureau of Labor Statistics (www.bls.gov/data/inflation_calculator.htm).

Figure 7-3. *National Party Share of Joint Fundraising Committee Receipts, 2008–16*

Millions of 2016 dollars

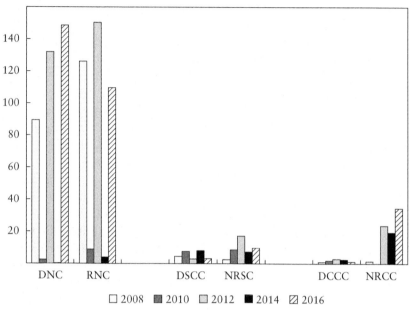

Source: Compiled by the authors from Center for Responsive Politics data. See Center for Responsive Politics, "Joint Fundraising Committees Recipients" (www.opensecrets.org/jfc/top.php?type=R&cycle=2016).

the DNC. This total was $200 million more than Donald Trump and the RNC raised in joint fundraising in 2016. Although Barack Obama raised far more from individual donors to his campaign than Mitt Romney did in 2012, Romney raised more ($493 million) than Obama ($461 million) through joint fundraising. In 2008, John McCain and the RNC raised $221 million, while Obama and the DNC raised $228 million that year. The drop in Trump/RNC joint fundraising is consistent with his challenges in fundraising generally.

Joint fundraising committees often host big-ticket fundraising events to attract wealthy donors and groups who appreciate the opportunity to rub elbows with the powerful and famous. Figure 7-3 shows how much each of the six national party committees received directly from participation in joint fundraising committees from 2008 to 2016. Clearly, the DNC and RNC in particular have successfully used JFCs to raise large sums during presidential election years.

Because there are no limits on the amount of federal money that can be transferred from a state party to a national party committee and no limit on transfers between federal party committees across states, funds raised by state parties via joint fundraising committees are often transferred to national party committees. Such transfers allow the national party committees to set up JFCs that direct far more to them than the JFC allocation formula gives them.[73] Here is how it worked in the case of the 2016 Hillary Victory Fund, the JFC that raised the most in 2015 and 2016 ($530 million).[74] The official reports show that the Clinton campaign was allocated $158.2 million from the Hillary Victory Fund, the DNC was allocated $107.5 million, and thirty-eight state party committees were allocated a combined $112.4 million.[75] However, the state party committees kept very little of the money allocated to them from the joint fundraising since virtually all of that money was immediately transferred to the DNC, allowing "a small number of elite Democratic donors to give hundreds of thousands of dollars to the DNC for the purpose of affecting the presidential campaign."[76] For example, the Oklahoma Democratic Party received $3,013,100 from the Hillary Victory Fund JFC, and every penny was then transferred to the DNC. A single donor's contribution to a national party committee was limited to $33,400 per year in 2016, and that contributor could also give up to $10,000 per year to any (and even all) state party committees. So, if those state parties transferred their JFC proceeds to the national party, the limits on how much a contributor may give to a national party committee would, in effect, be circumvented.

The joint fundraising committees that raised the most in the 2016 cycle were those connected to the presidential nominees. In addition to the Hillary Victory Fund discussed earlier, Clinton had a second JFC, the Hillary Action Fund, which raised a total of $46.6 million and was set up primarily as a fundraising vehicle for the DNC. Indeed, of the $39.2 million transferred out of the committee (the rest was for overhead and other expenses), Clinton received only $2.6 million (6 percent), but the DNC received $36.7 million (94 percent).[77] Donald Trump had two JFCs. The Trump Victory joint fundraising committee raised a total of $108.4 million, and of the $94.4 million transferred out of the JFC, the Trump campaign received $13.6 million (14 percent), the RNC received $51.1 million (54 percent), and $29.7 million (32 percent) was distributed in various amounts to twenty-one state Republican Party committees.[78] The Trump Make America Great Again JFC raised a total of $263.7 million, and of the $158.8 million transferred out, Donald Trump for President received $121.2 million (76.3 percent) and the RNC received $37.6 million (23.7 percent).[79]

Both parties' presidential nominees followed the same joint fundraising committee strategy by setting up one JFC as a fundraising vehicle primarily for their own campaign and one that raised funds mostly for the national party. Clinton followed Obama's example by setting up her JFC with the DNC the year before the presidential election, permitting individuals to give twice as much since contribution limits to national party committees are annual limits.[80] However, Obama did this as the party's *unopposed* nominee, while Clinton entered into a JFC with the DNC well before she defeated Bernie Sanders for the nomination. The Sanders team cried foul and accused the DNC of financial favoritism. Clinton's fundraising prowess helped the DNC pay down its debt, and, in return, Clinton had control over the funds. Former interim DNC chair Donna Brazile explained in her postelection book:

> The [Clinton] campaign was raising millions of dollars through the DNC, and because of the agreement they had made to pay off the party's debt I could not touch a cent. The states were raising money, too, but that money was not under the states' control either. All of this was in the hands of Robby Mook [Clinton's campaign manager], who wanted to maintain control of all the funds and spend them in the way that he saw fit.[81]

Brazile concluded that although the DNC's financial arrangement with the Clinton campaign "was not a criminal act, . . . it compromised the party's integrity."[82] Indeed, supporters of Bernie Sanders saw the DNC-Clinton JFC arrangement as proof that the process was rigged to ensure Clinton would win the nomination.

Below the presidential level, other joint fundraising committees raised money for the parties and various candidates. Team Ryan, House Speaker Paul Ryan's JFC, raised $65.6 million for the 2016 elections, and the NRCC received $20 million of it, Ryan's own campaign received $12.9 million, and $2.8 million was allocated to Prosperity Action, Speaker Ryan's leadership PAC.[83] Senator John Cornyn (R-Tex.) and RNC chairman Reince Priebus created the NRSC Targeted State Victory Committee in 2014 to direct funds to targeted Senate contests.[84] This JFC raised $8.3 million and distributed $2.2 million of its proceeds to the NRSC and $5.7 million to eighteen state Republican parties.[85] We expect to see increasing use of JFCs for candidate and party fundraising, especially by presidential candidates, because of the vast amounts they must raise to compete effectively for national office and also because the *McCutcheon* decision removed the aggregate contribution limit, making it easier to raise more from each big donor, who can write one large check that will be distributed to the various candidates and party committees in the JFC. Yet, we are not likely to see a national party committee establish a JFC with a presidential candidate again until after the party's nominee is selected.

New National Party Accounts

As noted, the parties can now collect even more from individuals and PACs for their new convention, legal/recount, and headquarters accounts created as a result of the 2015 CRomnibus deal. These accounts are embedded within each national party committee and to date have not been assigned unique Federal Election Commission ID numbers. Still, the FEC tracked how much each of these new accounts raised during the 2016 election cycle, as shown in table 7-4.

The RNC and DNC each received $18,248,300 in public funding for their 2012 conventions, and, if the public funds were still available, that amount would have been increased in 2016 to $19,598,700 to account for inflation.[86] Table 7-4 shows that the RNC raised more than the public subsidy it would have received and the DNC raised slightly less for their 2016 conventions. So, for this first round with the new convention committee accounts, the national parties generally raised about what they lost from public funds. The new national party convention accounts are in addition to the preexisting host committees both parties use to cover the expenses of the increasingly complicated made-for-TV productions. As discussed in chapter 2, since the 1980s, host committees have been allowed to raise and spend money from ordinarily prohibited sources (specifically, corporations and labor unions) in unlimited amounts to assist the locality in hosting the convention. Its purpose is to encourage "commerce in the convention city and the projection of a favorable image of the city to convention attendees."[87] In 2016, the Philadelphia Host Committee raised $86.8 million and the Cleveland Host Committee raised $70.1 million.[88] The Cleveland Host Committee was $6 million short of its $64 million fundraising goal and sought a late contribution

Table 7-4. *Contributions to the New CRomnibus Accounts of the
National Party Committees, 2015–16*

Dollars

	Convention	Headquarters	Recount/ legal	Total
DNC	16,755,965	6,953,019	4,089,189	27,798,171
DSCC	n.a.	7,068,150	2,931,767	9,999,917
DCCC	n.a.	7,321,678	2,693,120	10,014,799
Democratic Party totals	16,755,965	21,342,847	9,714,076	47,812,887
RNC	23,817,038	26,367,459	5,949,515	56,134,013
NRSC	n.a.	9,408,452	1,348,478	10,756,929
NRCC	n.a.	10,080,459	10,751,747[a]	20,832,207
Republican Party totals	23,817,038	45,856,370	18,049,740	87,723,149

Source: Federal Election Commission, "2015–2016 Election Cycle Data Summaries through 12/31/16: National Party 24-Month Data Summaries (1/1/15–12/31/16)" (https://transition.fec.gov/press/summaries/2016/ElectionCycle /24m_NatlParty.shtml) as of June 24, 2017.

a. There were no House recounts for the Republicans.

of that amount from conservative megadonors Sheldon and Miriam Adelson,[89] and the GOP host committee ultimately exceeded its goal. Some corporate sponsors who had supported host committees in the past did not in 2016, and some traditional big-name attendees, such as former presidential candidates John McCain and Mitt Romney and former presidents George H. W. Bush and George W. Bush, did not attend.[90] In the case of the Democratic convention, the Philadelphia Host Committee met its fundraising goal but only after the convention concluded.[91]

All six national party committees raised funds for their new headquarters and recount/legal accounts, but the RNC outdid all the others with the $26.4 million it raised for its headquarters account. Much of the money for the RNC headquarters account was transferred from the main RNC account and marked for specific purposes. For example, the RNC transferred $1,387,868 for "reimbursement for allocated staff salaries and other costs" on July 29, 2016, and it transferred $2,279,977 for "expenses reimbursement for 2014 identified headquarters building operating expenses" on October 31, 2015.[92] Some of these transfers refer to 2014 FEC Advisory Opinion 2010-14, which, among other things, allows the national party committees to allocate staff expenses based on the percentage of time individual staff members spend doing election-related work and, in this case, headquarters work.[93] This is one area where the parties could certainly enjoy some efficiencies of scale without actually violating the law, because they would not have to hire separate staff for their headquarters, convention, and recount/legal work. However, as noted, some observers have cautioned that the lack of clear rules from the Federal Election Commission to regulate how the parties may use these new accounts means that the parties are free to interpret how the money can be spent.[94]

Party Receipts from PACs

As Figure 7.2 indicates, the parties raise only a small portion of their money from political action committees (PACs). Yet, when we look at each party committee separately, we can see that the parties' congressional campaign committees (the DSCC, DCCC, NRSC, and NRCC) raise far more from PACs than their national committees (the DNC and RNC) do. Still, in 2016, PAC donations were only 6 percent of DSCC receipts, 4 percent of DCCC receipts, 8 percent of NRSC receipts, and 7 percent of NRCC receipts.

The PACs' focus on the House and Senate party committees is not surprising. Most PACs are connected to interest groups, corporations, or labor unions that are focused on policy results, and these organizations target their lobbying efforts on congressional committee and party leaders in particular.[95] Their PACs follow an access-oriented electoral strategy by concentrating most of their campaign contributions on incumbent congressional candidates they expect to lobby, who win reelection over 90 percent of the time, with the majority of PAC money generally going to each chamber's majority party. After the Democrats took control of Congress following the 2006 elections, PACs began to direct more money to the DSCC and the DCCC than to the NRSC and NRCC, and as the Republicans gained control of the House in 2010 and the Senate in 2012, PACs shifted more contributions to the NRCC and the NRSC. For the 2016 elections, PACs also could contribute to the parties' new convention, recount/legal, and headquarters committees. Yet these contributions are difficult to track because they are made to a national party committee's main account, and then the party committee earmarks the money for these specific purposes. Since BCRA kept the limit on PAC contributions flat (without adjustments for inflation each cycle), we expect PAC contributions to party committees to continue to decline as a fundraising source for the parties. For a discussion of PAC contributions to candidates, see chapter 3.

Member Contributions to Their Parties

A final category of funds for parties is money raised from their own elected officials and candidates. Federal candidates and officeholders are permitted to transfer unlimited sums from their principal campaign committee and $15,000 per year from their leadership PAC to any national party committee. In the 1970s and 1980s, members of Congress redistributed very little to their parties or to fellow candidates,[96] and "incumbents actively resisted even suggestions from party leaders that they might share their wealth for the benefit of the team."[97] Eric Heberlig and Bruce Larson found that House incumbents' contributions to their respective congressional campaign committees (the DCCC and NRCC) began to rise in 1994, when control of the chamber was seriously up for grabs for the first time in four decades, and incumbent transfers to the Hill committees (the DSCC, NRSC, DCCC, and NRCC) grew sharply in 2004 after the 2002 Bipartisan Campaign Reform Act banned soft-money contributions to the national party committees.[98] The DCCC collected $16.4 million from Democratic lawmakers in 2002 and $23.8 million after BCRA in 2004, and the NRCC raised $19.1 million in 2002 from its own members and $25.3 million in 2004 (amounts adjusted for inflation in 2016 dollars).

Congressional party leaders convince incumbents to give to the Hill committees and to the party's candidates in close races by using encouragement and peer pressure, by charging their incumbent members dues and setting fundraising quotas, and by using the parties' control over institutional positions of power such as committee and subcommittee leadership posts and important party positions as rewards. Heberlig and Larson found that House members' contribution strategies became more party oriented over time as the fight for control of the chamber intensified after 1994 into late the following decade (their analysis ends in 2008). Elected party leaders, committee chairs, and majority party members are more party centered and give more to their parties and fellow candidates than other incumbents do.[99] Indeed, the parties ask these leaders to do more than their colleagues because of the relative ease with which they are able to leverage their positions to raise more from policy-seeking PACs and individual donors. In 2016, the DSCC raised a good deal more from Senate Democrats ($19.1 million compared to the NRSC's $3.6 million) than it had in 2014 ($8.3 million compared to the NRSC's $4.2 million) as the party, and many other observers, thought that the Democrats had a good chance of taking control of the Senate (amounts adjusted for inflation in 2016 dollars).

Political party fundraising in 2016 differed in some interesting ways from that in 2012. For instance, the difficult relationship between the Republican National Committee and the party's eventual presidential nominee, Donald Trump, resulted in the RNC being the only one of the six national party committees to have a real decline in receipts from 2012 ($407 million) to 2016 ($343 million—both in 2016 dollars). The *McCutcheon* decision allowing individual contributors to donate more to party committees and without the constraint of an overall limit may have had a modest effect on the receipts of the five other committees, but the change was not dramatic. Ending public funding of the party conventions had little impact, as both parties were able to raise enough for their conventions through the new convention accounts. The DNC's joint fundraising with Hillary Clinton was quite controversial and caused a serious and consequential rift between Clinton and Sanders supporters that likely contributed to Clinton's general election loss. The next section discusses how parties spent the money they raised.

Party Spending

Political parties can spend money in a variety of ways to assist their candidates, and all modern party committees work to distribute their funds efficiently, where the money will do the most good to secure or maintain majority control of the various government institutions; that is, the parties direct most of their spending to the most competitive races. Moreover, the regulatory and political context of each election cycle influences how the parties spend their money. In 2016, there were no major regulatory changes that forced the parties to alter their central spending strategies. Yet the political context was a different matter entirely. The Republicans controlled the Senate and needed to defend twenty-four seats in 2016 to the Democrats' ten. Several of the incumbents in these seats decided to retire, putting partisan control of the Senate in play. The Republicans held fifty-four seats, and most experts predicted a gain of three to six seats for the Democrats.[100] As the Democrats needed five seats to win control of the Senate, there was intense interest in the seven seats considered in the "toss-up" category.[101] In the House, most agreed all along that Republicans would retain control, as they had a 247 to 188 lead going into the election. Democrats would need to gain thirty seats to attain a majority, but the best of predictions had them picking up ten to fifteen seats.[102] At one point in October, when Clinton held a six to nine percentage point lead in various polls, some speculated a Democratic majority in both the Senate and the House was a possibility, and the Clinton campaign actually started to shift resources into states with close Senate races.[103] During this same period, fundraising dropped for Clinton's Super PAC and rose for the Democratic Senate Majority PAC, a Super PAC that supports Democratic Senate candidates. In the end, Democrats gained only six seats, winning 194 seats in the House to the Republicans' 241. The Democrats won forty-eight seats in the Senate, a gain of two, to the Republicans' fifty-two. In an unusually unpredictable election year, the changing dynamics during the campaign season impacted how the parties employed their resources.

Party Candidate Contributions and Coordinated Expenditures

A national party committee may give up to $5,000 per election (primary and general election) directly to a federal candidate. Of course, this is a very small drop in the bucket, especially for a presidential candidate. This strict limit on direct party contributions reflects the notion that parties could act as "corrupt conduits" for donors who want to influence lawmakers.[104] Additionally, parties are permitted to spend money on behalf of their candidates when acting in coordination with them. These *coordinated expenditures* were limited originally to $10,000 in House races in 1974, but they are adjusted for inflation every election cycle. So, by 2016, the coordinated expenditure limits ranged from $96,100 to $2,886,500 for Senate nominees (depending on the state's population) and $48,100 for House nominees in most states and $96,000 for House nominees in states with only one representative.[105] Working directly with their candidates, the congressional campaign committees have used coordinated expenditures to pay for polls, the production of campaign ads, opposition research, and to compile lists of targeted voters.

Figures 7-4 and 7-5 show that the parties have never really spent much on direct contributions to their House and Senate candidates. This is primarily because the parties are limited in what they can contribute directly to their candidates without an adjustment for inflation. Before 2004, the parties relied more on coordinated expenditures, which have higher spending limits. Yet these party spending figures mask the vast majority of party spending from about 1996 to 2002, when both parties

Figure 7-4. *Party Spending on House Candidates, 2000–16*

Millions of 2016 dollars

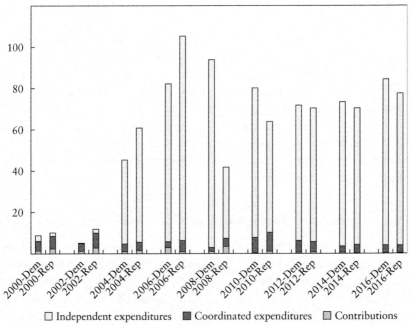

☐ Independent expenditures ■ Coordinated expenditures ☐ Contributions

Sources: Compiled by the authors from Brookings Institution, *Vital Statistics on Congress: Data on the U.S. Congress,* 2017 (www.brookings.edu/multi-chapter-report/vital-statistics-on-congress/); Federal Election Commission, "2015–2016 Election Cycle Data Summaries through 12/31/16: Party Committees."

relied most on the soft money they could raise in unlimited amounts from virtually any source, including corporations and unions (see figure 7-2).

Parties were permitted to spend soft money in unlimited amounts as long as that spending did not technically expressly advocate the election or defeat of a candidate for federal office, because the law allowed the parties to raise and spend soft money to promote "party building" activities, a restriction the parties interpreted quite broadly. Studies of soft-money spending found that much of it was spent in competitive presidential states and in close Senate and House races, and most of this spending was for candidate-specific ads, mailers, phone calls, and so on.[106] Almost none of this soft-money spending is reflected in figures 7-4 and 7-5, because the national party committees were able to spend their soft money more efficiently by transferring virtually all of it to state party committees with looser spending rules to produce and run mostly negative issue

Figure 7-5. *Party Spending on Senate Candidates, 2000–16*

Millions of 2016 dollars

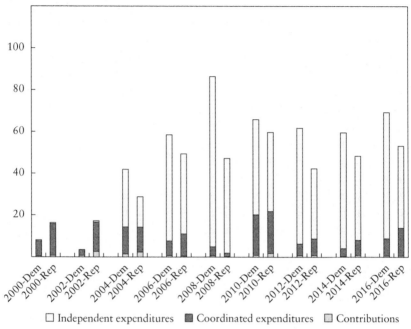

☐ Independent expenditures ■ Coordinated expenditures ☐ Contributions

Sources: Compiled by the authors from Brookings Institution, *Vital Statistics on Congress: Data on the U.S. Congress* (www.brookings.edu/multi-chapter-report/vital-statistics-on-congress/); Federal Election Commission, "2015–2016 Election Cycle Data Summaries through 12/31/16: Party Committees."

advertisements against their candidates' opponents.[107] They could use unlimited soft money for these ads because the ads, which presumably discussed policy issues rather than candidates, were not considered election-related communications intended to influence the outcome of an election under the very narrow interpretation of what was considered electioneering; that is, only communications that use one or more "magic words," such as "vote for," "defeat," or "support," referred to in the 1976 *Buckley* v. *Valeo* decision.[108] Reformers opposed to this use of unlimited soft money for elections, and lawmakers frustrated with the barrage of negative advertising against them, called these ads "sham issue ads" because they easily avoided using the "magic words" but were clearly intended to influence the outcome of an election.[109]

Once soft money was banned, parties could continue to spend limited amounts of money in coordination with their candidates. For the presidential election, Republicans spent $20 million in coordinated expenditures for Donald Trump, which is $3 million less than they spent to help Mitt Romney in 2012. The Democrats spent $22 million in coordinated expenditures to help Hillary Clinton, about $1 million more than they spent for Barack Obama in 2012. As with congressional candidates, direct party contributions were of no consequence for the presidential contenders. For the House, the DCCC and the NRCC each spent about $3.6 million on coordinated expenditures, an almost perfectly balanced effort (see figure 7-4). Party coordinated expenditures for Senate candidates looked different in 2016, as expected, with the NRSC spending $13.3 million and the DSCC spending $8.3 million (see figure 7-5), because the Republicans had more seats to defend during this cycle. Yet, while the 2016 coordinated expenditure numbers are higher in absolute terms than the 2014 and 2012 expenditures, the GOP spent less and the Democrats only slightly more on coordinated expenditures (in adjusted dollars) than they did in 2010, when this same class of senators was last elected (see figure 7.5).

Party Independent Expenditures

Since the Supreme Court's 1996 decision in *Colorado Republican Federal Campaign* v. *Federal Election Commission*,[110] the national party committees also have been permitted to make unlimited independent expenditures to help their candidates, as long as they do not coordinate with candidates and the expenditure is made from disclosed and limited contributions raised from permissible sources in limited amounts ("hard" money). Individuals and candidates themselves have been permitted to make unlimited independent expenditures since *Buckley* v. *Valeo* (1976). Yet newer groups, such as Super PACs, now do most of the independent expenditure spending because, since the 2010 *Citizens United* v. *Federal Election Commission* and *SpeechNow.org* v. *Federal Election Commission* decisions, they can *raise*, as well as spend, unlimited amounts of money from virtually any source for this purpose (while the parties must use hard money raised in limited amounts from only individuals, PACs, and their own candidates for independent expenditures).[111]

Figures 7-4 and 7-5 show how the national parties have allocated their resources using different types of spending (contributions, coordinated expenditures, and independent expenditures) in support of their House and Senate candidates from 2000 to 2016. Clearly, the parties' spending strategies have changed over time and the parties closely track one another in shifting their emphasis from one type of spending to another. The changes in the type of spending are influenced by changes in the rules governing their campaign finance activities. For instance, after the 1996 *Colorado Republican Federal Campaign v. Federal Election Commission* decision permitted the national parties to make unlimited independent expenditures, both parties, but especially the NRSC, immediately experimented with this new type of spending in Senate races, and by 2006 both parties had shifted almost all of their spending to independent expenditure spending for their House and Senate candidates.

One might wonder why this shift to independent expenditures did not happen sooner, since parties were permitted to make independent expenditures beginning in 1996. The answer is related to another change in the rules. Beginning mostly in the early 1990s and until passage of BCRA in 2002, the national parties did much of their spending using soft money, which they transferred to state parties to spend, mostly on candidate-specific "issue ads" (as discussed). This party soft-money spending does not even show up in figures 7-4 and 7-5, since the parties transferred most of their soft money to state party organizations to spend because the state parties could do so with fewer restrictions.[112] So, from 1996, when the parties were permitted to make unlimited independent expenditures, until 2002, when soft money was banned with BCRA, the parties saw little need to make independent expenditures, because they were doing fine using soft money to pay for campaign efforts against the opponents of their candidates in close races. Moreover, soft money could be raised more easily in unlimited amounts from virtually any source, while independent expenditures had to be paid for with hard money raised in smaller increments from sources that were more restricted. Once soft money was no longer available after 2002, the parties shifted wholeheartedly to independent expenditures in 2004.

Yet independent expenditures may be more valuable than the soft-money issue ads the congressional parties relied on before 2002. Since independent expenditures are paid for with limited hard-money receipts, they may be used to expressly advocate for the election or defeat of a specific candidate. However, since the parties cannot coordinate independent spending with their candidates, they have had to separate their independent and coordinated spending operations, and, as a result, "the parties make redundant outlays for polls and infrastructure before they make any meaningful IE investment in television ads or mail."[113] Moreover, such spending may not always be very effective and is certainly not preferred by candidates, who have no control at all over how the money is spent.

Independent expenditures have been used irregularly by the RNC and DNC in recent elections. Indeed, the national committees are affected more by the presidential election cycle than the congressional campaign committees are. The DNC made $1.1 million in independent expenditures in 2008,[114] only $15,487 in 2010, and made no independent expenditures at all in 2012, 2014, and 2016. Barack Obama declined public funding in the 2008 and 2012 general elections, as did Hillary Clinton in 2016, and, given their own robust fundraising, these presidential contenders did not have to rely on the DNC to fund campaign activities with independent or coordinated spending. Moreover, Obama and Clinton probably wanted to control the messaging of their campaigns and likely did not expect or want the DNC to spend on their behalf.

The RNC made no independent expenditures in the last two midterm elections but made $53.5 million in independent expenditures in 2008, $42.4 million in 2012, yet only $321,531 in 2016. Of course, since McCain took the public funds in 2008, he relied heavily on the RNC for campaign advertising and voter contact and mobilization, since his own funding was limited. However, Romney declined public funds in 2012, yet the RNC did quite a lot of independent spending, most of it for expenditures in opposition to Obama.[115] Indeed, most independent expenditures are used for negative advertisements against the party's (or group's) opponent, not for positive ads for their candidate.

The RNC was caught off guard by the nomination of Donald Trump as their party's presidential nominee in 2016, and it spent very little in independent expenditures. The RNC did, however, transfer an unusually large amount, $45.6 million (compared to only $33.4 million in 2012), to state and local party committees, most likely for ground operations and voter mobilization in states such as Florida, Pennsylvania, and Wisconsin.[116] Yet, the RNC did end the cycle with a large amount of cash on hand, $25.3 million, after leaving only $5 million in 2014 and $4.8 million in 2012.[117] The DNC ended the 2016 cycle with $10.5 million in cash on hand, but with $4 million in debts owed by the committee. At the beginning of the 2016 cycle, the interim DNC chair reported the DNC was about $10 million in debt as a result of spending in the 2014 cycle, and the Clinton campaign covered 80 percent of that debt in 2016.[118]

For House races, independent expenditures were relatively similar for both parties. The DCCC spent $80.4 million to the NRCC's $73.6 million. Recall that the Democrats expected to gain about twice as many seats as they did in the end, so the slightly higher spending reflects their optimism. In the Senate, however, we clearly see a divergence. The DSCC spent $60.4 million to the NRSC's $39.2 million on independent expenditures. It is impossible to conclude from these numbers that the Republicans were more "complacent" than the Democrats, but we can say simply that the Hill committees were not the primary or sole vehicle for demonstrating party support. Since the 2010 *Citizens United* decision, single-candidate and party-focused Super PACs have become important players in Senate elections, as the next section will show.

The Extended Party Network in 2016

Recently, many scholars of political parties have argued that parties should be viewed not as bounded institutions but rather as networks of affiliated actors that include party elected officials, candidates and leaders, and allied nonparty groups and activists. This concept is known as the extended party network (EPN).[119] In this view, nonparty groups can be important elements of contemporary U.S. parties. Paul Herrnson argues that the complementary activities of party-allied groups in each party's enduring multilayered coalition are evidence "of increased party influence that is missed by narrower definitions of parties."[120] He notes that many nonparty groups in the party coalitions formed in part in response to constraints on the activities of party organizations, such as campaign finance changes that have diminished the ability of parties to raise and spend money relative to nonparty groups such as Super PACs.

The *Citizens United* and *SpeechNow.org* decisions and two implementing rulings from the FEC resulted in the sanctioning of independent-expenditure-only committees (what have come to be called Super PACs) that can raise and spend unlimited sums of money from virtually any source as long as their activity is fully disclosed. After these changes to the rules, many believed that outside interests would come to dominate elections, effectively eclipsing the parties. While outside interests have certainly made good use of Super PACs, the parties have also benefited by the creation of *partisan* Super PACs. The Senate Leadership Fund (R), Senate Majority PAC (D), Congressional Leadership Fund (R–House), and the House Majority PAC (D), for example, enabled the parties to operate, in effect, a *second* independent expenditure operation in 2016. In fact, as with party committee independent expenditures, party-allied

Super PAC spending was also closely matched by party and chamber. For the House, the Democratic Party allied Super PAC (House Majority PAC) spent $47 million compared to $40 million spent by the Republican Super PAC (Congressional Leadership Fund).[121]

In 2016, the DSCC spent $20 million more in independent expenditures than its Republican counterpart, but the Democratic allied Super PAC (Senate Majority PAC) spent $75 million, $11 million less in 2016 than the Republican allied Super PAC (Senate Leadership Fund), which spent $86 million.[122] Although many big GOP donors were poised to spend millions on the presidential election, once it was clear that Trump was likely to be the party's nominee, they turned their attention to keeping the Senate in Republican hands. Indeed, by May, more GOP senators found themselves in increasingly competitive contests as Trump's poll numbers fell, and Republican donors gave to Senate Republican allied Super PACs, which proved to be effective vehicles for directing large sums to targeted Senate races.[123] Michelle Hackman wrote in the *Wall Street Journal* that "this year, the influx of spending in Senate races reflected the degree to which some top Republican outside groups, including outfits run by GOP strategist Karl Rove and the Koch brothers, opted not to spend on the candidacy of the party's presidential nominee, Donald Trump, and instead direct their considerable resources to Senate contests."[124] The Democrats, too, were determined to take control of the Senate, especially after the Senate Republican majority's refusal to even consider President Obama's Supreme Court nominee. This fierce competition for control of the Senate meant that a number of both parties' Senate-focused allied Super PACs saw record fundraising in 2016 (see chapter 3).

Partisan Super PACs also conduct important election-related activities traditionally performed by the parties themselves, such as opposition research. For the 2016 elections, America Rising PAC, "a new generation of Republican research and rapid response,"[125] raised $1.4 million, and American Bridge 21st Century, "a progressive research and communications organization committed to holding Republicans accountable for their words and actions," raised a whopping $19.9 million for opposition research.[126] Since Super PACs cannot coordinate with candidates or parties, these opposition research organizations "share" much of their research on websites for the parties and others to use. Spending by such partisan Super PACs generally extends the parties' activities beyond what the formal party organizations raise and spend themselves (see chapter 1). One Super PAC that contended it *could* coordinate with the Clinton campaign was Correct the Record.[127] This rapid-response communications group was active in both the nomination and general election phases. In the words of Bernie Sanders's campaign manager, Jeff Weaver, Correct the Record's activity against Sanders was "one of the most despicable aspects of the Democratic primaries," and the group's efforts no doubt contributed to the anti-Hillary sentiment already growing among Sanders's supporters.[128]

Conclusion

When we wrote about parties after the 2012 elections, we concluded that parties were holding their own in a high-stress environment, with competition from outside groups making them work harder to maintain a meaningful presence. Four years later, a changed regulatory landscape gave parties greater access to money, and they appear to have used the new fundraising opportunities effectively. Specifically, the *McCutcheon* ruling and the "CRomnibus" legislation gave the national parties distinct advantages over other campaign entities in attracting attention from wealthy donors. Even the loss of public funding for the presidential nominating conventions created an opportunity for more pleas to high-dollar donors to make up the loss. The parties also became the logical vehicle for creating party-linked joint fundraising committees. These JFCs, in particular, raise concerns about big money donors getting around the contribution limits, because contributions given to one party committee can be, and were, transferred to other party committees. Additionally, the parties benefited from the growth of party-allied Super PACs. In fact, of all the campaign finance actors, the parties seem to have made the most effective use of Super PACs, making them highly effective "insider" tools.

But perhaps the most important lesson about the robustness of the parties is in the unique example of the relationship between the Republican National Committee and the GOP's presidential nominee, Donald Trump. While the RNC dropped in overall receipts in 2016, it continued to run an effective fundraising and campaign operation despite its nominee. Just as significant, the four party Hill committees ran evenly matched, effective campaigns for control of their chambers apart from the presidential campaign antics.[129] In fact, the relative normalcy of party operations in an abnormal campaign environment supports our belief that political parties continue to pursue electoral control of institutions by incorporating changes in the regulatory environment in innovative, self-interested ways.

Notes

1. In poker, a "flush" is a hand of five cards all of the same suit but not in sequential order. It often is a winning hand, ranking only below a full house but above a straight.

2. Jonathan Martin and Alexander Burns, "As Donald Trump Incites Feuds, Other G.O.P. Candidates Flee His Shadow," *New York Times*, August 6, 2016; Jeremy Peters, "G.O.P. Worries Clout Is Fading in Western U.S.," *New York Times*, August 27, 2016, sec. A.

3. Donna Brazile, *Hacks: The Inside Story of the Break-ins and Breakdowns That Put Donald Trump in the White House* (New York: Hachette Books, 2017).

4. Ibid.

5. Mike Lux, cofounder and president of Progressive Strategies, LLC, and senior adviser for progressive outreach for the Democratic National Committee, interview by David Magleby, January 6, 2017.

6. Bob Cusack, "Trump Slams RNC Chairman, Calls 2016 Process 'A Disgrace,'" *The Hill*, April 12, 2016.

7. Marty Cohen, David Karol, Hans Noel and John Zaller, *The Party Decides: Presidential Nominations before and after Reform*, Chicago Studies in American Politics (University of Chicago Press, 2008).

8. Ibid.

9. Barbara Norrander, *The Imperfect Primary: Oddities, Biases, and Strengths of U.S. Presidential Nomination Politics*, 2nd ed. (New York: Routledge, 2015).

10. See, for example, Raymond La Raja, *Small Change: Money, Political Parties, and Campaign Finance Reform* (University of Michigan Press, 2008); Richard Pildes, "Romanticizing Democracy, Political Fragmentation, and the Decline of American Government," *Yale Law Journal* 124, no. 3 (December 2014), pp. 576–881; Jonathan Rauch, *Political Realism: How Hacks, Machines, Big Money, and Back-Room Deals Can Strengthen American Democracy* (Brookings, 2015).

11. Kyle Kondik and Geoffrey Skelley, "Incumbent Reelection Rates Higher than Average in 2016," *Sabato's Crystal Ball*, December 15, 2016.

12. Ashley Balcerzak, "Where the Money Came from, Not How Much, Mattered in the Presidential Race," Center for Responsive Politics, November 9, 2016.

13. Diana Dwyre and Robin Kolodny, "Party Money in the 2012 Elections," in *Financing the 2012 Election*, edited by David B. Magleby (Brookings, 2014), pp. 175–214.

14. *McCutcheon v. Federal Election Commission*, 572 U.S. ___ (2014).

15. Liz Kennedy and Seth Katsuya Endo, "The World According to, and after, McCutcheon v. FEC, and Why It Matters Symposium: Money in Politics: The Good, the Bad, and the Ugly," *Valparaiso University Law Review* 49, no. 2 (2015), p. 536.

16. Center for Responsive Politics, "Top Individual Contributors: Hard Money by Individual, 2016 Cycle" (www.opensecrets.org/overview/topindivs.php?cycle =2016&view=hi).

17. Jonathan S. Berkon and Mark E. Elias, "After McCutcheon," *Harvard Law Review Forum* 121 (June 20, 2014), p. 373.

18. *McCutcheon* v. *Federal Election Commission*, 572 U.S. ___ (2014).

19. Michael Malbin, "McCutcheon Could Lead to No Limits for Political Parties—with What Implications for Parties and Interest Groups?" *New York University Law Review Online* 89, no. 92 (2014), p. 103.

20. Robert Kelner, "The Practical Consequences of McCutcheon," *Harvard Law Review Forum* 127 (2014), p. 386.

21. R. Sam Garrett and Shawn Reese, "Funding of Presidential Nominating Conventions: An Overview," *Congressional Research Service*, May 4, 2016.

22. Peter Overby, "Say Goodbye to the Taxpayer-Funded Political Convention," NPR, March 26, 2014.

23. The Democratic National Committee (DNC) and the Republican National Committee (RNC), the Democratic Senatorial Campaign Committee (DSCC) and the National Republican Senatorial Committee (NRSC), and the Democratic Congressional Campaign Committee (DCCC) and the National Republican Congressional Committee (NRCC).

24. "Consolidated and Further Continuing Appropriations Act, 2015," P. L. 113-235 (2014), www.gpo.gov/fdsys/pkg/PLAW-113publ235/html/PLAW-113pub l235.htm, Section 101: Pub. L. No. 113-235 Section 101.

25. R. Sam Garrett, "Increased Campaign Contribution Limits in the FY2015 Omnibus Appropriations Law: Frequently Asked Questions," *Congressional Research Service*, May 17, 2015); Garrett and Reese, "Funding of Presidential Nominating Conventions."

26. Federal Election Commission, "Contribution Limits for 2015–2016 Federal Elections," 2015 (www.fec.gov/pages/brochures/contrib.shtml#Contribution _Limits); Garrett, "Increased Campaign Contribution Limits in the FY2015 Omnibus Appropriations Law," p. 3.

27. "Multicandidate committees are those that have been registered with the FEC (or, for Senate committees, the Secretary of the Senate) for at least six months; have received federal contributions from more than 50 people; and (except for state parties) have made contributions to at least five federal candidates. See 11 C.F.R. §100.5(e)(3). Consequently, most PACs attain multicandidate status automatically over time." See Garrett, "Increased Campaign Contribution Limits in the FY 2015 Omnibus Appropriations Law," p. 5.

28. Carrie Levine, "Limits Unclear on New Political Party 'Slush Funds,'" Center for Public Integrity, August 3, 2015.

29. Garrett and Reese, "Funding of Presidential Nominating Conventions."

30. Raymond La Raja, "CRomnibus Pays Off for Parties," *MassPoliticsProfs*, December 17, 2014.

31. See, for example, David B. Magleby, ed., *Outside Money: Soft Money and Issue Advocacy in 1998 Congressional Elections* (Lanham, Md.: Rowman and Littlefield, 2000); David B. Magleby, ed., *The Other Campaign: Soft Money and Issue Advocacy in the 2000 Congressional Elections* (Lanham, Md.: Rowman and Littlefield, 2003); David B. Magleby and J. Quin Monson, *The Last Hurrah? Soft Money and Issue Advocacy in the 2002 Congressional Elections* (Brookings, 2004).

32. Dwyre and Kolodny, "Party Money in the 2012 Elections."

33. *Citizens United* v. *Federal Election Commission*, 558 U.S. 310 (2010).

34. *SpeechNow.org* v. *Federal Election Commission*, 599 F.3d 686 (D.C. Cir. 2010).

35. In FEC Advisory Opinion 2010-09 in 2010 (Club for Growth), the FEC confirmed that the *SpeechNow* decision permitted unlimited contributions to independent-expenditure-only political committees in federal elections. See Federal Election Commission, "Advisory Opinion 2010-09: Club for Growth," July 22, 2010 (www.fec.gov/data/legal/advisory-opinions/2010-09/). In Advisory Opinion 2010-11 in 2010 (Commonsense Ten), the FEC exceeded the ruling in *SpeechNow* *.org* v. *FEC*, ruling that *Citizens United* allows independent-expenditure-only committees to accept unlimited contributions from political committees, corporations, and unions, not just from individuals. Within weeks, a new type of independent-expenditure committee, the Super PAC, emerged to take advantage of the new, more flexible rules about independent fundraising and spending. See Federal Election Commission, "Advisory Opinion 2010-11: Commonsense Ten," July 22, 2010 (www.fec.gov/data/legal/advisory-opinions/2010-11/).

36. Robin Kolodny and Diana Dwyre, "Convergence or Divergence? Do Parties and Outside Groups Spend on the Same Candidates, and Does It Matter?" *American Politics Research* 46, no. 3 (2018), pp. 375–401.

37. Mark Hensch, "Activists Turn Up Heat on DNC for More Debates," *The Hill*, August 30, 2015.

38. H. A. Goodman, "DNC Should Increase Number of Debates and Let Sanders (and Others) Battle Clinton," *The Hill*, September 8, 2015.

39. Mark Longabaugh, senior Sanders 2016 campaign adviser, interview by David Magleby, February 8, 2017.

40. Eugene Scott, "Sanders Campaign Drops Lawsuit against DNC over Voter Database Breach," CNN, April 29, 2016.

41. Candace Smith, "Jeb Bush: The Demise of the One-Time Frontrunner's Campaign," *ABC News*, February 22, 2016.

42. David Graham, "Which Republicans Oppose Donald Trump? A Cheat Sheet," *The Atlantic*, November 6, 2016; Roll Call Staff, "Republicans in Congress against Trump," *Roll Call*, October 12, 2016.

43. Rebecca Ballhaus, "Donald Trump, Republicans Finalize Joint Fundraising Deal," *Wall Street Journal (Online)*, May 18, 2016, p. 1.

44. Reid Wilson and Joe Disipio, "Clinton Holds Huge Ground Game Advantage over Team Trump," *The Hill*, October 22, 2016.

45. Ibid.

46. Becky Bond and Zack Exley, "Hillary Clinton's Vaunted GOTV Operation May Have Turned Out Trump Voters," *Huffington Post*, November 11, 2016.

47. Alex Roarty, "Democrats Say They Now Know Exactly Why Clinton Lost," McClatchy DC Bureau, May 1, 2017.

48. Edward-Isaac Dovere, "How Clinton Lost Michigan—and Blew the Election," *Politico*, December 14, 2016.

49. Deirdre Schifeling, executive director of Planned Parenthood Votes, interview by David Magleby, May 30, 2017.

50. Gabriel Debenedetti and Edward-Isaac Dovere, "Inside the Scramble to Oust Debbie Wasserman Schultz," *Politico*, July 25, 2016.

51. Stephanie Akin, "Timeline: Comey's Journey from Clinton Investigation to Unemployment," *Roll Call*, May 10, 2017.

52. Hillary Clinton, *What Happened?* (New York: Simon and Schuster, 2017), pp. 403–04.

53. Frank Newport, Lisa Singh, Stuart Soroka, Michael Traugott, and Andrew Dugan, "What the Public Learned about Donald Trump and Hillary Clinton during the 2016 Campaign," PowerPoint presentation at the Annual Meeting of the American Association for Public Opinion Research, New Orleans, May 18–21, 2017.

54. John Philleppe, chief counsel of the Republican National Committee, interview by David Magleby, February 8, 2017.

55. Maeve Reston and Stephen Collinson, "How Donald Trump Won," CNN, November 9, 2016.

56. Ibid.; Ben Kamisar, "GOP Hopes Data Investment Will Boost Midterm Odds," *The Hill*, June 2, 2017.

57. Joshua Green and Sasha Issenberg, "Inside the Trump Bunker, with Days to Go," Bloomberg, October 27, 2016.

58. Campaign Finance Institute, "President Trump, with RNC Help, Raised More Small Donor Money than President Obama; as Much as Clinton and Sanders Combined," table 2, February 21, 2017 (www.cfinst.org/Press/PReleases/17-02-21/President_Trump_with_RNC_Help_Raised_More_Small_Donor_Money_than_President_Obama_As_Much_As_Clinton_and_Sanders_Combined.aspx).

59. Federal Election Commission, "Advanced Data," 2017 (www.fec.gov/data/advanced/), see Trump and Clinton financial summaries for 2016; Campaign Finance Institute, "President Trump, with RNC Help, Raised More Small Donor Money than President Obama."

60. Maya Rhodan and David Johnson, "Here Are 7 Electoral College Predictions for Tuesday," *Time* (blog), November 8, 2016.

61. Josh Katz, "2016 Senate Election Forecast: The Democrats Have a 52% Chance of Winning the Senate," *New York Times*, sec. The Upshot, November 8, 2016. Note, however, that the political handicapping pros at the *Cook Political Report* and *Rothenberg and Gonzales Political Report* predicted that control of the Senate was a toss-up on the eve of the election.

62. Center for Responsive Politics, "Political Parties Overview: 2016 Election Cycle," May 18, 2017 (www.opensecrets.org/parties/); Center for Responsive Politics, "2016 Presidential Race," 2017 (www.opensecrets.org /pres16/); Center for Responsive Politics, "Most Expensive Races: 2016 Election Cycle," May 18, 2017 (www.opensecrets.org/overview/topraces.php?cycle =2016&display=currcandsout); Leigh Ann Caldwell, "These Are the Nine Most Important Senate Races to Watch on Election Day," *NBC News*, November 7, 2016; Inside Elections, "House Ratings," *Inside Elections with Nathan Gonzales*, November 3, 2016.

63. Chris Cillizza, "Hillary Clinton's 'Email' Problem Was Bigger than Anyone Realized," CNN, May 26, 2017; Jennifer Agiesta, "He Won. She Lost.," CNN, July 2017; Frank Newport and others, "What the Public Learned about Donald Trump and Hillary Clinton during the 2016 Campaign."

64. Newport and others, "What the Public Learned about Donald Trump and Hillary Clinton during the 2016 Campaign."

65. Cillizza, "Hillary Clinton's 'Email' Problem Was Bigger than Anyone Realized."

66. Jonathan Martin, Alexander Burns, and Maggie Haberman, "Cut Ties to Donald Trump, Big Donors Urge R.N.C.," *New York Times*, October 13, 2016.

67. Seth Gitell, "The Democratic Party Suicide Bill," *The Atlantic*, August 2003.

68. Data compiled by the authors from Center for Responsive Politics, "Joint Fundraising Committees," June 20, 2017 (www.opensecrets.org/jfc/top.php?type =R&cycle=2016).

69. Center for Responsive Politics, "1999 State Victory Fund Cmte: Joint Fundraising Committee Summary," 2017 (www.opensecrets.org/jfc/summary.php ?id=C00350553&cycle=2000).

70. Center for Responsive Politics, "Joint Fundraising Committees: Summary," May 16, 2017 (www.opensecrets.org/jfc/index.php).

71. Center for Responsive Politics, "Kerry Victory 2004: Joint Fundraising Committee Summary," 2005 (www.opensecrets.org/jfc/summary.php?id=C0039 8198&cycle=2004).

72. Center for Responsive Politics, "Joint Fundraising Committees: Summary."

73. Bob Biersack, "How the Parties Worked the Law and Got Their Mojo Back," Center for Responsive Politics, February 19, 2016.

74. A separate Hillary Action Fund raised another $46.6 million with the DNC.

75. Compiled by the authors from Federal Election Commission data. See Federal Election Commission, "Hillary Victory Fund: Committee Overview, 2015–2016" (https://www.fec.gov/data/committee/C00586537/?cycle=2016).

76. Biersack, "How the Parties Worked the Law and Got Their Mojo Back."

77. Compiled by the authors from Federal Election Commission data. See Federal Election Commission, "Hillary Action Fund: Committee Overview, 2015–2016," November 19, 2017 (www.fec.gov/data/committee/C00619411/?cycle=2016).

78. Compiled by the authors from Federal Election Commission data. See Federal Election Commission, "Trump Victory: Committee Overview, 2015–2016" (www.fec.gov/data/committee/C00618389/?cycle=2016). Note that these reported amounts do not include any of the JFC's funds allocated to state party committees that were later transferred to the national committee. One would need to look at multiple state party FEC filings to calculate exactly how much each state party received from a JFC and then turned around and transferred to another party committee, as detailed for the Democratic Party of Oklahoma. Thus, these state party transfers to national party committees not only get around the contribution limits but are also being made pretty much under the radar as well.

79. Compiled by the authors from Federal Election Commission data. See Federal Election Commission, "Trump Make America Great Again Committee: Committee Overview, 2015—2016" (www.fec.gov/data/committee/C00618371/?cycle=2016).

80. Magleby, *Financing the 2012 Election*; Brazile, *Hacks*, p. 97.

81. Brazile, *Hacks*, pp. 71–72.

82. Ibid., p. 98.

83. Center for Responsive Politics, "Team Ryan: Joint Fundraising Committee Summary," 2017 (www.opensecrets.org/jfc/summary.php?id=C00545947). Prosperity Action raised a total of $4.2 million for the 2016 elections and distributed $1.2 million in $5,000 to $10,000 contributions to 169 Republican House candidates and 14 Senate candidates. See Center for Responsive Politics, "Prosperity Action Contributions to Federal Candidates, 2016 Cycle," May 16, 2017.

84. Byron Tau, "GOP Launches New Big Money Effort," *Politico*, August 5, 2014.

85. Center for Responsive Politics, "NRSC Targeted State Victory Cmte: Joint Fundraising Committee Summary," 2017 (www.opensecrets.org/jfc/summary.php?id=C00617498). The remaining funds were spent on administrative and fundraising expenses.

86. This number was calculated using the 2012 amount multiplied by the inflation conversion factor for 2016 found on Robert Sahr's website: http://

liberalarts.oregonstate.edu/spp/polisci/faculty-staff/robert-sahr/inflation
-conversion-factors-years-1774-estimated-2024-dollars-recent-years/individual
-year-conversion-factor-table-0.

87. Federal Election Commission, "Convention Committees and Host Committees" (www.fec.gov/press/resources-journalists/convention-committees-and
-host-committees/).

88. Center for Responsive Politics, "Top Overall Party Committees,"
May 18, 2017 (www.opensecrets.org/parties/topparties.php?type=R&cycle
=2016&Pty=D).

89. Matea Gold, "Cleveland Host Committee Confirms That It Sought $6
Million from Adelsons to Fill Funding Gap," *Washington Post*, July 15, 2016.

90. Mary Kilpatrick, "Sponsored, Bye? In Cleveland, a Drop-Off in Corporate Support Has a Ripple Effect on Fundraising," *CQ Weekly* 74, no. 23 (July 18,
2016), pp. 43–44.

91. Julia Terruso, "After-Party Chores," *Philadelphia Inquirer*, August 7,
2016.

92. Federal Election Commission, "Republican National Committee 2015–
2016 Disbursements: Other Federal Operating Expenditures" (www.fec.gov/data
/disbursements/?two_year_transaction_period=2016&cycle=2016&data_type
=processed&committee_id=C00003418&min_date=01%2F01%2F2015&max
_date=12%2F31%2F2016&line_number=F3X-21B).

93. Federal Election Commission, "Advisory Opinion 2010-14: DSCC," FEC
.gov, 2010 (http://saos.fec.gov/saos/searchao;jsessionid=8A1D841757B2ABFAE
70337A8DA02FCCA?SUBMIT=ao&AO=3089).

94. Carrie Levine, "Limits Unclear on New Political Party 'Slush Funds,'"
Center for Public Integrity, August 3, 2015.

95. Thomas Holyoke, *Interest Groups and Lobbying: Pursuing Political Interests in America* (Boulder, Colo.: Westview Press, 2014).

96. Clyde Wilcox, "Share the Wealth: Contributions by Congressional Incumbents to the Campaigns of Other Candidates," *American Politics Quarterly* 17
(1989), pp. 389–408; Anne Bedlington and Michael Malbin, "The Party as an
Extended Network: Members Giving to Each Other and to Their Parties," in
Life after Reform: When the Bipartisan Campaign Reform Act Meets Politics,
edited by Michael Malbin (Lanham, Md.: Rowman and Littlefield, 2003),
pp. 121–37.

97. Eric S. Heberlig and Bruce A. Larson, *Congressional Parties, Institutional
Ambition, and the Financing of Majority Control* (University of Michigan Press,
2012), p. 9. See also Gary C. Jacobson, "Party Organization and the Distribution
of Campaign Resources: Republicans and Democrats in 1982," *Political Science
Quarterly* 100 (1985–86), pp. 603–25; Robin Kolodny and Diana Dwyre,
"Party-Orchestrated Activities for Legislative Party Goals," *Party Politics* 4
(1998), pp. 275–95.

98. Heberlig and Larson, *Congressional Parties, Institutional Ambition, and the Financing of Majority Control*, chapter 5. See also Marian Currinder, *Money in the House: Campaign Funds and Congressional Party Politics* (Boulder, Colo.: Westview Press, 2009), especially chapter 6.

99. Heberlig and Larson, *Congressional Parties, Institutional Ambition, and the Financing of Majority Control*, chapter 5; Eric S. Heberlig and Bruce A. Larson, "U.S. House Incumbent Fundraising and Spending in a Post–Citizens United and Post–McCutcheon World," *Political Science Quarterly* 129, no. 4 (2014), pp. 613–42.

100. Nathan L. Gonzales, "Senate Ratings | Inside Elections," *Inside Elections with Nathan Gonzales*, September 2, 2016.

101. These were in New Hampshire, Nevada, Pennsylvania (pure toss-up), Indiana, and Wisconsin (tilt Democratic), and Florida and North Carolina (tilt Republican).

102. Nathan L. Gonzales, "House Ratings | Inside Elections," *Inside Elections with Nathan Gonzales*, September 2, 2016.

103. Philip Rucker, Ed O'Keefe, and Mike DeBonis, "Buoyed by Rising Polls, Clinton Shifts to a New Target: The House and Senate," *Washington Post*, October 22, 2016.

104. Nathaniel Persily, "The Law of American Party Finance," in *Party Funding and Campaign Financing in International Perspective*, edited by Keith D. Ewing and Samuel Issacharoff (Portland, Ore.: Hart Publishing, 2006), pp. 222–23.

105. Federal Election Commission, "2016 Coordinated Party Expenditure Limits," 2016 (www.fec.gov/info/charts_cpe_2016.shtml).

106. See Magleby, *Outside Money*; Magleby, *The Other Campaign*; Magleby and Monson, *The Last Hurrah?*

107. Diana Dwyre, "Spinning Straw into Gold: Soft Money and U.S. House Elections," *Legislative Studies Quarterly* 21, no. 3 (1996), pp. 409–24.

108. *Buckley* v. *Valeo*, 424 U.S. 1 (U. S. Supreme Court 1976).

109. Diana Dwyre and Victoria Farrar-Myers, *Legislative Labyrinth: Congress and Campaign Finance Reform* (Washington: CQ Press, 2000), pp. 24–26.

110. *Colorado Republican Federal Campaign Committee* v. *Federal Election Commission*, 518 U.S. 604 (1996).

111. *Citizens United* v. *Federal Election Commission*, 558 U.S. 310 (2010); *Speechnow.org* v. *Federal Election Commission*, 599 F.3d 674 (2010).

112. Dwyre, "Spinning Straw into Gold."

113. Robin Kolodny and Diana Dwyre, "A New Rule Book: Party Money after BCRA," in *Financing the 2004 Election*, edited by David Magleby, Anthony Corrado, and Kelly Patterson (Brookings, 2006), p. 202.

114. More than half of the $1.1 million spent independently by the DNC in 2008 was spent in April and May, before the party's nominee was chosen. See

Anthony Corrado, "Financing the 2008 Presidential General Election," in *Financing the 2008 Election*, edited by David Magleby and Anthony Corrado (Brookings, 2011), p. 143.

115. Dwyre and Kolodny, "Party Money in the 2012 Elections," p. 207.

116. Brakkton Booker, "RNC Hires Staff to Supplement Trump's Lacking Ground Game in Critical States," NPR, September 2, 2016; Steven Lemongello, "How Did Trump Win Florida? A GOP Ground Game Years in the Making," *Orlando Sentinel*, November 16, 2016.

117. Federal Election Commission, "2015–2016 Election Cycle Data Summaries through 12/31/16: National Party 24-Month Data Summaries," 2017 (www.fec.gov/press/summaries/2016/ElectionCycle/24m_NatlParty.shtml).

118. Brazile, *Hacks*, p. 33.

119. The term "extended party network" was likely first used in Bedlington and Malbin, "The Party as an Extended Network."

120. Paul Herrnson, "The Roles of Party Organizations, Party-Connected Committees, and Party Allies in Elections," *Journal of Politics* 71, no. 4 (2009), p. 1221.

121. Center for Responsive Politics, "2016 Outside Spending, by Super PAC," July 6, 2017 (www.opensecrets.org/outsidespending/summ.php?chrt=V&type=S).

122. Ibid.

123. Nick Corasaniti and Ashley Parker, "G.O.P. Donors Shift Focus from Top of Ticket to Senate Races," *New York Times*, May 20, 2016.

124. Michelle Hackman, "Tight Senate Contests Set New Spending Records; Pennsylvania Race Has Already Topped $162 Million; New Hampshire and Nevada Also Have Hefty Price Tags," *Wall Street Journal (Online)*, November 7, 2016.

125. America Rising PAC, "About America Rising PAC" (www.facebook.com /AmericaRisingPAC/about); Joe Pounder, "An Opposition Researcher for the GOP Reveals His Secrets," *Time*, June 16, 2016.

126. Center for Responsive Politics, "2016 Outside Spending, by Super PAC."

127. Clare Foran, "A $1 Million Fight against Hillary Clinton's Online Trolls," *The Atlantic*, May 31, 2016.

128. Institute of Politics, *Campaign for President: The Managers Look at 2016* (Lanham, Md.: Rowman and Littlefield, 2017), p. 122.

129. Robin Kolodny, *Pursuing Majorities: Congressional Campaign Committees in American Politics*, Congressional Studies Series 1 (University of Oklahoma Press, 1998).

EIGHT   *Political and Policy*
Implications following the
2016 Election

DAVID B. MAGLEBY

This volume has examined the financing of the 2016 election, drawing distinctions between the presidential election and congressional elections. In this chapter, we return to the following questions: Does the amount of money spent still matter? How did changes in the rules and regulations impact the 2016 election? What are the policy implications and possible changes arising from the 2016 election?

Does the Amount of Money Spent Still Matter?

The answer is yes. Money is still a crucial part of elections. The question is raised because in 2016 the winning presidential candidate, Donald Trump, was outspent almost two to one by the losing candidate, Hillary Clinton. Trump and the outside groups that supported him spent $397 million, whereas Hillary and the outside groups that supported her spent $793 million.[1] The leader of the main Super PAC supporting Clinton, Guy Cecil of Priorities USA Action, holds the view that "money is still going to play an important role and even more so in larger states where it's very difficult for citizens to get to know their elected official firsthand."[2] Regarding Marco Rubio's campaign, his pollster, Whit Ayres, said, "The money would come in particularly when he was winning. Then the money would stop coming in when he started losing." Ayres concluded, "It is the ability to raise enough money [that allows candidates] to keep going."[3]

The 2016 presidential election illustrated the importance of strategic decisions with respect to campaign spending: how much money the campaign can raise, how the money is raised, and how the money is spent. In 2016, the Clinton campaign raised $563.7 million, while the Trump campaign raised $333 million. This discrepancy in fundraising may suggest that the Trump campaign was at a financial disadvantage, but the smaller amount of money raised by Trump's campaign was not as much of a problem as one might think. There are three reasons for this: first, the strategic advantage of small donors;[4] second, the unprecedented amount of earned media the Trump campaign had; and third, that much of the spending by Trump and his party and group allies occurred relatively late in the campaign.

The disparity between the 2012 and 2016 general election finances is striking in that the Trump campaign spent $250 million less than the Romney campaign and almost $200 million less than the Obama campaign in 2012, yet still won. One key to understanding the success of the Trump campaign is the role earned media played in the 2016 presidential election.

According to mediaQuant, a firm that measures and analyzes news coverage across traditional and social media, the media value, measured as "the monetized value of media coverage in print, broadcast and online news channels," of Trump's earned media coverage during the last month of the 2016 campaign was $537 million, compared to Clinton's $358 million earned media value that month. When mediaQuant compared Trump's and Clinton's earned media coverage for the twelve months preceding the 2016 general election, it found that Trump received over twice as much earned media coverage as Clinton, with Trump receiving $5.4 billion in earned media coverage compared to $2.5 billion for Clinton.[5]

Studies examining earned media coverage of candidates during the Democratic and Republican primaries likewise found a distinct Trump advantage in earned media coverage. A study by the Shorenstein Center on Media, Politics and Public Policy at the Kennedy School at Harvard University examined coverage of the leading Republican presidential candidate by eight news outlets during 2015, the year preceding the presidential election year.[6] The study concluded that Trump received $55 million in "ad equivalent" earned media coverage during that time, compared to $36 million for Jeb Bush, $34 million for Marco Rubio, $32.5 million for Ted Cruz, $24 million for Ben Carson, and $16 million for John Kasich.[7] In a subsequent study examining earned media coverage during the primary period itself (January 1–June 7, 2016), the Shorenstein Center found that Trump received more media coverage than any other Republican candidate throughout the primaries: "There was not a single week when Ted Cruz, Marco Rubio, or John Kasich topped Trump's level of coverage. During the time that Rubio was an active candidate for the Republican nomination, he got only half as much press attention as Trump. During the time they were still in the race, Cruz received roughly two-thirds the coverage afforded Trump while Kasich got only a fourth."[8] Moreover, even after Trump effectively secured the Republican nomination in late May, he still received more earned media coverage than either Clinton or Bernie Sanders during the last five weeks of the primary, even though Clinton and Sanders were still contesting the Democratic nomination.[9]

Two other studies of earned media during the primaries find similar results. An analysis of more than fifty newspapers by *The Atlantic* found that between July 2015 and August 2016 there were 18,640 stories about Clinton, 7,841 stories about Sanders, and 29,009 stories about Trump.[10] The *Tyndall Report*, which monitors news coverage by ABC, NBC, and CBS, found that the Trump campaign received over twice as much coverage (1,144 minutes) during the 2016 election campaign on the nightly newscasts of the three networks as the Clinton campaign did (506 minutes).[11]

Is earned media likely to become a substitute for campaign expenditures in future campaigns, as it was for Trump in 2016? Or was the 2016 election an anomaly because of Trump's unique style and personality so that few prospective candidates could generate the sustained earned media attention he did? In 2016, Trump had much more earned media coverage than either party's nominees did in 2008 or 2012.[12] The author of the *Tyndall Report* story described the basis for Trump's extraordinary earned media coverage: "Simply put, the Trump phenomenon is more newsworthy. . . . Compared with her [Clinton], he is more accessible, more outlandish, more entertaining, more flamboyant, more unpredictable and, by far, a more radical departure from political norms."[13] Unless another presidential candidate can capture the news media's attention in the future the way Trump did in 2016, we expect candidates' campaign financing in the future to more closely resemble the way Romney and Obama financed their races in 2012 and the way Clinton financed her campaign in 2016.

Strategic Spending

While the amount of money raised by a campaign is important, so is how that money is spent. Traditionally, survey research has helped gauge public opinion and allocate limited campaign resources. However, over the last sixteen years, microtargeting (using consumer data appended to voter files) and modeling (using algorithms to model the behavior of voters) have increasingly been used by campaigns to help target campaign resources.[14] Modeling is credited for the success the Obama campaign had in 2012 in fundraising, media advertising, and turnout.[15] A senior adviser to the Obama campaign described the significance statistical modeling played in the allocation of resources:

> The new megafile didn't just tell the campaign how to find voters and get their attention; it also allowed the number crunchers to run tests predicting which types of people would be persuaded by certain kinds of appeals. Call lists in field offices, for instance, didn't just list names and numbers; they also ranked names in order of their persuadability, with the campaign's most important priorities first. About 75% of the determining factors were basics like age, sex, race, neighborhood and voting record. Consumer data about voters help round out the picture. We could [predict] people who were going to give online. We could model people who were going to give through mail. We could model volunteers. . . . In the end, modeling became something way bigger for us in '12 than in '08 because it made our time more efficient.[16]

In 2016, the Clinton campaign likewise emphasized modeling to help allocate resources. However, following Clinton's surprising loss, allegations began to surface that the Clinton campaign may have relied too much on modeling, to the detriment of information from field operatives in battleground states. A *Politico* article in December 2016 quoted campaign operatives in Michigan as saying that the Clinton campaign ignored requests for a more robust ground game:

> Multiple operatives said, the Clinton campaign dismissed what's known as in-person "persuasion"—no one was knocking on doors trying to drum up support for the Democratic nominee, which also meant no one was hearing directly from voters aside from voters

they'd already assumed were likely Clinton voters, no one was tracking how feelings about the race and the candidate were evolving.
This left no information to check the polling models against—which
might have, for example, showed the campaign that some of the
white male union members they had expected to be likely Clinton
voters [were] actually veering toward Trump.[17]

The article goes on to say that "the anecdotes are different but the narrative is the same across battlegrounds, where Democratic operatives
lament a one-size-fits-all approach drawn entirely from pre-selected
data—operatives spit out 'the model, the model,' as they complain about
it—guiding [Clinton campaign manager Robby] Mook's decisions on
field, television, everything else."[18] While some of the complaints about
field operations in Michigan and other battleground states could be attributed to second-guessing by campaign operatives after the election,
other accounts of the Clinton campaign also describe a reliance on modeling at the expense of a more robust field operation. Her campaign staffers
reported that there was "No money. No paid staff. No advertising. No
literature. No bumper stickers. No yard signs."[19]

Big Data and Modeling

An advantage enjoyed by Democrats in 2008 and 2012 was superior
data files on voters and more advanced statistical modeling of persuadable
voters, predictable issue concerns of voters, and the propensity of individuals to make campaign contributions. Republicans acknowledged this
party deficit in their postelection report following the 2012 election. The
report noted, "The use of highly targeted and personal voter contact
based on data was an area where the Obama campaign clearly excelled in
2012."[20] As Republican National Committee (RNC) chair, Reince Priebus made investing in better data on voters a high priority. Ellen Bredenkoetter of the Republican-aligned Data Trust said, "One of the things
Reince Priebus . . . [and his] three chiefs of staff were really focused on
was building a data operation that can very easily integrate with whoever
the nominee was."[21] It appears that the investment made by the GOP in
data and field operations was important to Trump's victory.

Following the 2016 Electoral College defeat of Clinton, there are questions for the Democrats about whether the campaign put too much stock
in big data and computer models of the electorate. In response to a
question about why the Clinton campaign continued to invest in North

Carolina, Iowa, and Arizona late in the cycle, Deirdre Schifeling of Planned Parenthood said, "I think the overmodeling is the problem."[22] Steve Rosenthal, who was working for the Service Employees International Union in 2016, echoed this idea: "We created a generation of campaign automatons who believe that this is what the model says, so therefore that's what we do, and they're not taking into account what's different about this cycle."[23] Laura Quinn, whose firm, Catalist, is in the business of building big datasets for progressive groups, said, "The models don't tell you necessarily what to say [to voters]. Models are also heavily rooted in the past . . . you're assuming that patterns are more likely to hold than they're likely to be departed from."[24] Mike Lux, who worked at the Democratic National Committee during the general election, sees consultants as overly confident in their models. He said, "The political consultant class has created their own bubble and they're so convinced that their voter modeling is so fabulous. In fact, I think their voter modeling on both parties has a lot of holes to it."[25]

This concern about Clinton's campaign relying too much on data and analytics was important enough for her to comment on it in her book *What Happened?* She writes, "I'm convinced that the answer for Democrats going forward is not to abandon data but to obtain *better* data, use it more effectively, question every assumption, and keep adapting. And we need to listen carefully to what people are telling you and try to assess that too."[26]

Message versus Money

Money does not win elections unless there is also a message. Conversely, a message that connects with the electorate can make up for less money. This was especially evident in 2016 in the presidential primaries. In June 2015, Florida governor Jeb Bush was considered a favorite for the Republican nomination. He had name recognition, given that both his father and his brother had been president. His Super PAC had raised $100 million, which it was prepared to spend on his primary campaign. But Bush did not have a message that connected with the Republican primary electorate. In contrast, Trump spent only $73 million during the primaries, less than Bush, Cruz, or Rubio,[27] yet had a message that connected with the 30 percent of the Republican primary voters who consistently supported him.[28]

During the general election, it seemed that once again message was more important than money. Trump had a simple message, "Make

America Great Again." That message likely meant different things to different people, but it appealed to voters, irrespective of their backgrounds or circumstances, who were, for whatever reason, dissatisfied with the state of the country. Hillary's message was more complex and consequently more difficult for voters to understand and embrace. Dan Schwerin, Clinton's chief speechwriter, summed up the problem with Clinton's message: "Her stump [speech] has always been a long recitation of what she wants to do as President. We've rolled out a million detail policies. Our problem is missing the forest for the trees. We've never found a good way . . . that sums up her vision for how America would be different."[29]

Funding Strategies: Small versus Large Donations

While both John McCain in 2000 and Howard Dean in 2004 had some success raising small donations online, it was during the 2008 presidential election that the Obama campaign demonstrated the role that small donations can play in an election and the advantages of such donations. The Obama campaign raised $181.3 million through donations under $200 in the 2008 election, 24 percent of his total individual donations, and $218.8 million, 28 percent of his total individual donations, in the 2012 election.[30] In contrast, Clinton raised $42.4 million, 22 percent of her total individual contributions, through small donations in 2008, and McCain raised almost the same amount, $42.1 million, 21 percent of his total individual contributions, in 2008.[31] In 2012, Romney raised just 12 percent of his individual contributions, $57.5 million, through donations of $200 or less.[32]

In 2016, small donations were the backbone of the Sanders campaign and played a large role in the Trump campaign. During the primary, Sanders raised $99.7 million, 44 percent of his individual campaign contributions, through small donations,[33] and largely eschewed large donations and large fundraising events. The Trump campaign, in conjunction with the Republican National Committee, raised approximately $239 million in small donations during his campaign, 69 percent of his total individual campaign contributions.[34] The Clinton campaign, in contrast, raised just 22 percent, $136.8 million, of her total individual campaign contributions in amounts of $200 or less.[35]

Small donations are important to campaigns, because they give candidates a recurring opportunity for campaign contributions. While large contributions, particularly maximum contributions, give candidates an instant influx of cash, small donations mean a candidate can repeatedly solicit those donors. For candidates who face an uphill fight, these donations can reward momentum. While the Sanders campaign faced overwhelming odds to get the nomination, it was financially competitive with the Clinton campaign in large part because of its ability to raise money from small contributions.

Two of the Republican presidential primary candidates, Ben Carson and Rand Paul, raised more money through small donations than from large ones, and four other Republican candidates, Ted Cruz, Carly Fiorina, Mike Huckabee, and Scott Walker, raised at least one-third of their individual contributions in amounts under $200.[36] In the ten most expensive Senate races in 2016, five candidates raised roughly one-third of their individual contributions in amounts of $200 or less, and four other candidates raised roughly 25 percent of their individual contributions in amounts of $200 or less.[37]

While small donations are still not the norm in elections, the evidence does suggest that since 2008 they have become more and more a part of the fundraising mix for candidates. It is likely that this trend will continue, as candidates see the advantages of small donations and as campaign contributors understand the role that even small donations can play in a campaign. It may also be that the media will pay more attention to small donors in the future. One analysis of the 2017 Virginia Democratic gubernatorial primary suggested that one reason that former congressman Tom Perriello lost to Lieutenant Governor Ralph Northam was that Perriello "was unable to raise millions of dollars in small donations . . . and relied on a few wealthy donors to write six-figure checks."[38]

Super PACs

One trend that began in 2010, following the Supreme Court's *Citizens United* decision, was the creation of Super PACs to supplement candidate fundraising. In 2016, the Super PAC supporting Clinton, Priorities USA Action, and the Super PAC supporting Jeb Bush, Right to Rise, were the most prodigious spenders, but almost all the presidential candidates, with the notable exception of Sanders and Trump during the primaries, had a Super PAC supporting them.[39] As discussed in chapter 1, Super PACs played a wider range of roles in support of presidential candidates in 2016. Some focused on building databases, others on contacting individual voters, and still others on social media. The primary way Super PACs continue to spend money is on television advertising. Many

Senate candidates also benefited from Super PAC support.[40] Unless the *Citizens United* decision is overturned by a future Supreme Court, which at this point seems unlikely, or a constitutional amendment is passed to overturn the decision, which also seems unlikely, Super PACs will continue to be a part of the campaign finance landscape.

Social Media

Social media and e-mail were not new campaign tools in 2016, but both saw greater use than in previous elections. In 2008, and even more in 2012, the Obama campaign used e-mail and other social media to engage donors and voters. The Pew Research Center found that "the Obama campaign posted [on social media] nearly four times as much content as the Romney campaign and was active on nearly twice as many platforms. Obama's digital content also engendered more response from the public— twice the number of shares, views and comments of his posts."[41]

In the 2016 presidential election, all the presidential candidates used social media. Ben Carson, for example, had an aggressive Facebook strategy during the primary season.[42] However, the candidate who used social media most effectively was Trump. His use of Twitter during the campaign and since his election is unprecedented in its frequency. During the campaign, he used Twitter to drive his earned media coverage, as conventional media frequently covered the latest Trump tweet. He tweeted about his opponents, the pope, news reporters, his IQ, illegal voting, a rigged election, and public policies regarding immigration, such as his proposal to build a wall along the Mexican border. As Democratic pollster Mark Mellman said, "They [Trump's campaign] drove tremendous amounts of coverage that way, very smart, really the first sort of Twitter-driven election, if you will, social media-driven election in that sense. Again, it's not clear exactly if that could be replicated further down the ballots in that way and it's not even clear that other candidates who are more normal could replicate that."[43] A second longtime Democratic participant in campaigns observed of Trump, "He clearly knows how to change the debate and change the discussion. It's like, 'Pay no attention to what I'm doing over here because I'm tweeting this over here.'"[44]

While the media covered Trump's tweets in great detail, they largely missed his campaign's extensive use of Facebook. The Trump campaign, building on a prior business relationship with a marketing firm headed by Brad Parscale, used Facebook to identify donors and persuadable voters whom they could convince to vote for Trump or not to vote for

Clinton. Joshua Green and Sasha Issenberg reported near the end of the
general election campaign that the Trump campaign had

> three major voter suppression operations under way . . . aimed
> at three groups Clinton needs to win overwhelmingly: idealistic
> white liberals, young women, and African Americans. Trump's in-
> vocation at the debate of Clinton's WikiLeaks e-mails and support
> for the Trans-Pacific Partnership was designed to turn off Sanders
> supporters. The parade of women who say they were sexually as-
> saulted by Bill Clinton and harassed or threatened by Hillary is
> meant to undermine her appeal to young women. And her 1996
> suggestion that some African American males are 'super preda-
> tors' is the basis of a below-the-radar effort to discourage infre-
> quent black voters from showing up at the polls—particularly in
> Florida.[45]

Foreign Funding and Election Activity

The use of social media in the 2016 election generated substantial controversy after the election when it was discovered that the Russian government, working through individuals or groups, had run election-related
ads on Facebook and Google. The scope of Russian interference was
large, including hacking twenty-one state election systems.[46] At least
twelve Russian intelligence officers hacked into the computers of the
Democratic National Committee, 300 people affiliated with the Clinton
campaign, and the Democratic Congressional Campaign Committee,
with the intent of sharing information that would damage the candidacies
of Hillary Clinton and other Democrats. The Russians unsuccessfully
also attempted to hack into the computers of the Republican National
Committee.[47] They were able to successfully breach the accounts of staff
to U.S. senators John McCain and Lindsay Graham,[48] as well as some
Republican House members and supportive individuals and groups.[49]
The Russian hackers leaked their stolen e-mails in stages, largely through
organizations such as WikiLeaks, intending to do maximum harm to
Clinton and other Democrats.

Russia used social media to communicate directly with individual
Americans during the 2016 campaign. They often did this through the
Internet Research Agency, a Russian-owned entity, but their messages
often used other source names, such as "Back the Badge," which emphasized law and order themes; "South United," which showcased a

confederate flag and called for the South to rise again; "Blacktivist," which sought to dampen African American turnout; and "Being Patriotic," which emphasized themes like Hillary Clinton and Benghazi.[50] Russia also used social media to spread fake news stories to targeted audiences to reinforce their anti-Clinton predispositions.[51] Facebook media efforts included at least 80,000 pieces of content, which reached 126 million users. Twitter has identified 2,700 Russian- linked accounts, which posted 131,000 tweets between September and November 2016. The Russians also used bots, pumping out 1.4 million tweets viewed around 288 million times. YouTube had 1,100 videos underwritten by Russians and related to the election.[52] The Internet Research Agency purchased $4,700 in Google search and display ads.[53]

To fund their activity, the Russians paid Facebook in Russian rubles for some of the ads run on that platform[54] and used cryptocurrency, including bitcoin, for other transactions. By using cryptocurrency, the Russians were able to avoid transactions with traditional financial institutions.[55] Russia spent as much as $100,000 on Facebook advertising campaigns.[56] More broadly, the Internet Research Agency spent $1.25 million monthly, not all of which was used for U.S. election interference.[57]

The actions by Russia in the 2016 election pose critically important policy questions, discussed later in this chapter. More broadly, they demonstrate that, for purposes of regulation, spending in elections needs to include spending on social media. The Russian activity also shows how difficult it is for recipients of these communications to know who actually is communicating with them. The 2016 Russian electioneering may result in stricter laws and regulations.

Candidate Foundations

During the 2016 election, attention was focused on foundations closely identified with presidential candidates that may have directly or indirectly benefited their candidacies. After completing his term as Florida's governor in 2007, Jeb Bush formed the Foundation for Excellence in Education, and he remained active in the work of the foundation after leaving office. The foundation generated controversy in 2013 for paying for state legislators and state education officials to attend conferences where the guests were lobbied by for-profit groups who had donated to the Excellence in Education Foundation.[58] The foundation became an issue in 2016 because of Bush's success in raising large sums of money for his Super

PAC and the possible connection between donors to his foundation and those also giving to his campaign. In July 2015, Bush released a list of donors to his foundation, making transparent any connections to donors to his presidential campaign, including his Super PAC.[59]

In 1997, Hillary Clinton and her husband, then president Bill Clinton, formed the Clinton Foundation. By 2016, it had raised $2 billion, with most of its expenditures being for charity. The charity became an issue early in the 2016 campaign, as some claimed the Clintons were using Hillary Clinton's position as secretary of state to reward donors to the foundation, claims she denied.[60] Donald Trump used the allegations in his campaign against Clinton as evidence for his claim that she was "crooked Hillary."[61] Both the Bush and Clinton foundations helped cultivate relationships with individuals and groups who later donated to their campaigns and affiliated Super PACs. Given the increasing role large donors, corporations, and unions now play in funding candidates through Super PACs, foundations like the ones formed by Jeb Bush and the Clintons are likely to become more common.

The Donald J. Trump Foundation also was the subject of controversy during the 2016 election. Charges arose over a $25,000 contribution the foundation made to "And Justice for All," a political group supporting Republican Pam Bondi, the Florida attorney general. Foundations may not make political donations. In the fall of 2016, after the contribution was reported in the media, Trump was fined, and he replaced the money that had come from his charity.[62] The most visible involvement of the Trump Foundation in the 2016 election was his nationally televised charity fundraiser to raise money for veterans groups in Des Moines, Iowa. The event was held on the same night as a televised debate between other Republican contenders for the presidential nomination, in which Trump did not participate. The fundraiser raised $5.6 million, with $2.8 million going to the Trump Foundation. The event was organized and promoted by the Trump campaign, and campaign staff were involved in the allocation of funds from the event.

These activities of the Trump Foundation are the subject of a lawsuit filed by the New York attorney general in 2018.[63] The New York attorney general also wrote the acting commissioner of the Internal Revenue Service, referring evidence of possible violations of the U.S. Internal Revenue Code. The letter states that the New York investigation found that "(1) the president of the Foundation's board, Mr. Trump, used Foundation assets for personal gain; (2) the Foundation impermissibly intervened in a political campaign by, among other things, attempting to influence the outcome of the 2016 presidential election; (3) the Foundation failed to report excise tax liability properly; and (4) the Foundation engaged in deceptive and/or improper fundraising practices."[64] The most relevant issue for campaign finance is the second item. The letter details the time, place, and manner used by the foundation and the Trump campaign to engage in what it describes as "deceptive and improper fundraising practices." Among the specifics reported in the letter are that the campaign directed and coordinated the timing, recipients, and amounts of disbursements from the fundraiser. The event closely mirrored Trump campaign themes and slogans. In addition, checks to recipients following the fundraiser were distributed at Trump campaign events, and enlarged versions of the checks were displayed at the events with the Trump campaign slogan, "Make America Great Again!" printed on the check.[65]

How Independent Are Independent Expenditures?

The distinction between contributions given to candidates, party committees, and PACs, which are limited and disclosed, and independent expenditures, which are unlimited, is based on the assumption that independent expenditures are just that: independent. However, in practice, the Federal Election Commission (FEC) has struggled to set boundaries. The FEC has defined an independent expenditure as "an expenditure for a communication that expressly advocates the election or defeat of a clearly identified federal candidate; and is **not** coordinated with a candidate, candidate's committee, party committee or their agents."[66]

During the 2016 election cycle, Larry Noble, who was the general counsel at the Federal Election Commission from 1987 to 2000, stated, "We don't have coordination rules anymore."[67] Another longtime participant in national politics, Mike Lux, observed that in 2016

> the outside groups . . . have become more and more blatantly coordinated with the campaigns. . . . [I]n the 90s when I first started doing IEs, I was literally religious about the separation, right? . . . [T]he blatancy by which the outside groups now were coordinating and taking their signals from the campaign was striking. Obviously it helps that we can all see each other's ads instantly and know what the bias[es] are pretty instantly. So that's a part of it, but part of it is that the FEC no longer functions.[68]

What constitutes "independent" and what constitutes "coordination" are major issues that the evidence from 2016 suggests are unclear. Candidates such as Jeb Bush and John Kasich delayed the official announcement of their campaigns in 2016 in order to facilitate fundraising for Super PACs and coordination on message. In previous election cycles, candidates pushed the limits of coordination by making public extensive B-Roll footage, video files of the candidates that might be useful for independent groups making ads.[69] In 2016, Democrats, building on American Bridge, started Correct the Record, a new Super PAC aligned with Hillary Clinton, which served as a rapid-response messenger through social media. Correct the Record broke new ground in 2015–16 by claiming it would "work in coordination" with the Clinton campaign. The group claimed that it was not subject to the standard Super PAC prohibitions on coordination because the material it produced was directed to the web and through social media.[70]

The Campaign Finance Policy Agenda following the 2016 Election

Presidential candidate Donald Trump spoke often of how his opponents were owned by large donors through Super PAC contributions and, in Hillary Clinton's case, money given to the Clinton Foundation and to her directly in speaking fees. While Trump did not discuss specific ways he would change our "rigged" elections, he did differentiate himself by not endorsing a Super PAC, unlike other Republicans seeking the nomination, and by claiming that no interest or lobbyist owned him, because he was a self-financed candidate. At one of the televised Republican presidential nomination debates, Trump said, "So I will tell you I understand the game, I've been on the other side all of my life. And they have a lot of control over our politicians. And I don't say that favorably, and I'm not sure if there's another system, but I say this. I am not accepting any money from anybody. Nobody has control of me other than the people of this country."[71] At a later primary debate, he said,

I know the system far better than anybody else and I know the system is broken. And I'm the one, because I know it so well because I was on both sides of it, I was on the other side all my life and I've always made large contributions. And frankly, I know the system better than anybody else and I'm the only one up here that's going to be able to fix that system because that system is wrong.[72]

More broadly, Trump spoke of "draining the swamp," which appeared to include eliminating the corrupting effect of special interests. Now that Trump is in office, reforming the way elections are financed is not high on his reform agenda. Rather, Super PACs supporting Trump were formed early in his administration, in 2017,[73] as was a leadership PAC formed by Vice President Mike Pence.[74] Trump's campaign committee raised $43 million in 2017, and America First (his largest Super PAC) raised a reported $30 million, only $4 million of which was disclosed to the FEC.[75]

Legislative Agenda

There are also no indications that the Republican congressional leadership sees legislation on campaign finance as a high priority. Other policy concerns, such as tax cuts, health care, and government infrastructure, are high priorities for Republicans in 2018. Reform legislation has been introduced in both houses, but the last set of reforms to pass in either house was the DISCLOSE (Democracy Is Strengthened by Casting Light on Spending in Elections) Act, which passed in the House in 2010 only to fall three votes short of cloture in the Senate, with all fifty-seven Democrats and no Republicans voting for the bill.

Given the difficulty Congress has had in enacting even the most essential legislation, it is not surprising that legislation in the area of campaign finance has not generated much attention in recent years. Where there appears to be some bipartisan agreement is in the area of greater disclosure and requiring disclaimers in social media advertising. Both greater disclosure and disclaimers became more pressing with the use of social media by groups supported by the Russian government in the 2016 and 2018 elections. The fact that in March 2018, as part of the omnibus spending bill passed by Congress, the FEC was directed to report to the House and Senate "on the Commission's role in how it identifies foreign contributions to elections, and what it plans to do in the future to continue these efforts," is evidence of the growing legislative interest in the role of foreign money in U.S. elections.[76]

A group of bipartisan sponsors in both houses have proposed the Honest Ads Act, which would require more transparency for online political ads. Its Senate sponsors are Mark Warner (D-Va.), Amy Klobuchar (D-Minn.), and the late John McCain (R-Ariz.). The act requires digital platforms to make "reasonable efforts" to bar foreign nationals from running ads attempting to influence U.S. elections. The act would also require digital platforms with more than 50 million unique monthly visitors to maintain a publicly available record of advertisers who have spent more than $500 on ads in the previous year. The archive would include a digital copy of the ad as well as a description of the target audience, the rate charged, the candidate or office that the ad was supporting, and the contact information of the advertiser. Facebook and Twitter have both indicated they support the Honest Ads Act.[77]

Social media platforms have taken some action on these issues on their own. In 2018, Facebook began a policy of including a disclaimer saying "Paid for by" along with the name of the advertiser. The scope of the Facebook policy included news organizations running ads promoting their news coverage.[78] Facebook also has committed to retaining an archive of all political ads "for the next seven years, or through a full congressional election cycle," available at their website. Likewise, Twitter announced it was now requiring "those running political ads for federal elections to identify themselves and certify that they are in the United States." Twitter will now prohibit foreign nationals from targeting political ads to people in the United States.[79]

As the Supreme Court confirmation process for Judge Brett Kavanaugh unfolded in 2018, another issue related to foreign spending in U.S. elections unfolded. Could foreign nationals or foreign governments spend money on issue advocacy, which is ads that do not explicitly call for the election or defeat of a candidate and are run sixty days before an election? In his opinion in *Blumen* v. *Federal Election Commission* (Case 1:16-cv-00259-BAH, filed August 3, 2018), Kavanaugh, joined by two district court judges, ruled that two foreign nationals, because they were not U.S. citizens, could not spend money on express advocacy, but they could engage in issue advocacy, as defined in *Wisconsin Right to Life* v. *Federal Election Commission* (551 U.S. 449 (2007), 469–70), and that express advocacy is a communication that "is susceptible of no reasonable interpretation other than as an appeal to vote for or against a specific candidate." Communications that do not meet this test can be seen as issue advocacy and therefore are not subject to the same limitations. This decision was upheld by the Supreme Court a year later. One interpretation of this is that this means that in the context of foreign governments, such as the Russians in 2016 and 2018, running ads that do not meet the express advocacy standard is not prohibited. As more is learned about

Russian involvement in the 2016 and 2018 elections, this could become a subject for further legislation.

Legislation concerning the relationships between candidates and their Super PACs and other independent groups has also been introduced in Congress. The "Stop Candidate Super PAC-Candidate Coordination Act," sponsored by Representative David Price (D-N.C.), and a similar measure, the "'We the People' Democracy Reform Act of 2017," introduced in the Senate by Senator Tom Udall (D-N.Mex.), would prohibit single-candidate Super PACs, among other provisions.[80] Some elements of the Udall and Price proposals are also included in the Democratic Party's 2018 "A Better Deal for Our Democracy." Similar in some respects to the Republicans' 1994 "Contract with America," this document includes provisions about campaign finance and voting rights reforms, changes to the Federal Election Commission, stricter ethics laws, and other reforms. Should the Democrats secure majorities in Congress, the proposal may provide a roadmap of possible legislation for the lead-up to the 2020 election and beyond.[81]

Courts and Campaign Finance

Federal courts, especially the U.S. Supreme Court, have been at the center of reshaping campaign finance policy. Throughout this book, cases that fit this description have been discussed, including *Colorado Republican Federal Campaign Committee* v. *Federal Election Commission* (1996), *McConnell* v. *Federal Election Commission* (2003), *Wisconsin Right to Life* v. *Federal Election Commission* (2007), *Citizens United* v. *Federal Election Commission* (2010), *SpeechNow.org* v. *Federal Election Commission* (2010), *Arizona Free Enterprise Club's Freedom Club PAC* v. *Bennett* (2011), and *McCutcheon* v. *Federal Election Commission* (2014), all of which were decided by a single-vote majority.

At the federal level, those hoping for a reversal of *Citizens United* v. *Federal Election Commission* had high hopes once Merrick Garland was nominated by President Barack Obama in 2016 to replace Antonin Scalia, who died in February 2016. Their assumption was that Garland would side with the dissenters in *Citizens United* on the issue of Super PACs. But the Senate did not vote on Garland, and instead Neil Gorsuch was named by President Trump, confirmed by the Senate, and was seen as a likely supporter of the Court's recent rulings on campaign finance. The retirement in 2018 of Justice Anthony Kennedy and the appointment of Brett Kavanaugh to replace him further reinforces the current majority on issues related to campaign finance. It is also possible that with Gorsuch and Kavanaugh on the Court, the prior rulings upholding contribution limits and other limits, such as the BCRA soft-money ban, enacted by Congress could be overturned.

Under Chief Justice John Roberts, the majority on the Supreme Court has narrowed the definition of what constitutes corruption. The standard changed from the appearance of corruption in *Buckley* v. *Valeo* to the majority's language in *McCutcheon* v. *Federal Election Commission*, which defined corruption as "a contribution to a particular candidate in exchange for his agreeing to do a particular act within his official duties."[82] Roberts is also of the view that large Super PAC donations do not mean the donor gains access to the officeholder or undue influence as a result of the expenditure. He wrote, "Spending large sums of money in connection with elections, but not in connection with an effort to control the exercise of an officeholder's official duties, does not give rise to such quid pro quo corruption. Nor does the possibility that an individual who spends large sums may garner influence over or access to elected officials or political parties."[83]

At the regulatory level, recent years have seen little oversight from the FEC or from the Internal Revenue Service (IRS), and that is not likely to change. However, two lawsuits brought by the New York attorney general claim the Trump Foundation may have violated federal tax law as well as state tax law (letter to the Internal Revenue Service)[84] and may also have violated federal election law (letter to the Federal Election Commission).[85] These claims will be reviewed in the next two subsections.

The FEC

The FEC is a regulatory body "responsible for the civil enforcement of federal campaign finance law," which means it provides interpretations and rulings on the application of the law. It administers the disclosure of campaign finance transactions and, for participating candidates, administers the presidential public financing program.[86] The FEC has six commissioners, no more than three of whom can come from the same party, and all but one of the commissioners in the FEC's history have been either Democrats or Republicans. While the president appoints FEC commissioners, the pattern has been for the president to defer to the two Senate party leaders. It has not been uncommon for commissioners to reach the end of their term and continue to serve pending appointment of a replacement, what the FEC calls "holdover status." One commissioner, Ellen

Weintraub, has been in holdover status for more than a decade. When Ann M. Ravel reached the end of her term on April 30, 2017, she chose to vacate her seat rather than join the five other commissioners, all of whom were in holdover status.[87] In an op-ed in the *New York Times*, she gave the following reason for not serving beyond her term: "It pains me to report that the agency remains dysfunctional, more so than ever."[88]

With Weintraub's departure, the FEC has only four commissioners, all of whom are serving with expired terms, thus allowing President Trump to appoint as many as six commissioners. No more than three commissioners can come from one political party, but this would not prohibit President Trump from nominating three Republicans and three independents. In the history of the FEC, one independent has been a commissioner, Steven T. Walther, who was appointed by President George W. Bush in 2007 and is presently serving.[89] White House counsel Don McGahn was Trump's campaign counsel, and presumably he will have substantial input on appointments to the FEC.

For the FEC to take action requires agreement from at least four commissioners, and the party balance built into the FEC has effectively meant that either party can block action if the three fellow partisans vote together, although a 2-2, 3-2, or 2-3 vote also results in inaction.[90] Congressional Research Service (CRS) analyst R. Sam Garrett has said, "'Deadlocked' votes are the most prominent and enduring indicator of policy disagreements within the FEC."[91] Partisan deadlock at the FEC serves the political interests of those who would prefer a less regulated election finance regime, as the absence of four affirmative votes on rulings has allowed groups to test limits and push beyond past rulings or expectations. One prominent example is that the FEC was unable to agree on rules implementing the *Citizens United* and *SpeechNow.org* court decisions for nearly five years, leaving uncertainty about how these decisions altered prior FEC rulings through the 2010, 2012, and effectively the 2014 election cycles.[92]

FEC commissioners, not surprisingly, disagree even on the extent to which they are deadlocked. Ann Ravel, the former Democratic commissioner who resigned in February 2017, said 30 percent of the commission's votes ended in a 3-3 deadlock. This is disputed by Republican commissioner Lee Goodman, who, examining the data in a different way, said that only 9.7 percent of cases ended in a 3-3 deadlock.[93] If a case is deadlocked, then it is effectively closed and the case is dropped. At the close of 2015, there was a four-year backlog of cases.[94] There have been prominent, seemingly "open and shut" cases that have been deadlocked in the last few years. This has led to more frustration with the FEC and has significantly weakened its watchdog power over elections.

Quantifying how much deadlock there has been on the FEC depends, in part, on what is counted. On some "Matters under Review" (MURs), the FEC's most significant enforcement cases, there may be multiple votes. If all votes on the same MUR are 3-3, is each vote counted as a deadlock or is that one deadlock? The last time the FEC produced an "official, publicly available statistical summary" of votes was in 2009.[95] Using that summary's data, the CRS found the FEC was deadlocked or made no rulings on 13 percent of MURs and on approximately 17 percent of advisory opinions (AOs). The CRS tallied data for 2014 using the FEC's Enforcement Query System and found the FEC deadlocked or did not take action on 24 percent of MURs.[96] Using a broader measure, one study found that the outcome of 40 percent of votes on matters put to a vote by the FEC was not to take action.[97]

After the FEC decided not to make an official and publicly available summary of FEC activity, one reform advocacy group decided to develop a dataset themselves. Public Citizen's data extend from 2003 to 2014. Their study found increasing deadlock during the 2010 to 2014 period in one or more of these areas: enforcement actions, proposed audits, proposed rules, and advisory opinions.[98] Another analysis, which looked only at enforcement cases on the question of illegal coordination between Super PACs and candidates, found a higher level of agreement among commissioners.[99] One reason for this was the fact that the FEC had not agreed on new coordination rules, making it harder to agree on possible violations of rules established before Super PACs were permitted.

The lack of action at the FEC is seen very differently by those who favor deregulation of campaign finance and minimal regulatory interference, as compared to those favoring a more active FEC issuing rulings and taking action to enforce the law. As R. Sam Garrett of the Congressional Research Service states,

> Some contend that recent years have marked a particularly problematic period in which, amid policy stalemates, some areas of campaign finance law have gone without adequate interpretation or enforcement. Others respond, equally vigorously, that Congress purposely insulated the FEC from excessive partisanship in the wake of Watergate and in one of the most constitutionally protected

free speech areas made action more difficult. They also caution that the commission cannot or should not do via regulation what Congress declined to do by statute.[100]

Since the FEC began in 1975, it has had very little oversight from Congress. The Congressional Research Service tallied all "congressional hearings substantively devoted to FEC Oversight between 1995 and 2015 and found there had been a total of 5 hearings, with the most recent hearing in 2011."[101] One reform that both sides in the campaign finance reform debate likely agree with is to require the U.S. Senate to report to the FEC electronically. Senate candidates continue to report to the secretary of the Senate, who sends paper copies of the reports to the FEC, where they are entered into the FEC's computers. According to the FEC, this costs $876,000 and also delays access to the electronic data by Senate candidates.[102] The CRS has tallied the subject matter of legislative recommendations from the FEC for 2005–14 and found that in every congress over this period there was proposed legislation calling for mandatory electronic filing of Senate reports. With equal frequency, the FEC has called for legislation to broaden "existing prohibitions on 'fraudulent misrepresentation' of campaign authority, such as fundraising for fictitious political committees" and "to extend current restrictions on personal use of campaign funds to other kinds of political committees."[103] These are both areas of campaign conduct where the FEC seeks legislative action.

Those favoring a more active FEC favor its restructuring. In recent decades, the common elements of proposed legislation on FEC organization have included an uneven number of commissioners (three, five, or seven), with a single chairperson (often with a ten-year term) and often with appointed administrative law judges to preside over enforcement actions. Primary sponsors of this framework include the late senator John McCain (R-Ariz.) and Senator Russ Feingold (D-Wis.) and Representatives Christopher Shays (R-Conn.) and Martin Meehan (D-Mass.), all of whom were sponsors of the Bipartisan Campaign Reform Act. This proposed legislation was introduced in the 108th, 109th, 110th, and 111th Congresses (2003–10). Representative Derek Kilmer (D-Wash.) introduced a similar bill in the 114th and 115th Congresses (2015–16 and 2017–18).

Supporters of the current "bipartisan design" of the FEC see decisions coming from the current structure as less politicized than would be the case with an uneven number of commissioners.[104] Former FEC commissioner Brad Smith shares this view. He stated, "The bipartisan requirement, far from being 'designed for failure,' is what makes regulation palatable at all."[105]

As discussed earlier, the activity of the Trump Foundation in the 2016 campaign raises important regulatory issues for the Federal Election Commission. The attorney general of New York wrote the Federal Election Commission in 2018, referring evidence of a "possible violation of the Federal Election Act." Among the specifics of the referral were that the Trump Foundation had disbursed $2.8 million to influence the 2016 election, a contribution not allowed under the law. The letter reported a claim that the foundation and campaign had coordinated in ways also not allowed under the law. The letter also provided the FEC with evidence relating to the $25,000 contribution to the group affiliated with Florida attorney general Bondi.[106]

The high level of involvement by the Trump campaign in hosting, promoting, and benefiting from the Iowa fundraising event could set a precedent for other candidates in the future if the FEC, IRS, and state and federal courts do not rule that it was illegal. Trump gained the benefit of substantial media attention for his Iowa Trump Foundation fundraiser and then the additional benefit of distributing the proceeds from the fundraiser during the campaign. Donations to the foundation were not subject to contribution limits or disclosure requirements.

Another result of the FEC's gridlock has been inactivity in the area of regulations on political advertising in social media. A decade earlier, the FEC had excluded from regulations all internet communications "other than communications placed for a fee on another person's website." Following the discovery of the large-scale use of social media by Russian groups in 2018, reform groups called on the FEC to issue new and more expansive rules requiring greater disclosure and the placement of disclaimers in all political ads.[107]

The IRS

As discussed in chapter 2, the IRS has a regulatory role with regard to groups whose activities extend to elections. With a deadlocked FEC and a restrained IRS, we are in a period of limited regulatory oversight of campaign finance. Key issues, such as whether nonprofit social welfare groups (section 501(c)(4) groups) can devote more than half of their spending to election-related activity, have remained unresolved. The language of the Internal Revenue Code is that section 501(c)(4) groups are "social welfare" organizations "not organized for profit but operated exclusively for the promotion of social welfare."[108] However, in 1959, the Treasury Department issued a regulation that redefined the "exclusive" requirement to mean that "an organization is operated exclusively for the promotion of social welfare if it is 'primarily' engaged in promoting in some way the common good and general welfare of the people of the community."[109] Since "primarily" has not been defined by the Treasury Department or by the IRS, the requirement remains vague to this day. Presently, the IRS uses a "facts and circumstances test" to determine whether the activity of a section 501(c)(4) organization is primary or not.[110] Because "primary purpose" has not been defined, groups and their attorneys are left to interpret this in different ways. Absent clear boundaries, some groups have been willing to apply their own interpretation and spend nearly all funds raised by the group on electing or defeating a candidate. A case in point is Carolina Rising, a 501(c)(4) group that spent nearly $5 million in the 2014 North Carolina U.S. Senate race hoping to elect Republican Thom Tillis. In a detailed analysis of the group's spending, Robert Maguire of the Center for Responsive Politics found that up to 97 percent of the group's expenditures were spent in the election contest.[111]

The surge in groups seeking section 501(c)(4) status during and after the 2010 campaign and the differential treatment given conservative groups appears to have meant the IRS is less actively evaluating such groups. Given the perceived inaction on the part of the IRS and the fact that it has stated that "while an application is pending, the organization can treat itself as exempt from federal income tax law," it is not surprising that groups have formed, filed with the IRS and been active while awaiting IRS review.[112]

At the same time that the IRS was facing an increased number of applications from groups seeking approval as new 501(c)(4) organizations, Congress had cut the service's budget. Within the IRS, the cuts were not applied equally to all divisions. The service prioritizes the division that focuses on individual income taxes and other income-generating functions over the division that deals with tax-exempt organizations and pension funds.[113] As a result of budget cuts and in a move to reduce costs, the IRS designated the Cincinnati, Ohio, office rather than the Washington, D.C., office, which had been designated for decades, to conduct the reviews of groups applying for 501(c)(4) tax-exempt status.

The IRS appears to have also become less active in providing oversight of nonprofit groups involved in politics. The IRS was heavily criticized in 2013 for the way it targeted for more intense scrutiny applications from groups with the terms "tea party," "patriot," or "9/12 movement" in their names who were applying for status as section 501(c)(4) organizations. Following an FBI investigation, the Justice Department decided not to file any criminal charges, although several top officials, such as acting IRS commissioner Steven Miller and key division head Lois Lerner, stepped down under pressure.[114]

In the view of Marc Owens, who worked at the IRS for twenty-five years, including a decade as director of the Exempt Organizations Division, the IRS as a regulator was "pretty much kept locked away in 2016 and the little regulation there was, and I would put that in quotation marks, really occurred through the media and investigative reporters."[115] According to Owens, this decline in oversight came as a result of the combination of congressional demands on the IRS and declining funding.[116] More fundamentally, the culture and practices of the IRS are very different from those of an election commission charged with disclosing campaign finance activity and responding to requests for rulings on what is and is not permissible in the midst of an election campaign. The IRS culture values secrecy and not disclosure, and the timetable for reporting to the IRS is not attuned to the electoral calendar like the timetable for reporting at the FEC or state-level campaign finance commissions. FEC rulings on matters before the commission are public, while decisions by the IRS are typically private, although redacted "Private Letter Rulings," with all identifying information removed, may be released to provide guidance on tax questions.[117]

Criticism from Congress regarding how the IRS handled the 501(c) groups was strong and sustained. House Speaker John Boehner and Senate Republican leader Mitch McConnell both voiced concerns, as did others from both parties.[118] Some have been critical of Congress with regard to the IRS as well. Paul S. Ryan, now with Common Cause, states that in the period since the resignations of Miller and Lerner, there have been "laws passed by Congress prohibiting the IRS from doing rulemaking on the subject and prohibiting the IRS from expending resources for enforcement. I think we're going to see more weakening of the IRS and its ability to enforce laws in the area of the political arena. . . . The IRS is prohibited by an Appropriations Bill from engaging in rulemaking [with election finance]."[119] In part because of the delays in reviewing applications for section 501(c)(4) status, the IRS now states that "while an application is pending, the organization can treat itself as exempt from federal income tax."[120]

In July 2016, the IRS announced a ruling that tax-exempt section 501(c)(4) and 501(c)(6) groups are no longer required to identify donors of $5,000 or more on their annual tax returns to the IRS. Donor identities were previously required on the tax forms, but the identities were not made public. Given the controversy over possible foreign money being spent in 2016, and that some of that money may have been directed to section 501(c) groups, this ruling generated some controversy. Montana senator Jon Tester, for example, objected, saying, "We need more transparency in our campaigns, not less."[121] Less than a month after the IRS ruling, the U.S. District Court for the District of Columbia, ruling on a different question, overturned a 1980 FEC rule that nonprofit groups were not required to disclose donors if their contributions were not earmarked for specific advertisements. The case, involving the 501(c)(4) American Crossroads Grassroots Policy Strategies, is likely not the last word on the question. Subsequent court cases and legislation may clarify what is now an uncertain landscape for donors to 501(c)(4) and 501(c)(6) groups.[122]

Different Schools of Thought about How to Improve Campaign Finance

While comprehensive campaign finance reform legislation is not likely to be passed in the current political environment, some incremental changes are under consideration. Two broad approaches scholars and advocates have taken for improving campaign finance in the United States are to provide limits on the way money can be raised and spent on elections (reformers) and to remove limits as much as possible (deregulators). Within each group, there are important differences, but the critical distinction is whether the group believes that the government can effectively balance the competing demands of freedom of speech and fair elections. Reformers seek a system in which individuals have approximate equality to voice their views and vote based on information drawn from competitive elections. Deregulators give much more weight to freedom of speech, essentially arguing that there should be few or no restraints on individuals, corporations, and groups to spend money to influence elections.

The reform school has long favored public funding of federal elections, with contribution and expenditure limitations and full disclosure.[123] This

group sees the two decades following implementation of the amended
FECA as a success, with all major candidates for president accepting federal matching funds in primaries and the public grant and spending limits in the general election. While there were biases in the allocation of
PAC money to incumbents in congressional races, they also see FECA as
a success at the congressional level. There was widespread acceptance of
disclosure by candidates, party committees, and PACs, and independent
expenditures were much less than were seen in more recent years. The
reformers see BCRA as a fine-tuning of FECA, addressing two primary
problems: party soft money and interest-group electioneering under the
guise of "issue advocacy." Subsequent court and administrative decisions
have meant that party committees are again able to be major players in
independent expenditures and that wealthy individuals and groups can
spend unlimited amounts through Super PACs and large contributions
to party committees, as they once did through soft money. Before BCRA,
groups and individuals could spend on election-related activities anonymously through "issue ads," while today they can do the same thing
through section 501(c)(4) groups.

While the deregulation school has been successful in rolling back some
of the new limitations in BCRA through court cases and deadlocked or
inactive regulatory commissions or agencies, this has not limited the call
for further deregulation by individuals and groups who favor an even less
regulated system. In the extreme, the deregulators would remove all contribution and expenditure limits and some would limit disclosure.[124] As
with the reformers, the deregulators are not all of one mind with respect
to particular reforms,[125] but these two approaches are helpful in examining possible future changes in campaign finance in the United States.
For purposes of this analysis, we will examine the following areas of
possible reform: party committees, groups, disclosure, the FCC, lobbying,
and pay to play.

Party Committees

As discussed in chapter 7, those favoring fewer restrictions on money in
politics accomplished part of that goal through the 2014 case *McCutcheon*
v. *Federal Election Commission*, which eliminated the previous aggregate contribution limits on individuals giving to political parties. In
2016, this helped make it easier for presidential candidates to raise more
money in joint fundraising agreements. Additionally, those favoring fewer
limits on the political parties were successful in that Congress passed the

Consolidated and Further Appropriations Act of 2015, omnibus appropriations legislation that passed late in 2014 (sometimes called CRomnibus), which allowed national party committees to establish new accounts with increased contribution limits for specified purposes—one for legal, compliance, and recount expenses and another for building expenses. All six national committees (RNC, DNC, NRSC, DSCC, NRCC, and DCCC) set up these accounts. The RNC and DNC were also permitted to establish national nomination convention expense accounts.[126]

In recent years, the deregulation school has focused on lifting the rules on how political parties can raise and spend money. A group of legal scholars and political scientists has made the case that parties play a vital and distinct role in elections and that they have been left at a disadvantage by changing rules that permit Super PACs and section 501(c)(4) groups to raise and spend unlimited amounts in elections. It would be much better, they argue, if these funds were being raised and spent by the political parties, because they are more connected to the candidates, have an ongoing relationship with government, and are more supportive of challengers and open seat candidates.[127] This school attempts to build its case by pointing to an earlier time when parties were stronger. For some, this period preceded enactment of the Bipartisan Campaign Reform Act (BCRA), which banned the unlimited contributions parties could raise and spend through party soft money. For those favoring deregulation of parties, the parties have been weakened over a much longer period, dating back to the Progressive Era reforms of direct primaries and civil service laws limiting party patronage.[128]

The deregulators of parties have been criticized for ignoring the abuses of party machines in controlling nominations and patronage, and more recently studies that found the party soft money of the 1996–2002 period was used not as a way to strengthen political parties but instead as a way to direct unlimited funds into particular electoral contests. Some deregulators overlook the evidence that soft money was used by party leaders to curry favor with large donors, granting them unusual access to leaders, including the president in the White House or on Air Force One. In the view of the Supreme Court, this kind of access had at least the appearance of corruption and was a basis for the Court to uphold the limitation.[129] Deregulators also inflate the strength of political parties since the era of political machines and overlook that the less restrained parties in the soft-money era were not spending that unlimited money on "party building" nearly as much as on candidate-specific election activity in a small number of competitive races.[130] Moreover, since BCRA, the party committees have been able to actively support candidates in competitive races with limited and disclosed hard-money contributions.

The party deregulators won major victories with the *McCutcheon* decision and the CRomnibus legislation. Both gave the parties greater access to large donors and more funding. Deregulators are now pushing for increases in what parties can spend in coordinated expenditures with candidates. In 2016, the coordinated expenditure limits ranged from $96,100 to $2.9 million, based on the voting population in the states for Senate elections, and the maximum coordinated expenditure for party committees to spend in coordination with candidates was set at $48,100 unless the state had one representative, in which case the limit was $96,100.[131]

If the FECA-coordinated expenditure limits were raised, there is no evidence the party committees would use that opportunity in a large number of races. In fact, since the 2008 election cycle, the party committees have not been making maximum coordinated expenditures in most House and Senate contests. In 2016, for example, only 79 of the 870 candidates received the maximum coordinated expenditure in U.S. House races, and in the Senate 26 of the 68 candidates received the maximum coordinated expenditure.[132]

Those who defend the limits on parties contend that the courts have already gone too far in opening up new avenues to raise money from large donors through *McCutcheon* and that Congress went too far in permitting the parties to establish funds to which a donor could give an additional $100,200 per year to each of the new party committees. Having these accounts funded or available meant party leaders could allocate a larger share of their other receipts to independent expenditures in the battleground contests. More broadly, this school sees parties as more than adequately funded and believes that removing coordinated expenditure limits will not strengthen parties.

The proponents of tighter limits on parties and groups also point to extensions of the parties through the partisan Super PACs organized around each chamber of Congress (for Democrats, the Senate Majority PAC and House Majority PAC, and for Republicans the Senate Leadership Fund and Congressional Leadership Fund). Functionally, these groups play much the same role that party committees played using soft money pre-BCRA; in fact, some scholars have even called these partisan

Super PACs the "new soft money."[133] At the presidential level, this same function is served by candidate-specific Super PACs such as Restore Our Future for Romney in 2012 or Priorities USA Action for Obama in 2012 and Clinton in 2016. Taken together, the proponents of limits on contributions and expenditures argue that the system has already provided too many opportunities for wealthy individuals and groups to influence elections and that efforts should be made to scale back the means for influencing election outcomes rather than expand them.

Groups

Those favoring deregulation favor loosening the current bans on coordination between candidates and their party committees' independent expenditures in their races. Some also argue for striking limits on coordination between candidates and supportive Super PACs. Michael Gilbert and Brian Barnes argue that anticoordination rules are unworkable and possibly unconstitutional:

> Coordination rules do not target bargaining effectively, and it is not clear that they could. . . . Coordination rules simply cannot deter much corruption, at least not when wealthy and sophisticated actors—the very actors who cause the most concern—are involved. As a result, coordination rules may violate the Constitution. This is not because coordinated expenditures do not corrupt but because the coordination rules do not deter. They interfere with political speech without combating much corruption.[134]

Those favoring retaining the bans on coordination between independent spenders and candidates point out that the court rulings justifying unlimited independent spending were conditional on that spending being independent of the candidates. They contend that because of a lack of regulatory rulemaking and enforcement, we are already at a point where independent spenders can effectively communicate with each other, share staff, involve the candidates and congressional leaders in fundraising, and other similar activities. They point to candidates such as Newt Gingrich giving advice to his Super PAC in 2012 and Ted Cruz doing the same to one of his Super PACs in 2016.

Proponents of deregulation have already scored major successes in deregulating the system. Super PACs effectively remove individual contribution limits for those wanting to spend in support of a candidate or congressional party, and expanded use of section 501(c)(4) groups with few agreed constraints effectively allows individuals and groups to spend unlimited and undisclosed amounts of money on election-related activities. Removing the aggregate limits on party contributions means those wanting to spend through the political parties can effectively spend millions of dollars that way each cycle. Thus, the deregulation school has accomplished much of its agenda of removing limits on contributions and expenditures.

Rather than removing the limits on coordination between Super PACs and party committees making independent expenditures, reformers favor making them stronger. For example, the Brennan Center for Justice has written,

> These "shadow campaigns" mock the campaign finance system. When candidates help raise money for a super PAC and also have a say in how that money is spent . . . that spending becomes virtually indistinguishable from that of campaigns. As a result, the current limits on direct contributions to candidates, which the Supreme Court has long recognized as an important check on corruption, become meaningless. Allowing collaboration between super PACs and campaigns also threatens the efficacy of public financing systems, which depend on participation of candidates who are removed from big money.[135]

Absent changes in personnel and approach at the FEC or new legislation, it is likely that the current absence of clear boundaries on impermissible coordination will continue, at least through the 2020 election.

Disclosure

Disclosure of contributions, transfers, and expenditures has been a cornerstone of federal campaign finance law for more than five decades. It has consistently been upheld as constitutional by the Supreme Court.[136] Justice Antonin Scalia was an outspoken defender of transparency when it came to disclosing the source of campaign communications or limiting speech. In *McConnell* v. *Federal Election Commission*, he wrote, "The premise of the First Amendment is that the American people are neither sheep nor fools, and hence fully capable of considering both the substance of the speech presented to them and its proximate and ultimate source."[137] One purpose of the act Justice Scalia was ruling on was to provide greater disclosure of issue ads, which at the time did not provide information on the source of funds used to pay for this speech. As discussed in chapters 2 and 3, the nation again faced a situation where groups avoided disclosure by virtue of their nonprofit status.

Those favoring consistent and effective disclosure of outside "independent" spenders believe the current disclosure laws for Super PACs and political party committees should be in place for section 501(c)(4) donors. Given the numerous examples of 501(c)(4) groups spending heavily to promote or attack candidates in recent election cycles, they believe these groups should be required to disclose their donors. Fred Wertheimer, founder of Democracy 21 and a longtime advocate of campaign finance reform, stated to the *Washington Post* following the 2012 election,

> We need disclosure legislation, to bring an end to the secret money being laundered into our elections. That would play a very large role in preventing the misuse of 501(c)(4)s for campaign purposes, because it's being done now as a vehicle to hide donors. . . . We also ought to pass comprehensive disclosure legislation so citizens can once again fully know who is financing the campaign expenditures that are being made to influence their votes.[138]

501(c)(4) groups are not only spending heavily in congressional and presidential races but are also allowed to contribute to Super PACs. This transfer of funds permits donors to indirectly get their money into a Super PAC, where all of it can be spent on electioneering. One example of this in 2016 was the 501(c)(4) group One Nation, which gave $21.7 million to the Senate Leadership Fund Super PAC.[139]

The 2016 election raises an additional concern for those who feel that groups involved in election-related activity should fall under the FECA political committee rules. As noted in chapters 1 and 3, some section 501(c)(4) groups provided services to candidates that historically have fallen under FECA political committee rules. Services in this category include calendaring, promoting, and staffing candidate-specific rallies and events; voter mobilization for primaries, caucuses, and general elections; and other activities. By using 501(c)(4) groups for these activities, candidates were able to fund them through unlimited and undisclosed contributions.

The activity of 501(c)(4) groups is in addition to the expanded role candidate-specific Super PACs played in 2015 and 2016. For example,

Ready for Hillary, a Super PAC supporting Secretary of State Hillary Clinton, raised and spent money in 2015, building a list of 4 million names and e-mail addresses of supporters of her possible candidacy.[140] Once Clinton announced her campaign, she gained access to the Ready for Hillary list through what *Politico* described as a "data swap."[141] The list was seen at the time as "a data gold mine that will immediately bolster the Democratic front-runner's fundraising and organizing efforts."[142] In their book on the Clinton campaign, which was published after the 2016 election, Jonathan Allen and Amie Parnes report that Clinton campaign manager Robby Mook and other professionals on the Clinton campaign thought that "Ready for Hillary had grossly overexaggerated the group's lists. After accounting for bad e-mail addresses, one official later groused, 'It wasn't half a million names.'"[143] One group filed a complaint about the Ready for Hillary data transfer, but no action was taken on the matter by the FEC.[144]

Some publicized cases in 2014 and 2016 have raised the important regulatory question of whether the ability of 501(c)(4) groups to dedicate nearly all of their spending to electing a candidate by promoting their preferred candidate or attacking the opponent, or opponents in the case of a primary election, violates the law on what the primary purpose of the 501(c)(4) group is. Inaction by the IRS and FEC on cases like Carolina Rising for its activities supporting Thom Tillis in the 2014 North Carolina U.S. Senate race or Marco Rubio's 2016 Conservative Solutions Project[145] is likely to signal to other campaigns that candidate-specific 501(c)(4) groups will be allowed. For deregulators, the inaction of the FEC and the IRS is consistent with their view that spending should be unconstrained, but for those favoring disclosure and limits, these cases call for a much more active FEC and IRS.

Those favoring deregulation argue that the current system has far too many restrictions and limits and that individuals and groups should be able to exercise their freedom of speech without constraint. Some, such as former general counsel to the Obama 2008 and 2012 campaigns Robert Bauer, and Samuel Issacharoff, have recommended raising the disclosure threshold for individual donors from the current $200 to the maximum allowable contribution, which in 2016 was $2,700 for the primary and general elections. Bauer argues that "no one is 'buying' a candidate for public office for that figure, and the privacy interests of donors at that level or below should be protected."[146]

Some have argued that requiring disclosure of individual contributions can lead to harassment or threats to the donors. Justice Clarence Thomas made this point in *Citizens United*, where he recounted examples of intimidation or retaliation against donors in the 2008 California Proposition 8 gay marriage initiative and other examples and pointed out "the fallacy of the Court's conclusion that 'disclaimer and disclosure requirements . . . impose no ceiling on campaign-related activities, and do not prevent anyone from speaking.'"[147]

Justice Thomas's view was not shared by other justices, and Justice Scalia was a prominent defender of disclosure in the electoral context. In a different case, *Doe* v. *Reed*, Scalia wrote, "Requiring people to stand up in public for their political acts fosters civic courage, without which democracy is doomed. For my part, I do not look forward to a society which, thanks to the Supreme Court, campaigns anonymously (McIntyre) and even exercises the direct democracy of initiative and referendum hidden from public scrutiny and protected from the accountability of criticism. This does not resemble the Home of the Brave." With Scalia no longer on the Court and as other cases arise, the Court's strong endorsement of disclosure could diminish.

FCC

Disclosure of receipts and expenditures by candidates, party committees, and PACs has been used extensively by the news media, academics, and the public. Use of the data has been enhanced by privately funded groups such as the Center for Responsive Politics. Broadcast radio and television stations have long been required to keep on file documentation on paid ads run by the station on issues of public importance. The "local public inspection file" contains records of advertising that "communicates a message relating to any political matter of national importance, including: (i) a legally qualified candidate; (ii) any election to federal office; or (iii) a national legislative issue of public importance."[148]

Since 2012, the Federal Communications Commission has required broadcasters to upload these files.[149] The disclosure includes the sponsors of ads and the particulars of requests for ad placements, as well as when the ad ran.[150] Since 2014, all television stations have made this information available in electronic form.[151]

Before electronic disclosure, data on sponsors of such ads were required to be kept in paper form at the stations, and people had to go to the stations during normal business hours to review the data. Some scholars have used these data to track advertising falling outside the definitions or reporting periods of federal law.[152] Having the station's ad-buy data available electronically is a major improvement over the previous system. However, it remains difficult to track ad-buy data because the data are not uploaded in a common format and may not be complete.[153]

Academics have tracked television advertising over time using a method developed for large commercial advertisers that is more efficient than visiting all broadcast stations and reviewing the paper files for the relevant information. These data have been archived by the Wisconsin Media Project and more recently by the Wesleyan Media Project.[154]

However, there remain important limits to disclosure. Donors to section 501(c)(4) or section 501(c)(6) groups are not disclosed, and donors to these groups are likely aware that these groups can transfer funds to Super PACs but that the disclosed donor to the Super PAC is the 501(c) group and not the donors who funded the 501(c)(4) group. Those favoring enhanced disclosure put forward legislation in 2010. The proposed act was titled "Democracy Is Strengthened by Casting Light on Spending in Elections," or the DISCLOSE Act. It would have required groups spending $10,000 or more on express advocacy or its "functional equivalent" over the calendar year that includes the election to disclose their spending and donors to the FEC within twenty-four hours after hitting the $10,000 mark. The groups covered by the act included IRS section 501(c)(4), 501(c)(6), and 527 groups; corporations; unions; and Super PACs. For corporations, it required disclosure of political activity to shareholders. It expanded the BCRA disclaimer language to require television and radio stations to disclose in the ad the names of primary contributors to the organization sponsoring the ad and required the head of the organization sponsoring the ad to record a "stand-by-your-ad" statement. It prohibited spending by foreign nationals and by government contractors with contracts in excess of $10 million. The DISCLOSE Act passed the House but fell three votes short of the threshold needed to overcome a filibuster in the Senate.

Lobbying and Pay to Play

For some participants, campaign contributions and lobbying are linked. This is often the case for conventional political action committees (see chapter 3), where incumbents routinely host fundraisers attended by lobbyists representing groups that make a contribution to the incumbent's reelection campaign. One of the concerns about wealthy individuals participating by contributing to candidate-specific or congressional leadership–driven Super PACs, large party joint fundraising contributions, or candidate-specific 501(c)(4) groups is that those individuals, like conventional PACs, are contributing in order to enhance their access to congressional leaders or individual politicians. This form of contributing is often called "pay to play."

Pay-to-play concerns arose in recent cases involving associates of lobbyist Jack Abramoff, particularly Kevin Ring, and in a separate case involving Virginia governor Robert F. McDonnell. Kevin Ring was accused of giving Washington Wizards basketball game tickets to an attorney at the U.S. Department of Justice as an illegal gratuity. The prosecution was permitted by the court to introduce as evidence Mr. Ring's legal campaign contributions in order to provide the wider context of Mr. Ring's behavior. Witnesses at trial stated that campaign contributions were "sort of like the ante in a poker game," purchasing "a seat at the table."[155]

Former Virginia governor McDonnell and his wife, Maureen, were convicted in 2014 of accepting more than $175,000 in loans and gifts from a businessman McDonnell helped in what appeared to be an example of "pay-to-play" corruption. The U.S. Supreme Court unanimously overturned Governor McDonnell's conviction based on incorrect jury instructions on the meaning of an "official act." McDonnell's attorneys argued in their appeal that setting up meetings and arranging events for benefactors were not by themselves evidence of an official's corruption. Chief Justice Roberts, writing for the Court, said that McDonnell's actions were "distasteful" but that "an 'official act' is a decision or action on a question, matter, cause, suit, proceeding or controversy."[156] The Justice Department could have sought a second trial for McDonnell and his wife but did not.

The larger issue raised by the McDonnell case is whether elected officials and their donors will be able to avoid prosecution by avoiding actions beyond the scope Governor McDonnell engaged in. The McDonnell decision has been cited by lower courts in reversing the convictions of Sheldon Silver, who had been the Speaker of the New York State Assembly but had been convicted of corruption in 2015,[157] and Dean G. Skelos, majority leader in the New York State Senate, who had also been convicted of corruption in 2015.[158] In 2017, the Justice Department decided not to pursue a retrial of U.S. Senator Robert Menendez of New Jersey, whose corruption trial on charges of conspiracy, bribery, and fraud had resulted in a hung jury. As in the Virginia and New York corruption cases, the changed definition of corruption coming out of the *McDonnell* case played a role in the New Jersey case.[159]

Activity at the State and Local Levels

While political activity in changing campaign finance law and practice has been largely centered in the courts at the state and local levels, there has also been activity by legislatures, city councils, and through the ballot initiative process.

There were four statewide campaign finance ballot initiatives in 2016: one in South Dakota, one in Missouri, and two in Washington. In South Dakota, voters passed a measure revising state lobbying and campaign finance laws. Subsequently, the legislature, with the support of the governor, repealed the measure. In Missouri, voters overwhelmingly voted to reinstate campaign contribution limits.[160] In Washington, voters approved an advisory measure, Initiative 735, urging their U.S. senators and U.S. representatives to propose a federal constitutional amendment that free-speech rights are reserved for "individuals, not corporations; that spending money is not free speech under the First Amendment; that governments are fully empowered to regulate political contributions and expenditures to prevent undue influence; and that political contributions and expenditures must be promptly disclosed to the public." There was limited opposition to the measure. An initiative similar to this passed in Colorado in 2012 with 74 percent of the vote.[161] That measure instructed the Colorado congressional delegation to propose and support a constitutional amendment allowing Congress and the states to limit campaign contributions and spending and instructed the state legislature to ratify such an amendment.[162]

In 2016, an initiative to establish public financing in Washington, paid for by a nonresident sales tax (Initiative 1464), was defeated. The public funding mechanism was known as "democracy credits," which were three vouchers for $50 each that could be donated to qualified campaigns or candidates during even-numbered years. Candidates eligible to receive the credits would need to collect at least seventy-five private contributions of at least $10, commit not to accept private contributions exceeding half the maximum limit for the office sought, and promise they would not spend more than $5,000 of their personal funds on the campaign. The system was patterned after "democracy dollars," a similar reform enacted by voters in Seattle, Washington, in 2015. That system gave each voter three $25 vouchers that could be given to candidates who had agreed to campaign contribution limits. Proponents argued that the system would orient candidates more toward small donors and away from the wealthy. Opponents saw the system as likely to further benefit incumbents. The proponents were much better funded, at $4.3 million, than the opponents, at $28,000.[163]

In 2015, voters in Maine voted to allow publicly financed state candidates to qualify for additional funds with certain rules and limits in the Maine Clean Election Act. The measure's proponents also argued that the measure improved disclosure of who pays for political ads and increased penalties for violations of campaign finance law.

In addition to the "democracy dollars" initiative in Seattle, other local jurisdictions have also enacted campaign finance reform. The Portland City Council adopted a public financing system much like the one in place in New York City. Also in Oregon, voters in Multnomah County adopted contribution limits for candidates and Super PACs. Local measures like these are sometimes test cases both for viability and constitutionality.[164]

Conclusion

While Trump's campaign was financed in different ways and at lower levels than in previous presidential campaigns, much of the rest of the financing of the 2016 election marked a continuation of several long-standing patterns. Organized interest groups were especially important in financing congressional incumbent campaigns through PACs. Individuals making contributions to candidates remained the largest source of funds for presidential candidates, and wealthy individuals again played a predominant role in funding Super PACs and at least some of the 501(c)(4) groups. Conventional PACs and Super PACs in some cases reinforce each other, and, as noted, conventional PACs again made substantial independent expenditures in 2016.

The Clinton campaign was in some important respects an extension of the way Obama funded his 2008 and 2012 campaigns. Clinton built on a large base of individual donors but with less support from small donors than Obama had in 2008 or 2012 and less than Sanders had in 2016. We attribute this to her message not resonating as much with small donors and to her not being as energizing a candidate as either Obama or Sanders. Clinton clearly had access to the same tools of small-donor fundraising, lists and the internet, but Sanders outpaced her in ways that suggest other Democrats in the future may be able to build on the Obama and Sanders success stories with small-donor fundraising. Trump's success with small donors and his use of social media are indicators that Republicans could also engage small donors much more than they have in recent election cycles.

Clinton elevated the importance of her Super PACs in her overall campaign finance strategy, perhaps as a strategic necessity because she could not keep pace with Obama in 2012 or Sanders in 2016 in individual contributions from small donors, while Sanders dismissed having a Super PAC, which is not necessarily a model future Democrats are likely to follow. Rather, the mixed strategy of Obama in 2012, with a diversified set of donors, including small donors, those closer to being able to contribute the maximum, and those able to fund a Super PAC, is the more likely model.

Aside from Trump, the Republican presidential candidates funded their campaigns much as Newt Gingrich and Rick Santorum did in 2012, with an excessive reliance on Super PACs and 501(c)(4) groups. Jeb Bush is the 2016 candidate most likely to be remembered for putting too much stock in a large Super PAC bank account.

There is much about the candidacy and presidency of Donald Trump that is unconventional. He was able to exploit an extraordinary advantage in earned media during the nomination and general election phases of the campaign. He was able to position himself as the outsider, and as one of his campaign managers, Corey Lewandowski, stated, he had "the ability not to be beholden to special interests."[165] He used his own resources to help launch his campaign, but by the end his campaign was much less self-funded than he had touted it would be. The reality, however, is that his campaign benefited from Super PACs and at least one 501(c)(4) group, especially late in the campaign. The campaign also relied less on television and more on social media, especially Facebook. Future campaigns will be debating how to take better advantage of social media, in part because of the Trump campaign.

While the presidential campaign was in some ways unconventional, congressional elections were extensions of trends seen over several cycles. The incumbency advantage in fundraising remains undiminished; Republicans presently enjoy a structural advantage in several states in the way House district boundaries were drawn following the 2010 census. This and the incumbency advantage have meant there have been relatively few battleground districts. It is in those contests that independent expenditures by the party committees and spending by Super PACs and 501(c)(4) groups are most important. But as important as being competitive in that money chase is, the recruitment of candidates is even more important to the overall party strategy. Underperforming candidates in Ohio, Indiana, and Florida hurt Democrats in their quest for a Senate majority, and Republicans also had races slip away that could have been more competitive, such as in Colorado. At the same time, party leaders can point to prudent investments in candidates such as Todd Young in Indiana for Republicans, who won by nearly 10 percent of the vote, defeating a well-known former senator, and Jason Kander in Missouri for Democrats, who lost by less than 3 percent of the vote against a much-better-known incumbent senator.

Political parties were important to the outcome of the presidential and congressional races. The Trump campaign entered the general election with very little conventional organization on the ground in battleground states. The early and substantial investment by the RNC in building a database that could be used up and down the ballot in key states and in deploying sufficient field staff to assist in connecting such data to key races was important. The Super PACs connected to the congressional leadership played a very important role in both parties, and the infusion of late money into the Senate Leadership Fund and Congressional Leadership Fund, much of it from Sheldon and Miriam Adelson, was also important.[166] Rob Portman, in part because of the spending of his own Super PAC, was able to knock out Ted Strickland early enough that Republicans could shift resources to places like Wisconsin, Pennsylvania, Missouri, and North Carolina to hold four seats that could have gone the other way. Democratic outside money was also important in several places, including both the U.S. House and U.S. Senate contests in Nevada and the U.S. Senate race in New Hampshire.

Electoral politics is very much a team sport, with the sum of activity by the candidates, the party committees, and interest groups all part of the team effort. As discussed in this chapter and chapter 2, the trend over the past decade has been to lessen restrictions on the sources of money in politics and on how much different participants can spend. As a result, candidates (in part through candidate-specific Super PACs, 501(c) groups, and party joint fundraising), party committees (through the elimination of aggregate party contribution limits and allowing new accounts for particular party purposes), and groups (through Super PACs, 501(c) groups, and 501(c)(6) groups) are all now in a position to spend more money on elections than at any time since the Watergate scandal.

Could candidates and their party and group supporters do just as well or better if they spent less? Some argue that the combination of Trump's limited use of TV and greater use of social media is one way to reduce spending. Others point to the possibility that candidates who prioritize small donors can reap the Obama and Sanders benefit of more active volunteers. One or both of these approaches may be viable, but the reality remains that candidates will not want to risk their victory by overlooking an approach that maximizes money raised. Those who favor one candidate or oppose others and who have money to give will be identified and asked to contribute. For these reasons, the pattern of recent elections is likely to continue for the foreseeable future, with campaigns being likely to match or exceed spending by nominees from their party in previous elections.

Campaign finance since BCRA took effect and was largely upheld by the Supreme Court has been moving in the direction of fewer limits. This is the result of a series of Court decisions that permit unlimited contributions to independent-expenditure-only committees (Super PACs), including such spending from the general treasuries of corporations and unions. The *Citizens United* and *SpeechNow.org* decisions made it clear that individuals and groups faced no legal barrier to such unlimited spending. The move toward fewer constraints on the financing of campaigns has also come from the absence of an effective regulatory agency in this policy area. As discussed in this chapter, the Federal Election Commission, because of its inactivity, has fostered an environment where those who want to spend money to influence the outcomes of elections have more options to expend large, and in some cases unlimited, amounts of money. Since there are no clear or enforced rules on what constitutes coordination between a candidate and a Super PAC, some Super PACs have more actively involved the candidates in their activities. In addition, neither the FEC nor the IRS has enforced the rule that the primary purpose of a 501(c) group cannot be electoral politics. As a result, 501(c)(4) groups in 2014 and 2016 engaged in a wide range of activities and expended well over half of their funds on electoral politics.

Notes

1. Center for Responsive Politics, "2016 Presidential Race" (www.opensecrets .org/pres16/).

2. Guy Cecil, chief strategist for Priorities USA Action, interview by David Magleby, March 15, 2017.

3. Whit Ayres, founder and president of North Star Opinion Research, interview by David Magleby, April 25, 2016.

4. Both the Clinton and Trump campaigns raised roughly the same percentage of their money through donations of $200 or more, 70 percent and 69 percent, respectively.

5. Paul Senatori, "Can Media Prominence Predict an Election? Trump vs. Le Pen," *MediaQuant*, May 6, 2017.

6. CBS, Fox, NBC, the *Los Angeles Times*, the *New York Times*, *USA Today*, the *Wall Street Journal*, and the *Washington Post*.

7. Thomas E. Patterson, "Pre-primary News Coverage of the 2016 Presidential Race: Trump's Rise, Sanders's Emergence, Clinton's Struggle," Shorenstein Center on Media, Politics and Public Policy, Harvard Kennedy School, June 2016, p. 6.

8. Thomas E. Patterson, "News Coverage of the 2016 Presidential Primaries: Horse Race Reporting Has Consequences," Shorenstein Center on Media, Politics and Public Policy, Harvard Kennedy School, July 11, 2016.

9. Ibid.

10. Adrienne LaFrance, "Trump's Media Saturation, Quantified," *The Atlantic*, September 1, 2016.

11. *Tyndall Report*, "2016 Year in Review" (http://tyndallreport.com /yearinreview2016/).

12. According to the *Tyndall Report*, which looked at coverage on ABC, CBS, and NBC for 2012, the Romney campaign received 479 minutes of media coverage, while the Obama campaign received 157 minutes. In 2008, the Obama campaign received 745 minutes and the McCain campaign received 531 minutes. For comparison, in 2016, Trump's campaign received 1,144 minutes while Clinton's received 506 minutes (http://tyndallreport.com/yearinreview2016/).

13. Paul Farhi, "Trump Gets Way More TV News Time than Clinton. So What?," *Washington Post*, September 21, 2016.

14. Jeff Greenfield, "This Is How Your Personal Data Helps Candidates Predict Your Vote," *PBS NewsHour*, December 18, 2015.

15. David B. Magleby, Jay Goodliffe, and Joseph A. Olsen, *Who Donates in Campaigns? The Importance of Message, Messenger, Medium and Structure* (Cambridge University Press, 2018).

16. Candice J. Nelson, "Survey Research and Campaigns—Getting to the Future," in *Campaigns on the Cutting Edge*, 3rd ed., edited by Richard J. Semiatin (Los Angeles: Congressional Quarterly Press, 2017).

17. Edward-Isaac Dovere, "How Clinton Lost Michigan—and Blew the Election," *Politico*, December 14, 2016.

18. Ibid.

19. Jonathan Allen and Amie Parnes, *Shattered: Inside Hillary Clinton's Doomed Campaign* (New York: Crown, 2017), p. 169.

20. Henry Barbour and others, "Growth and Opportunity Project," Republican National Committee, March 2013, p. 35 (https://gop.com/growth-and-opportunity-project/).

21. Ellen Bredenkoetter, chief data officer for the Republican National Committee, interview by David Magleby, May 30, 2017.

22. Deirdre Schifeling, executive director of Planned Parenthood Votes, interview by David Magleby, May 30, 2017.

23. Steve Rosenthal, founder and CEO of America Coming Together Organizing Group and founder and president of The Atlas Project, interview by David Magleby, February 8, 2017.

24. Laura Quinn, founder and chief executive officer of Catalist, interview by David Magleby, January 4, 2016.

25. Mike Lux, cofounder and president of Progressive Strategies, LLC, and senior adviser for progressive outreach for the Democratic National Committee, interview by David Magleby, January 6, 2017.

26. Hillary Rodham Clinton, *What Happened* (New York: Simon and Schuster, 2017), p. 76.

27. Bill Allison, Mira Rojanasakul, and Brittany Harris, "Tracking the Presidential Money Race," *Bloomberg Politics*, July 21, 2016; Center for Responsive Politics, "Also Rans: 2016 Presidential Race" (www.opensecrets.org/pres16/also-rans).

28. "2016 National Primary Polls," *FiveThirtyEight*, July 1, 2016 (projects.fivethirtyeight.com/election-2016/national-primary-polls/republican/).

29. Allen and Parnes, *Shattered*, pp. 137–38.

30. Campaign Finance Institute, "President Trump, with RNC Help, Raised More Small Donor Money than President Obama; as Much as Clinton and Sanders Combined," February 21, 2017 (www.cfinst.org/Press/PReleases/17-02-21/President_Trump_with_RNC_Help_Raised_More_Small_Donor_Money_than_President_Obama_As_Much_As_Clinton_and_Sanders_Combined.aspx).

31. Campaign Finance Institute, "All CFI Funding Statistics Revised and Updated for the 2008 Presidential Primary and General Election Candidates," January 8, 2010 (www.cfinst.org/pdf/federal/president/2010_0106_Table1.pdf).

32. Campaign Finance Institute, "Money vs. Money-Plus: Post-Election Reports Reveal Two Different Campaign Strategies: 69% of Obamas Itemized Donors Started with a Small Contribution; Obamas Itemized Donors Averaged More than Five Contributions Each," January 11, 2013 (www.cfinst.org/pdf/federal/president/2012/Pres12Tables_YE12_AggIndivDonors.pdf).

33. Campaign Finance Institute, "President Trump, with RNC Help, Raised More Small Donor Money than President Obama; As Much As Clinton and Sanders Combined," February 21, 2017 (http://www.cfinst.org/Press/PReleases /17-02-21/President_Trump_with_RNC_Help_Raised_More_Small_Donor _Money_than_President_Obama_As_Much_As_Clinton_and_Sanders_Com bined.aspx).

34. Ibid.

35. Ibid.

36. Center for Responsive Politics, "Also Rans: 2016 Presidential Race."

37. Center for Responsive Politics, "Most Expensive Races" (www.opensecrets .org/overview/topraces.php).

38. Fenit Nirappil, "Why Perriello Lost: Too Little, Too Late," *Washington Post*, June 18, 2017, p. C6.

39. Center for Responsive Politics, "Outside Spending, by Super PAC" (www .opensecrets.org/outsidespending/summ.php?chrt=V&type=S).

40. Ibid.

41. Pew Research Center Journalism and Media Staff, "How the Presidential Candidates Use the Web and Social Media," August 15, 2012 (www.journalism .org/2012/08/15/how-presidential-candidates-use-web-and-social-media/).

42. Tessa Berenson, "The Secret of Ben Carson's Campaign Success: Face-book," *Time*, September 8, 2015.

43. Mark Mellman, CEO of The Mellman Group, interview by David Magleby, May 30, 2017.

44. Rosenthal, interview.

45. Joshua Green and Sasha Issenberg, "Inside the Trump Bunker, with Days to Go," *Bloomberg Businessweek*, October 27, 2016.

46. Associated Press, "U.S. Tells 21 States That Hackers Targeted Their Voting Systems," *New York Times*, September 22, 2017.

47. Nicole Gaouette, "FBI's Comey: Republicans Also Hacked by Russia," *CNN Politics*, January 10, 2017.

48. Josh Meyer, "Russia Hack of U.S. Politics Bigger than Disclosed, Includes GOP," *NBC News*, October 8, 2016.

49. Jim Sciutto and Pamela Brown, "Russia Hacked GOP Groups, US Intel Believes," *CNN Politics*, December 12, 2016.

50. Scott Shane, "These Are the Ads Russia Bought on Facebook in 2016," *New York Times*, November 1, 2017.

51. Gabe O'Connor and Avie Schneider, "How Russian Twitter Bots Pumped Out Fake News during the 2016 Election," NPR, April 3, 2017.

52. Mike Isaac and Daisuke Wakabayashi, "Russian Influence Reached 126 Million through Facebook Alone," *New York Times*, October 30, 2017.

53. David Meyer, "Facebook, Twitter and Google Reveal How Many People Saw Russia-Linked Posts," *Fortune*, October 31, 2017.

54. Shane, "These Are the Ads Russia Bought on Facebook in 2016."

55. Mark Mazzetti and Katie Benner, "12 Russian Agents Charged in Drive to Upset '16 Vote," *New York Times*, July 14, 2018, p. A1, 14.

56. Meyer, "Facebook, Twitter and Google Reveal How Many People Saw Russia-Linked Posts."

57. "Russia Spent $1.25M per Month on Ads, Acted Like an Ad Agency: Mueller," *Advertising Age*, February 16, 2018.

58. William March, "Jeb Bush's Education Foundation under Fire for Lobbying for Laws That Benefit Corporate Donors," *Tampa Tribune*, March 3, 2013.

59. Associated Press, "Jeb Bush Releases List of Donors to Education Foundation," *NBC News*, July 1, 2015.

60. Peter Schweizer, *Clinton Cash: The Untold Story of How Foreign Governments and Businesses Made Bill and Hillary Rich* (New York: Harper, 2015). On news reports on Clinton's meetings with donors at the State Department, see Stephen Braun and Eileen Sullivan, "Many Donors to Clinton Foundation Met with Her at State," Associated Press, August 24, 2016. On Clinton's denials, see Michelle Ye Hee Lee, "Here's How Trump Got the AP Story on Clinton Foundation Donors All Wrong," *Washington Post*, August 25, 2016.

61. Anthony Zurcher, "US Election: Why Is Clinton's Foundation So Controversial?" *BBC News*, August 23, 2016.

62. David A. Fahrenthold, "How Donald Trump Retooled His Charity to Spend Other People's Money," *Washington Post*, September 10, 2016.

63. Vivian Wang, "The Donald J. Trump Foundation, Explained," *New York Times*, June 14, 2018.

64. Letter from Barbara D. Underwood, Attorney General, State of New York, to David J. Kautter, Acting Commissioner, Internal Revenue Service, June 14, 2018 (https://ag.ny.gov/sites/default/files/irs_final_letter.pdf).

65. Ibid.

66. Federal Election Commission, "Independent Expenditures," 2017 (www.fec.gov/help-candidates-and-committees/making-disbursements-pac/independent-expenditures-nonconnected-pac/).

67. Larry Noble, senior director of ethics and general counsel of Campaign Legal Center, interview by David Magleby, March 9, 2016.

68. Lux, interview.

69. Paul Blumenthal, "Senate Candidates Find a Way to Give Those Friendly Super PACs a Helping Hand," *Huffington Post*, March 27, 2014.

70. Nicholas Confessore and Eric Lichtblau, "'Campaigns' Aren't Necessarily Campaigns in the Age of 'Super PACs,'" *New York Times*, May 17, 2015.

71. "Wednesday's GOP Debate Transcript, Annotated," *Washington Post*, September 16, 2015.

72. Donald Trump, "The CNN Miami Republican Debate Transcript, Annotated," *Washington Post*, March 10, 2016.

73. The Super PACs active in 2017 were America First, Great America, and the 45Committee. See Alex Isenstadt, "Gingrich, Giuliani to Lead Group Pushing Trump's Agenda," *Politico*, January 30, 2017.

74. Vice President Mike Pence became the first vice president to form a leadership PAC while in office, The Great America Committee, which was formed in 2017. See Elizabeth Landers, "Pence Raises $1 Million for His Leadership PAC," CNN, July 26, 2017.

75. Julie Bykowicz, "Trump Makes Fundraising Quick Work," *Wall Street Journal*, February 2, 2018, p. A5.

76. Megan R. Wilson, "Congress to Require FEC Report on Foreign Money in Elections," *The Hill*, March 22, 2018.

77. Luis Gomez, "Twitter, Facebook Back Honest Ads Act. Is Google Next?" *San Diego Union Tribune*, April 10, 2018.

78. Mike Snider and Jessica Guynn, "News Publishers Protest Facebook's New Political Ad Rules," *USA Today*, May 18, 2018.

79. Nellie Bowles and Sheera Frenkel, "Facebook and Twitter Plan New Ways to Regulate Political Ads," *New York Times*, May 24, 2018.

80. H.R. 3952, "The Stop Super PAC Candidate Coordination Act" (https://www.congress.gov/bill/115th-congress/house-bill/3952/text); H.R. 3848, "We the People Democracy Reform Act of 2017" (https://www.congress.gov/bill/115th-congress/house-bill/3848).

81. "A Better Deal for Our Democracy: Fixing Our Broken Political System and Returning to a Government Of, By and For the People," *House Democrats Leadership* (https://abetterdeal.democraticleader.gov/better-deal-for-our-democracy/).

82. *McCutcheon* v. *Federal Election Commission*, 572 U.S. ___ (2014), p. 4.

83. Ibid.

84. Underwood, Letter to Kautter, June 14, 2018.

85. Letter from Barbara D. Underwood, Attorney General, State of New York, to Commissioners Caroline C. Hunter, Ellen L. Weintraub, Matthew S. Peterson, Steven T. Walther, and Lisa J. Stevenson, Acting General Counsel, Federal Election Commission, June 14, 2018 (https://ag.ny.gov/sites/default/files/fec_final_letter.pdf).

86. R. Sam Garrett, *The Federal Election Commission: Overview and Selected Issues for Congress*, Congressional Research Service Report R44318, December 22, 2015, p. 1.

87. Commissioners are not necessarily appointed for full six-year terms but instead may be appointed for the remainder of the term of the person they are replacing. For example, in June 2008, the Senate confirmed Donald F. McGahn and Steven T. Walther to terms that expired ten months later. Both continued to serve beyond that date in "holdover status." Walther continues to serve, while McGahn left the commission in 2013, later serving as general counsel to the Trump presidential campaign and then as White House counsel.

88. Ann M. Ravel, "Dysfunction and Deadlock at the Federal Election Commission," *New York Times*, February 20, 2017.

89. Steven Walther's term expired April 30, 2009, but as has become the norm, he is continuing to serve until a replacement is named (www.fec.gov/press /resources-journalists/commissioners/).

90. For additional background on the design of the FEC, see Robert E. Mutch, *Campaigns, Congress, and the Courts: The Making of Federal Campaign Finance Law* (New York: Praeger, 1988), pp. 88–117.

91. Garrett, *The Federal Election Commission*, p. 11.

92. See Federal Election Commission, "Independent Expenditures and Electioneering Communications by Corporations and Labor Organizations," 79 Federal Register 62797, October 21, 2014.

93. Ashley Balcerzak, "Ann Ravel's Parting Shot," Center for Responsive Politics, February 23, 2017.

94. Peter Overby, "As Her Turn Leading the FEC Ends, Ravel Says Agency Is Broken," NPR, December 31, 2015.

95. For a detailed statistical analysis of FEC votes, conciliation agreements, and penalties under differing numbers of commissioners for this period, see Michael Franz, "The Devil We Know? Evaluating the Federal Election Commission as Enforcer," *Election Law Journal* 8, no. 3 (2009), pp. 167–87.

96. Garrett, *The Federal Election Commission*, p. 12.

97. Dave Levinthal, "How Washington Starves Its Election Watchdog: FEC Hamstrung by Political Bickering, Case Backlogs, Staff Departures—Even Chinese Hackers," Center for Public Integrity, May 4, 2016.

98. Angela Bradbery and Craig Holman, "Roiled in Partisan Deadlock, Federal Election Commission Is Failing," Public Citizen, April 2015.

99. Kenneth P. Doyle, "Campaign Finance: Analysis: Deadlocks Are Only Part of the Story at FEC," *Daily Report for Executives*, August 31, 2015.

100. Garrett, *The Federal Election Commission*, p. 1.

101. Ibid., pp. 29–30.

102. Federal Election Commission, "Fiscal Year 2018 Congressional Budget Justification," p. 22 (www.fec.gov/resources/cms-content/documents/FEC_FY _2018_Congressional_Budget_Justificiation.pdf).

103. Garrett, *The Federal Election Commission*, p. 15.

104. Scott Blackburn, "Delusions about 'Dysfunction': Understanding the Federal Election Commission?" Institute for Free Speech, October 5, 2015.

105. Brad Smith, "Do Commissioners Weintraub and Ravel Want the FEC to Fail?" Center for Competitive Politics, May 20, 2015.

106. Underwood, Letter to Hunter and others, June 14, 2018.

107. Democracy 21, "Democracy 21 Files FEC Comments Calling for Broad Ad Disclaimer Regulations," May 25, 2018 (http://democracy21.org/news-press

/press-releases/democracy-21-files-fec-comments-calling-for-broad-ad
-disclaimer-regulations).

108. Internal Revenue Service, "Types of Organizations Exempt under Section 501(c)(4)," October 12, 2016 (www.irs.gov/charities-non-profits/other-non
-profits/types-of-organizations-exempt-under-section-501-c-4).

109. Internal Revenue Service, "Guidance for Tax-Exempt Social Welfare Organizations on Candidate-Related Political Activities," November 29, 2013 (https://www.federalregister.gov/documents/2013/11/29/2013-28492/guidance
-for-tax-exempt-social-welfare-organizations-on-candidate-related-political
-activities).

110. Jennifer Mueller, "Defending Nuance in an Era of Tea Party Politics: An Argument for the Continued Use of Standards to Evaluate the Campaign Activities of 501(C)(4) Organizations," *George Mason Law Review* 22, no. 1 (2014), pp. 103–58.

111. Robert Maguire, "Political Nonprofit Spent Nearly 100 Percent of Funds to Elect Tillis in '14," Center for Responsive Politics, October 20, 2015.

112. Internal Revenue Service, "Contributions to Organization with IRS Application Pending" (www.irs.gov/charities-non-profits/charitable-organizations
/contributions-to-organization-with-irs-application-pending).

113. Marc Owens, partner with Loeb & Loeb, interview by David Magleby, March 16, 2017. See also Josh Hicks, "Shrinking IRS Struggles to Keep Up with Growing Number of Tax-Exempt Charities," *Washington Post*, January 9, 2015; Massimo Calabresi, "IRS to Rubber-Stamp Tax-Exempt Status for Most Charities after Scandal," *Time*, July 13, 2014.

114. Lauren French, "Lerner Still Hill's Favorite Piñata," *Politico*, September 23, 2015.

115. Owens, interview.

116. Ibid.

117. Robert W. Wood, "No Virginia, You Can't Rely on IRS Rulings," *Forbes*, October 7, 2010.

118. For Speaker Boehner's criticisms, see Ed O'Keefe, "Boehner on IRS Scandal: 'Who's Going to Jail over This Scandal?'" *Washington Post*, May 15, 2013. For Senator McConnell's criticisms, see Jonathan Weisman, "I.R.S. Chief Out after Protest over Scrutiny of Groups," *New York Times*, May 15, 2013. For comments by others in Congress, see Christi Parsons and Lisa Mascaro, "Obama, Lawmakers Denounce IRS for Targeting Conservative Groups," *Los Angeles Times*, May 13, 2013.

119. Paul S. Ryan, vice president for policy and litigation at Common Cause, interview by David Magleby, February 9, 2016. See also Lydia Wheeler, "Deal Blocks the IRS from Cracking Down on 'Dark Money' Groups," *The Hill*, December 16, 2015.

120. Internal Revenue Service, "Contributions to Organization with IRS Application Pending."

121. Peter Overby, "Dark Money Groups Get a Little Darker, Thanks to the IRS," NPR, July 17, 2018.

122. Peter Overby, "Judge Shuts Down Multimillion-Dollar Loophole in Election Law," NPR, August 6, 2018.

123. Scholars and advocates for reform generally favor limits on individual and PAC contributions and expenditures by individuals, party committees, and PACs as well as a more active regulatory agency. They are also critics of the deregulatory school. See, for example, Thomas E. Mann and E. J. Dionne Jr., "The Futility of Nostalgia and the Romanticism of the New Political Realists: Why Praising the 19th-Century Political Machine Won't Solve the 21st Century's Problems," Brookings, June 17, 2015; Lee Drutman, "How to Properly Diagnose the Chaos of American Politics," *Vox*, June 24, 2016; Lee Drutman, "Giving the Two Parties Even More Money Will Not Solve Polarization: And, No Empowering Small Donors Is Not Going to Make Politics Even More Polarized," *Vox*, November 20, 2015; Thomas E. Mann and Anthony Corrado, "Party Polarization and Campaign Finance," Brookings, July 15, 2014.

124. John Cochran, "Campaign Finance's Deregulation Option," *New York Times*, July 9, 2007.

125. Scholars and advocates who are skeptics of reform and often favor deregulation include Bruce Cain, *Democracy More or Less: America's Political Reform Quandary* (Cambridge University Press, 2014); Nathaniel Persily, "Stronger Parties as a Solution to Polarization in America," in *Political Polarization in America*, edited by Nathaniel Persily (Cambridge University Press, 2015), pp. 123–35; Jonathan Rauch, *Political Realism: How Hacks, Machines, Big Money and Back-Room Deals Can Strengthen American Democracy* (Brookings, 2015); Richard Pildes, "Romanizing Democracy, Political Fragmentation and the Decline of American Government," *Yale Law Journal* 124, no. 3 (2014), pp. 804–52; Raymond J. La Raja and Brian F. Schaffner, *Campaign Finance and Political Polarization: When Purists Prevail* (University of Michigan Press, 2015).

126. Federal Election Commission, "FEC Statement on Campaign Finance Provisions of the Consolidated and Further Continuing Appropriations Act, 2015 (H.R. 83)" (www.fec.gov/updates/fec-statement-on-campaign-finance-provisions-of-the-consolidated-and-further-continuing-appropriations-act-2015-hr-83/); Federal Election Commission, "Legislation" (www.fec.gov/legal-resources/legislation/).

127. La Raja and Schaffner, *Campaign Finance and Political Polarization*.

128. Mann and Corrado, "Party Polarization and Campaign Finance."

129. *McConnell* v. *Federal Election Commission*, 540 U.S. 95 (2003).

130. For both a broad overview and detailed case studies of soft money and issue advocacy spending, see David B. Magleby, ed., *Outside Money: Soft Money*

and Issue Advocacy in 1998 Congressional Elections (Lanham, Md.: Rowman and Littlefield, 2000); David B. Magleby, ed., *The Other Campaign: Soft Money and Issue Advocacy in the 2000 Congressional Elections* (Lanham, Md.: Rowman and Littlefield, 2003); David B. Magleby and J. Quin Monson, eds., *The Last Hurrah? Soft Money and Issue Advocacy in the 2002 Congressional Elections* (Brookings, 2004). For an assessment of how issue ads and soft money were used on television, see David B. Magleby, "The Impact of Issue Advocacy and Party Soft Money Electioneering," in *The Medium and the Message: Television Advertising and American Elections*, edited by Kenneth Goldstein and Patricia Strach (Upper Saddle River, N. J.: Prentice Hall, 2004), pp. 84–104. For a description of how these studies and the data gathered between 1998 and 2003 were used in the *McConnell v. Federal Election Commission* litigation, see David B. Magleby, "Party and Interest Group Electioneering in Federal Elections," in *Inside the Campaign Finance Battle: Court Testimony on the New Reforms*, edited by Anthony Corrado, Thomas E. Mann, and Trevor Potter (Brookings, 2003), pp. 147–74.

131. R. Sam Garrett and L. Paige Whitaker, "Coordinated Part Expenditures in Federal Elections: An Overview," *Congressional Research Service*, August 15, 2016, p. 1.

132. The following table provides the party coordinated expenditures at the maximum allowed for House and Senate general election candidates between 2008 and 2016.

Dollars

	House	Senate
2016	7,511,537 (79)	28,115,908 (26)
2014	7,934,848 (89)	14,735,493 (29)
2012	11,972,478 (140)	20,374,381 (29)
2010	15,600,741 (175)	34,380,551 (37)
2008	10,287,248 (126)	12,653,503 (27)

Source: Compiled from FEC data.

Notes: Figures in parentheses represent the number of candidates that received the maximum amount of party coordinated expenditures. The limits in 2016 range from $96,100 to $2,886,500 for Senate nominees, depending on each state's voting-age population, $96,100 for House nominees in states with only one representative, and $48,100 for House nominees in all other states. The limits in 2014 range from $94,500 to $2,755,200 for Senate nominees, depending on each state's voting-age population, $94,500 for House nominees in states with only one representative, and $47,200 for House nominees in all other states. The limits in 2012 range from $91,200 to $2,593,100 for Senate nominees, depending on each state's voting-age population, $91,200 for House nominees in states with only one representative, and $45,600 for House nominees in all other states. The limits in 2010 range from $87,300 to $2,392,400 for Senate nominees, depending on each state's voting-age population, $87,300 for House nominees in states with only one representative, and $43,700 for House nominees in all other states. The limits in 2008 range from $84,100 to $2,300,000 for Senate nominees, depending on each state's voting-age population, $84,100 for House nominees in states with only one representative, and $42,100 for House nominees in all other states.

133. Daniel P. Tokaji and Renata E. B. Strause, *The New Soft Money: Outside Spending in Congressional Elections* (Ohio State University, Moritz College of Law, 2014).

134. Michael D. Gilbert and Brian Barnes, "The Coordination Fallacy," *Florida State University Law Review* 43, no. 2 (2015), p. 402.

135. "Strengthen Rules Preventing Candidate Coordination with Super PACs," Brennan Center for Justice, February 4, 2016 (www.brennancenter.org /analysis/strengthen-rules-preventing-candidate-coordination-super-pacs).

136. *Buckley* v. *Valeo*, 424 U.S. 2 (1976).

137. *McConnell* v. *Federal Election Commission*, 540 U.S. 258 (2003).

138. Dylan Matthews, "Crossroads GPS and Priorities USA Were Created for the Purpose of Hiding Donors," *Washington Post*, May 15, 2013.

139. Center for Responsive Politics, "Outside Spending Summary, 2016" (www.opensecrets.org/outsidespending/detail.php?cmte=C00571703&cycle =2016).

140. Annie Karni, "Clinton Campaign Scores Ready for Hillary Email List," *Politico*, May 30, 2015.

141. Ibid.

142. Ibid.

143. Allen and Parnes, *Shattered*, p. 28.

144. Foundation for Accountability and Trust, "FACT Files Compliant with FEC Regarding Hillary Clinton," June 1, 2015 (www.factdc.org/single-post /2015/06/02/FACT-Files-Complaint-With-FEC-Regarding-Hillary-Clinton).

145. Robert Maguire, "Two (At Most) Secret Donors Funded 93% of Pro-Rubio Nonprofit," Center for Responsive Politics, May 3, 2017.

146. Robert F. Bauer and Samuel Issacharoff, "Keep Shining the Light on 'Dark Money,'" *Politico*, April 12, 2015.

147. *Citizens United* v. *Federal Election Commission*, 558 U.S. 483 (2010).

148. Federal Communications Commission, "The Public and Broadcasting," July 2008 (www.fcc.gov/media/radio/public-and-broadcasting).

149. The Campaign Legal Center, "Sponsorship Identification and the FCC's Online Political Files," September 29, 2016 (www.campaignlegalcenter.org /document/sponsorship-identification-and-fcc-s-online-political-files).

150. The FCC describes what is required to be disclosed as follows: "This file must contain all requests for specific schedules of advertising time by candidates and certain issue advertisers, as well as the final dispositions or 'deals' agreed to by the broadcaster and the advertiser in response to any requests. . . . Finally, the file must include the reconciliation of the deal such as a description of when advertising actually aired, advertising preempted, and the timing of any make-goods of preempted time, as well as credits or rebates provided the advertiser." See Federal Communications Commission, "About Public Inspection Files" (https://publicfiles .fcc.gov/about-station-profiles/).

151. Ibid.

152. See Magleby, *Outside Money*; Magleby, *The Other Campaign*; Magleby and Monson, *The Last Hurrah?*

153. Justin Elliott, "Political Ad Data Comes Online—but It's Not Searchable," *ProPublica*, August 2, 2012.

154. Wesleyan Media Project, "Data Access" (http://mediaproject.wesleyan .edu/dataaccess/). For the Wisconsin Media Project archive cite, which has data for 1996, 2000, 2002, 2004, and 2008, see Elections Research Center at the University of Wisconsin-Madison, "Wisconsin Advertising Project" (https:// elections.wisc.edu/wiscads/).

155. Samuel Issacharoff, Pamela S. Karlan, Richard H. Pildes, and Nathaniel Persily, *The Law of Democracy: Legal Structure of the Political Process* (St. Paul, Minn.: Foundation Press, 2016), p. 607.

156. *Robert F. McDonnell, Petitioner* v. *United States*, 579 U.S. 21, 28 (2016).

157. Benjamin Weiser, "Sheldon Silver's 2015 Corruption Conviction Is Overturned," *New York Times*, July 13, 2017.

158. Benjamin Weiser, "Dean Skelos's 2015 Corruption Conviction Is Overturned," *New York Times*, September 26, 2017.

159. Laura Jarrett, Dan Berman, and Sarah Jorgensen, "Justice Department Won't Retry Senator Bob Menendez," CNN, January 31, 2018; Matt Ford, "Has the Supreme Court Legalized Public Corruption?" *The Atlantic*, October 19, 2017.

160. Jason Hancock, "Missouri Voters Like Campaign Donation Limits, but Will the Courts?" *Kansas City Star*, November 11, 2016.

161. John Schroyer, "Amendment 65 Sent Message, but Action May Not Follow," *The Gazette*, December 25, 2012.

162. Carlos Illescas, "Amend 65: Voters Back Campaign Finance Measure, Despite Lacking Legal Legs," *Denver Post*, November 6, 2012.

163. Daniel Beekman, "Seattle Initiative Puts Spotlight on Campaign Financing," *Seattle Times*, October 26, 2015.

164. Corey Goldstone, "Voters Approve Numerous Campaign Finance Reform Measures on State/Local Level," Campaign Legal Center, November 14, 2016.

165. Corey Lewandowski, primary campaign manager, Donald J. Trump for President, quoted in Institute of Politics, *Campaign for President: The Managers Look at 2016* (Lanham, Md.: Rowman and Littlefield, 2017), p. 29.

166. Sheldon and Miriam Adelson together contributed $15 million on October 24 to the Senate Leadership Fund. This is in addition to the $20 million they contributed to the same group in August 2016. For more about the context of these gifts, see Jacob Pramuk, "Business Giants Piled Cash into GOP Senate Super PAC in Election's Final Days," CNBC, December 8, 2016.

Appendix: List of Interviews

Tiffany Adams, vice president, public affairs, National Association of Manufacturers, January 4, 2017

Whit Ayres, founder and president, North Star Opinion Research, April 25, 2016

Michael Beckel, reporter, Center for Public Integrity, March 9, 2016

Robert Biersack, senior fellow, Center for Responsive Politics, December 14, 2016; April 27, 2017

Ellen Bredenkoetter, chief data officer, Republican National Committee, May 30, 2017

Andrew Brown, technology director, Democratic National Committee, February 9, 2017

Martin Burns, manager, political intelligence, AARP, April 27, 2016

Brian Calabrese, federal liaison, NRA-ILA, January 4, 2017

Guy Cecil, chief strategist, Priorities USA Action, March 15, 2017

Amy Dacey, former CEO, Democratic National Committee, December 13, 2016

Jennifer Duffy, senior editor, the *Cook Political Report*, November 21, 2016

Preston Elliot, deputy executive director, Democratic Senatorial Campaign Committee, December 13, 2016; January 4, 2017

Rob Engstrom, senior vice president of political affairs and federal relations, national political director, U.S. Chamber of Commerce, January 5, 2016; November 21, 2016

Carla Eudy, president, Eudy Company, April 21, 2016

Geoff Garin, president, Hart Research Associates, June 1, 2017

Nathan Gonzales, editor and publisher, *Inside Elections*, November 21, 2016

Sam Gonzales, specialist in American national government, Congressional Research Service, June 23, 2015

Scott Goodstein, founder and chief executive officer, Revolution Messaging, March 15, 2017

Keegan Goudiss, director of digital advertising, Sanders 2016 campaign, and partner, Revolution Messaging, March 15, 2017

Hayden Hatch, legislative aide, NRA-ILA, January 4, 2017

Ariel Hayes, deputy political director, Sierra Club, February 10, 2017

Craig Holman, government affairs lobbyist, Public Citizen, March 16, 2017

Harold Ickes, previous president, Priorities USA, and cofounder, Ickes and Enright Group, December 12, 2016

Wesley Joe, researcher, Campaign Finance Institute, June 24, 2015

Jessica Johnson, independent expenditure director, National Republican Congressional Committee, December 14, 2016

Sheila Krumholtz, executive director, Center for Responsive Politics, December 14, 2016; April 27, 2016

Steven Law, president and CEO, Senate Leadership Fund, March 15, 2017

Linda Lipson, chief executive officer, Alliance for Justice, January 5, 2017

Mark Longabaugh, senior Sanders 2016 campaign adviser, February 8, 2017

Tom Lopach, executive director, Democratic Senatorial Campaign Committee, December 13, 2016

Mike Lux, cofounder and president, Progressive Strategies, LLC, and senior adviser for progressive outreach, Democratic National Committee, January 6, 2017

Jessica Mackler, president, American Bridge, March 27, 2017

Robert Maguire, political nonprofits investigator, Center for Responsive Politics, December 14, 2016; April 27, 2016; April 14, 2017

Meredith McGehee, policy director, Campaign Legal Center, March 11, 2016

Mark Mellman, CEO, The Mellman Group, May 30, 2017

Michael Meyers, president, TargetPoint, June 1, 2017

Sarah Morgan, political director, National Republican Senate Committee, February 22, 2017

Larry Noble, senior director, ethics and general counsel of Campaign Legal Center, March 9, 2016; February 9, 2017

Jason Ouimet, director, federal affairs, NRA-ILA Institute, January 4, 2017

Marc Owens, partner, Loeb & Loeb, March 16, 2017

Brandi Graham Pensoneau, federal liaison, NRA-ILA, January 4, 2017

John Philleppe, chief counsel, Republican National Committee, February 8, 2017

Mike Podhorzer, political director, AFL-CIO, March 17, 2017

Trevor Potter, founder and president, Campaign Legal Center, March 11, 2016

Joe Pounder, cofounder and president, America Rising, March 20, 2017

Carrie Pugh, political director, National Education Association, March 15, 2017

Laura Quinn, founder and chief executive officer, Catalist, January 4, 2016

Steve Rosenthal, founder and CEO, America Coming Together Organizing Group, and founder and president, The Atlas Project, February 8, 2017

Paul S. Ryan, vice president, policy and litigation, Common Cause, February 9, 2016

Doug Sachtleben, communications director, Club for Growth, March 8, 2017

Deirdre Schifeling, executive director, Planned Parenthood Votes, May 30, 2017

Clay Schroers, national campaigns director, League of Conservation Voters, January 5, 2017; March 16, 2017

Mike Shields, president, American Action Network and Congressional Leadership Fund, February 8, 2017

Rob Simms, executive director, National Republican Congressional Committee, December 12, 2016

Greg Speed, president, America Votes, January 6, 2017

Charlie Spies, leader, national political law practice, Clark Hill, February 10, 2017

Gail Stoltz, political organization consultant and contractor, National Education Association, March 15, 2017

Jennifer Stromer-Gally, professor, School of Information Studies, Syracuse University, March 2, 2017

Sharon Wolff Sussin, national political director, National Federation of Independent Business, January 5, 2017

Tim Tagaris, digital fundraising director, Sanders 2016 campaign, and partner, Revolution Messaging, March 15, 2017

Peter Valcarce, chief executive officer, Arena Communications, June 2, 2017

Kelly Ward, executive director, Democratic Congressional Campaign Committee, December 13, 2016

Andrew Welhouse, copywriter, Arena Communications, June 2, 2017

Fred Wertheimer, founder and president, Democracy 21, November 22, 2016

Contributors

Anthony Corrado
Colby College

Diana Dwyre
California State University, Chico

Jay Goodliffe
Brigham Young University

John C. Green
Bliss Institute, University of Akron

Richard L. Hall
University of Michigan

David A. Hopkins
Boston College

Robin Kolodny
Temple University

David B. Magleby
Brigham Young University

Molly E. Reynolds
Brookings Institution

Index

Figures and tables are indicated by "f" and "t" following page numbers.

Democratic Congressional Campaign
Committee (DCCC), 221, 228–29,
232, 256t, 264; independent
expenditures of, 286–87; individual contributions to, 266–70, 268t;
member contributions to, 279;
PACs and, 278
Democratic Governors Association,
88
Democratic National Committee
(DNC): building fund (2016), 69;
Clinton's relationship with,
203–04; e-mails and hacking, 7,
17, 211, 251, 261, 308; individual
contributions to, 266–70, 267t;
past debt of, 67, 194, 275, 286;
pre-2015 and post-2015 CRomin-
bus change to law, 254–55, 256t,
276; recount/legal expenses fund,
69. See also Building accounts;
CRomnibus legislation; Joint
fundraising committees; National
conventions; Party money; Recounts or legal expenses
Democratic Party: America Votes
coalition and, 117; Citizens United,
efforts to overturn, 98; committees, moneys raised by, 24; 501(c)
(4) groups and, 115; PAC contributions to, 91–92, 92t; presidential
general election financing, 200–04;
Senate races and, 94, 218; Super
PACs associated with, 105–06,
149t, 204, 225; top outside
spending in Senate and House races
(2015–16), 107, 107t. See also
Congressional elections; National
conventions; Nomination campaign, Democratic; individual
candidates and party committees
Democratic Senate Majority PAC
(Super PAC), 281
Democratic Senatorial Campaign
Committee (DSCC), 218, 221, 228,
229, 256t, 264; independent
expenditures of, 287; individual

contributions to, 266–70, 267t;
member contributions to, 279;
PACs and, 278
Democratic White House Victory
Fund, 16
Deregulation. See Regulatory
environment
Diaz, Danny, 176
DISCLOSE (Democracy Is Strength-
ened by Casting Light on Spending
in Elections) Act (proposed 2010),
313, 332
Distrust of politicians, 2
DNC. See Democratic National
Committee
Doe v. See name of opposing party
Donald J. Trump Foundation. See
Trump Foundation
Double counting due to transfers of
money from PAC to PAC or from
group to Super PAC, 37
DSCC. See Democratic Senatorial
Campaign Committee
Duffy, Jennifer, 35, 229–30
DuHaime, Mike, 11, 167

Early money, assumptions about
importance of, 3, 15, 133, 137,
233
Earned media: presidential campaign
and, 176, 209–10, 300–01; during
Republican primary campaigns,
300–01; Trump and, 1, 12–13,
166, 169, 173, 209, 300–01, 307
Electoral College winner, not popular
vote winner, 2, 187–89
Elliot, Preston, 218
Ellison, Larry, 153
E-mails. See Democratic National
Committee; FBI investigation of
Clinton's private server and e-mails
EMILY's List, 73, 89, 99t, 100, 226
End Citizens United (reform group),
98, 99t
Environmental Super PACs, 105
Erickson, Robert, 220

Washington Post on Senate races, 218
Washington state initiative on public
    campaign financing, 334
Wasserman Schultz, Debbie, 7, 17,
    203, 251, 261
Wealthy donors: Clinton's focus on,
    15, 198; compared to small donors,
    305–06; distorting influence of, 6,
    67–68, 70, 79; importance of
    campaign contributions of, 5–6, 21,
    305–06; JFCs and, 70; *McCutch-
    eon*'s effect on, 61, 133, 253–54,
    276, 326; new party accounts
    permitted by 2015 law and, 67–68;
    pay-to-play contributions by,
    332–34; reaction to Trump in
    Access Hollywood tape, 18, 264;
    Ryan and, 227; Super PACs and,
    138, 148, 310, 335; Trump's
    relationship with, 5–6, 198, 205.
    See also Adelson, Sheldon and
    Miriam; Koch brothers; *individual
    donors by name*
Weaver, Jeff, 145, 160, 289
Webb, Jim, 147, 158, 160

Weintraub, Ellen, 316–17
Wertheimer, Fred, 68, 329
Wesleyan Media Project, 109, 210,
    332
We the People' Democracy Reform
    Act of 2017 (proposed), 315
White rural voters, 260
White working-class voters, 210
Whitman, Meg, 199
WikiLeaks, 7, 19, 251, 261, 308
Wilks, Farris and Daniel, 152
Wisconsin, 35, 286, 337
Wisconsin Media Project, 109, 332
Wisconsin Right to Life v. *Federal
    Election Commission* (2007), 314,
    315
Women, Trump's treatment of, as
    campaign issue, 18, 187, 210, 263,
    264
Women's Vote (Super PAC), 115

Young, Todd, 337
Young Guns Action Fund, 106
Young voters, 16
YouTube, 309